Helen Sheehy

MARGO

The Life and Theatre of Margo Jones

SOUTHERN METHODIST UNIVERSITY PRESS

Dallas

Copyright © 1989
by Helen Sheehy
All rights reserved
Printed in the United States of America

First edition, 1989
Requests for permission to reproduce material
from this work should be sent to:

Permissions
Southern Methodist University Press
Box 415
Dallas, Texas 75275

Library of Congress Cataloging-in-
Publication Data
Sheehy, Helen, 1948–
    Margo : the life and theatre of Margo
Jones / Helen Sheehy. — 1st ed.
        p.   cm.
    ISBN 0-87074-296-5
    1. Jones, Margo.   2. Theatrical
producers and directors — United States
— Biography.   I. Title.
PN2287.J595S54   1989
792'.0233'092 — dc20   89-42892
[B]   CIP

Grateful acknowledgment is made to the
Collection of American Literature, Beinecke
Rare Book Room and Manuscript Library,
Yale University, for permission to quote from
the letters of Thornton Wilder.

For Tom Sheehy,

who shared the journey,

and in memory of my mother,

Wilma French Probst,

who showed me the way

Contents

Prologue

They were all looking at her—the technical director, the stage manager, the actors, and the playwright—waiting for her to tell them what to do. She felt terrible, physically ill at what she had just seen. The final dress rehearsal was over. They expected to be dismissed, to go to dinner and then get some much-needed sleep. How could she tell them that three weeks of rehearsal had been wasted—her direction, their acting, the entire production lacking in art, without one moment of beauty? She knew they were tired, worn out as she was. They had closed a play yesterday and the crew had worked all night and into Sunday morning changing the set and refocusing the lights. After the performance, she had gone back to her apartment at the Stoneleigh with the playwright to discuss this next production and, fortified by Scotch on the rocks, they had worked through the night, acting out the lines, playing the roles, until they had found the key to it. Or had they? She had fallen asleep or maybe she had passed out, and when she woke up it was Sunday, and she was alone.

She knew that the actors didn't believe their parts, that they had lost faith in the play. Somehow she had to make them believe. To do that, she had to believe in it herself or convince them that she did when the truth was, although few suspected it, she sometimes wondered if theatre was worth all the effort. From her seat in the top row of the darkened theatre, she looked at the actors standing in a circle of light, and at the stage manager peering out from the small window of the control booth, and at the playwright, who had given her his script with such hope and trust. She couldn't let them see her doubt. "Babies," she announced in a voice filled with energy and excitement, belying the puffy shadows under her eyes and masking the weariness she felt, "we're doing this playwright a terrible disservice. We have to restage and redo the entire show before tomorrow's opening-night performance."

They worked through the night, fueled by coffee and half-eaten sandwiches and driven by her determination. The air grew stale with the smoke from her Camels. She moved from actor to actor, whispering ideas for fresh characterizations, nudging them into the new staging, urging them to feel, really feel the emotions. Moment to moment, scene by scene, she reshaped the production. She relaxed briefly on the old maroon sofa in the control booth while the crew

1

changed all the lighting and sound cues to fit the new staging. When she left them to pace the theatre and check the performances from every angle, the lingering fragrance of her Tuberose perfume stayed with them. At times she would go back to her seat in the house and watch from there, pretending she was an audience member seeing the play for the first time. Her whole being empathized with the actors, felt what they felt and entered the world they had created. As they worked together and the hours passed, a curious thing began to happen. Her fatigue, her hangover, her doubts were forgotten, consumed in the process of creation, of making theatre. Finally, just before dawn, they were finished. She knew that the production was not great, possibly not even good, but now it had moments of beauty and truth, and she, who knew the cost of creating art, was grateful for moments.

The theatre was still, everyone too exhausted to speak. The actors sprawled on the floor, looking up into the lights and into the eyes of the director, who had bounded onto the stage, brimming with impossible vitality. She smiled in amazement at the worn-out company—and in a drawl laced with evangelistic fervor proclaimed, "But darlin's, we're doing what we love!"

EVERYTHING IN LIFE is theatre, she said, for it was her passion, her driving obsession. She had a rare and powerful gift, the ability to make art happen. Some called her a visionary and a prophet. She thought of herself in homelier terms, as a farmer or a gardener clearing the land, tilling the soil, sowing some seeds, and helping them grow.

The seeds she planted grew into the resident nonprofit professional theatre, America's national theatre. Before her, the focus was Broadway—New York and the commercial theatre. Despite occasional road shows, out-of-town tryouts, and a few struggling theatres, the rest of the country lay fallow. After her, the resident theatre took root, growing into over three hundred theatres, a towering tree with branches in every state. It flourishes because of the faith, hard work, imagination, and sheer will of this woman.

She found and nurtured the work of budding playwrights like Tennessee Williams, William Inge, Joseph Hayes, Jerome Lawrence and Robert E. Lee, and many others. She said, if we succeed in inspiring the operation of thirty theatres like ours, the playwright won't need Broadway. Her prophecy has come true, and now Broadway depends on the resident theatre for new plays. Who was this person named "a patron saint of playwrights" by Jerome Lawrence, characterized by Thornton Wilder as "fighter, builder, explorer, and mixer of truth and magic," and christened by Tennessee Williams the

Prologue

"Texas Tornado" and a "combination of Joan of Arc and Gene Autry—and nitroglycerine"?

Her work was ephemeral, but her pioneering vision of resident professional theatres producing new plays and classics has endured. Her name was Margo Jones. She was an American from Texas, an outsider from nowhere.

The Heart of a Girl

OWHERE WAS Livingston, a small town of about two thousand people set in the piney woods of Polk County in East Texas. Margo Jones, born on December 12, 1911, and christened Margaret Virginia, grew up in this quiet town, the second child of Richard and Martha Pearl Jones. The family lived in a two-story frame house decorated with Victorian gingerbread trim and separated from the town's main street by a white picket fence. On long summer evenings they gathered on the broad front porch to laze the time away in rocking chairs. Dad played the French harp and they sang hymns or special favorites like "Red River Valley."

Chinaberry and cottonwood trees provided shade, and day lilies, white roses, jonquils, blue iris, and red amaryllis grew in the yard. Margo told a friend that her mother would just open the door and fling her hand wildly, planting flower seeds everywhere. The century was new, times were tranquil, and life in Livingston idyllic. Once in a while a Model T chugged by the house, passing the horse-drawn buggies. Lying awake in her upstairs bedroom, Margo could hear all the gentle night sounds, the crickets singing and the frogs croaking from the creek out back, but another sound called to her. She knew it was a "devilish thing" to do, but sometimes she crept out of her bedroom in the early morning to go to the railroad station and watch for the four o'clock train to clatter up the grade, whistle blowing, on its way to *somewhere*—to Dallas, or Los Angeles, or New York.

WHILE MARGO YEARNED for excitement and a world outside the boundaries of small-town life in Livingston, the land must have seemed a rough Eden to her great-grandfather, Dr. Robert Batt Jones, and his wife Eliza Wingfield, who with their four grown sons moved from war-ravaged Mississippi to East Texas in the late 1860s.

A southern atmosphere permeated Livingston in the early years of this century. Many of the settlers had left the South after the Civil War to make a new life in the fertile lands of East Texas. Nourished by underground springs and the Trinity River, the land around Livingston bloomed with wild flowers: yellow jasmine and violets in January; sweet William, pansies, daisies, and bluebonnets in the spring; sweet peas and brown-eyed Susans in the summer; and red holly and redhaw berries in December. Wild blackberries, huckleberries, pecans, black walnuts, and hickory nuts flourished. Tangled switch cane, cedar thickets, and pine and hardwood forests sheltered deer, wild turkey, and bear.

Although the land was lush, times were hard, and Margo grew up hearing stories of the Jones family's journey to the West when, faced with defeat and poverty, "we pulled ourselves up by our bootstraps and started over." She heard too about the Old South of bygone plantation days, and about her cultured, highly educated family that had been devastated by the Civil War. The family traced its lineage to a Virginian, Captain Richard Jones, who served in the militia of his home state in the 1650s. Captain Jones's descendants lived and farmed around Petersburg, Virginia, where Margo's great-grandfather was born in 1798. After graduating from the College of William and Mary in Williamsburg, Virginia, Robert Batt Jones had earned his medical degree from Philadelphia Medical School, taken postgraduate training in London and Edinburgh, and then returned to Virginia. There he married Eliza Wingfield Harper, a member of the family that had settled Harper's Ferry, and they had six children, four sons and two daughters. They established their home in Enterprise, Mississippi, where Dr. Jones practiced medicine and farmed and the family prospered, enjoying the comforts of plantation living, made possible by an economy based on slavery. During the Civil War, Dr. Jones served as a surgeon, and his four sons, Virginius, Edward Ward, Joseph, and Robert, fought for the Confederacy. After the Civil War, the bankrupted family headed west to Texas to make another life. They found the rich red soil of Polk County ideal for growing cotton.

Hard work was often the theme of the family stories Margo heard—like the story of Uncle Willie Matthews, whose father had been killed in the Civil War. To help support his impoverished family, twelve-year-old Willie had driven a team of horses pulling wagonloads of cotton through the woods all the way from Livingston to Galveston, a two-hundred-mile round trip. Like so many other families who settled the Southwest, the Jones family would combine hard work and a belief in the value of education to make a new life.

Margo's grandfather, Edward Ward, who had served in the 28th Mississippi Regiment and Joseph E. Johnson's Tennessee Army, settled in Leggett, a small town north of Livingston. In the early 1870s he wed Mary Matthews, a native of Louisiana. They had nine children, four sons and five daughters. Their third child, born January 12, 1880, and named Richard Harper, was Margo's father. Edward Ward remembered the affluence and comfort of his childhood on the Mississippi plantation, surrounded by books and a genteel culture. He believed that the way out of poverty was through education, and he sacrificed to send his sons and daughters to college. Richard attended school in Polk County and Sam Houston Normal Institute in Huntsville. At the institute, one of Richard's sisters introduced him to her friend, Martha Pearl Collins, from Mason in central Texas.

Like the Joneses, the Collins family had fled the shattered South, moving from Virginia to Texas following the Civil War. William Braime Collins was a surveyor and in later years became a sheep rancher. His daughter, Martha Pearl, tall and slender with thick, dark hair and dark eyes, captivated Richard Jones. After they graduated from Sam Houston Normal Institute, both taught school for several years. During those years they corresponded, Richard addressing his fervent love letters to "Muriel," the nickname he gave her that she preferred then to Martha Pearl. In 1906, after a courtship of seven years and while they were both teaching school in Newton, Texas, they married, and the following year Richard brought his bride to Livingston.

Although their marriage was to endure, it suffered stresses and the conflict of two powerful wills. Martha Pearl confided to Margo years later, "Try to realize why I never encouraged you to marry. One can't tell a thing about a man until you are married." A photograph taken early in the couple's marriage suggests a less than perfect union. The new husband and wife, standing well apart, look sadly at the camera, lips tightened into thin hard lines. Martha Pearl had enjoyed living on her own and supporting herself for several years. Married at twenty-eight, a grown woman two years older than her husband, she found the adjustment to wedded life difficult. The youngest of five brothers and sisters, she missed her family and felt like an outsider among the clannish Joneses of Livingston, especially among Richard's five sisters—"the Aunts"—who all lived nearby and demanded their brother's attentions. Highstrung, with an artistic temperament and a love of books, oil painting, and music, Martha Pearl poured her talents and energies into religious devotion and her ambitions for her children.

Richard had ambitions as well. Hardworking and serious, with a brilliant logical mind, he created the position of county superintendent of schools in Polk County in 1907, earning the affectionate nickname "the Professor." In 1909 their first child, Stella Nell, was born, and two years later, a few minutes before midnight, Martha Pearl gave birth to a second daughter, Margaret Virginia—Margo. Two sons—Richard, born in 1915, and Charles, born in 1920—completed the family. Perhaps seeing an opportunity to break free of the confines of Livingston, Martha Pearl supported the family by teaching foreign languages, art, and music in the local schools while her husband studied law at the University of Texas in Austin. During World War I the family moved to Huntsville, Texas, where Richard worked as county agent. However, in 1921 they returned to Livingston, and Richard set up a law practice in a small frame building across from the courthouse.

MARGO LIKED TO visit her father at the courthouse, an imposing building with classic white pillars, high ceilings, and gray marble floors. Its sandstone foundation trembled when the trains roared by just a few yards away. Devoted to her father, Margo had decided that she wanted to be a lawyer too, and time after time she climbed the steep, narrow stairs to the second-floor District Court to sit quietly in the balcony and watch her father try his cases. Like most country lawyers, Richard practiced both civil and criminal law, and he served several terms as county attorney. Usually scholarly and serious in demeanor, Richard could become fiery and forceful in defense of what he considered to be right.

Once in a while Margo attended a traveling circus or a Chautauqua lecture that had set up tents in Livingston. The Livingston Opera House, like so many other legitimate theatres across the country, had closed its doors in the 1910s and reopened as a motion picture house. Although some Texas cities had theatre buildings as early as the 1830s and welcomed traveling acting companies, vaudeville troupes, and minstrel shows, Livingston, influenced by the local churches, levied a hefty $250 tax in 1857 against "transient" theatres. Amateur theatricals were acceptable, however, including a rage for "Tom Thumb weddings," in which children, dressed up as General Tom Thumb and his bride and members of their wedding party, enacted the event that had first caught the imagination of the country in the late 1800s. In her first performing role at four years old, Margo played a ringbearer in one such "wedding."

Like most children, she loved to play dress-up, trying on different characters from a brawny male in hip boots, gloves, and western hat to a delicate wood sprite wearing a wreath of flowers and castor bean leaves. Often she created her own dances to go with the costumes. "I thought that I was very attractive as a little girl," Margo recalled later. "I knew that I was pretty smart and I wasn't really unattractive, I guess, but I remember they used to say, 'Who's that fat little girl with the curly hair?'" Although Margo lost her baby fat and became in later years a glamorous figure, the "fat little girl" taunt remained with her. Dressing up, imagining other selves, creating theatre was a way of entering another world, becoming something other than the chubby little girl who wasn't as pretty as her older sister Stella Nell, a popular beauty with long, wavy hair and a sweet disposition whom Margo adored. Sitting in straight-backed chairs in front of their upright piano, she and Stella Nell often entertained the family with piano duets. Margo could play "by ear," but she also took music lessons and learned to read music. Besides piano, she played violin and ukulele. An early thrill was the first time that she ever saw "sheet music straight from a musical show in New York."

One day when Margo was eleven and sitting in the balcony of the courthouse watching the proceedings below, she suddenly realized that she "was in the presence of drama." She knew that she loved the courtroom sessions because they were like plays. "Up went a sheet in the barn where my sister and my brothers joined me in my first directing-producing venture," she remembered. "I was lucky to know so early what I wanted to do. It gave me a valuable head start."

A "chatterbox" with enormous energy, cat's eyes that changed with her moods from blue to gray, a square, determined jaw with chubby cheeks and dimples, and dark, curly hair, Margo seemed to move faster than anyone else. "Somehow I got to being ahead of myself in school," she said later. Behind her was her mother, pushing her. A neighbor recalls that Martha Pearl "loved to talk. Once she phoned and demanded that my mother go immediately to the window and look at the beautiful sunset. Of course, my mother missed the sunset because by the time Martha Pearl finished talking it was dark and sunset long past." Martha Pearl taught Margo to read before she entered first grade, enrolled her in elocution lessons, and encouraged her to write poetry, to memorize "pieces," and to appreciate "a beautiful sunset or a pale evening sky." According to her brothers, Margo and her mother often clashed, "because they were so much alike." She had a better, more egalitarian relationship with her father, and like many southern females she was a "daddy's girl," though not a petted, spoiled little girl but one who was expected to work and was valued for her intelligence. Margo worked in her father's law office, learning useful skills like typing and filing but also absorbing his logical and organizational skills and observing his gracious, persuasive manner. Her practical father advised her to make multiple copies of documents and letters, a habit she continued throughout her life even to the extreme of making copies of her most intimate love letters. A diverse clientele, young and old, rich and poor, black and white, visited the busy law office, and Margo, happy to be out in the world, learned to talk to them all with ease.

IN AN EFFORT to catch up with Stella Nell, who was two years ahead of her in school, Margo skipped the seventh grade, and she planned to skip one more grade so she and her sister could graduate together and enter college at the same time. She entered high school at twelve years old. Most of her classmates were older—fifteen, sixteen, and seventeen—and Margo felt "socially, terribly inferior." Scholastically, she maintained average grades, B's with a sprinkling of A's and C's, and an almost perfect attendance record. Her favorite subject was math, with English second, and she hated the mandatory home nursing course and home economics class. She played tennis and was in her words an "awful dumb player," but she was a strong swimmer.

With her family, Margo attended services every Sunday at a little country Christian Church nestled along Long Cane Creek, a few miles outside Livingston. On pleasant summer Sundays, everyone brought a covered dish to share and picnicked on the grounds. Although she didn't have a fine voice like her father, Margo sang in the church choir and especially loved the hymn "Shall We Gather at the River?" Church attendance and daily scripture readings at home, however, failed to stifle her adolescent devilry. "With my family as strict as they were, I was not about to do a lot of the things that kids in the same grade were doing," Margo recalled. Still, she and her best friend, Corene Brock, who lived across the street, sneaked cigarettes at slumber parties, and even in the little church where she had been baptized by immersion in the water of Long Cane Creek, Margo had a wild streak. Years later, she claimed to have been "one of the first girls to smoke with the men out behind the churchhouse between anthems at choir practice."

Teenage Margo "already liked a little booze," perhaps trying to do what her older classmates did or as a natural rebellion against the conservatism of Livingston. In 1901 there were numerous saloons in Livingston, and they were said to bring so much "shame and crime that women did not go to town on Saturday afternoon." The good people of the town voted to ban liquor in 1902, a decision that enraged the saloonkeepers, who set fire to the town businesses and destroyed them all except for one warehouse. "So much was sacrificed that the people have never allowed another open saloon in the town . . . keeping the whole of Polk County dry." Corene Brock remembered that "you were very careful who you offered a drink to in your house, or if you went to someone's house and they offered you a drink you were careful who was there and whether you took it or not. . . . I've always said [Livingston] was . . . narrow-minded . . . and unbending."

Livingston may have been narrow-minded, and it was certainly like thousands of small towns across the country in the early twentieth century with its life of church picnics, school functions, and hard work, but Margo's strict, educator parents nonetheless encouraged their daughter to broaden her mind and spirit. Although they were born in the nineteenth century, Richard and Martha Pearl Jones's values were shaped by the vast Southwest, new country where it was possible to create a new future not bound by the strictures of the past. As her brother Charles says, "All of our family were individuals each with completely different ideas as to what we wanted to do with our lives. . . . The love of family was always there even though we might not have always agreed with what another of the family was trying to do. [Our parents] gave us the desire to learn about everything and the opportunity to do what we wanted."

This childhood idyll, this springtime, ended quickly.

IN DECEMBER 1924, when Margo was thirteen and Stella Nell fifteen, they caught the flu. At that time, influenza was often a deadly illness, with bed rest and plenty of fluids the standard prescription for cure. The ailing sisters moved into their parents' second-floor bedroom, which opened onto a large balcony. Although ill herself, their mother nursed them.

In late December, a winter storm hit Livingston, leaving the trees shimmering with ice and the house laden with long, beautiful icicles. One day Martha Pearl checked on the girls, admonished them to stay in their warm beds, then went back downstairs. As she left she told Stella Nell, "You take care of Margaret."

The girls had been confined to their beds for weeks with little to do except gaze out the windows. Lying there, bored with the forced inactivity, Margo admired the frozen scene outside her window—a wonderland of glistening icicles hanging from the eaves and from the balcony. It wasn't enough to enjoy the beauty from a distance. She wanted to hold it close to her. She cajoled and begged and finally persuaded Stella Nell to go outside and get her an icicle. The loyal Stella Nell got out of bed and went onto the balcony, her breath clouding in the freezing air. She broke off an icicle and brought it back to Margo. Almost immediately the ice began to melt in the warm room. Then Stella Nell began to cough and her nose started to bleed.

The bleeding did not stop for ten days. On the tenth day, January 1, 1925, Stella Nell died. Margo blamed herself. At thirteen years old, she felt that her life was over. "I didn't think I could go on."

UNPREPARED FOR DEATH, the Jones family did not have a space reserved on Cemetery Hill, and so buried Stella Nell in Uncle Willie Matthews's cemetery plot. The whole family suffered. Martha Pearl, who had had a slender, girlish figure, gained weight, becoming matronly and old beyond her forty-six years. She devoted herself to religion and searched for answers in many different churches. Richard, who had lost his beloved law partner about the same time as Stella Nell's death, turned to work for solace.

Margo was profoundly changed. Her naturally curly hair, which she had grown out and wore in long curls over her shoulders, fell out and when it grew back it was straight. There were no illusions, no playacting that could change what had happened or bring Stella Nell back. At the impressionable age of thirteen, she had been singled out. Stella Nell's death left Margo as the oldest child and the only daughter in the family, imparting to her a special significance. In time, Margo accepted her sister's death, saying that "somehow God let me know that she had not gone, that she was just as much with me, that I must try to be the kind of person she wanted me to be." Margo decided, in effect, to live a life for two. She must achieve greatness not only for herself, but for Stella Nell. Art and work would be her salvation.

Margo doubled her work load in school and, as she had planned, skipped another grade, her junior year, to graduate with Stella Nell's class. In her senior year, although still the youngest in her class, she was at last accepted by her classmates, who had previously rejected her as a "perfect goodie-good." The pain of Stella Nell's death had lessened and she was able to enjoy her final year of high school. The "bunch," a group of girls who had been Stella Nell's friends, made her a part of their group. She attended "slumberless" slumber parties, afternoon teas, birthday parties, a "possum" hunt, and football games. She Charlestoned at dinner dances and drove around Livingston with her friends, hanging out at Fain's Filling Station or the White Kitchen, snapping "Kodaks." She won ribbons and trophies in debate and declamation and gave humorous readings, like "Betty at the Baseball Game" and "Husbands," on the radio and at clubs. In the senior-class play, *A College Town*, she acted the part of Molly, a honeymooner, who had one line. She passed notes in school, signing them "Margarette," chewed Beech-nut and Orbit fruit gum, watched the boys paint "Seniors '27" in the class colors of rose and gold on the Livingston water tower, and believed in the class motto, "Push, Pull, or Get Out." She dated Kenneth Kennedy, the dark-haired, good-looking senior class president, and attended the Senior Reception with him. Kennedy was the oldest boy and she was the youngest girl in the class, and Margo liked him and became "terribly upset" when she discovered he preferred a girl who was away at college. But she pressed the pink roses he had given her in her memory book and wrote, "Don't Ever Forget." She thought her senior year had been a "great success."

Margo soon had a new beau—Paddy Vance, a freckle-faced local boy a few years older than her. Alarmed that their daughter's new friend seemed to have serious marriage intentions, Richard and Martha Pearl encouraged Margo to continue her education instead. They needn't have worried. Margo had no plans to marry or to stay in Livingston. She had always been attracted to the wilder boys, with their "desire for adventure in life," because she shared that desire.

Early one morning in the fall of 1927, Margo left her home for the railroad station. This time she didn't have to sneak out of the house. She was fifteen years old and she was going somewhere. She said good-bye to her little brothers and her parents and boarded the train, leaving the piney woods of Polk County for the dry plains of Denton, in North Texas.

THE GIRLS' INDUSTRIAL COLLEGE of Texas (later renamed the College of Industrial Arts, then Texas State College for Women, and now Texas Woman's University) was founded in 1901 partly through the efforts of the Texas Women's Christian Temperance Union, which petitioned the state legislature to establish a college for women. The college with its red brick colonial buildings was located forty miles north of Dallas in the small town of Denton, "a clean town morally. There are no saloons here." In 1903, the first president of the college, Cree T. Work, emphasized that a "woman's sphere" should be as large as a "man's sphere," and that "woman's rights are as great as man's." The motto of the college, "The spirit of the need of the times demands ability to do, and we learn to do by doing," signaled that women were to be taken seriously as productive, full members of society. In this atmosphere of support and challenge, young women were prepared for the future.

In her freshman yearbook photograph, Margo looks even younger than her fifteen years. Her short, straight hair, combed flat against her head, emphasizes her round cheeks and snub nose. Although younger than her classmates, at her full height of five feet six inches and dressed in the college uniform of blue silk sports suit and white crepe middy blouse, Margo did not feel socially inferior as she had in high school. To set herself apart from all the other Margarets, however, she liked to be called Margo.

The social life of the campus centered on the auditorium, where productions of class plays and picture shows were presented. Students were also allowed to go to the picture show in town once a week, and seniors could go to town on any evening "in groups of three or more without a chaperone." On Sunday afternoons seniors could ride with their gentlemen callers in cars "provided two couples go in a five passenger car, and have secured permission from the Dean of Women in advance." Margo dated occasionally, going to the

The Heart of a Girl

movies or sometimes attending weekend house parties, but most of her time was devoted to work.

In 1930, the Depression forced millions of people out of jobs and onto breadlines. The college bulletin of that year reported that "undaunted by the persistent cries of 'hard times,' the College of Industrial Arts miss buckles down to real work and continues her college education in spite of the economic condition." Margo helped pay her expenses—tuition and room and board that amounted to approximately five hundred dollars a school year —first by waiting on tables, then by working at the college library, and finally by acting as secretary to the dean. Between her freshman and sophomore years she worked as a counselor in a Salvation Army camp and had a brief romance with a young man from Rice Institute who she thought "looked like Rudy Vallee." Other summers she worked at her father's law office in Livingston or attended college summer sessions.

College years are often when lifetime friendships are formed, but Margo, despite many casual friends and acquaintances, didn't have any intimate friends. She even preferred not to have roommates; when she did, she told her mother, she "made the best of it." Years later when she recalled her college years, Margo couldn't think of any significant personal experience then. She chafed at the pace of academia. Although outwardly gregarious, she often felt alone and apart, "not like the rest of them."

She competed in swimming, joined the Dramatic Club, and participated wholeheartedly in theatre productions, but busy as she was, Margo found time to write to her family every day, needing their support and love. Martha Pearl wrote back daily, sending son Richard to the railroad depot with the letter, and often with a box of freshly cut flowers as well, for her "precious Margie." In her letters, Margo told her family of her activities and her hopes and dreams. "I do love to do things," she wrote. "Maybe someday I'll get an M.E. degree and I don't mean a Master of Engineering—Instead it will be a Master of Experience. . . . I have made friends with the most important people on campus —both faculty and students. . . . I really think if one believes in their own life and future that they should invest in it. If you buy books, if you spend money in travel, if you buy a typewriter, take lessons in swimming or riding—any of these things you are really investing in yourself and you will get a high percentage of interest. . . ."

In her letters, Margo rarely talked about her classes, characterizing one class in particular as "junk." She was not an outstanding student, especially during her first two years at college. She received a D in English Composition and failed Survey of English Literature and had to repeat the course. She enjoyed a small success when several poems she had submitted to the school's literary magazine were accepted. The short poems are of middling quality, standard adolescent verse, but the fact that they were published must have given Margo a great deal of satisfaction. Not given to introspection, driven instead to "do things," she found it difficult to sit still long enough to write. She regretted her inability to write well, but recognized that her talents lay in action, not contemplation. It was in classes like Debate, Story Telling, Expressive Voice, Dramatic Art, and Modern Drama that she excelled.

BECAUSE THE COLLEGE did not have a drama department, Margo majored in speech and minored in education. She found her classes crowded with aspiring actresses. She was the only student interested in directing. "This was fortunate," she wrote later, "because I had a chance to direct much more than the average directing student. . . ." She acted in a few plays, but "always with the clear understanding that I was doing it to acquaint myself with the actor's viewpoint and problems."

While she was at Denton, Margo often attended performances at the Dallas Little Theatre. She hoped to see a professional production too, since once in a while professional theatre companies played Dallas and Fort Worth, their productions usually "star packages" that had been originally presented in New York. Such productions were infrequent now, though, unlike in the nineteenth century when enterprising actors and theatre companies traveled "the road" by horseback, wagon, boat, and train, bringing classics, comedies, and melodramas to a regional audience. By the early twentieth century, the increased expense of railroad travel and the competition of the movies had contributed to the slow decline of such traveling companies.

In fact, at the beginning of the twentieth century, American theatre lagged far behind English and European theatre. America had not produced a world-class dramatist or any acting ensembles of note, nor had it created a national audience devoted to fine theatre. Since 1896, American theatre had been held in a stranglehold by a powerful syndicate formed by New York businessmen. For sixteen years this syndicate and booking agency controlled most of the New York theatres as well as theatres across the country. From a business standpoint, the syndicate was quite successful: profits flowed into a central New York office. Without competition, the syndicate could raise prices to whatever the market would bear. But the destructive effects of the syndicate system were far-reaching. Repertory, the practice of a theatre company alternating a series of plays, was abolished in favor of presenting one play in a long run. Centralized control of plays and playwrights led to plays written with tried formulas or to adaptations of foreign hits. The star system and the lack of permanent theatre companies eliminated the training ground for actors and other theatre professionals.

Although Broadway boomed in the 1920s, presenting plays by Eugene O'Neill, Elmer Rice, Maxwell Anderson, Philip Barry, George S. Kaufman, Ben Hecht, and Charles MacArthur, anyone living west of the Hudson River rarely had an opportunity to see the best new plays. In 1931, noted Shakespearean actor and theatre owner Walter Hampden toured his production of Edmond Rostand's *Cyrano de Bergerac* to Texas, and Margo saw a matinee, her first professional theatre performance. She was enthralled. Later she would write that she had seen something wonderful, "right down to the leaves on the trees in the garden with the balcony." At the end of the play everyone in the audience left, but Margo sat in the theatre alone and silent. "New vistas opened . . . ," she said.

While working at the college library, she came upon the current issue of *Theatre Arts* magazine, and she soon discovered bound copies of past issues. There she learned of the Old Vic in England, the Abbey Theatre in Dublin, and the Moscow Art Theatre. She read of the work of two pioneering theatre companies based in New York, the Washington Square Players and the Provincetown Players, both founded in 1915. Led by George Cram Cook, the Washington Square Players produced new American plays by Cook, his wife Susan Glaspell, Zona Gale, and such foreign playwrights as Ibsen, Schnitzler, Chekhov, and Shaw—all playwrights who did not have a chance of being produced on the Broadway stage. The Provincetown Players produced the work of a young writer named Eugene O'Neill under the direction and with the set designs of Robert Edmond Jones. The commercial theatre did not want to risk an investment on such untried new work.

The influence of the European art theatres and the Provincetown Players was being felt in towns across the country where dedicated amateurs had begun to create community theatres, or "little theatres" as they were called at the time. Many theatre intellectuals of the period, including Kenneth MacGowan, one of the founders of the Provincetown Players, felt that the little theatres were the zeitgeist of the new theatre, a national theatre for America. The community theatres gave everyone who wanted it a chance to perform, and brought live theatre to a regional audience. Margo learned that whenever the established theatre became unresponsive to new writing and new techniques, art theatres, often founded by gifted leaders outside the theatrical mainstream, broke through tradition to reinvigorate the theatre and send it in a new direction.

"At first it was like one great big glorious binge," she wrote later. "But when I began to sober up a little I found that *Theatre Arts* was more than a great record of our American and World theatre—that it was a standard—a credo—a philosophy. . . ." Margo absorbed the philosophy of artistic idealism proclaimed by the magazine. She read Robert Edmond Jones's book *The Dramatic Imagination* and felt that he spoke directly to her when he said, "I know that there are young people in this country who will really create for the theatre of their time, who will bring something into existence there that never has existed before." Stimulated by one of her professors and by *Theatre Arts*, Margo "lit into the Greeks, Shakespeare, Ibsen, Chekhov, O'Neill as though they were my own personal discoveries . . . reading all their works." She read a minimum of a play a day, a practice she claimed to continue throughout her life. She had found her theatre family. .

DURING ONE OF Margo's last semesters of college, she heard that John William Rogers, a Dallas playwright and drama critic, planned to speak to journalism students about dramatic criticism. Somehow she finagled her way into the audience. In a discussion session after the lecture, Rogers asked Margo what she was interested in. "I'm going to be a director," she replied.

Struck by her intensity and by this unusual ambition for a young woman, Rogers sent her a pamphlet containing George Bernard Shaw's advice to directors. Margo underlined many of Shaw's thoughts on directing, such as the necessity on the part of the director for "tact, judgment, infinite patience, intense vigilance, consideration for others and imperturbable good manners," and his assertion that "women directors are at no disadvantage in comparison with men." Margo cherished the pamphlet, and said later that the attention and encouragement she received from Rogers "helped me tremendously at that moment in my life."

While she was at college, Margo sometimes worked on publicity for the school's theatre productions, dropping off press releases and stories at the *Dallas Morning News*. There she met the esteemed "Critic of the Southwest," John Rosenfield. The roly-poly Rosenfield told Texans what to like in drama, music, and art. In the 1920s he had led the drive to revive the Dallas Symphony Orchestra, but his first love was the theatre. He enjoyed Margo's enthusiasm for the theatre and began to serve as her mentor, guiding her taste, getting her theatre tickets, discussing plays, and advising her about publicity. With Rosenfield's help, Margo learned how to sell a story, find an angle, and promote herself and her ideas. "Figure," Margo said later, "that I'm 51 per cent creator and 49 per cent promoter."

The Heart of a Girl

After five years of study, Margo received a Bachelor of Arts degree in speech in 1932. She earned her Master's degree in 1933 from the Department of Philosophy and Education, since the school did not offer an advanced degree in drama. Her graduate course work focused on educational psychology, and the subject she chose for her thesis, "The Abnormal Ways out of Emotional Conflict as Reflected in the Dramas of Henrik Ibsen," incorporated her interest in both theatre and psychology. Writing that "an emotional conflict is the state of the mind that is the result of the thwarting of a powerful drive," she examined three characters' ways of dealing with emotional turmoil: Hedda's suicide in *Hedda Gabler*, Ellida's hysteria in *The Lady from the Sea*, and Irene's insanity in *When We Dead Awaken*. In her thesis, Margo supported the belief that a strong, ambitious drive should not be stifled or obstructed and, drawing upon what she had learned in her Advanced Mental Hygiene course, she suggested ways to solve emotional conflicts—ways that would lead not to abnormality but rather to mental health. The thesis is somewhat dull and dependent on psychological jargon; nevertheless it is remarkable that Margo was able to convince the philosophy and education department even to allow a thesis about three strong female dramatic characters. But the paper is even more extraordinary in that it is a personal justification for Margo's own ambition.

As epigraph for her thesis, Margo selected a telling quotation from Samuel Butler's *The Way of All Flesh*: "All our lives long, every day every hour, we are engaged in the process of accommodating our changed and unchanged selves to changed and unchanged surroundings; living, in fact, is nothing else than this process of accommodation." Margo's college years had been a process of accommodation, of change. She didn't like academia, but she knew that college was a necessary stop in her journey to do something, to be somebody, for herself and for Stella Nell. The girl still grieving and guilty over her sister's death had turned into a compelling woman. Her senior picture, taken in 1932, shows a young woman with short, fashionably wavy hair, wearing lipstick and a big, confident grin. All traces of baby fat have disappeared, revealing a broad, open face with a strong, square jawline.

MARGO COULDN'T WAIT to begin her life in the theatre. She received her M.S. degree at eleven o'clock on a sunny August morning in 1933, and that afternoon she walked through the door of the Southwestern School of the Theatre in Dallas, where the writer and critic John William Rogers taught playwriting. The school's co-founder, Louis Veda Quince, who had studied Stanislavsky's method at the Boleslavsky-Ouspenskaya School in

The Heart of a Girl

New York and acted with the Theatre Guild there, taught acting and directed the plays at the school. His partner, Frank Harting, who had worked with the Dallas Little Theatre, taught makeup classes and was business manager.

Harting remembers: "We were busy painting, and nailing, and hammering on a hot afternoon, long before air conditioning. I was painting one of the rooms and I looked up, and this young girl was there with a big smile on her face. She looked like a saddle-shoed country girl, just out of the boondocks. She said, 'My name is Margo Jones and I've been going to school over at Denton at Texas Women's College. John William Rogers told me about your school. And I don't have any money, but are you going to give any scholarships?'"

Harting said, "My God, I haven't thought about scholarships." Then the phone rang and Harting, covered with paint, couldn't answer it.

Margo said, "I'll get it, if you want me to." Harting told her to answer it and listened in amazement as she told an inquiring caller "about our school, who was on the faculty, what the hours were going to be." In fact, Margo had researched the school thoroughly before applying.

"Margo grabbed a paint bucket and a brush and said, 'Look, I'm a good painter, why don't you do something else, and I'll finish this room.'" From that moment on, Harting recalls, "she pretty much was running things. I mean, she could do anything that needed to be done, and do it almost better than anybody. She got her scholarship."

At the Southwestern Theatre School, Margo attended all the classes, learning method acting from Louis Veda Quince, makeup from Harting, playwriting from John William Rogers, and dance and eurythmics from local ballet instructor George Frierson. And she used her typing skills as a "glorified office girl." She never acted in a production, but she built scenery and worked on props and, Harting remembers, "She was a great influence on the whole morale of the school, and she made people happy. . . . She gave everybody a shot in the arm if things were not going right. She had a way of making you feel they were going to go right. She was a highly motivated positive thinker."

Margo stayed at the school almost a year and described the experience later as "a source of real inspiration." She knew, however, that she needed "to gain an understanding of theatre all over the world," and jobs, especially in theatre, were scarce. She had read in *Theatre Arts* about the Pasadena Playhouse, a renowned amateur community theatre in southern California. Founded by Gilmor Brown, a former stock company actor with Ben Greet's company, the Pasadena Playhouse's first home was an old burlesque house. Brown had replaced the horse and dog acts, strippers, and high-kicking dancers with productions of Shakespeare, Ibsen, and Shaw. The little theatre, nicknamed "the moth-eaten temple of drama," was condemned by the Fire Department in 1925, but a house-to-house community campaign soon raised enough money to build a new theatre on palm tree–lined El Molino Boulevard.

The Playhouse had received national attention in 1928 when it produced Eugene O'Neill's surrealistic play, *Lazarus Laughed*. Rejected by Broadway producers as too difficult and too expensive, with its enormous cast, complicated mob scenes, masks, and special music, *Lazarus Laughed* provided the impetus for the Playhouse School of Theatre Arts. There the forty-seven-year-old Brown encouraged his young students, gave them lists of plays to read, and through his example demonstrated what a life in the theatre could be. A close friend said that Brown "has no personal life. His life is the theatre." Margo emulated that devotion, telling him later, "I think you know what Pasadena means to me. It is my Faith and Love of what you have done here that makes me know that I must do the job that must be done. . . ."

Because of its proximity to Hollywood and despite its amateur status, the Playhouse attracted members of the film community, including actors, talent scouts, and agents. The actors, eager to be discovered, worked for no salary on the Playhouse stage. Attracted by the theatre's reputation and the glamour of Hollywood, Margo enrolled in the 1934 Pasadena Playhouse Summer School.

Before she took the bus for Pasadena, Margo visited her family in Livingston. She saw her old friend, Corene Brock, who was married now. "I don't know how I'm going to do it," Margo announced to Corene, "but this time next year I'm going to be on a trip around the world."

Headed to California at age twenty-two, Margo was taking her first trip out of Texas. But even the surprised Corene wasn't skeptical. She knew that when Margo said "she was going to be doing something, she would be doing it."

AT THE FIRST meeting of the Pasadena Playhouse Summer School, Margo saw that she was one of the youngest participants and the only woman interested in directing. Forty-three students from twelve states, many of them teachers in high schools and universities, had enrolled in the six-week session. Again, she felt inferior and asked herself, "What am I doing here?" But one of the students, a young theatre teacher from Tulsa, Oklahoma, named John Stine, was charmed by a caricature Margo had drawn of him and spoke to her. The two became close friends. They cut classes together, drank beer, and had long discussions about poetry. Margo was thrilled when she and Stine were chosen to co-direct the final summer-school play, a Chinese epic tragedy called *The Chalk Circle.* Margo also stage-managed the first production, *School* by T. W. Robertson.

One night, while a forest fire raged in the mountains outside of Pasadena, Margo and John labored on a set, hammering and nailing and "working like mad." Then—Margo remembered the moment dramatically—with "a red glow hitting against the sky," their supervising director, Jerome "Jerry" Coray, walked in.

"Something told me," Margo said later, "that we were going to be friends." Stine and Margo gathered the courage to ask him to have a drink with them after work. For three days they asked, and for three days he refused. Finally, he announced to their casts, "We're going to take time off now. I'd like to see Mr. Stine and Miss Jones."

Knees shaking, they followed Coray into a little room off a garage. There he snatched a bottle of gin off a shelf and set it on a table. "Goddammit, have a drink," he said.

Although it was the middle of the afternoon, the three proceeded to down a fifth of gin. But, Margo remembered, "The important thing is that there was a welded friendship. . . ." Normally, instructors didn't go out with students, but Jerry was different. He and Margo toured the hills and arroyos around Pasadena in his Studebaker convertible. Later, Margo remembered: "We'd sit on mountain tops and drink Seagrams 7. We'd look over the valley and see millions of lights or two million not even counting the stars. We talked a lot about life and everything and there will never be a time that I won't admit that there was something very physical, but it was so much more spiritual. . . ."

In fact, Jerry was her hero. She "worshipped him." Coray, several years older than Margo, darkly handsome and a talented director, encouraged her and treated her as an equal, and Margo said later "that the first time I ever fell in love, really in love, was with Jerry. . . . It was at a time when I did not need or demand the things that people in love later demand. . . . It was fun. . . . I had no desire to make it serious."

Shila Wardall, a wealthy young widow in her early thirties, studied acting at the summer school. She often asked Coray and Margo to visit her at her home in nearby Ojai. Although quite naive, Margo soon realized that Shila was "terribly in love with Jerry." At Shila's house they listened to music, talked, drank and, Margo remembered, "Jerry and I were like a couple of little puppies. In fact, we used to fight." Once when she saw them fighting, Shila asked Coray, "What do you get out of this?"

Coray replied, "Sex."

The Heart of a Girl

Margo thought his answer was "cute." She said later that she "was a corn-fed girl hitting into the middle of what seemed like tremendous glamour," and it is clear that she enjoyed her newly awakened sexuality, romanticized her involvement with Coray, and relished her role in what she perceived as a love triangle.

When the summer-school session ended and after Margo returned to Texas for a time, Shila arranged for Margo to stay with her and direct the Ojai Community Theatre. Margo directed the Community Players in several plays, most notably *Hedda Gabler*. She supervised and worked on all aspects of the productions, including makeup, set building, and lighting. But she soon found that Shila had an ulterior motive. Shila knew that if Margo was around, Jerry Coray would come around too.

IN THE SPRING of 1935, perhaps responding to hints or suggestions from Margo, who dreamed of traveling, Shila asked the younger woman to go with her around the world and help her edit a book her husband had written on Hindu religion. Shila agreed to pay Margo's expenses and to give her a small salary for the editing job as well. Despite her poor showing in English Composition and a creative way of spelling, Margo accepted the job with confidence. She knew that Shila hoped Jerry would go with them. After much discussion about the awkward situation, Jerry and Margo decided that he should go, and why not, it might be fun.

In May 1935, the three sailed from Los Angeles on a Japanese boat, the Tsu Maru. They docked in San Francisco for three days, then sailed on to Honolulu and then to Japan and China. They visited Shanghai, Peking, Hong Kong, Singapore, Saigon, and Cambodia. They sailed to India, to Africa, then to England and France.

In a picture taken aboard ship, Jerry stands between the two women with his arms around both. The three are draped with leis; Jerry and Margo look slightly dazed and Shila smiles broadly. The details of the trip remain unclear, the romantic involvements hazy. Margo cryptically said later, "It was a strange trip." She was young, out of her depth perhaps, in a "Noel Coward" arrangement she may not have fully understood. Whatever the situation may have been, though, she did not seem harmed by it. "All I know," she recalled later, "is that as a youngster I had a chance to go around the world with Shila and Jerry. I got to know people."

Whenever they were on shore, Margo went to the theatre. Although she didn't know any foreign languages, she understood the universal language

The Heart of a Girl

of the theatre—the ephemeral bond between actor and audience, the visual richness of gesture, movement, and light. As part of the audience, she saw theatres that were a necessary and beautiful part of their country's culture.

In September 1935, after seeing theatre in every major world capital, her ship docked in New York. "My first glimpse of New York," she said, "was the greatest thrill of all."

She arrived the same night that Joe Louis, the "brown bomber," knocked out Max Baer. During her stay she saw another memorable contemporary event—the Group Theatre's production of *Waiting for Lefty* by Clifford Odets. Founded in 1931 by Harold Clurman, Cheryl Crawford, and Lee Strasberg and modeled after the Moscow Art Theatre, the Group Theatre introduced the plays of Clifford Odets and created an ensemble of talented actors. A decade later the company disbanded for various reasons—some members went to Hollywood to work in the burgeoning film industry, the leadership became divided, plays were artistic successes but commercial failures, and the Group had failed to develop a loyal subscription audience. But on the night Margo saw *Waiting for Lefty*, a play about a union meeting of striking taxi drivers, she witnessed an audience so roused in support of Odets's workers that many roared out, "Strike! Strike!"

Although her first visit to the city was brief, Margo wrote later, "New York made me feel that I had to go to work for the present and plan the future. The theatrical air was exhilarating, and it filled my lungs."

JERRY AND SHILA returned to California, but Margo decided to find work in the theatre back home in Texas. On the ship, she had heard about the Federal Theatre Project. Founded in 1935 and funded by the Work Projects Administration, the Federal Theatre Project created thousands of jobs for unemployed theatre people, produced plays by leading playwrights, developed the Living Newspaper productions, which presented important social issues, and introduced audiences all over America to live theatre. "It seemed logical to me," Margo wrote, "to go to my home territory and participate in the enormous program Federal Theatre had mapped out."

Sponsored by the Houston Recreation Department, the Houston Federal Theatre in 1935 hired Margo as assistant director. In the six months she worked on the Federal Theatre Project, Margo began getting to know the important people of Houston, including the newspaper people, who encouraged her and wrote about her. Margo acted in and stage-managed *Pioneer Texas*, a successful Federal Theatre production dubbed *Amateur Texas* by local wits. In an article ostensibly intended to publicize the play, the interviewer seemed much more interested in Margo Jones.

"Most stage managers are men," the reporter wrote. "Ask about her plans. You should see the determination in her eyes, feel the confidence in her voice, conviction in every word when she tells you, 'My job is in the theatre. I'm going to be a director. Sounds pretty Horatio Alger . . . I guess . . . but I know—I know!'"

Although *Pioneer Texas* received good reviews and met a WPA administrator's criteria for plays "agreeable to Texans [that] would not cause unfavorable criticism," the Houston Federal Theatre did not receive wide public support and failed after a few months. One problem was the shortage of skilled actors and technicians. The government required that the project employ men and women from the relief rolls, and Houston, like many other cities in the country, did not have a large number of unemployed actors on the public dole. Since Margo had not been on relief she was one of the first to be let go.

"Texas was a hard nut to crack, and we failed to crack it," said Hallie Flanagan, the petite, dynamic director of the Federal Theatre Project. A westerner, born in South Dakota, Flanagan had directed the Vassar Experimental Theatre. Her appointment to head the Federal Theatre Project earned her the derision of the New York theatre establishment, or "the boys," as the *New York Times* called them, "the local gentry for whom the theatre does not exist outside Manhattan." Flanagan approached her enormous job of creating a popular regional art theatre with great enthusiasm and unswerving commitment. Despite fine productions such as the world premieres of T. S. Eliot's *Murder in the Cathedral* and Marc Blitzstein's *The Cradle Will Rock*, and Living Newspaper presentations of *Power* and *One Third of a Nation*, the Federal Theatre was undercut by critics who accused the project of communist leanings. The project was terminated by Congress in 1939. Hallie Flanagan's aim had been broader than just putting theatre people to work. "Our far-reaching purpose," she said, "is to organize and support theatrical enterprises so excellent in nature, so low in cost, and so vital to the communities involved that they will be able to continue after federal support is withdrawn."

Although the program failed, Margo's experience with the project had been a success. She had become familiar with the activities of the Houston Recreation Department and had learned about the plight of unemployed theatre people and, most important, she had absorbed Hallie Flanagan's vision of a national theatre.

The Heart of a Girl

IN THE LATE summer of 1936, out of a job and with a strong need to make contact with other theatre people, Margo decided to go abroad, to revisit London and Paris and to travel to Russia, the Mecca for any serious theatre person. Unlike Chekhov's three sisters who only dream of going to Moscow, the center of art and culture, twenty-four-year-old Margo was not interested in "dreams without action," and along with theatre people from all over the world she attended the fourth Moscow Art Theatre Festival.

In 1936 Texas celebrated the hundredth anniversary of its independence from Mexico. Margo managed to get herself selected as a Texas Centennial delegate to the Moscow Festival. Costumed in western shirt, chaps, boots, and Stetson, she posed for publicity photographs. Her parents probably funded the major expense of the trip, but to help finance it, she decided to write articles about the Festival and sell them to the local newspaper, the *Houston Chronicle*. Unfortunately, the paper didn't want to buy them. Not to be deterred, on the day she was leaving for the Festival, Margo ordered her taxi driver to stop at the *Chronicle*, and charged in to have a final word with the editor. He bought the articles.

How could he resist Margo Jones?

"She was absolutely compelling," one woman who worked with her remembers. "When she was with you and talking with you, you had the impression that there was nobody else in the world but you. Her smile and snapping eyes 'seduced' everyone around her."

With Zoe Leger, a Houston friend, Margo sailed from New York on the *Aquitania*, first for visits in London, Paris, Berlin, and Warsaw, then on to the Festival in Moscow and Leningrad.

"THE MOMENT OF passing over the border line of Poland into Russia was like stepping over the footlights . . . onto a stage where an exciting play was taking place," Margo enthused. Along with *New York Times* theatre critic Brooks Atkinson, playwright Lillian Hellman, designer Mordecai Gorelik, theatrical cartoonist Al Hirschfeld, and others from the United States and around the world, Margo was eager to experience the richness of the Russian theatre.

She arrived in Moscow in a cold, drizzling rain. The Moscow purge trials and executions, based on Stalin's accusations against his former comrades, some actually heroes of the Revolution, were making international headlines, but Margo in her single-minded focus on theatre talked only of plays and production techniques. Politics held no interest for her. Many of the plays, heavy with Bolshevik propaganda, bored her.

She was fascinated, however, by the Russian audiences. The theatres were

The Heart of a Girl

packed with hundreds of workers in heavy boots and colorful shawls sipping tea in the lounges and sitting in theatre boxes. She moved among them, watched them applaud and cheer for fifteen minutes after a performance, and marveled at their enthusiasm. Why couldn't theatre in America generate the same kind of excitement?

"They seem to find in their theatre," she observed, "not only glamour, but life itself." She might have been describing herself.

Margo and other Festival guests spent an afternoon crowded into the theatre of the legendary director Vsevolod Meyerhold, watching him rehearse Chekhov's play *The Anniversary*. "Though quite an old man," Margo wrote, "Meyerhold jumped about the stage with the agility of a youth and was able on a moment's notice to suggest to his actors the exact movement to portray their respective characters."

Meyerhold had begun his theatrical career as an actor with Stanislavsky's Moscow Art Theatre, then left to develop his own company and his own ideas. "The theatre [in Russia] is the director," Margo observed. Meyerhold's theatre reflected his personality, beliefs, and techniques. Unlike Stanislavsky, who approached acting from the inside, Meyerhold believed in developing a role from the outside, using dynamic movement called biomechanics, voice control, and directing techniques drawn from the circus, mime, and silent film comedies. Unfortunately, only a year later in 1937, Meyerhold's theatre was closed by the Bolsheviks ostensibly because it did not conform to the precepts of socialist realism. Actually Meyerhold had offended Stalin with his bold satires of Bolshevik bureaucrats. In 1939, shortly after Meyerhold made a speech in defense of artistic freedom, he was arrested and then executed.

Supported by the state, the six hundred professional theatres and the hundreds of amateur workers' theatres in Russia did not depend on box-office successes, like the plays of Broadway, but flourished in an atmosphere devoted to art. In one of her *Houston Chronicle* articles, Margo wrote that the "one great lesson we should learn from the theatres of Russia . . . is the deadening effect of commercialism on the theatre." She felt that the best hope for the American theatre was the Federal Theatre and the experimental little theatres and college theatres.

On her last day in Moscow, Margo attended a rehearsal of Gogol's *Dead Souls* and a dramatization of Tolstoy's *Resurrection* presented by the Moscow Art Theatre. Although, according to Margo, the play was long and tedious, the house was full and tensely quiet except for occasional bursts of applause. She felt that the performance was "the most finished production I have ever seen."

The next day the group left for Leningrad. After twelve hours on a train, where they had a cold lunch and no coffee, they arrived again in a chilling rain. But the "fine and old and well kept" buildings of Leningrad reminded Margo of Paris. Unlike Moscow, where the streets were filled with mobs of poorly dressed peasants, Leningrad, she said, "seemed to be filled with youth." Margo toured the Hermitage, famous for its collection of Western European art, visited the palaces of the Tsar, and saw a bad production of *Othello* and a propagandistic play, *The Sinking of the Fleet*. The Festival ended with a colorful production of a Pushkin tale by the Kirov Opera and Ballet.

"The Russian theatre," Margo wrote, "added to my belief that the theatre can mean and do much for the culture of a country. It gave me moments of exalted beauty and one can not ask more of any theatre." On the boat going home, Brooks Atkinson, the *New York Times* theatre critic, told her that for the next few months "he would be seeing an average of five plays a week and that more than anything else he would miss the enthusiasm of the Russian audiences."

Middle-aged and tweedy, with a slight New England twang, small, neat mustache, and round silver-rimmed glasses, Brooks Atkinson appeared sedate, but he shared Margo Jones's keen enthusiasm for the theatre. Theatre critic of the *New York Times* since 1925, the most influential theatre critic in the country, Atkinson had a reputation for integrity and fairness. The length of his reviews suggested his opinion of a play. A one-paragraph review usually meant a pan, often an amusing one. During a revival of Ibsen's *The Wild Duck* in 1938, the theatre audience could hear the whistle of a cruise ship from the nearby West Side pier. Noting the ship's departure in his review, Atkinson declared, "It proved that something was moving." He reread *Hamlet* once a year because it is "the great play that says everything." His reviews were clear and uncomplicated. After seeing Maurice Evans's *Hamlet*, he wrote, "Only the dopes will stay away from this one."

Atkinson called his work "the pleasantest job in the world." Unlike many critics, he laughed out loud in the theatre. Since he was color-blind, he often consulted others about the hues of the set and costumes. Although Massachusetts-born, Harvard-educated, and now a Manhattan resident, Atkinson was not an eastern provincial. He used his powerful position to encourage the development of theatre not just in the East but throughout the country. Most of all, he loved and respected theatre and its people, and they in turn respected him, after his death making him the only theatre critic to have a New York theatre named after him. He was the man Margo Jones had most wanted to meet in Moscow.

Years later Atkinson liked to tell the story of how he met the woman who, as he said, had "the mind of an adult and the heart of a girl."

The Heart of a Girl

He walked into the lobby of his Moscow hotel. A young woman who had been sitting on a sofa jumped up and rushed toward him. He saw an enthusiastic girl, her face glowing with vitality, her body leaning slightly forward exuding energy and a searching curiosity. Her slender frame seemed unable to contain the force of her personality. He heard her rich voice, trained in the rounded tones of drama school but shaded with the drawl of her Virginia ancestors, say, "Mr. Atkinson, my name is Margo Jones. You don't know me, but someday you will."

The Shining Hour

HE TAXI DRIVERS in Houston all knew her. And God help them if they called her Margaret or Maggie or Miss Jones. "Baby," she'd drawl, "this is Margo. Can you pick me up?"

Margo never learned to drive, perhaps because of a couple of bad experiences she had had in the past. At the age of five she was riding in an open Model T with her father when the car hit a bump and she was tossed out, unhurt, into a ditch. When she was in her teens, while riding with boyfriend Paddy Vance, their car overturned in front of her house. Again she was not hurt, but the experience was surely frightening. Perhaps these accidents were the reason she never learned to drive, but it is just as likely that she simply couldn't be bothered, that her energies were focused on matters more important to her. So she depended on taxis and friends to take her to work, to appointments, to parties, even to visit her parents in Livingston.

The cabbies stopped at her little theatre on the banks of Buffalo Bayou, where the lights still burned at 2:00 or 3:00 A.M. They often drove her to an all-night diner where she drank cup after cup of black coffee, ate her favorite Rice Krispies, and plotted and planned and dreamed.

Filled with the idealism and naiveté of youth, boundless enthusiasm, and the rhetoric of a visionary inclined to purple prose, Margo had one consuming grandiose ambition: to create the most exciting theatre in America. "I saw no reason," she said, "why I couldn't have it in Houston."

HOUSTON SPRAWLED for miles on the flat Gulf plain. It was a city of contrasts, a big, ugly city that still held onto its small-town roots. Segregation, slums, and poverty tarnished the brilliance of the Rice Hotel, the opulent luxury of the department stores, and the formal elegance of estates like Ima Hogg's "Latin Colonial" Bayou Bend. In Houston, the perfume of yellow roses, white azaleas, camelias, and night-blooming jasmine mingled in the air with the odors of crude oil, smokestacks, cow manure, and dirt.

A hundred years before Margo Jones came to Houston determined to create a theatre, the city imported theatre, like the rest of its art, from the East. Houston audiences stopped their fighting, drinking, gambling, and speculating to visit the town's fashionable new theatre built by theatrical impresario

The Shining Hour

Henri Corri, who billed himself as the "founder of the legitimate drama in the glorious Republic of Texas." Here, professional touring companies played Shakespeare, Restoration comedies, popular farces, and melodramas featuring actors like the young "Irish Roscius" Joseph Burke and seventeen-year-old Joseph Jefferson. In fact, Houston built a theatre before it built its first church. The Young Men's Society of Houston debated the question "Have theatres an immoral tendency?", but could find no opposition. Although the rougher elements frequented the theatres, smoking, spitting, and swearing, the reputable classes attended too and managed to keep some decorum.

In this raw town, theatre offered a stimulating diversion from the rigors of frontier life. It was a place where if the audience were lucky they could gawk at President Sam Houston, or witness a knife fight between gamblers in the lobby, or see the leading lady gallop a horse onstage, or watch an unfortunate actor playing Richard III accidentally set his ostrich plumes ablaze on the spermaceti chandeliers.

IN THE LATE fall of 1936, when Margo returned from Moscow, Houston had a thin veneer of sophistication, but beneath that veneer it was still a frontier town with a special Texas affection for promoters and pioneers. And, despite the Depression, it was a town booming with new wealth. Since her position with the Federal Theatre Project had ended, Margo took a job with the Houston Recreation Department teaching playground directors to put on children's plays in the city's parks. She wanted to direct, however, and felt that her best chance lay with the amateur little-theatre movement.

Houston already had a little theatre, primarily devoted to imitations of lighter Broadway hits. Houston audiences rarely had an opportunity to see classic plays or serious drama by contemporary playwrights. Margo did not attempt to get involved with the Houston Little Theatre, which presented plays popular with an older, more conservative crowd. The group already had an established director anyway, and Margo wanted to have her own theatre, where she could control the artistic choices. Instead she surrounded herself with a group of young Houston artists, musicians, actors, and writers, who considered themselves the "Left Bank" of the Bayou. Included in the group were Zoe Leger, the writer friend who had accompanied Margo to Moscow; Arthur "Sonny" Koch, a handsome, blonde engineer; artists Carden Bailey, Gene Charlton, Nione Carlson, and Maudee Carron; actor Sidney Holmes and his wife Malvina; and Rice Institute student and budding writer William Goyen. The group christened shy Bill Goyen the "Houston messiah," because he hailed from the town of Trinity in East Texas and because he refused to get out of his car when he first met them because he thought they were so wild. Jean Rauch-Barraco, a successful Houston oral surgeon and the only female in the 1933 class of the Dental College of the University of Texas, was friendly with the group. Dr. Barraco and her husband were patrons of the arts, and a friend recalls that "Doc was close to anyone in town with talent." "Doc" Barraco became Margo's dentist and her lifelong friend and confidante.

While she formed close relationships with her friends, Margo's interaction with her family, particularly with her mother, was often difficult. Martha Pearl had become more and more religious and disapproving of Margo's career choice. Her parents never visited her in Houston, and had little understanding of her life there. When friends drove her to Livingston for an occasional afternoon or weekend visit, Margo did not want her parents to know about her smoking and drinking—to them she was still their little Margaret. While she was at home, she stopped smoking "cold turkey," and the strain contributed to the brevity of her visits. When Jewish friends Sidney and Malvina Holmes drove Margo to Livingston, they were greeted by Martha Pearl, who thought them quite exotic and called them "God's Chosen Children."

However, Margo's parents did provide a financial supplement to her meager salary. Her father's law practice, like most rural law practices, was primarily devoted to land law, involving disputed titles to tracts of land. Common court practice assigned a percentage interest in the contested acreage to the winning lawyer. By this method and through purchase of land, on which he usually reserved the mineral rights, Richard Jones had acquired substantial land holdings. Locally in Livingston, he became known as the "land man." In 1932, oil had been discovered on one of his properties, producing an income fluctuating between eight hundred and a thousand dollars a month. A few years later, he deeded the land with its oil income to his three children. The two hundred to three hundred dollars that Margo received nearly every month for the rest of her life allowed her to travel and to devote herself full-time to theatre.

Not always comfortable with her parents, Margo saw more of her brother Richard, who lived in Houston now, and whom she had even persuaded to appear in one of her productions. Still, Margo garnered most of her support and sense of family from her friends. They gathered to play records, often the best new jazz or classical recordings, to dance, read poetry, or just talk.

One rainy Houston afternoon Margo led the group to a Houston restaurant she had found that ignored the local law and served mixed drinks. Carden Bailey remembers that "Margo always managed everything. She got the two biggest raincoats, hung them on the hooks on either side of the booth, and then buttoned them together so no one could see in. We sat there the whole afternoon drinking sidecars, first sidecar I ever had." Self-assured to some, to others Margo was naive "Miss Livingston." Bored by her single-minded focus on theatre, they sought to educate her about art and music and, with little success, urged her to read literature other than plays.

To artist Maudee Carron, however, the twenty-five-year-old Margo was a "goddess"—a goddess who smoked Camel cigarettes, drank Scotch when she could afford it, danced wildly and spontaneously, trailing colored scarves à la Isadora Duncan, preferred to sit on the floor, talked about theatre for hours, obsessively and passionately, and collected turtles of every size and shape, made of carved wood, precious stones, jade, and ivory.

Turtles? her friends wondered.

Margo had begun her collection at college when a boyfriend gave her a turtle pin. Then she had received two small turtle figures she called Shakespeare and Ibsen. A man she met in India gave her a jade turtle that she named Whimsey. Others were given her in Japan and at various stops around the world. By the time she arrived in Houston, she had several hundred turtles, all with names having to do with the theatre, all gifts. She claimed never to have bought one for herself: "I just hint for them," she said. Maudee Carron made her a little book titled "Turtle Soup," filled with lovely color washes, drawings, and a story: "Once she had been Margaret but mar-was so british and was so everything but mar-go was anything and so everything. . . . Once she found a turtle. . . . No, turtles that breathed died and her turtle must be immortal in stone or jade."

Some of her friends thought Margo's turtle collection a ridiculous affectation. Others saw it as a symbol: "We'll all make it," Margo would say; "We'll all get there, baby." Margo enjoyed the collection and always took several with her when she traveled—the only possessions she owned except for her clothes, books, and records—and the turtles often earned her some free publicity when a reporter wanted to talk about something other than theatre. The plodding turtle hardly seems an appropriate symbol for energetic Margo but, of course, the tortoise in the fable outpaced the distracted hare, a victory for single-minded endurance.

DURING HER YEARS in Houston, Margo lived with Leola Prestridge, a former Livingston classmate, in various rented rooms. One two-room apartment next to a skating rink where organ music blared day and night had "sickening pink walls" and a landlady who demanded they pay her quarters for the electric bill whenever they ironed. Margo did not like sharing an apartment, but sharing saved on expenses. She didn't spend much time at home

The Shining Hour

anyway and she slept late since she usually stayed up most of the night talking or rehearsing. The two women got along well, although they had little in common. Leola, quite religious and two years older than Margo, worked regular hours as a secretary for an insurance company. Back home in Livingston Leola had admired Margo, wishing sometimes that she looked like her dynamic friend, and she didn't seem to mind living now in Margo's shadow. It was a good thing. As one friend asserts, "Only Leola could have lived with Margo. Margo was a slob."

Soon after Margo began her job with the Recreation Department, she discovered that the department owned a small building, a former incinerator and sometime mule barn on Buffalo Drive near the Bayou, which had a little seventeen-by-thirty-five-foot proscenium stage, space for about 125 seats, dressing rooms, a prop room, and a small kitchen. Margo persuaded the City Council to let her have the building free of charge to produce plays. She would continue her regular teaching duties, she assured them, and would direct plays on her own time.

In the local newspaper she announced the birth of a new theatrical group —the Houston Community Players—and invited Houstonites to come audition for the first production. For the Players' first show she chose Oscar Wilde's *The Importance of Being Earnest,* in part because it was in the public domain and she wouldn't have to pay royalties. Also, the cast was small and the sets didn't have to be realistic. Nine people showed up for auditions, including Sonny Koch. Margo cast them in the nine roles of the play. Six cast members donated a dollar apiece to finance the production. Margo persuaded her artist friends, Carden Bailey and Gene Charlton, to design the set and costumes. According to Bailey, who designed a number of sets for the Community Players, he always gave in to Margo's demands "because you couldn't do anything else. She sweet-talked you until it became bullying. And she got you to thinking, 'Well, gee, this would be nice if I could do this, maybe I *could* do it.' . . ." The designers created a stylized black and white set, described by Margo as "off-modern." The Recreation Department budget paid thirty-seven dollars for black duvetyn drapes for the stage. Against the duvetyn, the designers set white objects—a tennis net and tennis balls suspended from above for the garden scenes, and boxes and packing crates covered with white cardboard and topped with white porcelain vases for the scenes in the drawing room. The actors were costumed in black and white. According to a newspaper clipping, the direction was stylized: "for each smart saying of Wilde's, the actors have a smart stage movement; for each epigram they have hilarious gestures." The play opened on December 3, 1936.

From the beginning Margo put her personal stamp on the theatre. For example, she felt that opening night, even for a two-night run, should be an event. Usually she wore slacks or a jump suit for ease of movement scrambling up and down ladders and building sets. On opening nights she shed her everyday jump suit and, fashionably dressed with her hair coiffed, she greeted her audience as they arrived and shook their hands as they left the theatre, thanking them for coming and enthusing about the next production. She treated the theatre as her home and tried to make her audiences feel comfortable, like welcome guests as well as important participants in the theatrical experience. The Players charged twenty-five cents admission and ran *The Importance of Being Earnest* two nights. The production received just one review, favorable, but because of Margo's skills as a promoter the Players had already begun to attract considerable public attention.

The proceeds from *The Importance of Being Earnest* paid for the royalties on the next production, in February 1937, Elmer Rice's dramatization of the Reichstag Trial, *Judgment Day*. For this production too Margo had no budget for set or props, and the play demanded a realistic courtroom setting and a large cast that would crowd the small playhouse stage. What to do? With her usual talent for imaginative problem-solving Margo persuaded District Judge Allan Hannay to allow her to present the play in his courtroom, using county lighting and county-owned furniture. In addition, she gained the judge and his wife as enthusiastic patrons of her theatre, and the newspapers gave free publicity to this unique theatrical event. The production played to standing-room-only audiences.

In March, Margo directed one of her favorite plays, *Hedda Gabler*, and earned praise from the Houston theatre critics. Finally, the first season of the Houston Community Players closed with the rollicking Russian farce, *Squaring the Circle*, which featured "ladders, ropes, sawhorses, and barrels, all painted a violent red and skeletonized against a black backdrop." Made confident by their successes, the Players raised their ticket price for this production: admission would now be thirty-five cents.

When *Squaring the Circle* closed, Margo left Houston for a six-week visit to the West Coast. To her eyes, every season was theatre season in California with its flourishing movie industry, major broadcasting studios, and professional and amateur theatres. She wanted to see as much theatre as possible, get ideas for her upcoming season, but most of all she hoped to see Jerry Coray. They had talked a few times on the telephone, always when Margo called him.

In California, she saw Alfred Lunt and Lynn Fontanne in the Pulitzer Prize–winning play *Idiot's Delight*. She attended a disappointing production of *Dead End*, and she saw *Boy Meets Girl*, a road show that had played Houston the previous season. At the Pasadena Playhouse, she visited with Gilmor Brown and enjoyed a new play by Fulton Oursler and Aubrey Kennedy called *Nude with Pineapple* and also *Fly Away Home*, a satire by Dorothy Bennett and Irving White. The most memorable production she saw, however, was Jerry Coray's Federal Theatre production of Paul Green's play *Johnny Johnson*. With a cast of over a hundred, fifteen sets, and a full orchestra playing the Kurt Weill score, the production with its red lights bursting over the dark bodies of soldiers and lonely Texas boy holding a lasso and singing of the Rio Grande, left a vivid impression in Margo's mind. "Play after play can be produced," she said, "and amuse and entertain an audience yet not give one moment that clings in the mind after the theatre is empty and dark." She left California inspired by the theatre she had seen, and still infatuated with Jerry Coray. Involved in his directing, he continued to serve as Margo's mentor, but it appears that he did not share her romantic feelings.

Although Margo was in love with Jerry Coray and thought of him often, she did not pine for him. Theatre came first and men second. Margo adored men and while she loved to "talk girl talk" with Virginia King, an attractive Houston actress and model, she had little time for dates. When she did go out it was usually with someone involved with her theatre. Or sometimes a group of ten or fifteen of the Community Players rented a weekend bungalow in the Galveston Bay area. They separated the cottage into a men's area and a women's area for sleeping although they spent little time sleeping and most of their time drinking. Malvina Holmes recalls that many of the Players drank heavily, trying out different drinks, even going through an absinthe period at one point.

One weekend at the bungalow, the group was drinking grapefruit juice and vodka. As a joke, they stopped putting vodka with Margo's grapefruit juice. When she insisted on more to drink, they kept giving her straight grapefruit juice, and she kept getting more and more "drunk." Finally, everyone staggered into their beds, and Margo, thinking she was deliriously intoxicated, leapt from bed to bed, dancing and singing. To get some peace, they finally told her what they had done. She didn't care and kept on dancing.

Her most ardent admirer at this time was blonde engineer Sonny Koch, who often acted as her chauffeur as well as her escort. Years later Margo said, "I had the devotion of a sweet and wonderful boy named Sonny Koch. He was a guy who asked me to marry him every fifteen minutes. He was good-looking. . . . He was talented. . . . I should be grateful to Sonny because there was somebody always nearby who believed in me with all his heart."

The charismatic Margo attracted many acolytes, admirers, and devotees and received romantic letters and love poetry from both sexes. One smitten young woman gave Margo a handwritten book of poems, seventy-six pages long and inscribed to Margo Jones on her birthday, December 12, 1940. Margo's friends hooted at all this adulation, and one friend, using the pseudonym "Twisted Column," wrote a comic epistle, saying in part, "I would whist that you be kind; I think your folicle [*sic*] matting is divine. . . . Madam, in conclusion, may I offer my poor love, unworthy and unknown as libation to you as a Greek. Alas, for it being all more or less Greek."

Why did Margo Jones receive so much attention and adulation? Fifty years after their association with her in the Houston Community Players, admittedly then in the springtime of optimistic youth, people still speak of their great love for Margo Jones, about how she rarely talked about herself, about how she brought out the best in them, about her "pure energy," about how she "always put other people first somehow, even though she had this driving ambition." Olivia Lockhart Glahos, a young Players actress who later became an anthropologist, remembers that "Margo worked entirely on nerve and enthusiasm and vitality and belief. [She was] a super salesperson. . . . one of those people that everybody would like to have a piece of."

I N T H E F A L L of 1937, at the beginning of her second season with the Players, Margo made a deal with the Houston Recreation Department to use the proceeds from the group to pay her salary and all production costs. In return, the Recreation Department freed her from her teaching duties. She could now devote herself full-time to developing the Players. She did everything. She chose the plays, produced them, held auditions and cast the actors, directed the plays, built sets and costumes and, with a cadre of volunteers, she set about selling two-dollar season subscription tickets. By the third season, they had sold twenty-seven hundred season subscriptions. Legend had it that Houston businessmen when summoned to the phone would tell their secretaries, "If it's that Jones woman, tell her I'm out of town, but I'll take ten tickets."

The success of the first season drew one hundred new members to the Community Theatre's second season. Margo chose Kaufman and Hart's *Merrily We Roll Along* with a cast of seventy-five to open the season, followed by Irwin Shaw's *Bury the Dead*; Thornton Wilder's *The Long Christmas Dinner*; the new play, *Nude with Pineapple*, that she had seen at the Pasadena Playhouse; Shakespeare's *Macbeth*; Molière's *The Learned Ladies*; James Warwick's *Blind Alley*; and P. G. Wodehouse's *Candlelight*. And she found time to direct the Houston Newspaper Guild in Hecht and MacArthur's popular *The Front*

The Shining Hour

Page. An extraordinarily ambitious season for a company made up of volunteers and with virtually no budget!

Houston Players member Malvina Holmes recalls that the Theatre "was the most wonderful place in the world for every misfit and lonely person. The Community Players was like a psychiatrist's couch to many people who were lost. We were all poor as church mice and . . . we had all the musicians, the painters, costume designers, everybody came there. It was the culture."

And when they came to the Players, they were welcomed by Margo Jones, who had no time for the pettiness and the politics that plagued so many community theatres. Of course, since the Players had no rules, no dues, no officers—just Margo, who ran the organization as a benevolent autocrat —there was little opportunity for dissension. Margo knew what she wanted, and she always got her own way.

Acclaimed theatre director Nina Vance, who founded Houston's resident professional theatre, the Alley, began her career with the Houston Players. She had heard about the theatre group on the Bayou and about their custom of having Sunday brunch. She put on a big hat and a dress "because I thought that's what you did on Sundays and I went." Nina Vance, then Nina Whittington, expected to discuss playwrights or acting techniques; instead the ever-pragmatic Margo took one look at her and said, "You're new, baby. How many tickets can you sell?"

Nina replied that she had just arrived in town and so didn't know many people yet. Undaunted, Margo advised, "Baby, you take the phone book and you start with A and you go to Z."

"It was the most brilliant lesson I ever learned," Nina said later. "There is where my Houston theater begins."

Like so many others, Nina Whittington stayed to sweep the floor, to act in leads and walk-ons, and to do whatever Margo told her to do. Margo preached a philosophy of total dedication. "It's just as important if you hammer the sets and scrub the floors," she would say.

Since all work was strictly volunteer, most Players held full-time jobs during the day and worked at the theatre early into the morning. Margo would say, "Babies, it's two o'clock, go out and get something to eat and be back at three." Maxine Mesinger, a young volunteer who later became a well-known Houston newspaper columnist, recalls Margo's discipline: "If Margo said we were going to work seven days a week until three in the morning, nobody bitched; and if they bitched they weren't welcome in our group. . . . You couldn't be around Margo and not be dedicated. She had a fire. . . ."

A number of people who went on to garner fame in the theatre world gathered around that fire. Actor Sidney Holmes, who looked like a young Charles Laughton, worked at a bedspring company but appeared in almost every Players production during their six seasons and later worked at the Alley Theatre. Reigh (later changed to Ray) Walston, a young, skinny redhead from Laurel, Mississippi, set linotype for a printer during the day and little dreamed that the Houston Players would be the beginning of a long and successful theatre, television, and film career. Novelist and poet William Goyen acted in plays while he studied at Rice Institute. German-born Joanna Schreiber, who later changed her name to Joanna Albus, worked for Eastern States Petroleum, became a close associate of Margo's, and later founded her own professional theatre in Houston. Others included writer Cy Howard and actor Larry Blyden.

Ray Walston remembers well his first role for the Players. He auditioned for a part in Maxwell Anderson's *High Tor*, the first play of the 1938 season. "I got the part of a sailor and said one word. . . ." But by the end of the season, Walston had captured a lead, Petruchio in *The Taming of the Shrew*. How does he explain this remarkable leap in just a few short months? "Margo could instill in the actors a confidence—she could convince actors that they were the greatest actors that ever lived."

Margo had a gift for selecting plays, inspiring actors, and casting just the right person for a role, and she had a natural ability for promotion and publicity. She had to work at directing. She loathed blocking, moving actors around on the small proscenium stage. She often stayed up all night in her favorite diner, drinking coffee and moving tiny toy figures across a diagram of the set. Or sometimes she would empty a big box of kitchen matches onto her living room floor and block the actors' movements with the matches. "Of course," remembers actress Virginia King, "that blocking would all be changed." Often Margo procrastinated until the cast insisted that she direct their movements. Then she would give them basic movements and tell them to do whatever they were comfortable doing. Ray Walston recalls that "first and foremost she was a great promoter—a great general—she could put things together and get things done quicker and better and more thoroughly than anyone I've ever known. She didn't have any particular style or knack or one way of directing."

When tensions ran high, Margo sometimes exploded into anger. According to Walston, "She could be so angry inside, but she would have a big, strong grin on her face and say, 'Now, listen, darling, let me talk to you, baby.'" She directed intuitively, smoking cigarette after cigarette, running her fingers through her short, permed hair, cajoling, commanding, and cursing. During one rehearsal she became so involved in a scene that she chewed on, then discarded, a page of the script, later growing frantic when she couldn't find it.

With a company of volunteers, Margo could not afford to make enemies. One of her favorite sayings was "Culture is getting through life with as little friction as possible." She depended on charm and persuasion to get her actors and technicians to do what she wanted. She also liked to create little rituals for her casts. On the opening night of Chekhov's *Uncle Vanya*, for example, she called the actors together. They saw she had a bottle of Russian vodka and, Ray Walston recalls, "a lot of little bitty glasses."

"Everybody just follow me," Margo said, and loyally though uncertainly they all trooped after her to the back of the playhouse and then to a dark area below the stage. With a dramatic flourish, she poured the vodka and the actors dutifully gulped it down. Unfortunately, the point of the Russian drinking tradition as preparation for *Uncle Vanya* was thoroughly lost on at least one cast member—Ray Walston, who was nervous and remembers thinking only about getting upstairs and finishing his makeup.

Margo had little time and perhaps little inclination for actor training and coaching. With amateur actors, the first step was making them believe in themselves—and this she accomplished. "She had complete enthusiasm," Virginia King remembers. "Everybody was 'baby'. . . . You just got carried along by her impetuousness and tremendous drive . . . until you just believed. . . . It was great!"

Company members brought nails from home to build flats and platforms, but most productions depended on imaginative staging and lighting effects rather than elaborate sets. Audiences grew accustomed to, but sometimes regretted, the sparseness. When the Players produced Wilder's *Our Town*, which had startled Broadway audiences the year before with its bare stage setting, one audience member congratulated actor Joe Finkelstein, saying, "Oh, Joe, I loved it, but I wish you could have afforded scenery." Sonny Koch with his engineering background became the group's electrician and lighting designer. In the first year or two, they used a primitive salt-water dimmer system. According to Sonny, "You take a ten-gallon pickle crock and fill it with salt water and you have a broom handle with a pie tin on the end of it. You have one line on the pie tin and the other end on a piece of metal that's hooked to the inside of the crock. And the electricity goes through the salt water from one to the other. And the closer they come together . . . when they touch at the bottom you have full lighting. But if you separate them, then the lights get dimmer. It's very dangerous. . . ." As the Players grew in number, they were able to purchase standard lighting equipment, and by 1942—just six years after their first production—they had acquired over fifteen thousand dollars worth of equipment, produced more than sixty plays, and grown from the original nine to about six hundred members.

Margo seized any opportunity to drum up business and promote the Players. Before her production of Shakespeare's *As You Like It* opened, she went to a local high school, where she spoke to an auditorium of restless students. Knowing that she had to get their attention somehow, she asked, "How many of you know Whiskers Savage?" Dozens of hands shot up at the mention of the popular local fighter. "Good," continued Margo. "Then you'll be interested to hear that Whiskers is coming to rehearsal tomorrow night to show our actors how to do the wrestling scene properly." Then she quickly contacted Whiskers Savage and persuaded him to attend rehearsal, where he was mobbed by the dozens of high school students who had come to see their favorite fighter and who stayed on to buy tickets for the play.

To involve the public she presented many large-cast plays and urged participation at every level. When she needed 150 dancers for Cy Howard's new musical *Going Up!*, to be presented at Houston's Music Hall, she announced a jitterbug contest with the "prize" a part in her production. She entered the Players in the Texas One-Act Play Contest, and they received statewide attention when they won several years in a row. The Players formed the Junior Community Players and presented children's plays. They offered acting classes, stocked a drama library, held play readings, initiated a six-week apprenticeship program, started a theatre class for teachers and clubwomen, presented programs for civic organizations and charities and, in the early forties, performed at army bases too.

At one point, feeling the need for press attention but having no specific occasion for it, Margo talked Houston mayor Oscar Holcombe into proclaiming "Theatre Week" and then ghostwrote the proclamation for him. Even when she managed to get away for a brief vacation, she continued to court the press. Upon arrival in Mexico City for a two-week stay, she dashed off a letter to *Houston Post* theatre critic Hubert Roussel, who poked gentle fun at her in a subsequent column.

"Margo Jones, the dynamo and director of the Community group, is in Mexico City but what good does that do?" he wrote. "Allegedly on a vacation to recover from stresses . . . she rushes out for one look at the town and then levels at this corner a voluminous airmail letter revealing that she is having a wonderful time planning her next show, *Johnny Johnson*, and that she wishes everybody were there because the climate of Mexico City is fine for rehearsing. And she has been to Mexican productions of *Rain* and *La Tosca* on the same night or perhaps simultaneously. And she has the complete seasonal program of the Pan-American theatre digested in elaborate detail. And she has been to the flower market, and it made her sorry because she realizes now they should have sent to Mexico for a funny wreath to be used in *Room Service* and she is living in the Astek [*sic*] hotel indicating missing at least one day of her schooling."

In December 1938, the Players presented *Special Edition*, a new play by Harold Kewpie Young, city editor of the *Houston Post*. In the playbill for that production, Margo summed up the philosophy of the Players:

> They hope to continue developing a group that can present plays that will be satisfying and exciting to audiences and will be judged as either good or bad productions—not as just "pretty good considering they are amateurs." They feel that the word amateur has a bigger and deeper meaning, that the word amateur means working for the love of it. They also hope to provide a training ground for actors and technical workers who want to make theatre their profession. They want to encourage playwrights by providing a stage and actors for the presentation of original plays. Above all, they want to remember that "the play is the thing." And if audiences come and are thrilled by the magic of theatre, then they will consider their work well done and the compensation golden.

It was a golden time for the Community Players, and they had a golden-girl director. However, despite her apparent total belief in the Players and even Hubert Roussel's elevating them to semiprofessional status in his newspaper reviews and articles, Margo began to see the limits imposed by inadequate rehearsal time and amateur actors. Her friend Maudee Carron criticized the Players' productions, saying that the acting did not always ring true, and she urged Margo not to compromise her art, telling her she was made for finer things.

GRADUALLY MARGO BEGAN to venture more into the theatre world outside Houston, and the theatre world began to hear more about her. In December 1939, her picture appeared in *Stage* magazine when she was named one of twelve outstanding little-theatre directors outside New York City—the only woman selected. She attended the Confederacy of American Community Theatres in Washington, D.C., in the spring of 1939 and was named Director of the South. As a member of the National Theatre Conference, an organization of directors of community and university theatres formed to serve the noncommercial theatre, Margo traveled to the annual meetings in

New York. She was elected to the Executive Council of the NTC, serving with Gilmor Brown of the Pasadena Playhouse; Frederick McConnell, the autocratic director of the Cleveland Playhouse; Barrett H. Clark, a renowned critic, author, and the executive director of Dramatists Play Service; Allardyce Nicoll, noted author, theatre historian, and chairman of the drama department at Yale University; and Hallie Flanagan of Vassar.

During her stays in New York then and for many years after, Margo sublet Rosamond Gilder's spacious, book-filled Gramercy Park apartment while Gilder traveled, usually to Europe to report on theatre there. Gilder, editor of *Theatre Arts* and a brilliant writer and influential figure in the theatre world, had become Margo's valued friend.

In 1941 the National Theatre Conference sponsored a new-play project to offer the best new plays for production outside of New York before they were presented on Broadway. When William Saroyan made his new play, *Jim Dandy*, available to theatres outside New York, Margo wrote, "This is the first step toward the decentralization of the American theatre." She believed that if more playwrights of Saroyan's stature would make their plays available to theatres across the country, actors could find work outside New York, repertory companies would be established, and playwrights could attach themselves to producing groups, leading to a renaissance in the American theatre.

On her trip to Washington, D.C., in 1939, Margo saw a theatre-in-the-round production by the Blue Room Players of Portland, Oregon. As part of the program for the Conference, they performed a light comedy in a hotel ballroom. Impressed by what she had seen, Margo knew that she could do the same thing in Houston. Because the playhouse was not air-conditioned and Houston summers were blazingly hot and humid, the Players had been unable to offer a summer season. But what if they could use an air-conditioned hotel ballroom? On the train back to Houston, Margo startled the person sitting next to her by jumping out of her seat exclaiming, "Why not?"

First, she had to convince the City Council of Houston. She stood before them. She had wheedled, charmed, coaxed, and backscratched. Now it was time for hardheaded directness. She looked at the men in the Council and said, "Honey, I don't care what it costs, you got the money. Houston's got the money. Give me the Grand Ballroom in the Lamar Hotel. What the hell's a ballroom when you haven't got a damn ball? When you can have *theatah*, when you can have plays. Wonderful, magical plays. Honey, we got to have some magic, some wonder. Give me that ballroom."

They did. In June 1939, the Houston Players launched their first summer season, in the round, in the air-conditioned Lamar Hotel ballroom with a production of *Louder Please* by Norman Krasna, followed by *There's Always Juliet* by John Van Druten, *The Second Man* by S. N. Behrman, *The Circle* by Somerset Maugham, *Springtime for Henry* by Ben Levy, and *Room Service* by Murray and Boretz. At first, her actors were terrified by the intimacy of theatre-in-the-round, but Margo's enthusiasm and the audience's enjoyment of the light summer fare bolstered their confidence. Margo soon discovered that she enjoyed the intimacy of the round stage, the closeness of audience and actor. Even the blocking, which she usually dreaded, became fluid and natural. The need for expensive flats and backdrops was eliminated; lighting, costumes, and a few props and pieces of furniture could set the scene. Although she later founded the first professional arena theatre in America, Margo was frank about her role as pioneer. Asked if she had invented theatre-in-the-round, she truthfully replied, "No, honey, the Greeks did."

Performing in a hotel ballroom sometimes had its surprises. One memorable evening during a rowdy convention at the Lamar, a brass band marched into the lobby. Alarmed, Margo raced out of the ballroom. Would they leave, please? The play was about to begin. The band ignored her. Instead of making a scene or calling for the manager, Margo summoned the full force of her southern charm. Playfully, she began to direct them, joining in their spirited music, and before they knew they were being manipulated, she started to lead them like a drum major. She paraded them around the lobby, through the door, and out into the street, then returned to the quiet ballroom to watch the play. Asked about what had happened, Margo replied nonchalantly, "Why, honey, I just marched them down the street so they wouldn't disturb the actors."

The six-play summer season moved to the Texas State Hotel in 1940 and to the Rice Hotel in 1941. The plays were presented free of charge to nearby army camps, and men in uniform were admitted free to all productions.

In 1940 Norris Houghton visited the Players to research his new book, *Advance from Broadway*, a report on theatre outside of New York. Margo told Houghton that her most successful productions "have been the classics. I always have to sell standing room for Shakespeare, Ibsen, or Chekhov." Houghton had found that many other community-theatre directors depended on light comedies and recent Broadway hits, and he wondered, "Is it perhaps those dramas a director cares for most, and in which he consequently outdoes himself, are those which the public most heartily enjoys? May it not be possible that the reason the classics are not supported in some places is because they are not well-enough done . . . ?" In his book Houghton described Margo as a "young woman with a mop of unruly close-cropped golden curls and twinkling blue eyes."

"What's the idea of giving me blonde hair?" Margo asked when she saw him next.

"It's a halo, darling," Houghton replied.

Margo may have found success with the classics, but she was also drawn to new plays. She presented Harold Young's *Special Edition*, then discovered Richard Shannon and Cy Howard and premiered their plays *Howdy, Stranger* and *Going Up!*, both huge musical spectaculars.

AT THE END of her summer season in 1941, Margo returned to California to see theatre, look for new scripts and, of course, see Jerry Coray. One day they happened to meet in Gilmor Brown's office at the Pasadena Playhouse. Coray whispered, "I know a script you should do." The script was *Sunrise in My Pocket* by Edwin Justus Mayer, a playwright who had two Broadway plays to his credit, *The Firebrand*, starring Joseph Schildkraut, presented in 1924, and his best play, *Children of Darkness*, featuring Mary Ellis and Basil Sydney and presented in 1929. Coray introduced Margo to a film actor who had a copy of the play. She read the script, a story about "a mournful Indian who has been educated at Harvard, a bellicose pirate, a cowardly swindler and a frontier strumpet, all marching with heroic Davy Crockett to fight for freedom at the Alamo," and she knew it would be perfect for her Houston Players. But she had no idea how to get in touch with the playwright. She phoned Brooks Atkinson, who as *New York Times* theatre critic would know how to reach Mayer, and Atkinson, who liked Mayer's work and of course liked Margo as well, used the telephone call as the basis for an article in the Sunday *Times*. He also took the opportunity to praise Margo Jones's courage in presenting high-quality, risky scripts and to chastise Broadway producers for their timidity and for "condescending to public taste."

When Margo called him at home, Atkinson wrote, "prudent members of the family poured ice water on the telephone while [she] described her discovery." Atkinson quickly supplied Margo with a telegraphed introduction to Mayer, who happened to live just a few miles away from her hotel in Los Angeles. It took her scarcely fifteen minutes to convince Mayer to allow her to present the play in Texas. "Think of it," she said, with customary hyperbole, "a story of Davy Crockett, Travis, Bowie, and all the other Texas heroes, played right in Texas, with actual descendants of these famous people playing the leading roles."

Mayer gave her the play, autographed to his "dear friend—Margo Jones," and promised to attend the opening. Overwhelmed as many were by Margo, Mayer wrote Atkinson later that he would have given the persuasive young woman his "furniture, bank balance and collection of Wilkie buttons if she had mentioned them" too.

Unfortunately, actress Virginia King, who played Annie, the only woman in the play, remembers *Sunrise in My Pocket* "as the worst thing we ever did. The script wasn't so bad—but what we did with it was godawful. I died at the Alamo—fell off a wall—great fun." For once, Margo may have lost her concentration on the theatre: about halfway through rehearsals of *Sunrise in My Pocket*, she had learned that Jerry Coray had gotten married. "I guess that if 50 million pounds of cement had hit my head and gone right through me at the time the shock would not have been greater," she said. She had been directing the show not only for herself but to make Jerry proud of her. Although Margo had had other romantic involvements, Jerry was her first love. His belief in her and her love for him had sustained her and she was left with a "great void and vacancy." She felt that "never, never, never, could anything even come close to what I had with Jerry." In fact, as with all her important romances Margo had idealized their attachment, turning it into theatre, into a romantic drama with Jerry acting the role of handsome leading man while she played the part of lovestruck ingenue. The pain and sense of loss were real, however, and to fill the void she began to work even harder.

D U R I N G   T H E   1941–42 season of the Houston Community Players, Margo lost over a hundred of her best actors and technicians to the army and the war effort. To compensate, she used Ellington Army Base personnel and chose plays with smaller casts. The season included the *Sunrise* premiere, attended by Mayer and New York producer Milton Shubert, *Going Up!*, *Rope's End*, and *Design for Living*. She staged Patrick Hamilton's *Rope's End* in three-quarter round at one end of the Playhouse with the audience on three sides. She found breaking the barrier between actors and audience by eliminating the proscenium frame to be quite effective.

The last play of the winter season, Noel Coward's delightful, sophisticated comedy about a ménage à trois, *Design for Living*, was not only directed by Margo but starred her as the irrepressible Gilda, with Ray Walston as Leo. William Rozan portrayed Otto, Sidney Holmes acted Ernest, and Nina Vance had the small part of Helen Carver. Members of the Players were astonished and somewhat horrified that Margo had chosen to play Gilda, especially since they knew she couldn't act. Virginia King had felt the role was hers, and was very upset. But Margo would not be dissuaded.

She identified closely with Gilda. An artist, at the end of the play Gilda leaves her husband to live with Otto and Leo, the two men she loves.

The Shining Hour

Like Gilda, Margo had chosen to live differently, outside normal social conventions. For her there would be no marriage, or children, or nine-to-five job. Also, Virginia King remembers, Margo wanted to play Gilda because the role was "so sophisticated and we were all wrapped up in being sophisticated."

"She was not very good," Ray Walston recalls. "On opening night Margo felt that the pace was too slow, so on one of her entrances she stormed in, slammed the door, and two paintings fell off the wall." The critics were kind, however, calling Margo's a "good bustling performance" and saying that she brought to the stage "the same qualities of drive and excitement that have made her the moving spirit of a restless organization."

While Margo planned her summer season, she continued to correspond with Eddie Mayer. She made countless phone calls on his behalf trying to build support for a New York production of *Sunrise* starring Raymond Massey even though Massey didn't seem interested in the role. "If everybody doesn't watch out," Margo declared, "I'm going to blink my last three eye lashes at some Texas oil king and get the backing and do it in New York myself." When the last production of the Community Players summer season, *The Shining Hour*, closed, Margo headed east for a working vacation. She was to direct *A Quiet Wedding* at a Long Island summer theatre.

While visiting New York to see plays and find new scripts, Margo met with agent Audrey Wood to discuss a possible production of *Sunrise* in Erwin Piscator's Studio Theatre at the New School. With her husband, William Liebling, Audrey Wood ran the Liebling-Wood theatrical agency. Wood had been schooled in the commercial theatre by her father, William Wood, who was the business manager for various Broadway theatres and who managed touring companies as well. Her father had introduced her to a game called play reading. "Manuscripts of unproduced plays mysteriously and continuously flooded our apartment," Wood recalled. "I can still remember a time when there were so many that my mother used to hide them behind the upright piano which she cleverly arranged cater-cornered in the parlor just for this catchall purpose." An only child, devoted to her father, Wood often advised him on play choices. Once, after reading all the Pollyanna novels, young Audrey tearfully urged her father to take out a road company tour of the popular story, which had been made into a silent movie starring Mary Pickford. The tour was a disaster, closing after just a few weeks on the road. "Despite my error, he continued to let me read plays for him," Wood said later. The rejection of *Pollyanna* laid the groundwork for Wood's tough, no-nonsense approach to the theatre and the submerging of the part of her that loved

Pollyana's optimism and gladness. Although tiny in stature, under five feet, Wood carried herself with great dignity. Red hair pulled back into a twist framed her rather large, broad face. She listened intently, spoke in a business-like, even curt manner, and had a reputation for shrewdness, thorough professionalism, and devotion to her client's every need.

Wood liked the young Texas director, her buoyant optimism and spirit reminiscent of Pollyanna's. Margo asked Wood if she had any interesting new scripts. "If you want to read a beautiful play," Wood said, "take this home with you and send it right back to me." On the title page of the manuscript Wood handed her, Margo saw a funny scribbled note: "Please do not leave in the shower or pass around promiscuously." One of Wood's clients was a young writer named Tennessee Williams; the manuscript was his first full-length play, *Battle of Angels*. Heavily influenced by D. H. Lawrence, filled with passionate sexuality and genuine poetic feeling, the play had been produced the year before by the Theatre Guild, which had initially championed its experimental nature, Williams's talent, and his work's challenging themes. However, stung by the adverse reception to the play in its Boston tryout, the Theatre Guild chose to close there rather than risk bringing the production to its New York subscribers.

Margo placed the script in her briefcase to read on the train back to Texas, but was so curious that she began reading it in her hotel room, read it straight through, and on the train reread it several times more. When the train stopped in St. Louis she rushed to a phone booth to call Audrey Wood to tell her how much she loved it. She asked, "Who is this boy?" Later, she wrote Wood that "I don't believe I'd be stretching it much to say I'd read it a dozen times. . . . I believe the play has more beauty, theatre and guts than any script . . . that I've read. . . . If you have any other scripts of Mr. Williams that I might read, I'd appreciate your sending them to me."

SOON AFTER her return from New York, on Labor Day weekend, Margo resigned from the Houston Community Players. Earlier that year, in a letter to Edwin Mayer, she had written, "I believe in this theatre a lot and come hell or high water I'm going to build up the most perfect theatre in the world—right here in the provinces." Hell and high water didn't come, but the hard reality of World War II intruded, and Margo closed the theatre that had been her life for the past seven years. She had moved beyond community theatre with its inadequate rehearsal time and amateur actors. She also sensed the decline of the community-theatre movement, saying "I think we brought a curtain down on an era and strangely enough, I think it was time for it to

The Shining Hour

come down." She closed her final season with *The Shining Hour*, the play's title an appropriate curtain line for the Community Players.

Next she headed for a teaching position at the University of Texas in Austin. Perhaps a university would be a "place where drama might continue during these stressing times." She packed her bags, her books, her turtles, and her worn copy of Tennessee Williams's play *Battle of Angels*.

Margo's friend Nione Carlson said later that "everybody knew that Margo had a sixth sense when she picked up a script. I think she was a visionary. She had a perfect ear—her genius was to put her finger on the person with genius." She also had an unshakable, almost arrogant faith in her own judgment. In Williams's writing, Margo found a voice for all the unarticulated yearning in her soul and a playwright who inspired her vision.

In a few months, Margo would meet Mr. Williams, a fellow "cottonchopper." She'd call him "baby" and would buy the beers.

Images of Magnificence

MARGO SWEPT INTO Austin like a strong east wind. Her first stop might have been the *Austin Tribune*, stirring the editors into gusty prose, for they hailed her arrival with a four-column story and picture on the front page of the "Stage, Screen, and Broadway" section titled "NEW STAR IN THE THEATRICAL HEAVEN— Famed American Director at University on Rockefeller Fellowship." The story characterized Margo as a "believer in the decentralized theatre . . . [a believer] that a great theatre is possible all over America."

James Parke, chairman of the University of Texas drama department, had arranged for Margo to be his wartime replacement, teaching his classes while faculty member Lawrence Carra took over as acting chairman. Through her connections in the National Theatre Conference, Margo received a Rockefeller Fellowship to fund the teaching. Parke, who knew Margo from their work together presenting theatre at army camps, had a background in professional theatre, but most of the faculty were academics, and resented the attention Margo received. After all, she didn't have a Ph.D. And, Margo admitted, she was about as academic as she was a "jet planer."

Almost immediately she got in trouble with the academic dean, E. William Doty. They had known each other socially in Houston, meeting at parties and at Community Players productions, so when Margo saw him at the university, she greeted him with warm affection and "chucked him under the chin." He coolly informed her that this was just not done. Later in the year, Doty demanded that Margo appear in his office and explain her unusual method of grading: students in her classes either received an A or an F. When the dean attempted to describe different levels of grading, Margo interrupted, "Oh no, oh no, darling, you either belong in the theatre or you don't."

For those students who belonged in the theatre, opportunities flourished at the University of Texas. The drama department presented plays in cooperation with the Curtain Club, which had been founded years earlier by noted playwright and critic Stark Young. Departmental offices were located in the imposing Modern Language Building, "MLB." Next door, Hogg Auditorium housed a five-hundred-seat theatre and dozens of bats; the Experimental Theatre (actually a converted lecture hall) seated one hundred to two hundred people, and a theatre-in-the-round seated an audience of 150. Three theatres with a series of plays booked in each, a strong faculty, and active student participation offered excellent theatre training.

Theatre training to Margo simply meant creating theatre, learning by doing. The University of Texas drama students crowded around her, warming to her enthusiasm, which was not the surface enthusiasm of a cheerleader but the deeper kind signified by the root of the word itself, divine inspiration. They thought she was very colorful—the only faculty member who insisted that they use her first name. She enthralled them with her talk of the theatre and fascinated them with her Bohemian behavior. She swore, drank whiskey, and often let her students teach themselves because she liked to "just let things happen." She announced to her classes, "Kids, you have to smoke because if you don't smoke, then I can't smoke, and if I can't smoke, I'll go crazy."

Her first directing assignment at the university was Maxwell Anderson's war drama *The Eve of St. Mark*. The National Theatre Conference had commissioned the playwright to write a play that could be performed with minimal production elements. In an effort to decentralize theatre and bring the best new work to groups outside New York (an effort Margo vigorously campaigned for as an NTC officer), the play was offered first to amateur theatres around the country before it was produced on Broadway by Anderson's Playwrights' Company. Sentimental and patriotic, the play attempts to express America's spirit at the start of World War II. On Broadway, it ran for 307 performances, one of the few plays about the war that proved successful, since wartime audiences in general preferred musicals, revues, and escapist fare like the long-running comedies *Life with Father*, *My Sister Eileen*, and *Arsenic and Old Lace*.

Margo rehearsed *The Eve of St. Mark* in the small Experimental Theatre. Moving restlessly around the hall in her worn red kidskin ballet slippers, she directed the play intuitively, relying on her instincts and experience. When spirits flagged, she gave inspiring talks, creating what one actress called an atmosphere "of high energy, high involvement, high concentration." As with the Houston Community Players, she tended to let the actors create the specifics of their roles and to offer emotional support and belief rather than coaching.

Actress Louise Latham, fresh from a ranch in the Texas Hill Country and the Hockaday School in Dallas, played the young girl in *The Eve of St. Mark*. She remembers that "what I learned from [Margo] was how to be a professional. People took fire around her and she was so powerful you either embraced her and went along with her dream, or you couldn't take it." Margo told Latham, "Someday I'll have a professional theatre and you'll work for me." Opening in Austin on November 9, 1942, just a month after the play had premiered in New York, *The Eve of St. Mark* received generally positive reviews.

Margo's intuitive directing style, however, irritated acting drama department chairman Lawrence Carra. Yale-trained and the protégé of Yale professor Alexander Dean, author of *Fundamentals of Play Directing*, Carra helped write the text and completed it after Dean died. Intended for community-theatre and college directors who work with amateurs, the book presents directing as a craft that focuses not on guiding actors but on planning stage pictures that tell the play's story. For example, certain movements are weak or strong, certain areas of the stage are more important or less important, and certain positions are best for a love scene or a conflict. Carra held to the book's precepts with a rigid faith. He attended Margo's rehearsals and observed her talking to actors, listening to their suggestions, and at times relying on trial and error to plan a scene. Carra, who was about the same age as Margo but was without her extensive directing experience, often interrupted her rehearsals saying, "This isn't staged right." Not used to anyone overseeing her work or telling her what to do, Margo felt hurt and angry. She didn't understand or want to learn about a directing technique made up of rules, diagrams, and fundamental principles. Carra rightly disapproved of Margo's stubborn refusal to accept advice or criticism, but perhaps he was also a bit jealous of this "new star" who was so very popular with the students.

IN ADDITION TO her academic duties, Margo kept up with the national theatre scene. She traveled to Washington, D.C., as head of a committee with Barrett Clark and Hallie Flanagan to judge a national one-act play contest sponsored by the Treasury Department to encourage investment in War Bonds. She maintained a heavy correspondence with other directors, writers, and theatre personalities and made speeches and read plays for the National Theatre Conference.

In November 1942, Margo returned to New York for the annual meeting of the Conference. The real purpose of the trip, however, was to meet Tennessee Williams. Her interest in the playwright had mounted when she read his early one-act plays, *American Blues*, which Audrey Wood had sent her. One of her first tasks at the university had been to call all the students she knew who owned portable typewriters, and put them to work at her apartment typing extra copies of *Battle of Angels* since she had to send the script back to Wood.

As she had promised, Audrey Wood introduced Margo to Thomas Lanier Williams, nicknamed "Tennessee" by his college classmates. Born in Colum-

Images of Magnificence

bus, Mississippi, in March 1911, nine months older than Margo, Tennessee was depressed by the failure of *Battle of Angels*, plagued with cataract problems, and desperately poor. Margo felt an immediate empathy for this writer whom she had grown to love through his work. Although they were about the same height, Margo's energy and booming self-confidence made her appear quite imposing. Excessively shy around strangers, Tennessee, overwhelmed and somewhat intimidated by his first meeting with the exuberant Margo, quickly took her to his friend Paul Bigelow's nearby apartment, in a brownstone just off Fifth Avenue. It was early morning, and Bigelow made coffee and immediately took to Margo, who, he says, "had a wonderful wide-open, Texas personality."

Soon the nervous Tennessee announced that he had an errand to run, and left. Margo stayed, and she and Bigelow got on famously as the day wore on and Tennessee did not return. Bigelow mixed Black Velvets, a voguish combination of champagne and stout then considered the very symbol of sophistication. Margo of course had to try one. Late that evening and after many more Black Velvets, Tennessee still had not returned. Margo went back to her hotel.

Her persistence won out, however, and the next day and for several days after, she and Tennessee met and talked for hours. Margo bought the beers since, she said, "the baby didn't have a penny." Indeed, the last few years had been grueling ones for Tennessee, financially and artistically. With the assurance of a prophet, Margo told him that his writing was beautiful, sensitive, eloquent—filled with humor, simplicity, and imagination. She told him that he was brilliant and would be a great figure in the theatre. To Tennessee, these words were like a fresh breeze, lifting his spirits, dispelling the disappointments, and setting him on a new course. He said later, "She did restore my faith in having some possible future as a playwright." In these early meetings, Margo and Tennessee found a common bond in their southern heritage and family situations. Each had a strong, domineering mother, and each had a beloved older sister who had suffered a tragedy that left psychological scars on her sibling. In Williams's case he would transform the tragedy of his fragile, mentally ill sister Rose into great art, *The Glass Menagerie*. Margo had found salvation in promoting the art that she believed in and working to build the theatre that was still just a vision.

That fall she returned to the University of Texas with more plays by Williams, including *Stairs to the Roof*, *You Touched Me*, and *The Purification*. She shared her enthusiasm for Williams with her students, one in particular, graduate student Theodore Apstein. He had heard Margo give a speech a year earlier and her commitment to new plays had inspired him. When she arrived at the university, Apstein sought her out. The only serious playwriting student at the school, Ted Apstein, born in Kiev of Russian-Jewish parents and raised in Germany and Mexico, had begun training to be an engineer at Cal Tech when he was only sixteen years old. Homesick and ill, Ted had left California and returned to Mexico City. He later came back to the United States and enrolled at the University of Texas. Although his refugee parents had urged him to study business or engineering, he instead majored in English and Spanish at the university and devoted himself to writing plays.

"Ah, children, I worship talent!" Margo often drawled to her eager students. In playwright Ted Apstein she found talent and a confidante, and he found a challenging mentor, who urged him to work harder and spend more time writing. Perversely, when Ted refused to spend his nights in drinking sessions with Margo and her students, she told him that he should play more. At the university, Margo directed two of Apstein's plays—a farce, *Sporting Pink*, and a drama, *A Choice of Weapons*.

They talked in Margo's small rented room two blocks from campus or over cup after cup of coffee in local cafés. Margo rarely talked about her personal life, but with Ted, perhaps because he was an empathetic writer, she shared her family problems. She showed him letters that she had received from Martha Pearl, disturbing letters filled with clippings of war atrocities. Margo's brothers, Richard and Charles, were in the service, and Martha Pearl didn't understand her daughter's interest in theatre. Why wasn't Margo involved in the war effort? These letters upset Margo, and she wrote back defending her choice of career, detailing her activities in an effort to make her parents understand her life. In Margo's voluminous correspondence with her parents, this would be a constant theme—a universal theme, perhaps, shared by all artists who attempt to explain, Why Art? In a letter to her parents written several years later, Margo summarized her feelings:

> Mother, Dear, I know how hard it is for you to understand why it is that I use the kind of energy that I do on my job. I have always wanted so for you two to understand. Some people become good doctors to try to help the physical ailments of mankind; some people become good educators to try to make mankind wiser and more understanding; some people grow flowers to bring happiness to people. I truthfully believe that putting on wise and true plays lifts the spirit and makes for better understanding among mankind. . . . Perhaps it is because I am my Mother's and Father's daughter and have a passionate desire to try to be of real use in this world. I believe that fine literature, fine music, fine painting and fine theatre

express the spiritual qualities of the creative people in this world; and I believe that the creative people have a perception about life that makes it good to try to impart to others.

She signed the letter "Love from your little girl, Margo," perhaps sensing that they would always view her as a child, not as the mature artist she was. In letter after letter to her parents, Margo, their only living daughter, sought to explain and justify her life.

DURING HER YEARS in Austin, Margo rented a room in a private home an easy walking distance from campus. She liked her sweet, elderly landlady, Mrs. Markey, and Mrs. Markey became devoted to her, making sure that she ate regularly and even washing her clothes and cleaning her room. Simply furnished with a bed and dresser, a few chairs, a small bookcase, and her turtle collection, Margo's room glowed on evenings and weekends with candlelight and fervent discussions.

Ted Apstein and some of the other students fell a little bit in love with their young teacher. Perhaps, Ted wondered years later, if there hadn't been the teacher-student barrier . . . Another young man, Paul Moor, a gifted music student, first met Margo when she asked him to advise her on background music for *The Eve of St. Mark*. Although romantic involvements between faculty and students were strictly forbidden, their working relationship blossomed into an affair. Perhaps in unconscious imitation of her involvement with her teacher Jerry Coray, Margo encouraged Moor's devotion.

"She was a person of enormous magnetism," Moor remembers. "I was fascinated with her from the very beginning—most people were fascinated by her and she dominated almost every group that she was a member of." The two spent a great deal of time together, having lunch, meeting for coffee, reading poetry by candlelight in Margo's apartment. Moor gave her a thick volume of poetry and writings by Rabindranath Tagore, a Hindu poet, playwright, and philosopher. Margo had first read Tagore's work in India, where she had visited his school. She treasured the book and Tagore's ideas about the freedom of art, where "tireless striving stretches its arms towards perfection." A few years later, apparently having become embarrassed by the attentions of a boy barely twenty years old, Margo dropped Moor completely. Although she explained her decision to him, Moor remembers that her rejection "destroyed me. I was almost literally in shock for about two years." Margo continued seeing Sonny Koch, now a captain in the Corps of Engineers who was stationed at Fort Leonardwood, Missouri, under assignment to train draftees to build bridges, airfields, and military camps. She wrote Sonny affectionate letters, and he sent cigarettes and marriage proposals to his "bebe."

O N E   D A Y   Margo approached Ted Apstein and said, "Darling, I've got to read something to you. It is the most beautiful play." Ted walked to Margo's room that evening. She turned off the lights and lit several candles. Then she began to read *The Purification*, a one-act play written in verse. Margo read all the parts herself, with voice breaking and tears running down her cheeks.

Not particularly impressed with *The Purification* or as moved as Margo had been, Ted felt slightly resentful of her interest in this unknown playwright named Tennessee Williams. However, when Ted made his first trip to New York City that fall, Margo gave him fifteen dollars for theatre tickets (at that time orchestra seats were $3.60—he could see four shows), and arranged for him to meet Tennessee Williams and agent Audrey Wood. Tennessee arrived at Ted's cheap hotel room nursing a terrible cold and carrying a box of Kleenex, but as a favor to Margo, he advised Ted about which plays to see, which ones to avoid, and he took him to the theatre. Audrey Wood, to whom Margo had sent a copy of Ted's play *Sporting Pink*, told the young man that he didn't know what he was writing about, but said that she felt he had a little bit of talent. Years later, Wood became Ted Apstein's literary agent.

Margo collected all the Williams plays and poetry she could. Back in Texas, she tried to get the drama department interested in showcasing his work, and even though she wrote Wood that she had everybody "pretty excited," they were not willing to risk a major production on an untried play. Margo persisted. She wrote Audrey Wood that she was eager to produce *You Touched Me* by Tennessee and Donald Windham. "Maybe we could get some New York people down to see it and maybe all this would do some good. . . ." But the drama department refused to produce the Williams play and thereby missed an opportunity to "do some good" for an emerging playwright.

Margo would not give up. She had accepted a position as the director of the Summer School at Gilmor Brown's Pasadena Playhouse at a salary of $170 a month, and Brown had assured her that he'd try to fit *You Touched Me* into the schedule. Tennessee, already on the West Coast, had begun work at MGM in Hollywood at, he thought, the shockingly extravagant salary of $250 a week. Ordered to work on a movie he called a "celluloid brassiere" for glamorous Lana Turner, Tennessee spent most of his time writing his own play *The Gentleman Caller*.

Margo wrote Tennessee in the spring of 1943 that she had gone "completely off my nut about [*You Touched Me*]. That is the one I want to do at Pasadena

Images of Magnificence

. . . this summer. I honestly think something pretty terrific can be done about it. . . . I feel something can really be accomplished in a hurry. A really fine production of it should and I believe will call the attention of every important person on the Coast. . . . Honestly, I've not been so excited about anything in a long time."

Margo completed her teaching duties at the University of Texas in the late spring of 1943 (probably with collective sighs of relief all around). Before going home to Livingston for a few days' visit with her family, she made a brief trip to New York to judge some plays on war savings for the Treasury Department, saw nine Broadway shows, and just missed seeing Tennessee, who had recently returned to California.

MARGO ARRIVED in California in June 1943 and spent the first evening there with Tennessee. Talking nonstop, popping cigarettes in and out of her mouth, Margo overwhelmed him with her ideas for *You Touched Me*. He listened in amazement as she outlined her plans with a lawyer's logic and an evangelist's fervor. She would cast it with the best Hollywood actors, important producers would come to see it, would fall in love with it, and in no time at all they'd be on Broadway. She had supreme confidence and verbal witchcraft, Tennessee thought. There was no telling what she might get away with. So the shy, boyish southern writer, tanned from the Santa Monica sun and slightly pudgy, with terrible eyesight but brilliant poetic vision, became caught up in Margo's whirl of ideas. He christened her the "Texas Tornado."

Tennessee told his roommate, writer David Greggory, about this "ball of fire" named Margo Jones. When he met Margo, Greggory felt that Tennessee had understated the case. "She was a juggernaut," he remembers. "Hell bent to make Hollywood recognize his remarkable talent." With their faith in Tennessee's talent in common, Margo and Greggory became good friends.

Margo talked to everyone about Tennessee's talents and wrote letters hailing him as the most important new writer along with her other favorites Ted Apstein and Horton Foote. Five years younger than Margo and Tennessee, Foote, trained as an actor, had just begun to feel his way as a playwright. He took for his theme family life in a small Texas town closely based on his own hometown of Wharton, Texas. After meeting Horton at a party that summer with Tennessee, Margo read his work and encouraged him. "I think she felt I might pay off someday," Foote recalls. But he realized that Margo was primarily interested in Tennessee. "She thought he was a genius," Foote says. "It was almost a religion with her." Struggling with his own writing, developing his own aesthetic, Foote felt a bit like a "poor relation" around the more flamboyant Margo and Tennessee. Margo's theatre contacts all over the country, including Brooks Atkinson at the *New York Times*, Rosamond Gilder of *Theatre Arts*, Gilmor Brown, and Frederick McConnell, heard about this new playwright Tennessee Williams. In a sense, she acted as Williams's unpaid promoter, making agent Audrey Wood's job immeasurably easier. With Margo's encouragement, Tennessee began to believe that he might indeed make it to Broadway.

Margo's job as director of the Summer School took second place to her task of arranging a major production of *You Touched Me* at the Playhouse. Unwilling to give main stage space to a new play, Artistic Director Gilmor Brown finally promised a production in the small Playbox Theatre.

No longer a "moth-eaten temple of drama," the Pasadena Playhouse was now the most prestigious amateur little theatre in the country. Certainly its facilities were among the most elegant. A row of sentinel palms guarded the imposing Spanish facade of the building, and tubs of flowers and plants lined the sidewalks. The entire theatre facility, estimated to have cost over six hundred thousand dollars, contained class and rehearsal rooms, costume and scene workshops and storerooms, property rooms, staff offices, a dining room, Gilmor Brown's posh red and beige study, a library, a greenroom, a recital hall with a platform stage at either end, the Playbox Theatre, which seated fifty, and the Spanish-style main theatre, which seated 832. From the flat roof used for fencing and dance classes and monthly board meetings, the arc lights of Hollywood could be seen lighting up the sky.

Margo roomed with actress Nancy Spencer, a staff teacher at the Playhouse. Nancy, a native of Houston, had acted in Margo's summer productions at the Lamar Hotel in Houston. A tall, beautiful blonde, she had graduated from Smith College with a degree in theatre arts and had come to the Playhouse on a hundred-dollar-a-month National Theatre Conference fellowship the previous fall—the first woman to receive that fellowship.

Nancy and Margo lived in the upstairs apartment of a two-story frame house on a side street a few blocks from the Pasadena Playhouse. The landlady, a little "wizened Cockney with a brown face and brown hands," lived downstairs. Their apartment included a tiny kitchen, a living room with a studio couch, a sleeping porch, several small bedrooms—and lots of mice.

According to Nancy, she did most of the cooking since "Margo was completely undomestic." They combined their ration books, but by the time they had finished rehearsals and gotten to the grocery, there was rarely meat left to buy. So they ate a lot of eggs that summer, and "practically ironed" the sugar sack to get the last bit of sugar. They bought liquor when they could afford it

Images of Magnificence

and, of course, Margo continued to smoke her favorite Camels. For unknown reasons, war shortages at the Playhouse included tomato catsup and Kleenex, and Nancy remembers that actors ate plain French fries and wiped off makeup with a "grungy old towel."

At the Playhouse, Margo's enthusiasm attracted the students, Nancy recalls, "like honey draws flies." She directed them in Ted Apstein's *Sporting Pink* and his version of a British thriller, *The Velvet Tower*. In Argentina on a fellowship studying theatre, Ted did not hear from Margo when she decided to lop off the last scene of *The Velvet Tower*—a decision difficult to comprehend since the final scene of the play, a murder mystery, reveals the who, how, and why of the murder. Later, Ted got a letter from Margo: the last scene just didn't work, she said, and so she cut it. It was more interesting that way, she said; now the audience had to figure out the mystery's solution on their own.

Margo's attention was focused on the revisions she and Tennessee were making on *You Touched Me*. Although the adaptation of D. H. Lawrence's story of the same name had been suggested by Donald Windham, Tennessee had made the play his own. Windham, a southern writer ten years younger than Williams, lived and worked in New York and was, to his chagrin, left out of most of the revision process.

With Margo's help, Tennessee made important changes in the Lawrence short story. Set in rural England in the early years of the century, the story describes the efforts of Captain Rockley to marry off one of his spinster daughters, Matilda, to his adopted son Hadrian. Williams reworked the story into a delicate, romantic comedy set during World War II. He changed Matilda's sister, Emmie, into a proud virgin aunt and added to the cast of characters Reverend Melton, a capon-like church rector who pays court to her. In Williams's play Captain Rockley, a drunken reprobate, attempts to seduce the maid and generally keeps the home in an uproar. Matilda, described as having the fragile quality of glass, undergoes a sexual and emotional awakening through the attentions of Hadrian, her stepbrother. His vitality and manly forcefulness bring life to the repressed household. All ends happily with the couples paired off in unions that properly mingle spiritual and carnal love.

While he and Margo revised *You Touched Me*, Williams's chief new project was a play titled *The Gentleman Caller*. He read the unfinished script aloud to her, seeking advice and support. Echoes of this play, later to become *The Glass Menagerie*, reverberate through *You Touched Me*. The maiden aunt, Emmie, sounds very much like Amanda in *The Glass Menagerie*. She chides Matilda about her posture, telling her to sit up straight. Emmie's lines have a southern cadence as well. She speaks breathlessly of alarming gas pressures and disturbing heart palpitations. *You Touched Me,* a gentle play in which the sensitive young heroine lives happily ever after with her stepbrother, who is also her gentlemen caller, has all the marks of an exercise for *The Glass Menagerie.*

Tennessee and Margo spent hours in her upstairs apartment huddled over the script, with Margo watching over Tennessee like a doting mother. He smoked cigarettes in a long holder and when one had burned down, he would look around absentmindedly for something to dig it out with. Margo, who didn't carry and rarely used a comb, kept a bobby pin in her pocket to pry out the cigarette. Tennessee would insert a fresh cigarette, and the two would return to work. Often he would miss the last bus to Santa Monica and would stay over, typing into the early morning on Margo's typewriter. She may have pampered him, but it is clear from the journal that Tennessee kept that summer that she also didn't hesitate to tell him when she didn't like his work.

Margo gave freshly typed copies of the play to Hollywood actors and sent a copy to Lemuel Ayers, who had received acclaim for his sets for the Broadway hit *Oklahoma.* Determined to persuade Ayers to design the sets for Tennessee's play, Margo planned a dinner party for him, his wife, and Williams. Since she didn't know how to cook, she talked Nancy Spencer into preparing the meal. Nancy borrowed silverware from some friends in Pasadena and fixed an elegant dinner, but the meal ended in disappointment when Mrs. Ayers demanded that Tennessee give her husband the rights to do the sets for the New York and London productions of his play also. Without his agent Audrey Wood's permission, Tennessee certainly couldn't sign away rights to future productions. Margo would have to find another designer.

Often dragging the reluctant Williams along with her, Margo cultivated her contacts with the Hollywood community. They had cocktails with the lovely young actress Ruth Ford, who they felt would be just right for Matilda. Ford liked the part and the play, but would have to arrange her schedule around the movie she was making for 20th Century–Fox. Other Hollywood actors tentatively cast for parts in the play included Agnes Moorehead, Carl Benton Reid, and Henry Morgan.

At the end of the summer, Margo secured a leave of absence from the University of Texas to direct *You Touched Me* at the Cleveland Playhouse and, later in the fall, at the Pasadena Playhouse. With the written recommendation of Hallie Flanagan, who felt that Margo was one of the few people in the country helping new playwrights, she also managed to receive transportation expenses and a salary from the National Theatre Conference. Awed by Margo's achievements on behalf of his play, Tennessee wrote to Donald Windham,

Images of Magnificence

"The girl is rather monumental in force of character. . . . She is never tired or bored herself and can't imagine weariness or boredom in other people. She wore me out this summer! But she will always be, as a personality, the most vital accident of my life. . . ." Tennessee wrote to Margo in Cleveland, reporting on his progress with *The Gentleman Caller*, enclosing a poem and offering encouragement, and calling her a combination of "Joan of Arc and Gene Autry—and nitroglycerine!" In a later letter he told Margo that he would fight for her to direct a New York production of *You Touched Me*, but warned that he couldn't afford to turn down an opportunity in New York if one were offered.

THE RED BRICK Cleveland Playhouse, one of the most successful little theatres in the country, had operated continuously since 1915. Seasons at the Playhouse rarely included new plays. Artistic Director Frederick McConnell and his audiences preferred lighter fare and Broadway's proven hits. Margo, the first female director at the Playhouse (and the last for almost thirty years), used the playbill for *You Touched Me* as a forum for her ideas, stating that "too often the theatres of the provinces prefer waiting for Broadway approval—prefer not taking a chance on an 'unproved play.' This lack of courage has its price. . . . Therefore when authors appear on the horizon, able, even in the hectic days of war, to write a beautiful and important play—it is our job to see that the play is presented."

As usual, Margo found opportunities to talk to the press during her stay in Cleveland, not only about *You Touched Me* and Tennessee Williams, but about her ideas for the decentralization of the American theatre, ideas that were becoming stronger and clearer. She told reporters that the vitality of theatre rested on doing new scripts, not simply following Broadway's lead but discovering new playwrights and presenting their work. She believed that theatre should be "as good in Podunk as in New York."

Margo sat cross-legged on the edge of the Playhouse stage, smoking her Camels, and rehearsed her actors, among them Carl Benton Reid, Houston Community Players alumnus Ray Walston, and twenty-one-year-old acting apprentice Anne Pitoniak, a recent graduate of the University of North Carolina who was just beginning her career in the theatre. While she was at the Playhouse, Margo met with the apprentices and talked to them about starting a theatre. "She spoke with intensity and her eyes shone. There was a joy she had that inspired us. Here was a theatre person with a strong connection with what she was doing," Pitoniak remembers. "Although we had never heard of Tennessee Williams, after Margo told us about him, we were very much in awe."

Images of Magnificence

Margo kept Tennessee informed of rehearsals, sometimes calling in the middle of the night with news of cuts or requests for fresh material. At first Tennessee planned to travel to Cleveland for the opening, but he changed his mind when Margo's "vague but terrifying comments stopped me in my tracks." Those comments probably had to do with the actions of Frederick McConnell, with whom Margo had clashed. Like Margo's colleague at the University of Texas, McConnell was appalled at her loose directorial style. Finally, at the end of the second week of rehearsal, after continuous arguments with Margo over cuts he wanted to make in the script, an upset McConnell said, "I can't stand this any longer, Miss Jones. You can stay in the auditorium, but I'm taking this play over." Worried about Williams's untried work and concerned about Margo's seeming failure to move actors around the stage in snappy patterns, McConnell took charge in the last week of rehearsal, telling the actors where, when, and how to move. Outwardly gracious and accommodating, Margo sat in the auditorium during the final week of rehearsal swallowing her anger, for she had no real power to fight McConnell.

Before the opening, which would be the world premiere of *You Touched Me,* she attended a dinner party given by the Cleveland Playhouse's president. She dressed elegantly for the occasion, in a black dress highlighted with a brilliant red sash, but her stomach, she reported, was "turning absolutely upside down."

Left out of the revising process and out of the New York advance publicity about the play, Donald Windham did attend the Cleveland opening. Photographers snapped his picture at the opening, but his photograph appeared in a local paper with a caption identifying him as "Tennessee Williams," an error which amused Tennessee a great deal, Windham somewhat less.

The usual glamour of a Cleveland Playhouse opening had been subdued by the war. The ladies wore street-length dresses and last year's formals. Many of the men wore their uniforms instead of the usual top hats and tails. The play received an enthusiastic reception and generally good notices.

Audrey Wood, who had attended the premiere with her husband, celebrated with the company at a cocktail party after the play. When she told Anne Pitoniak, "You remind me of a young Lynn Fontanne," the excited apprentice, overwhelmed by the compliment, promptly spilled her glass of Scotch into the lap of the powerful Miss Wood. Tennessee's agent returned to New York with a sheaf of good notices to give to New York producers; however, Margo felt that McConnell's cuts and directing choices had damaged the script. She returned to Pasadena eager to reinstate the cuts and to begin rehearsals on the production now scheduled for late November at the Pasadena Playhouse.

But first she had to recast the play. The Hollywood actors, including Ruth

Ford, had refused to ride buses back and forth to Pasadena. Ford wanted to do the part, but she was currently making a movie. She asked for a car to pick her up from the movie lot, but the Playhouse budget would not allow it. Ford recalls that she "was longing to play the role. I loved the play and believed in [Tennessee's] talent. [He] never forgave me for this." Hollywood actor Onslow Stevens, who was on the staff of the Pasadena Playhouse, played Captain Rockley; others in the cast were local actors.

In early November, Tennessee's father, Cornelius Williams, visited Los Angeles. Tennessee invited Margo to meet him that weekend for drinks with his salesman father and some of Cornelius's co-workers. Bored with the company and full of free liquor, Margo began to move wildly around the room, pirouetting and whirling, dancing to her own inner music. Her drinking and dancing shocked Cornelius, although as a drinking man who loved a good time he had a lot in common with Margo. He told his son that the Williams family had "never had a sober man or a drunken woman" in it, and he warned him against marrying the wanton Margo. "He had the idea I planned to," an amused Tennessee wrote to Donald Windham.

At times, Margo's Texas friends teased her about marrying Williams. But while she loved his talent and, in a way, loved him, Margo had an earthy understanding of Tennessee's sexual preferences, and no plans for marriage to the playwright or to anyone else.

"Margo," Nancy Spencer's mother lectured, "I don't care if you only stay married two weeks, you should have some normalcy in your life!"

"Oh, I don't ever want to get married," Margo replied. "There's no room for it in the theatre."

You Touched Me opened at the Playbox Theatre at the Pasadena Playhouse on November 29, 1943. Legally not a part of the Playhouse, the Playbox Theatre, supported by a loyal group of subscribers, provided a space for experimental theatre. Professional critics were not allowed and the playwrights received no royalties.

The audience liked the play, Tennessee declaring to Donald Windham that it left "the old dowagers in stitches." Although no reporters were allowed, word of the play's success traveled quickly around Hollywood. Studios called to ask for revised copies of the script. Mary Hunter, director of the Actor's Company in New York, phoned Tennessee to report that she was securing backing for a New York production. Margo, of course, believed that she would direct the play, somehow, in New York. Aware of this, and perhaps feeling a bit guilty about his encouragement of both directors, Tennessee wrote Windham that

"Margo will not be crushed over being left out of a possible Broadway production. I told her right along that she would have to take her chances on that and she knows it. There is a core of real unselfish interest in the woman. . . ." He recognized Margo's devotion to a dream that was larger than any one Broadway production.

After a night of celebration, Margo left Pasadena early one December morning. Smiling and crying a little, she waved good-bye to Tennessee from her train window. Tennessee wrote her soon after, "Life seems unreal now that you have left us. A posthumous existence."

EARLY IN 1944, Margo returned to the University of Texas to teach her classes and direct plays. She continued to enjoy her students, but after receiving a reprimand for rehearsing them during mealtime, she wrote Tennessee that her students were wonderful, "they do catch sparks," but "I can not stand the stifling academic life. . . . The only concern here is to keep the deans and parents pleased—there is no thought or knowledge of art. . . ."

She continued to press the drama department to do new plays and succeeded in scheduling a new-play slot for a major production that spring. The department had solicited new scripts, among them Tennessee Williams's *The Purification*. In a meeting to select the new play, all agreed with Dr. E. P. Conkle, playwriting teacher and resident playwright, who said, "I don't think there's any doubt that Mr. Williams is by far the most distinguished writer represented." Although he liked the play, Carra, the department chairman, felt that it presented too many production problems to stage it during the year and suggested instead that the play be produced that summer. Outraged, since she would be in Pasadena again for the summer and unavailable to direct the play, Margo cried out, "And I commit suicide!"

The drama department decided to ask Mr. Williams for another play that didn't present so many production problems, but he wired that his new script wasn't ready. He wrote Margo that he had been working on a verse play titled *Cockcrow*, set during the Renaissance with the plot revolving around the trial of a scientist for heresy. Tennessee predicted that when the present war was over, there would be a period in which old truths would be seriously questioned, and he hoped that the play would parallel that postwar experience of reexamining beliefs. He asked that Margo not hurry him for a final draft. The department scrapped the idea of doing an original play altogether and instead scheduled a popular standby, Noel Coward's *Tonight at 8:30*. Disappointed, Margo wrote Tennessee that this was her last attempt to "knock some sense into this department's head." She also wrote, "Your *Cockcrow* sounds wonderful. I won't hurry you. For I do know it takes months for anything fine to really come to life."

FOR THE PAST several years, Margo had been gradually formulating a vision, a concrete plan that would change the shape of the theatre in America. In her travels around the world, to the Moscow Art Festival, to New York and California, she had talked to writers, actors, directors, producers, and critics, and had "found out that everybody . . . who had ideals were discussing the same thing: a way to have theatre, to establish the fine companies which could produce the kind of theatre we all dreamed of." She decided to "restudy every word I could find written on the history of idealistic theatres the world over." She read and reread about the Moscow Art Theatre, the Abbey Theatre, the Jacques Copeau theatre, and the Washington Square Players. She thought, "we dream beautifully, but what are we doing about it? Why do we keep talking? Do we enjoy conversation more than action? I can't believe that!" In a late-night session in her Austin room on December 7, 1943, Margo articulated what she came to call "The Project."

Curtain Club member Ed Torrance and artist Maudee Carron, her old friend from Houston, listened raptly as Margo talked and talked with enthusiasm and determination of her hopes and ideals for the theatre. The amateur, little-theatre movement had failed, had not become the national theatre as so many had hoped it would. Margo felt the stirrings of a new movement in the theatre, and took personal responsibility for its birth. She spoke of establishing a network of fully professional resident theatres outside of New York—theatres that would be devoted to presenting new work and the classics. The theatres would be noncommercial and inexpensive, would provide jobs for theatre artists and technicians, would not tolerate the star system or long runs, and would become a truly national theatre for America.

While visiting Dallas in early 1944, Margo went to see her old friend and mentor, John Rosenfield, the highly respected critic of the *Dallas Morning News*. A native of the city, Rosenfield had attended the University of Texas, and after the First World War had gone to New York, where he studied at Columbia University. His father used to say, "I sent him to Columbia, but he went to the Metropolitan Opera," for John spent most of his time there and at the theatre and the movies. He worked for the *New York Evening Mail* as a movie reviewer and later for Paramount Pictures as a publicist. Paramount transferred him back to Dallas, but when the company asked Rosenfield to move again to New York, he decided to remain in his hometown. His family had settled in Texas before the Revolution, and he wanted to help make Texas a place where, he said, "children would grow up knowing about theatre, about music, about art." He landed a job on the *Dallas Morning News* reviewing plays, movies, and musical events, and headed up the Amusement Department at the paper.

Soon, Rosenfield became an important figure in the cultural life of Dallas as it grew from a small provincial town to a major city. *Time* magazine reported that "culture in Dallas has blossomed like a rose on the dry plains of the Southwest, thanks largely to Rosenfield." Barely five feet six inches tall, with dark hair and very pale skin, Rosenfield was enormously fat, weighing in at more than two hundred pounds. "Rosey" was a heavyweight not only in size but in Dallas political and cultural circles as well as having a national reputation and a byline in the *New York Times*. His standards were high, his knowledge of theatre and music encyclopedic, and he wasn't afraid to skewer hometown performances and visiting Broadway companies alike. He had kept in touch with Margo since her days as a student, and Margo had taught his son, John Rosenfield, Jr., at the university. When Margo visited him and told him about her dream to establish a permanent, resident theatre, Rosenfield saw an opportunity for Dallas and asked, "Why don't you do it here?"

Margo agreed, but replied that she didn't know how she could do it anywhere until she was sure that everything was right. She had reached the conclusion that the theatre would have to be subsidized somehow, that it would take a lot of money. She knew that she would need time to travel and to study in order to develop and organize the plan, and she would need a means to support herself while she was doing this. Rosenfield suggested that she put her ideas down on paper, then come back and see him. His friend, David H. Stevens, the innovative Director of the Humanities at the Rockefeller Foundation, might be interested in supporting such a plan.

Margo returned to the University of Texas and set to work on a formal written proposal to present to the Rockefeller Foundation. In April, she directed her final play at the university, André Obey's spectacle drama *Noah*. This play marked, she exaggerated, the 167th production she had directed since graduating from college.

Now thirty-two years old, Margo embarked on her new direction in life characteristically: she talked to the press. In an April 1944 interview she rehearsed her Rockefeller grant material, declaring that "something is wrong with our dramatic art when families all over the country cannot grow up in small cities and see all of Shakespeare and Ibsen and fresh, fine plays by young, unknown playwrights, instead of having to wait for traveling, warmed-over Broadway productions." She spoke of a "creative vs. business system" and of three outstanding young playwrights—Tennessee Williams, Horton Foote, and Ted Apstein.

June Moll, a young drama department instructor who was one of the few friends Margo had made on the faculty, remembers that Margo talked about her theatre plans constantly. "I really felt all the while," Moll says, "that Margo felt that she had not only the drive, the know how, but the Right to start the theatre." Margo talked to her students about her plans, as they huddled around her, warming themselves on her creative fire. In theatre designer Robert Edmond Jones's words she urged them to "keep always in your souls some images of magnificence."

With John Rosenfield's approval, Margo sent off her Rockefeller application dated May 20. The typed, four-page letter describing her plans was filled with intensity, idealism, and logic. Sounding once again like an evangelistic minister, Margo wrote, "I believe passionately in Art as a form of Salvation, and that the things art brings—beauty and spiritual growth—are the most important things in human life."

"I believe in decentralized theatre. I believe there is no reason why good theatre should be bottle-necked in New York and Hollywood. I believe in a dramatic map for America that will include great native playhouses in every town large enough to want one." She requested a year's fellowship of twenty-five hundred dollars plus travel expenses. In closing, Margo wrote, "This is a job that has to be done. I have an inner compulsion about it that is stronger than any feeling I've ever had. . . ."

In July, while she waited to hear if her grant had been approved, Margo directed *The Purification* at the Pasadena Playhouse Laboratory Theatre. Although she wired Tennessee that the performance had the simplicity he wanted, including guitar music "out of heaven," and urged him to "steal a plane and fly here," Williams did not see the production. He was in Provincetown working on *The Gentleman Caller.*

Written in heightened, intense verse, *The Purification* concerns incest between brother and sister and the sister's murder by her husband. The atmosphere of the play trembles with guilt, longing, and pain. Completed shortly after his sister Rose's lobotomy, the play has in it Williams's own guilt over his sister's fate. The character of Elena, the lost girl, the dead sister, hovers over the play.

Perhaps it's just as well that Tennessee didn't see the production, since Gilmor Brown had forced Margo to cut several lines, including references to "eager" genitals, breast bones, and groin clasping. Despite the changes, however, actress Rebecca Hargis, who played the mother in the play, remembers

Images of Magnificence

that "there is no doubt that magic occurred during *The Purification*, and I thought Margo achieved heights she never hit again. We were all innocent then and filled with wonder and so was the play." In a gesture of respect and love and as a measure of their shared pain over their lost sisters, Rose and Stella Nell, Tennessee dedicated *The Purification* to Margo Jones.

They had become intimate friends, sharing their hopes and problems primarily through telephone conversations and letters. Margo sent Tennessee a copy of her Rockefeller application. "Do me a favor Tennessee — read these plans carefully — read them . . . and let me know your reactions at once. . . . I'm glad Ten to be living in a world with you — I've said it many times before and I here repeat — The beauty of your plays gives a very real meaning to the things I'm trying to do."

Williams in turn kept her informed of his progress on *The Gentleman Caller*. He wrote that he had revised the "nauseous nauseous thing I read you in Pasadena. . . ." In August he wrote that he was having *The Glass Menagerie*, formerly *The Gentleman Caller*, typed up and was sending her a copy. He felt that it needed rewriting and condensing, and asked for Margo's opinion of this version. "It contains my sister," he said, "and that was the object."

Margo heard from the Rockefeller Foundation in early summer. Her application had been approved. She would receive a stipend of $150 a month and an allowance for travel. She was "damn thrilled," but worried that this might not be enough money because, she said, "It will be pretty hard to get around on that and look like an even half way respectable girl . . . and tip enough to get a smile, and ride a taxi so as not to arrive hot or cold or bedraggled at some destination that may in the long run help this theatre to be something. . . ." Before she began her travels, however, a required physical exam revealed that the robust, extraordinarily energetic Margo Jones was anemic, her condition surely the result of a work life too busy to allow time for nutritious, or even regular, meals. This surprising news sent Margo into a deep depression, but her spirits soon lifted as the iron and calcium supplements she took built up her system to Rockefeller-acceptable levels.

In a headlong burst of enthusiasm, Margo wrote her friend James "Jay" Laughlin, the founder of New Directions publishing, that her plan had been approved and she was to start right away. Although their backgrounds couldn't have been more different — Laughlin was an Easterner, the tall, elegant heir to a Pittsburgh steel fortune, educated at Choate and Harvard — Margo knew that Jay Laughlin would understand her dream, for he had founded New Directions in 1936 with an enthusiastic sense of mission and a firm belief that the art of the writer took precedence over the commerce of the publishing

Images of Magnificence

industry. Laughlin trusted his own taste and published the work of writers like Ezra Pound, William Carlos Williams, Dylan Thomas, Vladimir Nabokov, Djuna Barnes, Lawrence Ferlinghetti, Federico García Lorca, and Tennessee Williams before they had become well-known and successful.

Margo hoped that her work in the theatre would parallel what New Directions meant to literature. "I'm reading three and four new scripts a day —talking to people galore and spending a bit of time on the organizational part of all this," she wrote Laughlin. Not pausing for periods, using dashes just to catch her breath, Margo enthused, "I must find the 20 most amazing people in the country—not only must their talent and imagination and ability in the theatre be the best but their far sightedness in the entire plan must be in terms of images of magnificence—."

The young publishing pioneer encouraged Margo's efforts, offered his help in tracking down funds for the theatre, and suggested that New Directions publish any remarkable plays to which her movement gave birth.

In late August, Margo received a letter from Tennessee. "Right after the war," he told her, "there is bound to be a terrific resurgence in the arts. . . . Many, many boys will come out of this war with a desperate thirst for creation instead of destruction. There is your chance, Margo!—I believe that you are a woman of destiny!"

She believed it too. "I'm not trying for a good theatre," she said. "I'm trying for a great one."

Let Me Talk My Dreams

"I T MUST BE great . . . I am determined . . . We can have a real art theatre . . . I am dedicating my life to this . . . I believe . . . I have taken an oath. . . . " The words poured out in a flood of feeling, unembarrassed passion, and conviction. At thirty-three, Margo had not yet learned cynicism and sour disillusionment. She sensed that World War II marked a turning point. Despite the war in progress, popular songs like "Accentuate the Positive" and "Swinging on a Star" heralded a new optimism. The country had advanced scientifically, new industries had been created, and productivity and prosperity had soared, ending the Great Depression. Now was the time for art too to progress, for a new theatre distinctly American, not modeled after European theatres, to meet the challenges of a post-war world.

"I believe," Margo said, "that the biggest war job I can do is to keep faith with the hundreds of artists that I know who are scattered over the world who want to see when they return a theatre that was worth the blood and sweat and tears." Margo wrote to her brother Charles, who was serving in the navy in the Pacific, asking for his thoughts on her plan for a theatre. He responded with a long, encouraging letter, told her to follow her star, and added some prudent advice. "I know you have unbelievable vitality," he wrote, "but realize that others may not be so blessed."

MARGO BEGAN HER Rockefeller Fellowship in late summer of 1944. She planned to travel across the country to study theatres and learn all she could about their financial organizations, technical setups, personnel, and philosophies. Most important, she wanted to "talk to every idealist in the theatre, spend time in Hollywood and New York . . . learn everything I can about the latest and best lighting methods, watch ballet rehearsals, watch the best directors at work, get to know young playwrights" and, she summarized with characteristic hyperbole, "learn everything new possible!" She tempered her intense idealism with a practical vision of a theatre that provided jobs and security. "A mere way of life," she said, "is terribly important. You don't get good theatre unless you put in eight hours a day, get eight hours sleep and three meals a day that you know you can pay for." She believed too that a distinguished theatre could only be created through distinguished playwriting.

In her mind, the question of which came first, the theatre or the play, was like the riddle of the chicken and the egg—one could not exist without the other. The mission of her theatre would be to find exciting new playwrights and to present their plays.

California seemed the logical place to begin since she had just finished her work at the Pasadena Playhouse. In late September 1944, Dallas critic John Rosenfield traveled to Los Angeles to interview Margo and discuss ideas for the proposed Dallas theatre, the model of a theatre that she hoped would soon flourish in every large city in the country. In effect, the intellectual critic and the intuitive idealist were now a team. For Margo's theatre to succeed, it would need considerable public support. Rosenfield planned to build the necessary support through his influence with the important, moneyed people of Dallas and through articles focusing on Margo and her work. Rosenfield relished his behind-the-scenes role, and although he had sincere, altruistic motives in encouraging the arts in Texas, he had strong personal ambitions as well and a desire to one-up his rival, John William Rogers, who worked for the *Dallas Times Herald*. When he returned to Texas, Rosenfield splashed Margo's photograph, past history, and future plans for a theatre on the front page of the *Dallas Morning News* Arts Section. In the article, Margo enthused that Dallas was her home country and the "freshest cultural center between New York and San Francisco."

Margo visited playwright Dan Totheroh in Carmel and picked up several new scripts, then traveled to Palo Alto to study the city subsidy of their community theatre. She visited San Francisco and learned about the financing of their opera. At the University of California, she met with Henry Schnitzler, the son of playwright Arthur Schnitzler, and talked theatre philosophy and plays.

In October, the new script Tennessee had promised to send finally caught up with her. Just a few days earlier, James Laughlin had sent her the New Directions–published edition of *The Purification*. Thrilled with the dedication "to Margo Jones" and with the play, she kept it with her constantly. Margo had read hundreds of plays—classics, new scripts, verse dramas, potboilers, and Broadway hits—but whenever she opened a new script, she was filled with anticipation. She approached each script with "wonderment," one of her favorite words, reading not as a critic but as a lover. Once, when she received a shipment of poetry and plays from New Directions, she wrote publisher Jay Laughlin that "the box arrived. . . . I know no way except with sentiment to thank you. They arrived on a day when I most would have grabbed the hand of some one to talk—over beer, over coffee, over anything—there was no one and then all of a sudden I got pitched into the middle of so many hands to hold. . . ." When she read new work, she responded personally and immediately—either she fell in love or she didn't. For her, there were no half-measures.

S H E   B E G A N to read the *The Glass Menagerie*, a "memory play" in two parts, the final version of the script Tennessee had read to her the year before. Margo knew that the play, set in St. Louis in the 1930s and based on Tennessee's family, was semi-autobiographical, and she felt close to the southern family that carried the name "Wingfield," the name of her Virginia great-grandmother, though this may have been merely a fortunate coincidence, since it is likely that Tennessee actually chose the name from his own childhood memories of a Mrs. Wingfield who was a friend of his grandparents in Mississippi.

In *The Glass Menagerie* Tom Wingfield, the narrator and a character in the play, invites the audience into his memory, offering "truth in the pleasant disguise of illusion." The plot concerns the efforts of his mother, Amanda, a strong-willed, manipulative former southern belle who clings to memories of her past, to find a husband for Tom's sister, Laura. Shy and slightly crippled, Laura is "exquisitely fragile," like the glass animals she collects. The father of the family appears only in a photograph, for he left his wife and children years earlier. Amanda badgers Tom, a poet trapped in a deadening job at a shoe factory, to find a gentleman caller for his sister. Finally Tom brings home Jim O'Connor, a clerk at the shoe factory who has befriended him. Laura knew Jim in high school and was attracted to him. For a brief moment, as she dances with Jim, in a scene lit by candles, Laura glows with hope. Then, in their dance, they bump into the table and Laura's special glass unicorn falls off and breaks. Laura's hopes are shattered too when she learns that Jim is engaged to be married. Jim departs, and Tom leaves as well, to wander the world, pursued by memories of his sister and mother. Tom the poet, the narrator, ends the play, distanced from Laura and Amanda, but still with them in spirit. His lines, spoken directly to the audience, have the cadence and lyricism of poetry:

> I left St. Louis. I descended the steps of this fire-escape for a last time and followed, from then on, in my father's footsteps, attempting to find in motion what was lost in space—I traveled around a great deal. The cities swept about me like dead leaves, leaves that were brightly colored but torn away from the branches. I would have stopped, but I was pursued by something. It always came upon me unawares, taking me altogether by

surprise. Perhaps it was a familiar bit of music. Perhaps it was only a piece of transparent glass—Perhaps I am walking along a street at night, in some strange city, before I have found companions. I pass the lighted window of a shop where perfume is sold. The window is filled with pieces of colored glass, tiny transparent bottles in delicate colors, like bits of a shattered rainbow. Then all at once my sister touches my shoulder. I turn around and look into her eyes . . . Oh, Laura, Laura, I tried to leave you behind me, but I am more faithful than I intended to be! I reach for a cigarette, I cross the street, I run into the movies or a bar, I buy a drink, I speak to the nearest stranger—anything that can blow your candles out! (*Laura bends over the candles.*)—for nowadays the world is lit by lightning! Blow out your candles, Laura—and so good-bye . . . (*Laura blows out the candles.*)

Margo closed the script. Here indeed was magic and wonderment—a poetic vision far beyond Tennessee's earlier work. The play encompassed not just the ordinary lives of common people, but reached out to suggest the end of an era swept away by new forces loose in the world.

She longed to direct the play, to be involved with its production somehow, but she was committed to the Fellowship and needed John Rosenfield's support if she was to have the theatre she wanted. And so, in a letter written to Rosenfield soon after she had read the play, despite the fact that she and Tennessee had discussed opening her proposed theatre with it, Margo merely mentioned *The Glass Menagerie* in passing, writing instead of her work on the Project.

Margo interrupted her travels when she received word that her little brother Charles, now a rangy man more than six feet tall, would be visiting Livingston on a brief leave from his naval duties. Although Charles was nine years younger than Margo, they shared a special closeness and almost the same birthday: Margo was born a few minutes before midnight on December 1 2 and Charles was born a few minutes after midnight on the same day. Despite their age difference, the brother and sister were good friends. Charles liked to hear about his sister's projects. "She was an encouragement to me," he says. "I would read up on things she talked about. When she traveled, I traveled with her in my fantasies." At home in Livingston, when Margo needed a cigarette desperately, she and Charles would hide out behind the barn and smoke and talk—about life and art and dreams.

While she was in Livingston, Margo received a letter from Tennessee with the news that *The Glass Menagerie* had been optioned by New York producer

Eddie Dowling, who planned to direct the play and star in it. Tennessee wrote of his complete surprise that Dowling liked his play, and also of his fears of facing a commercial production alone. He was so overwhelmed by the situation that he had left New York to visit his family in St. Louis. Sustained by her energy and faith in his work, he hoped that there was some way she could be involved with the production. I need you with me, he told her. Margo had always believed that Tennessee would make it to Broadway, and she wanted to be there with him. She began to form a plan.

The Rockefeller Foundation had approved a trip to St. Louis, and she used the opportunity to talk to Tennessee about the play and her possible involvement with it. Tennessee wired Dowling in New York that Margo Jones would be a wonderful assistant director.

While she waited to hear from Eddie Dowling, she continued her scheduled tour. She visited the University of Iowa, where she had a long discussion with Tennessee's former playwriting instructor E. C. Mabie, and on her way to New York she revisited the Cleveland Playhouse and saw a production at Jasper Deeter's Hedgerow Theatre near Philadelphia. She made it to New York in time for the November meetings of the National Theatre Conference. While in New York she received a formal offer from Eddie Dowling to work with him on *The Glass Menagerie.* Audrey Wood, who along with Williams had recommended her to Dowling, signed on as Margo's agent. Before taking the job, Margo talked with David Stevens at the Rockefeller Foundation to request a leave of absence from her fellowship. She told Stevens that her directing job would "be worth its weight in gold in experience." Stevens agreed, and granted her request.

Margo also sent an awkward letter to Rosenfield explaining her decision to suspend work on the Project. Fumbling for words, she wrote, "I hope it will be possible for you to let the people of Dallas know that if we're to create this theatre in Dallas that it will be the interest and work of our own town and that Rockefeller's gave me my study fellowship to make me better able through knowledge acquired to be able to carry the plan out." She knew that her decision left Rosenfield in an embarrassing position. He had gained the support of Dallas mayor Woodall Rogers and the president of the Park Board, who had told him that the city was willing to back a theatre if Rosenfield could work on gaining community support. When she took the directing job, it at first appeared to Rosenfield that Margo had abandoned the Project.

To Margo, interrupting her Project to work on a new play in the commercial theatre was consistent with her goals. After working in little theatres and university theatre, the logical career move for an ambitious director was to the world of professional New York theatre. She had strong ambitions, wanted to be known and respected, but, as Tennessee Williams had observed earlier, she had a core of unselfish devotion to a dream larger than mere personal ambition. She believed fervently in Williams's writing; she had directed the premieres of two of his plays and championed his work to all who would listen. She convinced John Rosenfield, who in turn explained to the people of Dallas that she needed the experience of a Broadway play, and that as soon as the play opened, she would resume her travels and study. Also, Margo wanted to learn firsthand about the operations of a commercial theatre venture. As a savvy promoter, she knew that if *The Glass Menagerie* was successful it would only enhance her appeal to the people back home, and if it failed she had nothing to lose except time.

ALTHOUGH MARGO did not think of herself as a "woman director," she now had an opportunity few women were afforded in the professional theatre—a chance to prove herself on Broadway. Eighty-seven productions opened in the 1944–45 Broadway season; only four were directed by women. The hierarchical power structure of theatre mirrored society in general. Top executive positions were held by men. The women directors who worked the most—Margaret Webster, noted for her productions of Shakespeare, and Eva Le Gallienne, actress, translator, and director—created their own opportunities with their short-lived American Repertory Theatre, which they established in 1946 with producer Cheryl Crawford. In an attempt to seize control over their plays' interpretations, several women playwrights, including Rachel Crothers, Rose Franken, and Lillian Hellman, occasionally directed their own work. The women directors who made it to Broadway had to be talented, often even more talented than their male colleagues, for opportunities for women directors to work in the small, inbred world of the commercial theatre were rare, and jobs depended upon contacts. Margo's "contact" with Tennessee Williams and Audrey Wood had earned her the right to work in a commercial production, and that job in turn might lead to more contacts and more work.

Contacts, publicity for her project, learning her craft, all were important, but although Margo preached the doctrine of art theatres in the provinces, the world of New York theatre, Broadway, tempted her with its sophistication, glamour, and famous names. And to be on Broadway with a beautiful, poetic play filled with compassion and truth smack in the middle of the escapist entertainment, show business schmaltz, and glitz and glitter of Times Square was irresistible. Margo would have an opportunity to carry her banner of art versus commercialism, regionalism versus centralism into the very heart of the theatre capital.

When Margo reported to work on December 1, 1944, she learned that the co-producer and director of *The Glass Menagerie*, Eddie Dowling, had already completed most of the casting and hired the staff as well as designer Jo Mielziner. The fifty-year-old Dowling had cast himself in the role of Tom, the play's narrator, a decision that surprised Tennessee, who had conceived Tom as a much younger man. But Dowling had an assured talent, years of experience, and a trim physique, and when he applied a bit of shoe blacking to his scalp, the audience would probably never notice his thinning hair. Of course, the play is Tom's memory, and the presence of an older Tom, Tennessee realized, might be quite effective.

Born in Woonsocket, Rhode Island, in 1894, the young Dowling had worked as a cabin boy on ocean liners, made his first appearance on the stage at the age of fourteen in the Providence Opera House, toured England with a choral group in his late teens, and then returned to America to play vaudeville. Solid work in legitimate theatre followed and in 1939 Dowling produced and acted in William Saroyan's *The Time of Your Life*, which won the Pulitzer Prize. He was the first person agent Audrey Wood had approached to produce *The Glass Menagerie*. The timing was fortuitous since his most recent production, *Men at Sea*, had opened and closed in October.

Dowling secured the backing of Louis Singer, a wealthy New York City investment banker who was also a patron of the arts; since Singer had no background in or understanding of theatre, Dowling dubbed him a "virgin" from Wall Street. Singer's partner, Joel Schenker, was out of the country, and the play they had originally planned to produce with Dowling, *The Compassionate Congressman*, had been replaced by *The Glass Menagerie*. This play would be Singer's first solo producing venture, and he was understandably nervous about his seventy-five-thousand-dollar investment.

Dowling had worked with actress Julie Haydon in several plays, including *The Time of Your Life* and Saroyan's *Hello Out There*. He called her the "wraith of God" and felt that her angular, ethereal beauty would be just right for the fragile Laura. The thirty-four-year-old Haydon, a native of Oak Park, Illinois, had studied theatre in Chicago, then moved to California where she made her stage debut in Hollywood appearing with the nineteenth-century star, Minnie Maddern Fiske, in *The Lower Depths*. Haydon met, fell in love with, and later married the influential theatre critic George Jean Nathan.

It was Nathan who suggested to Dowling that Laurette Taylor play the part of Amanda. Dowling delivered the script to Taylor, who stayed up all night

Let Me Talk My Dreams

reading it, then exclaimed, "I've found it. . . . I've found the play I've been waiting for!" Born on April 1, 1884, the daughter of playwright Charles Taylor, Laurette Taylor had been one of the most popular actresses of the earlier twentieth century. Like Dowling, Taylor had begun her career as a child, appearing in vaudeville as "La Belle Laurette." She had acted in stock companies in roles as diverse as Topsy in *Uncle Tom's Cabin* and Marguerite in *Faust*. She had married playwright Hartley Manners and achieved her greatest success in his play *Peg o' My Heart*. When Constantin Stanislavsky and his Moscow Art Theatre toured America in 1924, he met Laurette Taylor, saw her work, called her America's greatest actress, and asked her to appear with the Moscow Art Theatre.

Taylor's career had floundered, however, following the death of her beloved husband. Their life together with their two children had been a blissful one. They lived on Long Island in a happy, hectic household surrounded by theatre people and guests. One visitor, playwright Noel Coward, based his comedy *Hay Fever* on their antics. But in 1928 when Hartley Manners died, Taylor suffered, taking refuge in liquor and, she said later, "going on the longest wake in history." Afterward she worked sporadically, for she could not be depended upon to learn her lines or show up for rehearsal on time, and her great talent lay in waste. Now, with this offer to play Amanda, the middle-aged woman desperate to find a husband for her daughter, Taylor had an opportunity to return to the stage. She felt that the secret of the role was capturing the duality of the character. Underneath Amanda's stout, shrill exterior breathed the soul of the young belle of Blue Mountain who had once had seventeen gentleman callers. Taylor could identify with Amanda's duality. When she was a young woman, Taylor was a vibrant actress with a mass of reddish gold hair, large brown eyes with heavy lids, expressive eyebrows, and a sensuous mouth. With age and drinking, her once slim figure had grown stocky and matronly. Her oval face had become flabby and round, her eyes faded and nearsighted. But just beneath the dulled surface one could glimpse from time to time the bright image of the beautiful young woman who had captivated audiences in America and London.

Dowling had tried unsuccessfully to cast the role of the gentleman caller. He had hoped for actor Dana Andrews, but when Margo signed on, she began auditioning actors for the part. Soon she reported to Dowling, "I've just found a man who reads the gentleman caller out of heaven. It's such a pity we can't use him."

"Why not?" Dowling asked.

"Well, he's so old," Margo said shrewdly, knowing full well that Anthony

Let Me Talk My Dreams

"Tony" Ross, fresh out of the service where he had appeared in the show *This Is the Army*, was just thirty-eight years old—if anything, too young to play a contemporary of Eddie Dowling's. Flattered by her comments, Dowling approved her choice. Rehearsals began in various places, Dowling's office, the hotel across the street, even Donald Windham's apartment.

Margo quickly settled into the routine of rehearsals. She managed to secure Joanna Albus, her friend from the Houston Players days, a position as production assistant on the play, and thus was assured of a willing, able assistant to type script changes, take notes, write letters, and run errands. Since their work together in the Houston Players, the women had remained close friends. Margo depended on Joanna's organizational skills and her efficiency not only professionally but personally as well. Although Joanna wanted to be an actress, she took on the role Mrs. Markey had assumed in Austin. She began to attend to the myriad details of Margo's life—taking out her cleaning, doing her shopping, and dealing with the dozens of daily tasks beyond the ken of a director busy with Art. Margo seemed to have a knack for finding people to attend to her personal needs while she focused her energies on her career. In return, she shared her theatre plans with Joanna, and together they planned to found the Dallas theatre. A few years older than Margo, Joanna was a striking woman—tall and dark-haired with classic features. Intense, somewhat shy and quiet, Joanna was content, for the moment, to remain in the background.

Initially, Dowling and Margo split the rehearsals, with Margo staging the gentleman-caller scene with Julie Haydon and Anthony Ross while Dowling rehearsed his scenes with Laurette Taylor. Margo was also responsible for most of the blocking, and according to assistant stage manager Willie Gould it was her idea to play much of the gentleman-caller scene on the floor. Although Tennessee had suggested that Dowling hire Margo as his assistant, she was named co-director, with increasing responsibilities as the pressures of the rehearsal period began to mount.

Rehearsals are a time of exploration and discovery of the world the playwright has created. Often the playwright has offered up his or her inner life, most private thoughts, emotions, and conflicts to public scrutiny. Actors settle into that world, becoming intimate with other actors who have been strangers just a few days before, and in doing this, they leave themselves vulnerable. In a very short time, the actors face basic questions about human nature and motivations—What does their character want and believe in? What does the playwright believe? Often, questions and emotions are dredged up that they would be reluctant to discuss with their closest friends. They have to trust the

Let Me Talk My Dreams

instincts and taste of a director who watches their characterizations unfold. In this self-contained world allegiances shift, tensions explode, pettiness and bickering surface. However, at the same time, rehearsals are filled with great excitement and commitment, for despite their differences, everyone involved in a production is united by a common goal, a sense of mission to create something larger than themselves, which is the theatre event—a performance shared with an audience, a celebration rooted in humanity's most ancient needs and rituals.

The company Eddie Dowling had assembled included Louis J. Singer, a nervous, first-time producer; Laurette Taylor, an alcoholic former star making a comeback; Julie Haydon, an excessively shy actress with George Jean Nathan, a powerful, meddling critic, at her side; Margo Jones, a young director with no commercial theatre experience; and Tennessee Williams, a relatively unknown playwright with a few small productions to his credit and one major flop. With this cast of characters, problems during rehearsal were inevitable.

Laurette Taylor's work in rehearsals alarmed the other members of the company, and Dowling even thought of replacing her. She peered through a large magnifying glass at her script, mumbled her lines, and made no apparent effort at characterization. Margo's directing notes urge Taylor to lighten her thick southern accent. Actually, Taylor was immersing herself in the role, exploring all facets of the character, becoming Amanda.

Sixty-three-year-old critic George Jean Nathan, the dean of American theatre critics, had founded *The Smart Set* magazine years earlier with H. L. Mencken. The magazine published the early plays of Eugene O'Neill, and Nathan had written dozens of books about the theatre and supposedly had never missed a New York premiere. Armed with his formidable reputation and impressive credentials, Nathan felt that Tennessee really didn't understand the theatre and needed help fixing his play. He and Dowling decided that a drunk scene for Tom should be included in the script. Dowling wrote an outline and then he, Singer, and Nathan met with Tennessee to inform him of their plan. After this unpleasant scene, Tennessee went to Margo's hotel room, where she was celebrating her birthday with a group of friends. Upset that anyone wanted to tinker with the writer's script, Margo insisted that if there was going to be a drunk scene, Tennessee should certainly write it. During the rehearsal period and even into the run, Dowling ad-libbed a corny drunk scene; finally convinced that such a scene for Tom was inevitable, Tennessee later wrote his own version, which was inserted in the production.

Margo's role as co-director began to take on another aspect. As Tennessee had intended when he recommended her for the job, she became his advocate, his staunchest supporter, and defender of the play against the forays of Dowling, Singer, and Nathan. In her mind the playwright, not Dowling, was the star and deserved her loyalty.

O N D E C E M B E R 1 6 the group left for their pre-Broadway tryout in Chicago. Advance publicity there had been arranged by Singer's representative Alex Yokel, the production supervisor. Using an old producer's trick on the unsuspecting locals, Dowling and Singer had promised Chicago mayor Edward Kelly that *The Glass Menagerie* would be the first venture of a new civic repertory theatre they planned to open in Chicago. Kelly reciprocated with letters of praise and support that were widely quoted in ads for the play.

Most of the company were united in their active dislike of the stingy producer Singer and his hired flack Yokel, who had so little understanding of the play. In a November newspaper interview promoting *The Glass Menagerie* and attempting to sell it to the Chicago audience, Yokel had lamely described the play as "a strange affair materializing the thoughts of three people"—a description that almost certainly would send audiences to *Kiss and Tell*, *Oklahoma*, *Ten Little Indians*, or *The Voice of the Turtle*—all popular productions that were currently playing Chicago.

Met in the city by icy cold winds whipping off Lake Michigan, the company began rehearsing in the smoking lounge of the nine-hundred-seat Civic Theatre; designer Jo Mielziner needed the stage to work on his set. Margo and Mielziner had liked each other immediately, and Margo worked closely with him on the technical aspects of the production. Assistant stage manager Willie Gould remembers that director Dowling "didn't have a clue" about any of the technical elements.

Mielziner had a reputation for calmness and unruffled detachment. The youthful-looking forty-four-year-old designer felt that his mission was "to aid and abet the actors." He had been a captain in the Army Air Force during the war, and *The Glass Menagerie* marked his return to the stage.

Mielziner was born in 1901 in Paris, where his mother worked as the Paris correspondent for *Vogue* magazine and his father was a portrait painter. His mother was a descendant of nineteenth-century actress Charlotte Cushman, and both parents were theatre lovers, introducing their son to theatre in Paris, London, and New York at an early age. After seeing Robert Edmond Jones's imaginative set design for *The Man Who Married a Dumb Wife* in New York in 1915, Mielziner knew that he wanted to become a designer. While traveling abroad on a scholarship, he managed to meet his idol, revolutionary theatre designer and writer Gordon Craig, who talked with him for three days, showed him drawings, and encouraged him. In New York in 1923, designer Lee Simonson helped Mielziner get his first job with the Theatre Guild. Led by Craig and Robert Edmond Jones, set designers of the 1920s were rebelling against realism in settings. The influence of movies had also begun to be felt. When Mielziner began designing sets and lights on Broadway in 1924, audiences, used to movies, would no longer accept three-minute waits while stagehands changed the sets. Designers used elevators, cables, turntables, conveyor belts, and scrims to facilitate fluid staging.

In the stage directions for *The Glass Menagerie*, Williams described the absent father's photograph as considerably larger than life-size, symbolizing the father's dominance over the family. He also wanted to use magic lantern slides to illustrate the family's memories. For example, when Laura mentions blue roses, an image of blue roses was to appear on a screen. Mielziner wisely advised against these techniques, saying that they would interfere with the actors and distract the audience's attention from the play. Williams agreed.

As the opening date neared, rehearsals grew increasingly hectic. Tennessee wrote to Donald Windham that Margo was like the leader of a jolly, wayward scout troop. In their free hours, most of the company (excepting Haydon and Dowling) spent the time drinking. Margo continued her habit of Texas-style drinking, and to relax she sang hymns with Willie Gould. During this time Tennessee introduced her to William Inge, the shy young drama critic of the *St. Louis Star Times*. Inge wanted to become a playwright, and Margo encouraged him, told him about her plans for a real playwrights' theatre, and urged him to send her his scripts.

Sonny Koch, on leave from Fort Leonardwood, joined her in Chicago to press his marriage proposals, but spent most of his time watching Mielziner work on the lights. Earlier, Sonny had written Margo that he wanted them to "make the tie that will bind—so softly, gently, freely—a tie that will bring happiness not only to us, but to my folks and yours, too." Margo adored Sonny and admired his clean-cut, blonde good looks, but replied that she felt inadequate personally, was too involved with theatre, and simply was not ready for marriage. Sonny assured her that her personality was not inadequate—it was entwined with her theatre personality—and he knew and loved them both. Consumed with the job she had to do, Margo continued to put Sonny off, but he held out hope and asked her to work on that "marryin' mood."

Worried about costs, Singer attempted to cut expenses wherever he could. Originally, experienced Broadway designer Rose Bogdanoff had been engaged to design the clothes, but she had been forced to withdraw because of illness. According to the playbill, the clothes were provided by Brooks Costume, although Eddie Dowling wore a favorite pea jacket from his last production and other costumes were purchased from the Salvation Army. Preoccupied with sets and lighting, Mielziner had time only to advise about the costume choices. In a letter to Audrey Wood, Margo complained about the producer's stinginess. "In many cases, it's absurd—Laurette and Julie have had to buy their own clothes and sew them—Joanna, my friend, has had to help them and so have I. . . . At the last minute Jo Mielziner thought Julie should have a dress not white and to get it little Tennessee had to go out and buy it and Mr. Singer wouldn't pay for it. It turned out that Eddie finally paid $20.00 of it and Tennessee paid $10.00."

Margo, Tennessee, and stage manager Randy Echols scurried around to secondhand stores finding props, like the old typewriter Tennessee wanted. Luckily, Steuben Glass supplied the glass menagerie of unicorns, squirrels, horses, cows, and deer.

The set had translucent walls, reflecting, Mielziner felt, Williams's exploration of the inner self. They allowed the action to flow rapidly from scene to scene. To cut costs, Singer wanted Mielziner to use canvas to back the set. Mielziner said, "I can't light canvas." Instead he demanded and got the more expensive lightproof black velour. Once the set was in place, Mielziner worked with two electricians he had brought from New York and with the stage managers, Randy Echols and Willie Gould, hanging and focusing the lights. The crew had two days to finish the lighting since the play was scheduled to open on Christmas night. They worked around the clock, taking time off only for dinner breaks. According to Willie Gould, Mielziner "decided to take every move in the play and light it." In Act One, there were 102 light cues, and Mielziner said, "this is the most difficult light job I've ever done."

Margo sat out front during the technical rehearsals, taking notes, checking the blocking as the actors got used to the set, timing the music and sound cues, ironing out problems with light cues, prop and costume changes, and checking acting interpretations, especially Eddie Dowling's tendency to hoke up his performance. When stuck for the correct line, Dowling sometimes delivered inappropriate ad libs, calling the menagerie "little glass guys" and referring to Laura as "old-timer." According to both stage managers, no one, including Eddie Dowling, dared to give acting notes to Laurette Taylor, although Margo and Tennessee did work with her extensively on her southern accent. Also, Margo continued to protect the play from Singer's interference.

Budgets, expenses, and projected receipts continued to worry Singer. As an inexperienced producer, he had little faith that the chaos of the moment could turn into money at the box office. To guard his sizable investment,

Singer called together Eddie Dowling, Tennessee, and Margo and told them that the play should have a happy ending, that Laura should marry Jim. Margo waited for the men to talk. Dowling didn't say a word. She waited for Tennessee to answer. Tennessee didn't speak.

"Tennessee," Margo began quietly, "don't you change that ending. It's perfect." Then she looked up at Louis Singer, her cat's eyes narrowing. Making her hand into a fist, she said in a menacing tone, "Mr. Singer, if you make Tennessee change the play the way you want it, so help me I'll go around to every critic in town and tell them about the kind of wire-pulling that's going on here."

Singer stared at the fierce young woman who was making her commercial directing debut with *The Glass Menagerie*. She had no clout other than her convictions. The original ending remained.

MIELZINER AND his crew finished the lighting about three hours before the preview curtain. The entire company of *Winged Victory* with its cast of soldier-actors playing next door had been invited to the Christmas night preview; the opening had been rescheduled for December 26. Willie Gould had only a sketchy light cue sheet, and had to ad-lib the cues to the two electricians. To manipulate all the dimmers, pulling them down or up at the appropriate moment, one electrician tied a rope around his waist, the other used a stick to control several dimmers at once.

Margo made the rounds of the dressing rooms, checking that the actors had everything they needed and offering last-minute support. In Laurette Taylor's dressing room, fifteen minutes before curtain, she found Taylor bent over the sink, wringing out a robe she was to wear in scene three. Unhappy with the color, she had dyed it. Margo couldn't believe her eyes as Taylor calmly handed the robe to stage manager Randy Echols and asked, "Could you find a way to dry this for me?" According to Margo, Echols "didn't bat an eye," just grinned and said, "Yes, Miss Taylor." He found a radiator, dried the robe, and Taylor wore it in scene three.

Throughout the rehearsal period, Randy Echols had heard Margo say many times about the play, "It's magic — it's sheer magic." She had slaved, she said, to keep the peace and to serve the play. Undoubtedly, her natural optimism had buoyed spirits during the grueling rehearsal period. The reward was the first performance of *The Glass Menagerie* before the soldier audience when the actors, especially the gifted Laurette Taylor, moving in Mielziner's evocative set and symphony of light, created something beyond words and silence, beyond the physical reality of sets and costumes, and forged that mystical,

Let Me Talk My Dreams

ephemeral bond with the audience that is the real language of the theatre. Together, this unlikely group of collaborators had created something larger than themselves, something true, and the soldier audience cheered.

The question was, could they do it again on opening night with the Chicago critics present? Members of the audience, who had braved the icy Chicago streets, paid a top price of $3.60 for their theatre seats and shared their playbills because of the wartime paper shortage. Paid for by fourteen pages of ads selling liquor, including James E. Pepper Bourbon, Red Horse Liqueurs, Blatz Beer, Schenley Reserve Whiskey, Delecta After Dinner Liqueurs, and Old Grand-Dad, the playbill urged them to "Buy War Bonds." But when the play began, the outside world was forgotten. The spell remained.

Afterward, the company went to Riccardo's, a nearby restaurant that Margo favored because she thought the owner looked like John Barrymore. There Margo warmed herself with a hot rum drink, and the group waited for the papers. Two Chicago critics, Ashton Stevens of the *Herald-Tribune* and Claudia Cassidy of the *Daily Tribune*, had the power to close a play with adverse reviews. The elderly Stevens looked frail, but his sharp barbs and polished prose had become a legend in Chicago. Once, after attending a very bad play, he had walked out of the theatre and found a murdered gangster lying under the marquee. "They shot the wrong man," he quipped in his column. Another time when he was asked if his theatre seats were satisfactory, he snapped, "No, I cannot only see, but I can hear every word." His colleague, Claudia Cassidy, who looked like actress Tallulah Bankhead, was characterized by theatre people as the Medusa of the Midwest, who had the power to turn actors to stone. Cassidy felt that critics were the "world's best audience, with the privilege of communicating what they discover." In his review of *The Glass Menagerie* Stevens wrote, "The play leaves you in the air. But I like this air. It is rare, rich." Cassidy declared that the play understood people and that she was caught in its spell. Both searched for superlatives to describe Laurette Taylor's incandescent performance, and they returned to the theatre again and again to see the play and communicated its appeal to their readers.

Attendance and box-office receipts were initially low. Eddie Dowling reminded Singer that he had promised him an artistic success, not a financial one. With the publicity provided by the newspaper critics and with growing word of mouth, however, the audience began to build. By the third week, operating expenses were met by the box-office receipts, and by the fourth week, the nine-hundred-seat theatre was sold out, and customers were turned away.

On December 27 Alex Yokel gave Margo her $150-a-week paycheck and reminded her that since the play was running now the check would be her last one. But Margo knew that the production still needed polishing, and with the support of Tennessee, Eddie Dowling, and Audrey Wood, she stayed on salary in Chicago for three weeks after the opening.

She hadn't forgotten about her Project. In her free time, she visited Northwestern University, the University of Chicago, and the Goodman Theatre. She saw *Winged Victory, Kiss and Tell, Oklahoma,* and *The Voice of the Turtle,* and she renewed ties with several of her former University of Texas students who had roles in the productions. The *Glass Menagerie* company was invited to functions around town, and Margo, often the appointed speaker, used the opportunity to talk about both the play and her Project.

When one local university invited the company to a tea, fifty theatre students attended and had a chance to observe the legendary Laurette Taylor at close range. Taylor arrived, seated herself in an armchair, looked around the large Commons room, and asked, "My God, do they pray in here?"

Tennessee, Margo, Julie Haydon, and Anthony Ross sat on the floor at her feet. "Julie," Taylor remarked, for no apparent reason, "manages to love everybody. I wish I knew how she does it."

Margo delivered an inspiring talk to the theatre students, urging them to go out and get what they wanted in the theatre. The students invited the company to come see their production of *The Inspector General,* but were deflated when Taylor announced that she had already seen Stanislavsky do it.

In late January, Margo said good-bye to the company and traveled to New York, where she planned to stay until *The Glass Menagerie* opened on Broadway. War news dominated the newspapers as Germany desperately fought the Allied advance, and Roosevelt, Stalin, and Churchill planned to meet at Yalta in early February. Theatregoers flocked to Broadway and the 1944–45 season was one of the best New York had had in years. To qualify for the Pulitzer Prize, *The Glass Menagerie* had to open in New York by March 31, and the booking situation was tight.

Margo resumed work on her Project, contacting playwrights and reading plays. In the small world of the theatre, word traveled quickly, and Margo learned that she had become a "hot" director. According to Randy Echols, "Eddie [Dowling] didn't give a damn except about his own performance. Everybody on the street knew that he hadn't directed." While this assessment may be unfair, it was clear that Margo had contributed a great deal to the success of the play, functioning not only as a director but as a production manager as well, overseeing all aspects of the complex production. Even before *The Glass Menagerie* opened on Broadway, the Leland Heyward Agency asked her to direct a musical version of *Volpone*, Sam Hoffman asked her to stage his new production, and producers showed renewed interest in Edwin Mayer's play *Sunrise in My Pocket*. Still she wrote John Rosenfield that although she loved her experience with *The Glass Menagerie*, what she wanted more than anything was to "get going on our theatre which seems to me the answer to a crying need. . . ."

She attended rehearsals for a musical version of Edwin Mayer's *The Fire-brand*, saw an "awful" production of Rose Franken's play *Soldier's Wife*, and took in *Pelléas and Mélisande* at the Met. She especially loved Margaret Webster's production of *The Tempest*, starring the distinguished black actor Canada Lee as Caliban. Walking through the snow back to her room at the Royalton Hotel, she thought that of all the productions she had seen, the plays of Tennessee Williams and William Shakespeare were the finest.

Margo's sojourn in New York ended abruptly one cold, rainy morning in early February when her phone rang at 7:00 A.M. It was John Rosenfield in Texas. He had formed a group of prominent citizens interested in a theatre for Dallas. They all agreed that Margo Jones was just the person they needed. Her gamble on *The Glass Menagerie* had paid off, giving her the imprimatur of a commercial Broadway success, which, ironically, was just the impetus needed for a nonprofit, art theatre for the Southwest. Rosenfield told her if she "wanted to grab this iron while it was hot she should get down here. . . ."

Margo notified Joanna Albus, and they left that day on the first train to Texas.

WHEN THE TRAIN called the Spirit of St. Louis rumbled out of New York City's Pennsylvania Station, Margo and Joanna, unable to purchase seats at the last minute, balanced on their suitcases in the crowded aisle, jostled by homebound soldiers. They changed trains in St. Louis, boarding the Blue Bonnet bound for Dallas.

During World War II, Dallas, surrounded by cotton and oil fields, had become the "War Capital of the Southwest." It was there that North American Aviation built more fighters, bombers, and trainers than any other company in the United States. Employment had soared as manufacturing, banks, and businesses boomed. Dallas was a city receptive to change, a city that believed growth was limitless, and a city that believed in the power of the individual. After all, almost everybody who was anybody in Dallas had begun at the bottom—even Herbert Stanley Marcus of the famed Neiman-Marcus department stores had started out sweeping up his brother-in-law's general store.

The city had been founded on the three forks of the Trinity River, the same

Let Me Talk My Dreams

river that flowed near Margo's hometown of Livingston. It was settled in the 1840s by John Neely Bryan, who envisioned a city built around the river that would be a terminal for shipping and commerce. He lured settlers with the promise of a trading center where they could make their fortune, but when the early settlers arrived, they found only a few crude log cabins and a narrow, crooked river too shallow and unpredictable to navigate. Many passed through the town to settle in the more fertile country of East Texas. Others stayed, building businesses and industries, creating opportunities for themselves where none existed before. When the railroad arrived in 1872, the future of the town was assured. As one historian has said, "Dallas is an example of a city that man has made, with little help from nature and practically none from Providence."

Dallas was the frontier and had attracted its share of desperate characters, like Belle Starr, who scandalized the town because she wore fringed buckskin pants, gambled, drank whiskey, and lived with outlaws. For entertainment, the settlers had enjoyed fistfights, horse races, rat killings, bearbaitings, cock-fighting, gambling, and dance halls. Often, in an effort to clean up the town, the solid citizens hired someone to set fire to the more notorious establishments. As the town grew, more sophisticated entertainment was desired, and in 1873 Dallas got its first theatre, Field's Opera House, a small auditorium on the second floor of a wooden building on Main Street. A few years later Craddocks Theatre opened, and then citizens built the Dallas Opera House in 1883. Touring companies played Dallas, featuring many stars of the late nineteenth and early twentieth century, such as Edwin Booth, Maurice Barrymore, Lillie Langtry, Tommaso Salvini, Johnston Forbes-Robertson, Alla Nazimova, Anna Held, Sarah Bernhardt, and Lillian Russell.

In 1905 Karl Hoblitzelle introduced vaudeville to Texas and almost single-handedly changed the public's attitude toward commercial theatre. He replaced the sleazier vaudeville acts with family-oriented entertainment and brought motion pictures to audiences all over Texas. Winning a victory over the protests of the churches, he scheduled movies to play on Sundays. Most people worked a six-day week and were free to relax only on the Sabbath.

Movie theatres supplanted the playhouses, and by the 1920s Dallas didn't have a permanent theatre for legitimate drama and touring companies. As the amateur little-theatre movement began to sweep the country in the 1920s, the Dallas Little Theatre was organized, prophetically, in an undertaking parlor. At first, like dozens of other little theatres throughout Texas, the community venture prospered, winning awards and popular support for its schedule of Broadway hits; but the Dallas Little Theatre presented its last productions in

Let Me Talk My Dreams

1943, a victim of the same lack of vitality and failure to grow and change that had killed so many little theatres across the country.

ON SATURDAY, February 10, 1945, as the Blue Bonnet drew closer to Dallas, Margo knew that here was her opportunity to turn her dreams into action. The fact that she scarcely knew anyone in town didn't discourage her. She had started at the bottom before. Although she believed that her theatre and other theatres like it could be successful anywhere in the country, she felt that it would be easier for her to work among Texans, who would understand her. She was one of them. Like the pioneers before her, who had created Dallas out of sheer will, aggressiveness, and an ability to adapt and change, Margo planned to create a theatre where none had existed before. She simply had no doubts. Those would come later.

Rosenfield had arranged for Margo and Joanna to stay at Eugene and Ruth McDermott's home in the lovely Preston Hollow section of Dallas. In fact, Rosenfield had asked Ruth McDermott to invite a few people interested in a theatre for the city to a meeting at her home on Sunday. Ruth McDermott had been active in the Dallas Little Theatre, and she and her husband were wealthy, civic-minded, and interested in the arts. Unfortunately, when Margo arrived in Dallas, Eugene McDermott was out of town with, according to John Rosenfield, the sad duty of locating a sanitarium for his wife, who suffered from a drinking problem.

When Margo and Joanna stepped off the train, they were met by a chauffeur. Ruth McDermott, who had recently broken her leg and was confined to a wheelchair, had sent a driver and limousine to fetch them—a gratifying luxury after the cramped, exhausting train trip. Even the weather seemed to welcome them. An early spring had come to Dallas, bringing sunny skies and sixty-degree temperatures. Jonquils and snapdragons were ready to burst into bloom, and the nurseries were filled with peach and apple trees, roses, sweet William, and crape myrtle. New York, with its gray skies and wintry cold, seemed a world away.

The next evening, Sunday, February 11, the "few" people Ruth McDermott had invited began to arrive. In Texas terms, a few people apparently meant seventy of Dallas's most prominent citizens—wealthy, sophisticated men and women who summered in Europe, shopped in Paris, and attended theatre in London and New York. Texas writer George Sessions Perry wrote later that Margo knew she could count on Dallas's "cultural war horses, who just automatically rally round and run interference for anybody trying to write a good book, paint a good picture or organize a good theatre. . . . They like their culture mixed with action, impact, excitement, adventure and glittering success." They liked to brag about their culture too, claiming that Dallas, a stopover point for transcontinental air travel, was the beginning of the East, a baby Manhattan. And, they boasted, Dallasites bought more books per capita than residents of any other city in the country. Through the Texas Institute of Letters, Dallas awarded five cash literary prizes each year and held so many literary teas and luncheons that a starving writer could grow fat just attending them.

Margo wrote later to Edwin Justus Mayer that she "didn't think that the Eddie Dowling–Laurette Taylor experience could be topped, but believe me experiences here in Dallas have." Among the many who crowded into the McDermotts' huge drawing room that day, Margo chose to sit on the floor, in the curve of the grand piano. She usually sat on the floor when circumstances allowed it, but with the instincts of a director she must have known that today the informal gesture would set her apart—would make her the focus of attention. At the McDermotts', Margo was meeting for the first time the wealthy men and women she would privately characterize later as the "oil-derricks," "cotton fields," "lumber mills," "printing presses," and "ranches" of Texas.

Betty Winn, a prominent leader in Dallas civic affairs who was there that Sunday, recalls now that she expected the guest of honor to look sophisticated, tall and dramatic, to look like someone who had just returned from directing a play on Broadway. Instead, she saw a thirty-three-year-old woman, five feet six inches tall, wearing no makeup except lipstick, with short, wavy brown hair, a turned-up freckled nose, a square, slightly jutting jaw, and bright, small eyes. Winn found Margo "plain . . . and not in the least bit theatrical looking, but every time she smiled she shed light." She remembers that Margo "looked like a country girl, acted like an enthusiastic child, and yet had a will of steel and a mind like a steel trap. So it was an odd combination. Everybody felt at ease with her."

To prepare the group, debonair Lon Tinkle, editor of the book section of the *Dallas Morning News* and chairman of the French department at Southern Methodist University, gave a brief history of theatre in Dallas. Then the two rival newspapermen who had known Margo since her college days, who had encouraged her and believed in her, John William Rogers of the *Dallas Times Herald* and John Rosenfield of the *Dallas Morning News*, introduced Margo and presented a survey of her background.

Her audience was crowded into the drawing room, the kitchen, the dining room, even the sun porch of the McDermotts' home. They waited expectantly for her to begin. She stood up and spoke, without notes. She never used notes or wrote out a speech. "Let me talk my dreams," she would say.

She said that if this theatre was to be "of the past, striving to exist on box-office hits," they could count her out. She said that this theatre in Dallas would be nonprofit. It would be a permanent, professional resident theatre that would be a model for theatres like it all over the country, a national theatre for America. She said that this theatre in Dallas would be a true playwright's theatre, presenting original scripts and providing playwrights with an outlet for their work. And this theatre would revive the classics: Dallas citizens would be able to say in twenty years, "My children have lived in a town where they could see the best plays of the world presented in a beautiful and fine way." She said that this theatre would present work of high quality—fine theatre—because, Margo believed, "bad theatre is worse than no theatre at all." This theatre would "go beyond the dreams of the past and would mean even more to America than the Moscow Art Theatre meant to Russia, the Abbey to Ireland, or the Old Vic to England; [it would be] a theatre that will carry on, but adapt to our Country and time, the ideals of the Stanislavsky's, the Copeau's, the Craig's; a theatre of our time: an art theatre."

Elizabeth Ann McMurray, owner of McMurray's, a successful Dallas bookstore that with typical Texas hyperbole promised "Books! Every title—Every author—Every publisher," said later that when Margo spoke that evening, "It was riveting, dramatic, one of the most thrilling things I have ever heard." The ability to communicate her dreams, to share them with an audience, was perhaps Margo's greatest gift, a natural talent like throwing a fast ball or having perfect pitch. Her technique was simple, her manner relaxed and almost casual. She gave them straightforward, plain talk, but plain talk that was imbued with sincere enthusiasm and keen excitement, grounded in a thorough knowledge of the theatre, and, above all, charged with a passion to draw others into her vision. Like a savvy politician or a crafty trial lawyer or a Bible-thumping evangelist, Margo could sway listeners to her cause with personal charm, a flexible voice (at times with a pronounced Texas drawl, at times with no drawl at all, depending on the situation), and an adroit sense of timing.

That night, standing in the curve of the McDermotts' grand piano, Margo knew when she had finished speaking that her talk had been a success. Her audience burst into loud, prolonged applause. And they had gotten off easily—she hadn't asked for money.

Just then, like the final scene of a well-made play, the double doors of the drawing room were flung open, and a nurse wheeled Ruth McDermott into the packed room. Ruth had been listening to a sermon on the radio, and the minister had closed his talk with a piece of verse that she now repeated: "You can feel the breeze, can't you? You can see the stars, can't you? You can smell the flowers, can't you?" Then, in a quiet, soft voice, Ruth said, "And to prove my faith in Margo Jones, here is my check for ten thousand dollars."

Actually, Margo had rehearsed a version of this scene earlier that afternoon when, after hearing Margo talk about her plans, Ruth McDermott had written out a ten-thousand-dollar check that John Rosenfield had promptly torn up, explaining that they couldn't accept it since they hadn't begun fundraising yet and wanted to inform people of their plan first. Now, with a rapt audience, Margo relished the dramatic moment. She walked to Ruth McDermott, graciously accepted the check, kissed her on the cheek, and said, "Bless you."

Ruth McDermott later wrote to Mrs. Brooks Atkinson that "enthusiasm reigned!" The energy and pandemonium grew so intense that a small group retired to the library to discuss how to proceed and ended by forming an organization called Dallas Civic Theatre, Inc.

The next day E. L. DeGolyer, a business associate of Eugene McDermott's who was a prominent oil geologist, philanthropist, and later the publisher of the *Saturday Review*, told Elizabeth Ann McMurray over coffee at her bookstore that "the time will come when people will be divided into two groups, the ones that were at that meeting and the ones who weren't, because this is going to make history."

Margo endorsed the ten-thousand-dollar check over to the Dallas Civic Theatre, but before the check was cashed, Eugene McDermott returned to Dallas. Distressed when he learned of his wife's gift, he asked to meet with John Rosenfield, Lon Tinkle, and Margo Jones. He was concerned about his wife's condition, afraid that they might have taken advantage of her. He demanded an explanation. Margo told McDermott about her plans for a theatre and what it would mean for Dallas and the country. After listening to her, McDermott not only supported the gift but agreed to become chairman of the theatre's board of directors. With characteristic understatement, he said later, "Margo had a way with persuasion."

The forty-five-year-old McDermott respected Margo's passion for theatre and her pioneering spirit, for he was something of a pioneer himself. Born in Brooklyn, with a trace of New York lingering in his voice, Eugene McDermott —Gene or "Mac" to his friends—had moved to Dallas in 1930 and, with the financial backing of Amerada Corporation's young president, E. L. DeGolyer, and along with J. C. "Doc" Karcher, had founded a small geophysical service firm. Using a seismograph process that McDermott and Karcher had developed to map faults within the earth, the firm began to extend that technology into oil exploration. During World War II, their sound-wave process was used to locate enemy planes and ships and to detect submarines. In 1951, this firm became the giant Texas Instruments Corporation, which went on to produce the first portable transistor radio and develop the first silicon chip, effectively inaugurating a new age in electronics. A scientist, inventor, scholar, and successful businessman, a pioneer in the electronics industry, Gene McDermott, silver-haired, earnest, and motivated by ardent curiosity, was also an involved philanthropist, who gave of himself as well as his wealth. Although in the beginning of their long association McDermott and Margo sometimes clashed, they were to form a bond unusual between scientist and artist, for they were kindred spirits. McDermott confessed to friends that he "had moments of thinking poetry more important than science." He thought "poetry was a kind of knowing and that science was another kind of knowing." He valued and understood Margo's dreams for a theatre as another kind of research and development, an experimental process, and allowed Margo "to run her own show." Part of his job, he felt, was "to keep other hands out of it."

On March 16, 1945, Dallas Civic Theatre filed its charter with the State of Texas. Officers of the forty-eight-member board of trustees were Eugene McDermott, president; E. L. DeGolyer, first vice-president; Lon Tinkle, second vice-president; R. Franklin Rodgers, treasurer; and Betty Winn, secretary. Other board members included Tennessee Williams; Jo Mielziner; Jed Mace, an interior decorator and designer; Elizabeth Ann McMurray; John Rosenfield; Mrs. T. E. Braniff, wife of the founder of Braniff Airlines; Hermes Nye, a lawyer who was also a folklorist and novelist; DeWitt Ray, a banker; and Arthur Kramer, Jr., who would later become president of A. Harris department store in Dallas as well as business manager for the board of trustees.

Margo was named managing director and placed on salary. Joanna Albus also drew a salary as Margo's assistant, but she hoped to become a member of the acting company. Margo and Joanna set up office and residence on the grounds of the Burford estate in Turtle Creek. The main house was described later by poet William Burford, who grew up there, as a "marvelous house, like a great F. Scott Fitzgerald fantasy. Here we were in Texas, living in a kind of Italian Tuscan part Moorish house." Burford's mother, Caroline Skelly Burford, who had been active in the Dallas Little Theatre, offered Margo a small, pink stucco guesthouse, originally built as a children's playhouse, as headquarters for the theatre. The house had knotty pine walls, a fireplace, a view of the Dallas skyline, and a rooster weathervane perched on the roof. Margo named the little house "Cockcrow," after Tennessee's play of the same name and as a reminder that their work there heralded a new age in theatre history. Williams and *The Glass Menagerie* company remained very much on Margo's mind. She talked on the phone with Tennessee frequently and wrote him often. He wrote sporadically, apologizing for his failure to write regularly but saying that Margo would understand since she knew him so completely that she could forgive him anything. Tennessee knew that this was conceited of him, but he also believed that it was the truth. Margo wrote to Eddie Dowling, Julie Haydon, Laurette Taylor, and Tony Ross. She said that she missed them and wished she could hand them a "bunch of Texas flowers." She wrote to Chicago critic Ashton Stevens to thank him for his wonderful words, which had saved a beautiful play, and also told him all about the beginnings of her Dallas theatre. As Margo had hoped, Stevens published her letter in his column—more free publicity for her theatre. Even her former adversary, the producer Louis Singer, heard from Margo. She did not hesitate to flatter him, telling him she had loved working with him, sending regards to his charming wife, and adding, oh, by the way, she had a new play, *Sunrise in My Pocket*, that she wanted him to read right away because it was just the play he had been looking for, and although she had something else she was doing, she wanted to "carry the torch for *Sunrise*." Clearly, Margo wanted to keep her options open if for some reason her Dallas theatre did not work out.

In letter after letter, Margo trumpeted her plans for her new theatre in Dallas and what it would mean to theatre in general. And through the letters and the many phone calls she made regularly to Rosamond Gilder at *Theatre Arts*, to George Freedley, author, theatre critic, and curator of the New York Public Library's Theatre Collection, to Edwin Justus Mayer and Brooks Atkinson, to Hallie Flanagan and Gilmor Brown, and to other theatre people around the country, she maintained ties with her professional peers, shared common goals and ideas, and alleviated the isolation she must have felt in Dallas. She believed in a decentralized theatre, but the side effect of decentralization was loneliness, the same loneliness felt by any pioneer exploring new territory. In Dallas, Margo *was* the theatre, and she liked that, but when phone calls and letters weren't enough, she usually found a reason to take a train or plane to New York or California.

In her many letters written in 1945, spreading the news of her theatre, the tone she struck never seemed self-serving, but echoed the lofty, high-minded, and visionary style of her favorite theatre writer, Robert Edmond Jones. She left it to others like Mary Morris of Carnegie Tech's theatre department to give her personal recognition. Morris wrote: "Margo, I am sure you are a pioneer,

Let Me Talk My Dreams

that there will be a long string of others following in your wake. . . . It's what we all want. It's the only thing for the theatre in America. I am wishing you every kind of success, knowing how long the road is once one has started on it, and all the difficulties it presents."

Difficulties were far from Margo's mind, however. Her theatre had been chartered, its board elected and bylaws written. The plan was to begin presenting plays in the fall of 1945. For her and Joanna, the most important task was to find a theatre space, but they also read dozens of scripts, attended parties, gave speeches, and began preliminary work on finding a company and a technical staff.

When *The Glass Menagerie* opened at the Playhouse Theatre in New York on March 31, 1945, Margo was there, in the company of loyal beau Sonny Koch. In an outstanding Broadway season filled with box-office and artistic successes like *Harvey, Dear Ruth, I Remember Mama,* and *Carousel, The Glass Menagerie* won acclaim from both critics and audiences. Brooks Atkinson was abroad working as a war correspondent, but Burton Rascoe of the *New York World-Telegram* wrote, "I can't say anything adequate to Miss Taylor's creation of The Mother. . . . You can't describe a sunset," and critic Robert Garland of the *New York Journal-American* said, "The craftsmanship—the playwriting, which is memorable; the playacting, which is flawless; and the production, which is inimitable—makes of *The Glass Menagerie* a masterpiece of make-believe." Along with the playwright, the designer, and the actors, Margo received her share of praise and critical attention. The reviewer for the *New York Post* wrote that the direction of Eddie Dowling and Margo Jones was "a smooth collaborative effort that fuses all the elements of a stagecraft into an almost perfect symphonic interpretation of the author's original conception." Margo collected all the reviews and notices and carefully pasted them in her *Glass Menagerie* scrapbook.

Upon her return to Texas, the Dallas Theatre Board hosted a reception to honor her. They wanted to hear all about her New York trip. Once again Margo saw that the sanction of a Broadway success gave her credibility, as well as a glamorous aura, with the folks back home.

On May 1, the Dallas Civic Theatre held an open meeting in a local hall. Five hundred people jammed into the room. Introductions were made, city officials spoke, and then Margo took the floor. One reporter who attended noted that she had a tremendous stage presence, but "her one fault is not to stop for a drink of water, giving the audience a chance to breathe." When a drunken man in the front row began heckling her, she at first ignored him, but when he persisted, Margo demanded the right to be heard, her Texas drawl

Let Me Talk My Dreams

becoming louder and more pronounced. When no one came to her aid, she took charge. Placing her hands on her hips, standing with her feet wide apart, and looking, as she recalled later, "not very lady-like," Margo demanded, "Will one of you men get him out of here or will I have to do it myself?"

Right on cue, stirred to action by this challenge to southern manhood, a muscular bouncer from a local bar sat down next to the offending heckler and intimidated him into silence. The audience cheered wildly, and why not, for Margo had given them not a boring speech but an event filled with drama and conflict. And she still hadn't asked for any money! Joanna said later that Margo "wowed them." Others wondered if she might have planted the heckler in the audience and staged the whole thing herself to create an exciting "scene."

Although *The Glass Menagerie* had lost the 1945 Pulitzer Prize to Mary Chase's play *Harvey*, the Drama Critics Circle had selected it as the best new play of the season. Soon Margo was on the train again to travel to New York to attend the award dinner. With her increased public appearances and contact with the well-dressed women of Dallas and New York, Margo gradually had begun to notice that her wardrobe was somewhat inadequate, but could bring herself to buy only an expensive new blouse for the Critics dinner. Afterwards she went to an *Oklahoma* cast party, then to the Stork Club with George Jean Nathan and Julie Haydon.

During her ten-day stay in New York, where she said "the real people are actually pulling for our success [in Dallas]," Margo declined numerous job offers, including a tempting one from MGM, met with actors, designers, and playwrights, collected an armful of new scripts, and hired designer Jo Mielziner to come to Dallas to consult on their theatre building. She attended several readings of *You Touched Me!* with Tennessee. Director Guthrie McClintic, Katharine Cornell's husband, had added an exclamation point to the title and planned to produce the play on Broadway that fall. Thrilled that the play was receiving a commercial production, and harboring no resentment against McClintic, Margo gleefully said to Tennessee, "I told you so."

Her old friend Rosamond Gilder hosted a small dinner party in her Gramercy Park home for Margo and Tennessee. On her final evening in New York, Margo went to a party given by Laurette Taylor and said good-bye to the *Glass Menagerie* company. She also had dinner with her former teacher Frank Harting, who had an important public relations job now with General Motors in New York, and tried to convince him to come to Dallas as business manager of her theatre. Harting declined, but did use his influence to arrange for train reservations to Dallas for Margo and Tennessee. Exhausted from a continuous round of interviews, parties, and receptions, Tennessee planned to

Let Me Talk My Dreams

spend some time in Dallas resting before traveling on to Mexico for a vacation. He told a *New York Times* reporter that Margo planned to start "a real creative theatre down there and she wants me to come and work with her. I want to do it. That is my real interest. I find very little that interests me here."

This time, on the train trip to Dallas, accompanied by a now-famous, award-winning playwright, Margo avoided the cramped coach. Instead she and Tennessee traveled first-class in a spacious drawing room with private dining and washroom facilities—the largest, most elegant accommodations the railroad offered.

It is highly unlikely that Tennessee got much rest during his stay in Dallas. Keenly aware of the publicity value of her friend's visit, Margo arranged for newspaper coverage, photographs, and a meeting with John Rosenfield. Earlier, Margo had informed her board that Tennessee planned to work on his next play in Dallas, so during his visit she urged Williams to complete a new one-act play. Another small guesthouse next to Margo's on the Burford estate had been refurbished for Tennessee's use. She wanted to make him as comfortable as possible, since her wish was that Tennessee remain in Dallas as the theatre's resident playwright. She assigned a non-salaried staff member, her former University of Texas student actress Rebecca Hargis, to look after him. Margo and Joanna were still the only paid staff members, and although Rebecca was officially the office secretary, who set up a script filing system, she was actually a gofer. She would go for the paper, for coffee, for lunches, and she chauffeured Margo and Tennessee, found Tennessee's wallet, which he constantly misplaced, fetched Margo drinks, and happily sat at their feet, stagestruck and devoted.

During May, Margo had investigated several prospects for a theatre space. She wanted an accessible downtown theatre location and although a former stock house, the Circle Theatre, which was currently a rundown motion picture house, was available, the eighteen-thousand-dollar yearly rent was much too high. As a temporary solution, Margo turned to the Globe Theatre on the grounds of Dallas's Fair Park.

When Dallas hosted the 1936 Texas Centennial Exposition, 277 acres had been set aside for the huge fair. Permanent buildings, representing the most advanced architecture of the 1930s, were constructed not only for the annual State Fair but as a year-round center for museums and cultural resources. The Globe Theatre, a replica of Shakespeare's Elizabethan playhouse, had been dedicated in 1936 with water from the Avon River obtained by B. Iden Payne of England's Stratford Theatre. The Dallas Park Board and the State Fair Association agreed to provide the Globe rent-free to the Dallas Civic Theatre.

Let Me Talk My Dreams

When Jo Mielziner visited Dallas and examined the Globe Theatre, he felt it was a fire hazard and might not meet building codes, but with no other building available, he agreed to draw up remodeling plans that included new lighting equipment, an all-purpose unit set, and a completely new auditorium. The renovations, budgeted at thirty thousand dollars, complied with specifications of the Dallas Building Inspector and Fire Marshall.

With a theatre building assured, Margo announced in July that the Dallas Civic Theatre would hereafter be named Theatre '45, the name to change yearly into infinity, she said. She had read about a theatre in Prague, Czechoslovakia, that changed its name with each year, remaining always contemporary.

With renewed energy, she and Joanna continued to read and catalog hundreds of scripts submitted by playwrights around the country. On the "A" list were unproduced plays by Edwin Justus Mayer, Arnold Sundgaard, Oran Jannings, Lynn Riggs, Horton Foote, Dan Totheroh, E. P. Conkle, William Inge, and Tennessee Williams. Margo once told a reporter, "When I pick up a script I say to myself, 'It could be Shakespeare.' . . . You see, honey, I want to live in a golden era of the theatre. Shakespeare was the reason for such an era. Imagine if we had twenty professional theatres doing six new scripts a year — and we would have more good plays if we had more productions." Margo knew that playwrights were generally an insecure lot who needed nurturing and encouragement. She read each new script not once but several times and wrote each playwright a personal letter with a detailed critique. William Inge, who had sent her two scripts, *The Vermin's Will* and *Farther Off from Heaven* (later revised and renamed *The Dark at the Top of the Stairs*), received encouraging letters from Margo, an expression of definite interest in *Farther Off from Heaven*, and an introduction to agent Audrey Wood. Inge said later, "She was always so willing to give of herself to the writers she believed in. She could always find time to encourage one, to help him believe in himself again."

With the aid of volunteer Ross Lawther, a lawyer and playwright who could take dictation as fast as she could talk, Margo answered hundreds of letters of application from actors and technicians who wanted work at Theatre '45. She attended four or five functions a week where people crowded around her as she drummed up support for the theatre. In a July *New York Times* article on the front page of the Sunday Arts Section, Margo announced her plans to decentralize the American theatre. She felt that decentralization would solve the problem of hundreds of unemployed actors and provide playwrights an outlet for their work. Her theatre, she said, would be a blueprint for the future. Other theatre leaders rallied to the cause, inspired by Theatre '45. Katharine

Cornell said, "A permanent repertory theatre, such as the one planned for Dallas, is what we've all dreamed for, hoped for and fought for." In an article written for the *Dallas Morning News*, Rosamond Gilder said that Theatre '45 could inspire a new age of theatres that would replace the four hundred stock companies that formerly existed in cities throughout the country.

On vacation in Guadalajara, Mexico, Tennessee received an urgent telegram from Margo requesting a short article on the playwright's attitude toward her Dallas theater, to "show Dallas and the country what we are trying to do. Wire when I can expect it, Love, Margo." Williams complied almost immediately, for this was a topic he and Margo had discussed at great length. He wouldn't have been surprised, he wrote,

> if Margo had said "inform the world" . . . for great theatre is an international thing. . . . But unfortunately America has not produced her share of playwrights—men such as Chekhov, Shaw, Ibsen, Lorca, Shakespeare —who have voices that carry beyond the national frontiers. I think this may be due considerably to the fact that there has been no great and lasting theatre here that could offer the sort of climate in which such dramatists could develop. . . . At the present moment there is no art theatre in America. . . . There is about to become what I hope and believe will be a true art theatre in America. Now don't be alarmed by that alarming word art. Art is actually a very straightforward thing, as plain and honest as daylight and about as necessary.

In July 1945, perhaps at Margo's request, writer John Lineweave spoke for the audience in an open letter to Theatre '45. The public had heard from critics, playwrights, actors, and directors; now it was time for the audience's voice to be heard. Unlike some theatre people, Margo loved to be part of a play's audience. In fact, some of her actors felt that she sometimes held unnecessary run-throughs just so she could watch a play. Although criticized at times for lacking a personal directing style or a particular artistic signature, Margo did think both as an artist and as an audience member. She wanted an art theatre that would connect with its audience, for the goal of all her efforts was the union of artist and audience in the theatre experience. In Lineweave's letter, he wrote that "we have won the battles against Germany, and we are winning the battles against Japan—and we are growing ever more aware, depressingly enough, that there are other greater battles ahead." As a member of Theatre '45's audience, Lineweave asked the theatre to "attract and nourish a share of sanity, talent and craftsmanship, and thereby make for us a living thing. In a manner of speaking, we want you to write a love letter to this aching world."

Let Me Talk My Dreams

All the attention and even adulation that Margo received during this period was enormously gratifying and ego-building, but what she rarely spoke or wrote about publicly was the grinding tedium and dreary labor required to bring a theatre into being. In speeches and articles, her plans sounded bright and positive, but the reality was quite different. The reality was red, burning eyes from hours of reading script after script; a stiff neck from hours of phone calls; a hoarse voice from hours of giving speeches and making small talk at cocktail parties; and aching shoulders from hours spent hunched over a typewriter, sweating in the ninety-seven-degree heat of a Dallas summer. The reality was lack of sleep, skipped meals, too many cigarettes, and too many drinks with no time to take a vacation or have a personal life. The reality was smiling endlessly, entertaining a constant stream of guests who might prove important to the theatre. The reality was correspondence files bulging with requests—actors wanting jobs or recommendations, writers wanting their manuscripts read and their egos massaged, reporters wanting stories with good quotes, board members wanting inside gossip or to meet somebody famous, family and friends wanting letters and attention. Margo juggled all the demands without complaint, except for a rare outburst to Sonny Koch about having to attend yet another function at the house of some "rich bitch," for she had gotten exactly what she wanted—the chance to turn her dreams into action.

In late July, twenty-three-year-old June Moll, a practical, forthright midwesterner who had listened to Margo's theatre plans at the University of Texas, finally gave in to her persuasion. Thinking, "What the hell. I'll give it a try," June resigned her position at the University of Texas and joined the Theatre '45 staff. June and her husband Jim, who was in the service, were both talented directors and, Margo hinted, they would have an opportunity to direct at Theatre '45. For the time being, however, June took over the processing of the hundreds of scripts they received. Margo continued to read every script, of course, but she and Joanna began to focus most of their time on a major fund-raising effort. Mabel Duke of Watson Associates, a Dallas public relations firm, was hired to promote the campaign.

Margo did manage to take a few days off at the end of July to travel to Livingston for a joyous reunion with her brother Richard, home on leave. The Jones family, which now included Richard's petite, dark-haired wife Bea, whom he had married in 1939, was united for the first time in years. The only one missing was Charles, still with the navy and stationed overseas.

On August 14 Margo with the rest of the country heard the news that Japan had surrendered. She wrote her mother that she had wanted to call her immediately, but had decided to leave the lines clear for all the boys who would be calling home. The end of the war brought new energy to the theatre campaign, but Margo admitted to her mother that she felt a bit humble and strange talking about her Project the day after peace was announced.

Margo's motto became "Don't open until everything is as near perfect as humanly possible." The fund-raising effort, headed by banker DeWitt Ray, was producing results, but the remodeling of the Globe would take time and the proposed opening date was changed to early 1946.

When Tennessee visited Dallas again that summer, Margo treated him to a daily swim and a steak dinner, a luxury since beef was a rationed commodity even in cattle country. She coaxed him to join her at speaking engagements and fund-raising functions, which she took very seriously. Tennessee didn't always understand. One evening when a fund-raising cocktail party was scheduled, instead of going with Margo, Tennessee jumped in Rebecca Hargis's car, a battered 1933 Ford that Margo hated. Theatre '45 had the use of a late-model Cadillac loaned to her by Eugene McDermott, more appropriate transportation to the elegant homes of wealthy Dallasites. Then, on the way to the party, Tennessee insisted that Rebecca stop at a drive-in restaurant, where they stayed for over an hour. They finally arrived at the fund-raiser a good two hours late, and Margo was furious. "Don't ever do this again," Margo shouted. "We can never raise money when you show up late in that beat-up old car!"

A member of the Theatre '45 board of directors, Tennessee attended their meetings, but, according to board member Jed Mace, he would at times jump up abruptly and go outside and run across the lawn. "We thought he was talented, but nutty," Mace remembers. In late-night sessions with Margo and her staff, Tennessee thought it was ludicrous hearing a group of idealists talking budgets and bottom line. Margo reminded him that money had to be raised and, turning her persuasive powers on him, asked him to donate fifteen hundred dollars to the campaign. Tennessee seemed agreeable but said that he would have to check with Audrey Wood first. Weeks later, he wrote Margo that Audrey would not allow him to give the money.

Although Tennessee supported Margo's theatre plans, he could not be persuaded to stay on as the theatre's resident playwright. Tennessee's social life suffered in Dallas, and he told Bill Burford, "I can't meet anybody here. I don't know where to go, what to do." When the restless Tennessee left town, June Moll and Joanna Albus moved into his vacant guesthouse. Still they needed more room and a central location, so Theatre '45 branched out to a downtown office in the Baker Hotel. They worked sixteen-hour shifts, building a mailing list, reading plays, giving talks, answering mail, writing articles, creating budgets, keeping records, and, always, raising money. With Audrey Wood's help, Margo began to learn about the workings of Actors' Equity and the Dramatists Guild, but she was starting to feel the strain of trying to handle both business and artistic decisions. What she needed, she said, was a "high-powered business manager."

By early October, over thirty-eight thousand dollars had been given or pledged. On October 8, however, the city manager announced that the Globe Theatre had been condemned as a fire hazard. Even though months earlier the Building and Fire Inspectors had granted Theatre '45 permission to occupy the Globe, they had reversed that ruling. Other building owners with properties similar to the Globe, properties that had been condemned, had insisted that Theatre '45 receive equal treatment. The financial campaign came to a sudden stop, and morale plummeted.

Margo and the board of trustees regrouped, extracting a promise from the city to include a theatre in their plans for a new Civic Center and meanwhile attempting to lease a theatre temporarily. When efforts to find a suitable building failed, the board decided to build. However, since new construction in Dallas had virtually halted during the war, there was an acute housing shortage. Building priority would go to erecting homes for returning veterans.

The outlook was bleak. Even the name, Theatre '45, was an embarrassment, for 1945 was drawing to a close, and they still didn't have a theatre. Frustrated, disappointed, but not defeated, Margo vowed to continue. On December 5 she wrote Tennessee, "Way down deep in my heart I know . . . that somebody has got to do a job like this and make it work." However, a week later the *Dallas Morning News* announced that Margo Jones would be in New York from January 15 to March 1 directing *On Whitman Avenue*, a new play written by Maxine Wood and to star Canada Lee, the talented black actor whom Margo had seen earlier that year as Caliban in *The Tempest*. The board of trustees had granted her a leave of absence. Eugene McDermott reported that no building had been found yet for Theatre '45, but several possibilities were under consideration.

While Margo had vowed to continue to work on Theatre '45, as a practical woman she knew that for the moment the plan was stymied. By taking the directing job, she could not only save the theatre money by going off salary, but could also gain more experience and invaluable press. And she could do what she loved most—direct a brand-new play. Unfortunately, when Dallas skeptics heard that Margo had taken a Broadway directing job they wondered if all that high-minded talk about an art theatre had been just that—just talk, after all.

Blooded on Broadway

NEW YORK. Broadway. "It may seem glamorous," Margo wrote June Moll, "but believe me it's a phony business—once in the stream a lot of things can happen but the stream is muddy and stupid—true, there are little undercurrents of beauty and even clear pools here and there, but the water is tainted water—how could it be otherwise with the cesspools of commercialism pouring into it each day."

Tainted water or not, Margo liked being in the theatre's mainstream. Her buoyant optimism and refusal to dish dirt with cynical New York theatre people marked her as an outsider, something of a naïf. She didn't mind playing the outsider role; it was a time-honored part for Texans and other southerners encountering the provincialism of New York. In fact, like many southerners she enjoyed pulling northern legs, broadening her Texas drawl to cartoon proportions, regaling credulous locals with tales of cowboys and Indians, acting out the stereotype of the country bumpkin in the big city while laughing inside at the astonishing ignorance and arrogance of New Yorkers who believed the civilized world ended at the Hudson River. She managed, however, to stir genuine interest in her ideas for decentralizing theatre among what she called the "real people," the people open to a fresh face with new ideas. Margo intended to meet as many people as possible during her stay in New York, people who might help her theatre. "I think," she wrote her mother, "one of the greatest things about anyone's work lies in the people they get to know."

One of the "real people" she met in New York was Haila Stoddard, an actress who was venturing into producing. Stoddard had optioned Edwin Justus Mayer's *Sunrise in My Pocket* and signed Margo (paying her a retainer of one thousand dollars) to direct the play. Reciprocally, Margo invested four hundred dollars in Stoddard and Jack Kirkland's new production, *Georgia Boy*.

Two years younger than Margo, Haila Stoddard had had the proverbial "born in a theatre trunk" childhood. In her case, her crib was a cigar box in the train depot of Great Falls, Montana, which her actress mother was passing through. Stoddard's first major role was that of the blonde ingenue Pearl in the

Blooded on Broadway

national touring company of *Tobacco Road*, starring Henry Hull. On tour she met and then later married *Tobacco Road* playwright Jack Kirkland. The attractive, vivacious Stoddard liked to bring theatre people and movie people together at her elegant, gray stone house on 63rd Street. Invitations to Stoddard's home were coveted, for she had a reputation for giving fabulous parties. In Margo she found a "kindred spirit."

Soon after arriving in New York, Margo attended a party at Stoddard's. This gathering, one of the most glamorous soirées of the season, was in honor of Yul Brynner, the twenty-five-year-old star of the musical *Lute Song*. Stoddard had helped launch the talented gypsy, who played the guitar and sang beautifully. Brynner arrived with his co-star, Mary Martin. William "The Thin Man" Powell strolled in with a young woman draped in pink maribou on each arm. Josh Logan, who had recently signed to direct Stoddard and Kirkland's production of *Georgia Boy*; Raymond Massey, whom Margo wanted as the lead in *Sunrise*; Linda Darnell, 20th Century–Fox's sexy new star and like Mary Martin a Texan; and dozens of other actors, theatre people, and hangers-on attended, enjoying the Scotch and champagne and the excellent food. Edward G. Robinson arrived late and sat on the floor with Margo to listen to Brynner and Mary Martin sing show tunes. Joanna Albus was there too, standing shyly on the sidelines, observing, judging the others who, like herself, looked on. She saw envy in their faces, and began to feel that emotion herself.

More parties. Julie Haydon's strange party for Maxine, her dog, backstage at the Playhouse Theatre; and Laurette Taylor's cocktail party where Margo enthusiastically told Spencer Tracy the story of *Sunrise in My Pocket*, and sent him home with the script. At Sardi's, she met directors Harold Clurman and Elia Kazan, who had just opened Maxwell Anderson's new play *Truckline Café*, featuring Marlon Brando, only to close it after thirteen performances. She had dinner with Norris Houghton, Beatrice Straight, and other members of Theatre, Inc., a nonprofit group formed in 1945 to encourage new playwrights and to develop a theatre for the people. Margo planned to spend more time with them, for their projects and ideals were similar to her own. Unfortunately, although this group sponsored a New York tour of London's Old Vic with Laurence Olivier and Ralph Richardson, and presented Shaw's *Pygmalion* with Gertrude Lawrence, their theatre soon folded.

Margo threw her own cocktail party in her room at the Royalton Hotel and casually included Jerry Coray and his actress wife, Ann, on the guest list. Although she had gotten over her distress at Coray's marriage, Margo still had special feelings for him, her first love, and did not want to lose his friendship.

Blooded on Broadway

Several of Margo's old friends from the Houston Players and the University of Texas were in town. Ray Walston (who had moved to New York to launch his stage career) and his new wife invited her for breakfast. She attended the wedding reception of former University of Texas theatre department chairman Jim Parke; and she picnicked on hamburgers and Scotch in her hotel room with playwright Ted Apstein. "Almost everywhere I go I run into old friends," Margo wrote her parents. She found time to have lunch with a new acquaintance too—a young man who wanted to talk to her about how to become a producer. "Get him," Margo told June Moll. "Nobody knows as far as I can see."

At a party at Ruth Ford's, she talked with actress Blanche Yurka about their recent work on a committee to read and judge proposals for financing a national theatre. New York producer Horace Schmidlapp had selected the committee, which included, in addition to Margo and Yurka, George Freedley, Basil Rathbone, and designer Lee Simonson. Schmidlapp had offered a one-thousand-dollar award for the best financing plan. Margo did not like any of the seventy-six financing plans she read since most of them focused on a central New York office sending out touring companies. Decentralization, she felt, was the way to develop a truly national theatre.

And, of course, she saw plays. She enjoyed Garson Kanin's *Born Yesterday*, found it "very clever, beautifully done," a play that "has something to say and does it with laughter." She found the Pulitzer Prize–winning play *State of the Union* "slick and fast" but empty. She didn't like Maurice Evans's *Hamlet*. In fact, Broadway was beginning a decline—there were twelve fewer productions than the year before. The artificial prosperity of the war years was drawing to a close. More and more people were moving to the suburbs and going to the movies for entertainment. Prices were going up too, and as in Dallas there was a problem with theatre houses. New York theatres were being demolished, many eventually to be replaced by television studios. Shows that were in out-of-town tryouts had difficulty finding theatres to move into when they came to New York.

While social engagements filled her nights, *On Whitman Avenue* occupied her days. She liked and respected Canada Lee, the co-producer and star of the play. Before rehearsals began, Margo spent a restful weekend with Lee and his family at their house in the country, managing to go to sleep both before and after dinner. The talented forty-year-old Lee had begun his career in the boxing ring, but after sustaining a blow that left him blind in one eye, had left boxing for show business. He had honed his acting skills with the Harlem Players, and had been Banquo in Orson Welles and John Houseman's Federal

Blooded on Broadway

Theatre production of *Macbeth*. He had played the explosive, angry Bigger Thomas in Welles's production of *Native Son*, adapted from the Richard Wright novel, and Caliban in Margaret Webster's production of *The Tempest*.

Although she had been hired by producers Lee and Mark Marvin as director for *On Whitman Avenue*, Margo soon developed a rapport with the two men, and they included her in production decisions, or what she termed the "managerial headaches." She wrote June Moll that their biggest problems were finding a theatre and "sweating out getting the bond put up for [Actors'] Equity because the limited partnership papers from the backers have not all been sent in and though the money is in the bank, it can't be touched until the papers are signed and the bond can't be put up until they are signed and you can't really sign big actors till the bond is up." She worked closely with Donald Oenslager, a leading Broadway designer who had begun his career years earlier with the Provincetown Players, as he redid his set for the present production because of rising prices.

She spent many evenings with playwright Maxine Wood working on the script. Wood, a native of Detroit, had drawn on postwar racial problems and the issue of segregated housing in writing *On Whitman Avenue*. Set in Lawndale, a fictional Detroit suburb, the plot follows a black war veteran (played by Canada Lee), his wife (acted by Lee's real wife, Vivienne Baber), and his family as they rent the upstairs of the Tilden house in Lawndale, then fight the efforts of Mrs. Tilden and her neighbors to evict them. The play exposes hypocrisy and prejudice: "You can't think one way and act another," a character says. While the play suffers from some repetitive writing, the resolution eschews melodrama and opts for realism as the veteran, forced to leave Whitman Avenue, takes his family back to the crumbling housing projects of the city.

Casting the seventeen-character play occupied a great deal of time. Margo chose Joanna Albus for the small part of Edna, a neighbor. An elated Joanna wrote June Moll, "I feel like an individual again. . . . You remember how often we felt like the extra spoke in the wheel and what a horrible feeling that is." Margo and Canada Lee sent scripts to well-known actors like Melvyn Douglas and Fredric March and his wife Florence Eldridge, and auditioned an average of 150 actors a day. "It nearly kills me," Margo wrote her family, "to see how many good people want jobs. That's the reason my job in Dallas is so important—one must decentralize this business." Will Geer, a tall, lean midwesterner with extensive credits in film and theatre, signed on to play the tolerant Ed Tilden, owner of the two-family home. Perry Wilson was chosen for the important role of his liberal daughter, who rents the apartment to the black family.

As a youngster, Margo had gotten to know black people through working at her father's office and had learned racial tolerance from him and developed a social conscience under his tutelage. Perry Wilson recalls that the cast was surprised that Margo, a southerner, would choose to direct the play, and remembers that Margo was shocked by the racist attitudes exposed in it. Although Margo was offered many directing jobs in New York, it is a measure of her commitment that she chose to direct *On Whitman Avenue*, a play that would certainly raise a few eyebrows in Dallas. In radio talks, speeches, and interviews while she was in New York, she talked of her work with *On Whitman Avenue*, and though she spoke also of Theatre '46 and wrote regularly to board members and to John Rosenfield, she worried that she was not doing enough to promote the theatre.

And what was happening with Theatre '46? June Moll, the only paid staff member in Dallas (assisted by volunteers Ross Lawther, his wife Selma, and Rebecca Hargis), charged with fund-raising, script reading, and keeping the office open, felt like a neglected country cousin. Although Margo and Joanna wrote often, calling themselves the New York branch of Theatre '46, their news of parties, famous people, and Broadway shows only served to heighten June's resentment at her thankless job. The businesslike June considered the social aspect of her work—"being charming to a lot of people with a lot of money" —"a lot of damned nonsense." Her husband Jim had returned from the war and wanted to get on with his life as a theatre director. Although Margo had vaguely promised directing work with Theatre '46, both Molls soon discovered that they were considered extensions of Margo, and would not be able to achieve any recognition on their own. Also, June quickly realized that the theatre in Dallas *was* Margo, was fueled by her vision, and that only Margo could raise the money to fund it. June wrote frankly to Margo that she and Jim wanted to take a leave of absence to find directing work. "We're not resentful," June said. "We just realize that the job here has to be done by one person."

Margo said that she loathed her inability to be the "kind of person that made it possible for all of us to function on the same basis." She believed, however, that the practical knowledge she was gaining, learning by doing, and especially the producing experience and the contact with actors, would prove invaluable to her Dallas theatre. In an impassioned letter, she wrote June that "the job we're doing there [in Dallas] is the most important job to be done in the theatre in America—each day I live up here I know more and more that that job must be done—the country is crying for it—the actors are begging for it—the designers must have it—the playwrights have got to have it—I have known about this place for a long time but until you really live it you can not know the real stupidity of the whole thing—no matter how long it takes—we must create the theatre we have dreamed and planned and are working on—it has got to be done."

These words seemed empty talk to June, who suspected that Margo wanted a career in the commercial theatre. If Theatre '46 was so important, why wasn't she in Dallas, raising money and finding a theatre building?

In fact, Margo was engaged in a delicate balancing act, weighing her needs as a theatre artist with her vision for a national, decentralized theatre. Directing, collaborating with playwrights, actors, and designers, was her daily bread. To stay in Dallas without a theatre building, even for a year, meant she would starve as an artist. To work only in the commercial New York theatre meant that she would neglect her plans for a nonprofit professional theatre outside New York. The solution to her problem as Margo saw it was to do both—to work as an artist and to achieve her vision.

"She had a vision," remembers Perry Wilson. "She was a very different figure from Antoinette Perry and some tough Broadway directors I had worked with—she was a southern lady." In rehearsals of the play Margo, as was her practice, sought first to create a warm, nurturing atmosphere where actors felt free to make contributions and develop their characters. She moved around the theatre in her worn red ballet slippers, smoking Camels, making notes, calling out instructions. She tended to concentrate more on the play's overall shape and flow from scene to scene and on character groupings and stage pictures than on specifics of actors' performances. This method had worked well on *The Glass Menagerie*, especially since the two stars, Laurette Taylor and Eddie Dowling, knew enough about acting technique to fill several textbooks. Canada Lee, Will Geer, and Perry Wilson, gifted, experienced actors, also flourished in this environment. The risk of this method was that sometimes actors needed and wanted strong, detailed direction, and without it, their performances and the production suffered. Some of the *Whitman* actors, used to being told exactly what to do by a director, felt lost. According to Perry Wilson, the actress playing Mrs. Tilden needed help in bringing some long speeches alive, and Margo had great difficulty in helping her with specific readings. Through positive reinforcement and belief (she knew that the actor's enemy was doubt), Margo coaxed and jollied and appealed to the actors to find the truth in a role, the real feeling, the real emotion. She didn't know how to tell them how to create this truth, but she knew when they had achieved it. In fact, after casting the person she felt to be right for a part, Margo felt that the actor should find the role himself and make it his own. In the 1940s this was an unusual approach for a director to take—most directors tended to be quite authoritarian. Actors, unless they were stars, didn't expect to be consulted.

For the most part, however, the rehearsal period went well. Margo developed a close friendship with playwright Maxine Wood, who stayed with the production and worked on the play through rehearsals and out-of-town tryouts. Perry Wilson recalls that Margo was like a coach with a team, giving pep talks and inspiring the company with her enthusiasm not only for the play, but for her theatre vision. Wilson felt that Margo's stirring talks were "a search for a more communal feeling with the actors." Like most dedicated directors, Margo loved the rehearsal period, the time when the outside world disappeared and only the work remained. Rehearsals were like a comforting home, the bed she slept in, the food she ate, giving structure and purpose to her life. The first performances of a play, the tryouts in front of an audience, were always a wrenching experience, a culmination and a loss, for it meant a return to that other world of everyday concerns.

The first tryouts were at the Erlanger Theatre in Buffalo, New York, for five days. The production received favorable reviews. The local press interviewed Margo and she talked about the play and announced, with some embellishments, her plan to decentralize the theatre. "My own theatre in Dallas," she told them, "will guarantee fifty-two weeks of employment to thirty actors and will have on its staff three playwrights." Wanting them to know that she remained committed to these goals, Margo clipped this article and others that mentioned her Dallas theatre and sent them to Theatre '46 board members and to John Rosenfield at the *Dallas Morning News.*

Next the company moved to Detroit, Maxine Wood's hometown, for a three-week run. During the war years, thousands of blacks had moved from the South to Detroit to work in the defense industry, a right guaranteed them by the courage of A. Philip Randolph, head of the Brotherhood of Sleeping Car Porters, who in 1941 had threatened President Roosevelt and Congress with a march on Washington, fifty thousand strong, if they did not do something to end discrimination in the defense industry. Roosevelt promptly issued an Executive Order known as the Fair Employment Practices Commission. Of course, this order did not affect private employers. Detroit was a troubled city, with a history of race riots, and gains made by blacks in the workplace and their distinguished record in the war did not offset the ingrained prejudice. In Detroit, members of the *On Whitman Avenue* company themselves encountered the racism the play depicted so vividly. Several restaurants refused service to Gus Smith, who played the grandfather. The local police, suspicious of the racially mixed trio of Canada Lee, his black assistant, and the red-haired stage manager riding together in a taxi, stopped them for questioning and even subjected them to a body search.

However, Detroit welcomed its hometown playwright, and Wood's play generated good reviews and packed houses. The prospects looked bright for a successful New York run.

Nineteen forty-six seemed to be the year for plays dealing with racial issues, the surfeit perhaps embodying an optimistic feeling that a new day was coming. Perhaps, as one writer put it, there would be "a double victory—a victory over fascism abroad and jimcrow at home." *Deep Are the Roots* by James Gow and Arnaud d'Usseau was written, d'Usseau said, for "whites who *think* they are progressive, liberal. . . ." Directed by Elia Kazan, the play enjoyed a long run, and a London tour, and gave many black actors jobs and Hollywood offers. Less successful was *Jeb*, Robert Ardrey's play about postwar discrimination, in which actor Ossie Davis played a black serviceman who returns to his southern home, where he faces the white townspeople and demands the right to work. Love between a black woman and a white man was the subject of *Strange Fruit* by Lillian Smith, a play excoriated by black critics and avoided by black audiences as yet another white writer's failure to understand the black experience.

On Whitman Avenue opened in New York at the Cort Theatre on May 8. Margo felt at home in this theatre on 48th Street because it was directly across the street from the Playhouse Theatre, where *The Glass Menagerie* was enjoying a long run. She spent a good deal of time on both sides of the street, checking on her productions and seeing her friends.

On opening night, Margo made her usual rounds, passing out personal notes for every company member and receiving gifts, including several of her favored turtles, in return. Then she took her place in the audience, joining the ever-faithful Sonny Koch and June and Jim Moll, who had arrived for the opening. The Molls couldn't help noticing that Margo's biography in the playbill announced that she would soon be working on two upcoming Broadway productions, a play called *Possessed* and Mayer's *Sunrise in My Pocket*, starring Raymond Massey. She was described there in striking terms. When producer Mark Marvin had asked her for information for the playbill and for some adjectives describing herself, Margo had told him that "energetic" and "enthusiastic" were the most frequently used, but as a woman she preferred "the dazzling dynamo from Texas," an appellation given her by George Freedley. "Forgive me my vanity," she told Marvin.

When the curtains parted, the audience saw a pretty, two-story Donald Oenslager–designed house surrounded by colorful flowers and green grass—a nice suburban home on nice Whitman Avenue. They watched as a nice family moved into the second floor of the house—the father, a returning war veteran; his pregnant wife; his little brother, who liked to build model planes; and his old grandfather, who loved to garden. A nice, ordinary family except for their black skin. Filled with anger and biting sarcasm about a pressing national problem, the play was a plea for racial justice. According to one observer, audiences gasped when the black child challenged the white boy, saying, "You ever hear of Joe Louis?" and cheered when Will Geer as Ed Tilden said, "I don't know how you can tell a man to fight for his country then not be able to live in it."

With a few exceptions, however, the critical response to the play was overwhelmingly negative. While Robert Garland of the *Journal-American* praised Canada Lee's performance and Margo Jones's helpful direction, he said that playwright Wood "sets out to prove a point which needs no proving, a point upon which all clear thinking men and women are ardently agreed." In fact, a few weeks later in St. Albans, Queens, life imitated art. When Canada Lee learned that St. Albans residents enforced Jim Crow laws and had evicted a black family from their home, he offered the white residents free tickets to *On Whitman Avenue* in an effort to help them change their minds. Obviously not clear-thinking, they turned down the offer.

Lewis Kronenberger of *PM* reported that Canada Lee overacted, that Margo Jones's direction was shaky, and that the play dealt with types, not people. Other critics said the play was clichéd, bogged down in preaching, not theatre. Only a few critics lauded the play, among them Vernon Rice of the *New York Post*, who called it the drama on the "Negro question we have all been waiting for." He commended the performances of Canada Lee and Will Geer and admired Margo's direction, especially her stage groupings. The play, he said, "may be dynamite . . . but if it is, then it is time that it is put to its proper use." Black critics felt that white playwright Maxine Wood had written about the black experience with honesty and understanding.

Throughout the 1945–46 season, critics and theatre artists had engaged in battle. Critics had blasted Irwin Shaw's *The Assassin,* Maxwell Anderson's *Truckline Café,* and Hecht and MacArthur's *Swan Song,* and the artists had retaliated with letters and barrages of their own. A writer said the season should be remembered as "the battle against the critics." Tellingly, the Drama Critics Circle could not agree on the best play of the 1945–46 season, and did not present an award that year.

The *On Whitman Avenue* company entered the fray. Will Geer stumped the city, giving talks and promoting the play. *People's Voice,* the Harlem Negro weekly, editorialized against the New York drama critics. Margo, Maxine Wood, critic Vernon Rice, and members of the company participated in a public forum held at the 136th Street Library. Even former First Lady Eleanor Roosevelt got into the act, writing in support of the play in her newspaper column, "My Day." All of the attention paid off, and audiences for the controversial play began to build. Both Margo and Maxine Wood took 50 percent cuts in their royalties in order to keep the play running.

Although Theatre '46 board members expected Margo back in Dallas by March 1, delays in the opening of *On Whitman Avenue* had put off her return by over a month. She lingered in New York until late May, finding it difficult to leave the *Whitman* company. Finally, after a "swell farewell party," Margo boarded the train for Dallas. During a several-hour layover in St. Louis, she visited William Inge. He read the first act of a new script to her, probably a revised version of *Farther Off from Heaven*. Although Margo usually preferred poetry to realism in plays, she found Inge's story of a middle-class Kansas family touching and poignant, and recognized and encouraged his budding talent.

Dallas was green and lush after a wet spring. Margo settled in to her little house, "Cockcrow," on the Burfords' Turtle Creek estate, had her hair done, bought some cotton dresses, dashed off notes to the *Whitman* actors, talked endlessly on the phone, and began planning how to build her theatre, brick by brick.

Her staff had dwindled to volunteers Ross and Selma Lawther and young Rebecca Hargis. While they were in New York, June and Jim Moll had told Margo that they were taking a leave of absence to work at a summer theatre in Ann Arbor, Michigan. Joanna Albus remained with the play in New York, happy to be close to her family in Yonkers, and to be working as an actress. In a letter to Rosamond Gilder at *Theatre Arts*, Margo, ever mindful of the importance of positive press coverage, assured Gilder that work on Theatre '46 was progressing, that the script department flourished, the public relations division was at work every day, and the personnel department continued to interview potential company members. What Margo didn't mention was that *she* was all the departments and divisions.

As June Moll had warned, nothing had happened with the theatre situation in Dallas during Margo's absence, and a hot, lazy Texas summer was not the best time to build momentum. Still, Margo continued to give talks, read scripts, and correspond with playwrights, actors, and technicians interested in working at the theatre. In June, a committee headed by Mrs. T. E. Braniff, theatre board member and wife of the airline magnate, was formed to find a theatre. They located a handsome city-owned stone building in Fair Park that had been used as a natural resources museum. The committee estimated that renovation would take five months and about seventy-five thousand dollars, and proceeded to study the plan.

In late June, Margo heard from actress Nancy Spencer, who had been her roommate at the Pasadena Playhouse. Nancy announced that she was giving up the theatre to marry a doctor and live in Boston. To Margo she left her "images of magnificence." In reply, Margo chastised Nancy for her lack of enthusiasm about marriage, telling her if she truly loved her doctor, her life would be exciting. Now thirty-four years old, although she claimed to be thirty-two, vainly lopping two years off her age for reporters and even for official records, Margo was thinking about marriage as well. The previous Christmas in Houston, Sonny Koch had pressed his marriage proposal, and Margo, during a visit that December with Malvina and Sidney Holmes, had kept them up all night as she paced and tossed and turned, debating with herself, wondering if it would be fair to marry Sonny when she knew that her work came first. Sonny was handsome, intelligent, devoted to her, and he loved the theatre. She couldn't bring herself to tell him an emphatic "no," but after years of waiting patiently, Sonny Koch knew the answer. Since Margo avoided conflict, there was no dramatic breakup, no climactic scene, just a gradual drawing apart. "After World War II ended," Sonny recalls, "it became clear to me that Margo didn't want to get married. I wanted to get on with my life." He ruefully adds, "I finally came to my senses."

In July, like most of the movers and shakers in pre-air-conditioned Dallas, Margo left town for a cooler climate. She packed dozens of scripts to read and traveled to Colorado to cover the Central City operas for the *Dallas Morning News* and to savor a few days in the mountain air. Nestled in the Rocky Mountains, the former gold-mining town of Central City hosted a gala four-day celebration centered around productions at the old opera house. Margo mingled with other visitors to the festival, who arrived in costumes ranging from cowboy outfits to court regalia. After seeing Mozart's *The Abduction from the Seraglio* and Verdi's *La Traviata* in English translations, she danced in the streets and partied until dawn. In her article about the festival she praised the "sheer exuberance" of the youthful companies, an exuberance that brought opening-night audiences to their feet, tossing bouquets at the performers.

When she returned to Dallas, she received a wire from Haila Stoddard informing her that because of money troubles the fall production of *Sunrise in My Pocket* was postponed indefinitely. Margo felt badly for playwright Edwin Mayer, but welcomed the news since the cancellation freed her to consider an even more attractive job offer.

Blooded on Broadway

The Playwrights' Company, the most distinguished producing company in New York, had asked her to direct Maxwell Anderson's new play, *Joan of Lorraine*, starring Ingrid Bergman. Founded in 1938 by playwrights Maxwell Anderson, S. N. Behrman, Elmer Rice, Robert Sherwood, and Sidney Howard, the Company presented their own plays, which included Anderson's *Key Largo*, *The Eve of St. Mark*, and *Storm Operation*; Rice's *Two on an Island* and *Dream Girl*; and Sherwood's *Abe Lincoln in Illinois*, *There Shall Be No Night*, and *The Rugged Path*. Composer Kurt Weill joined the group and wrote *Knickerbocker Holiday* with Anderson and *Street Scene* with Langston Hughes and Elmer Rice. Through her agent, Audrey Wood, who had negotiated a lucrative contract, Margo accepted the offer and thereby rose to the upper ranks of New York commercial directors, joining an all-male fraternity of Playwrights' Company directors that included Guthrie McClintic, Josh Logan, Garson Kanin, and Alfred Lunt.

Why would the Playwrights' Company choose a young woman director with only two Broadway shows to her credit to launch a new play starring a major film actress? Possibly their first choice had been unavailable, but Margo had a reputation as a playwright's director, a director who respected the writer's work, and she had experience working with new scripts, including Anderson's own *The Eve of St. Mark*. Her friend Jo Mielziner, who had designed many Playwrights' Company productions, gave Margo the *Joan of Lorraine* script initially and probably recommended her to Maxwell Anderson.

The Theatre '46 board agreed to Margo's continued absence from Dallas. June Moll argued that taking the job was a mistake, would not bring any prestige to Theatre '46, and urged Margo to stay in Texas and work on finding a theatre space. But Margo insisted that she could continue to follow the progress of the theatre-building situation closely and direct Anderson's play. She told June that if taking the New York job would delay the opening of her theatre for even five minutes, she would turn the offer down. Her decision was too much for the Molls, and although they remained in contact with Margo, who kept them informed of the theatre's progress, they did not return to work with her in Dallas.

On August 1, Margo flew to New York to meet with Maxwell Anderson and to clear up some problems with *On Whitman Avenue*. Two cast members had left the company and producer Mark Marvin had hired their replacements. Margo rehearsed with the new actors, talked with producers Marvin and Lee about restoring Maxine Wood's royalty cuts, and checked to see that the production and performances remained consistent.

The women in the company, especially Joanna Albus, told her about their wonderful new company manager, hired as a summer replacement. Intrigued by their reports, for she needed a top-notch business manager for her Dallas theatre, Margo arranged to meet the new man at a restaurant next door to the theatre. They chatted for a while, and then met again that night with Joanna along, since the manager and Joanna had been dating. Years later Margo remembered that from the first moment of their meeting there was really "no doubt it was just one of those things."

The man was Manning Gurian and he would change her life. Although Jewish and Brooklyn born, raised, and schooled—a singularly different background from Margo's—Gurian shared her love for the theatre, except to him the theatre was a way to make money, not art. When he was fourteen years old, he had worked as a movie usher, and after high school he had become chief usher for Earl Carroll's *Vanities*. He had paid his way through St. John's University Law School employed as Florenz Ziegfeld's office boy, and had worked his way up in the Ziegfeld organization to the box office and finally into management. He had earned a law degree but had abandoned the legal profession to work as a commercial theatre manager with producers like Norman Bel Geddes and Rodgers and Hammerstein. During World War II, he had served in the Signal Corps and in the Special Services.

When Margo met him, Gurian was in his middle thirties and was darkly handsome like Jerry Coray, with thick, wavy brown hair, prominent eyebrows, a strong nose, and a full, sensuous mouth. Gurian's soft-spoken, charming manner, dark eyes, and penetrating gaze had earned him a reputation as a ladies' man, a man who genuinely liked women, liked being around them, liked taking care of them. Margo found him personally and professionally irresistible. Gurian's brief affair with Joanna ended abruptly and his interest shifted to Margo. Although Joanna was hurt, she attempted to hide her feelings, for she was a mature, experienced woman and still devoted to Margo. Gurian found Margo "stimulating and exciting" and emotionally strong, filled with high spirits and girlish laughter. He admired her dedication and idealism; as he recalls, she "wanted nothing except theatre that worked and for people to be happy—she wanted nothing for herself."

Their love affair began slowly. Margo did not feel it was serious—she was just having fun and "taking pleasure in being with someone," she said later. Since they both had demanding jobs, their time together was sporadic, and in a choice between love and the theatre, the theatre usually won.

AFTER COMPLETING her duties with *On Whitman Avenue* (which had just reached its hundredth performance and would run, surprisingly, until the middle of September), Margo traveled to Maxwell Anderson's home in

Blooded on Broadway

Rockland County in upstate New York to discuss *Joan of Lorraine*. Anderson had completed the play, originally titled *Warrior's Return*, in November 1944. He wrote it, as he wrote all his plays, in a nine-by-twelve ramshackle cabin in the woods behind his house. A lot was at stake with this script. His most recent play, *Truckline Café*, had been a resounding failure, and some critics speculated that Anderson was in a decline, his career having reached its height during the late 1920s and 1930s with a string of box-office and critical successes, including *What Price Glory?*, *Winterset*, *Elizabeth the Queen*, *Mary of Scotland*, and *High Tor*.

Margo and Anderson made a strange pair. The shy playwright, nearly sixty years old, craggy faced and scholarly looking with large ears, thinning hair, and a reddish moustache, towered over the exuberant, loquacious Margo. Anderson was the son of a Baptist minister, a man he remembered as a "good mixer . . . a wonderful orator . . . and in the pulpit the most persuasive man I ever heard." The family had lived in Pennsylvania, Ohio, Iowa, and North Dakota, moving from parsonage to parsonage. Anderson thought his father's religious beliefs were a fake, "put on," and he recalled, "I've never been able to stand anything affected since." He had rejected his father's dream that he become a minister and, like Margo, had made theatre his religion instead, "devoted entirely to the exaltation of the spirit of man." However, his view of the theatre was Apollonian and intellectual, while Margo believed that theatre should be a Dionysian celebration.

Their common ground was the script of *Joan of Lorraine*. For years Anderson had wanted to write about "a play in rehearsal" because, he said "I have wanted an audience in the theatre to share the excitement of seeing a play come to life on a bare stage." In *Joan of Lorraine*, an acting company rehearses a play based on the story of Joan of Arc. Anderson's theme is "the problem of what to believe, and how a man defends his belief in a world of power politics and disillusion." The play weaves together the actual story of Joan of Arc with the story of the lead actress, Mary Grey, who quarrels with the playwright's and director's conception of Joan's character. Anderson shows that through faith and a series of compromises the greater good can be achieved, in this case both for the acting company rehearsing the play and for Joan of Arc. In his discussions with Margo, Anderson laid out his purposes and goals carefully, for just as Masters, the hard-edged director in the play within *Joan of Lorraine*, was the mouthpiece for Anderson and his philosophy, so Margo was charged with presenting the playwright's point of view. Anderson needed the persuasive Margo as his advocate to help control the star, Ingrid Bergman, who had already urged him to refocus and rewrite his script.

Blooded on Broadway

Anderson's Playwrights' Company colleagues had originally scoffed at his plan to ask Ingrid Bergman to play the dual role of Joan of Arc and the actress Mary Grey. Why should a famous film actress take a chance on a Broadway play? Urged on by his wife at least to ask Bergman if she wanted the role, Anderson did just that. After a long delay and protracted negotiations, with a frustrated Anderson vowing never again to get involved with movie people, Bergman finally signed the contract, saying that for years she had longed to play Joan of Arc and had even studied Joan's actual words and testimony.

After a short trip back to Texas, Margo flew to California to meet with Bergman. The trip had two purposes—first, to ensure the compatibility of the director and the star of *Joan of Lorraine*; second, to begin work on the script and to talk about Bergman's approach to the role. The actress was finishing work on a new movie, *Arch of Triumph*, based on the novel by Erich Maria Remarque (famous for *All Quiet on the Western Front*) and produced by a new company called Enterprise Productions. Although the film reunited Bergman with her *Gaslight* co-star Charles Boyer, she thought the story was depressing and felt uncomfortable during the filming and unsure of her performance. Also, her personal life was in turmoil. Though married to Dr. Petter Lindstrom, a dentist, she had just fallen in love with the noted photographer Robert Capa.

Margo spent hours on the set watching Bergman work and marveling at the talent of the tall, twenty-nine-year-old actress whose luminous face was familiar to millions from movies like *Intermezzo, Casablanca, Spellbound,* and *Notorious.* The women got along well. Bergman liked the Texas director, introduced Margo to her co-stars and producers, was friendly, down-to-earth, and direct. She researched the Maid of Orleans in great detail, reading translations of her life, other authors' versions of her story, and trial testimony. She became much more involved in creating her portrait of Joan than in acting the part of Mary Grey, and wanted to include as many of Joan of Arc's actual words in the play as she could, in effect to rework the script into a story primarily about Joan. Margo's objective was to protect Anderson's play as much as possible. She told Bergman that while Anderson welcomed her suggestions, the final decision had to be his for "as Masters says: Anybody can advise him, but it's up to him to decide." Margo made copious notes of her conversations with Bergman for later discussion with the playwright.

To prepare for the upcoming rehearsals, Margo enlisted Michel Bernheim of Enterprise Productions to assist her with the French names and French pronunciations in *Joan of Lorraine*. It is likely too that she renewed contacts with story department heads at Columbia and Paramount pictures as well as

Blooded on Broadway

with Jacob Wilk and Jack Warner of Warner Brothers, whom she had met the previous December when they summoned her to Little Rock, Arkansas, for a consultation about new plays and possible film scripts.

While Bergman remained in California, Margo flew to New York for pre-production meetings. She took a bus to Anderson's country home, delighting in the green woods and the "sun slanting through the trees," casting an "ethereal light." She spent the day there, discussing her notes with Anderson over a Japanese dinner.

The time-consuming task of casting the twenty-three-character play, five women and eighteen men, began on September 7. Margo worked from the Playwrights' Company's thirty-eighth-floor offices in the International Building, seeing about one hundred actors a day over a three-week period. "Scarcely an hour passes," she wrote her parents, "that some young talented person from Pasadena or Cleveland or Houston or Austin doesn't show up."

One of the young men she auditioned caught her eye immediately, not only because he was handsome, but because she recognized his talent. His name was Sam Wanamaker, and he was a native of Chicago with just a few Broadway credits and several radio serials on his resumé. During the war, he had served in the Special Services, where he played Tom in a production of *The Glass Menagerie*. In fact, Margo, taken with what she termed his "extraordinary talent," wrote to Enterprise Productions and suggested they produce a movie of *The Glass Menagerie* with her directing and Wanamaker playing Tom. She told the producers that after *Joan of Lorraine* opened, Wanamaker would be much in demand. Margo wanted to cast him for the dual leading role of Masters, the hard-boiled Broadway director, and the Grand Inquisitor, but Maxwell Anderson took one look at the boyish, twenty-seven-year-old Wanamaker and muttered, "No." After all, the character of Masters was Anderson's persona in the play, his voice. Even the name Anderson had chosen for the character indicated the importance of a masterly personality. How could an inexperienced actor serve as the mouthpiece of a dominating playwright, portray a powerful director, *and* hold his own opposite the charismatic Ingrid Bergman?

Margo turned her persuasive powers on Anderson. Wanamaker had read the part expertly, better than anyone else. Maybe a moustache would make him look older? Finally Anderson agreed, and Wanamaker began growing a moustache. The rest of the casting went smoothly. Romney Brent, who had an extensive list of credits both in New York and London, signed on to play the Dauphin. Since *On Whitman Avenue* was to close in the middle of September, Margo cast Joanna Albus in a small part. Lee Simonson, one of the

Blooded on Broadway

founders of the Theatre Guild and a pioneer in stage design, had been hired to design the costumes, lights, and minimal set.

In early October, Margo picked up Bergman at the airport and rehearsals began. Because of the shortage of theatre space, the company rehearsed in one theatre's lounge area and on the stage of a different theatre in the set of another play. Margo had some problems with the character of Masters, finding it difficult to separate herself and her feelings from the fictional director. In the play, Masters tells the actress Mary Grey that "actors should just have dinner, Mary—they shouldn't try to think." Mary replies, "But they have to think or they can't act." Masters's hard-nosed philosophy and aggressive personality were completely different from Margo's collaborative, gentler approach to directing. Despite these minor problems, after the first week of rehearsal Margo was in high spirits, excited about the company of actors she had assembled and about the play. She told Bergman that "somehow I feel that I was born to work on this with you and Max and Sam and all the others."

Perhaps feeling guilty that she had neglected her family during recent months, Margo wrote them dozens of letters during this time, informing them of her work with Bergman and the plays she had seen. Martha Pearl, who was in poor health, was staying with her sister in Amarillo. Margo's father and brother Charles lived a bachelor existence in Livingston, concentrating on their work. Charles's thoughts were often with Margo, though, and he followed her career with great interest. In fact, when he bought and developed a section of Livingston, he named a new street Whitman Avenue in his sister's honor.

October was a beautiful month in New York. Knowing Margo's fondness for flowers, Will Geer brought her a bunch of tiny chrysanthemums from his country garden; she saw Manning Gurian; and she attended productions of *Lysistrata, Hear That Trumpet,* and *Cyrano de Bergerac* (which reminded her of the first professional play she had seen in Fort Worth when she was twenty). None of the productions matched Laurence Olivier's *Oedipus,* though, which she had seen earlier that year. New York theatregoers marveled at the versatility of Olivier, who played the tragic hero and then dazzled audiences by acting the superbly comic lead in Sheridan's *The Critic,* both in the same evening. Margo considered the Old Vic's powerful production of *Oedipus* her greatest theatrical experience. With Maxwell Anderson and Ingrid Bergman, she saw the Theatre Guild's production of Eugene O'Neill's *The Iceman Cometh.* This play ended O'Neill's twelve-year absence from the Broadway stage, but the production was not very successful, static and constrained by the limitations of the proscenium arch. Unfortunately, stagecraft and stage design had not caught up with playwrights like O'Neill and Tennessee Williams, who were taking dramaturgy in a new direction, moving away from neat, well-made plays into a more free-flowing form.

Margo kept her Theatre '46 board members and John Rosenfield informed of her activities, sending Rosenfield anecdotes and information for his weekly column. Mrs. Braniff visited New York, and Margo rushed from rehearsal to meet her for lunch. They talked about the theatre building; it seemed that the city was reluctant to give them a permit. Margo planned to return to Dallas after the opening of *Joan* and to deal then with the building issues but now, with all her energies focused on the play, she needed to buy time. So, she told Ross Lawther, she used the "oil man's technique" on Mrs. Braniff and did not discuss the problem but instead "tried to charm and reckon and beckon enough" so that Mrs. Braniff "would be set for talking business the next time."

To promote *Joan of Lorraine*, Margo, wearing a chic black dress, lipstick, and eye makeup, posed for *Vogue* magazine photographers with Sam Wanamaker looking over her shoulder. Rehearsals continued to go well. Stage manager Alan Anderson, the playwright's son, remembers the New York rehearsals as "very peaceful, with no crises." In a letter to Ross Lawther, Margo summed up her feelings. "I wish I could tell you," she wrote, "the real joy that I'm having with this production. I have never felt, as a worker in the theatre, that I was hitting so on all eight. Every day is a sheer pleasure; one or two days have amounted to complete ecstasy! Practically every member of the cast has an extremely high intelligence and sensitivity and ability. The result is that directing is so exciting that I can hardly stand it. Even when I have been up all night, I never get tired working with that author and company. Ingrid continues to be a complete darling." Margo was having the time of her life and felt that only one thing could make her happier—the opening of her Dallas theatre.

The company moved to Washington, D.C., for a three-week tryout. Although the entire run had sold out in advance because of Ingrid Bergman's popularity, Maxwell Anderson was worried about his play. He didn't like making changes in his scripts, but Bergman and her assistant Ruth Roberts wore him down with constant meetings, bringing him new lines for Joan of Arc that they wanted him to incorporate into the play. He resisted, but finally capitulated somewhat, and the play became more a story about Joan of Arc and less about Anderson's original concept.

To make matters worse, when the company arrived in town, they learned that their theatre, Lisner Auditorium on the campus of George Washington University in the Foggy Bottom section of Washington, enforced a Jim Crow policy. Blacks were not allowed in that theatre or in Washington's National Theatre, where they were permitted onstage but not in the audience.

Blooded on Broadway

An outraged Bergman told Maxwell Anderson that if she had known of this policy, she would not have agreed to perform in Washington. Although certainly not a bigoted man or a believer in racial discrimination, Anderson tried to calm her down, asking her not to say anything to stir up trouble in her interviews. He knew that going along with the situation in Washington would be compromising his principles, but his play was about compromise—Masters makes a deal with a corrupt theatre owner, and Joan of Arc compromises in little things to achieve a greater good. A man of integrity, Anderson believed that compromise was necessary, even essential, in keeping one's faith.

Bergman did not follow his advice, and told reporters at a news conference the day before the opening that she "deplored racial discrimination in any form" and would never come back to Washington. The cast and especially Margo, who had just dealt with the problem of racial discrimination in *On Whitman Avenue*, agreed with Bergman, but like her they were bound by their contracts to work.

Even without the added complication of a segregated theatre, the tryout of *Joan of Lorraine* promised to be like many tryouts of new plays, a special form of hell for everyone involved. The risk of presenting an untried play, with the attendant fears of failure plus all the normal pressures of opening with last-minute technical and script changes, demanded mental toughness and emotional strength. The additional strain of daily rehearsals followed by evening performances followed by all-night production meetings required great physical stamina.

On Tuesday, October 29, the play opened at Lisner Auditorium. The Committee for Racial Democracy had organized a mass meeting to protest the Lisner's racial policy and greeted the opening-night audience with pickets and leaflets. Backstage tensions were high as Margo made her usual rounds, handing out personal notes and good wishes to a nervous company facing its first test in front of an audience.

When the play opened on the bare, cavernous stage of the Lisner, the audience applauded the first sight of the famous film star. Soon, though, because the theatre was stifling hot and the acoustics terrible with numerous dead spots, the audience grew restless, coughing and fidgeting. The architectural configuration of the auditorium was such that audience members in the back of the theatre could hear but not see, while those sitting in front could see but not hear. The abrupt transitions from the Joan of Arc scenes to the acting-company scenes left the audience confused. A reviewer for the *Hollywood Reporter* attended the opening and praised Bergman's performance but felt that the play had "too much to say and took too long to say it." Another,

Blooded on Broadway

local reviewer said that the stage was large enough to play touch football on and complained that he couldn't hear a word. Despite all the problems, the play ended to thunderous applause. The controversy was not forgotten, though. While some people complimented Ingrid Bergman at the stage door, others spat on her, calling her a "nigger lover."

The next day and in subsequent rehearsals Margo and the designer Lee Simonson worked on the technical problems. The lighting cues in between scenes were changed, making transitions clearer and smoother; heavy drapes were strategically hung to lessen the acoustical problems; and the "tormentors," the drapes on the sides of the stage, were moved in to narrow the space, making it seem less vast.

During a rehearsal break, a *Washington Post* reporter interviewed Margo. She talked about the challenge of working on *Joan of Lorraine*. As usual, though, she also used the interview as an opportunity to promote her vision. "All over the United States, this side of the Hudson, the need . . . is in the air," she told the reporter. "One successful repertory house anywhere out in the hinterland would sow the seeds of countless others." The reporter left Lisner Auditorium with the conviction that what the theatre most desperately needed was "more dynamic practitioners with the courage, clear vision, and abiding faith of Margo Jones."

Because of her clash with Anderson, the publicity flap over the play, and the thought of possible failure in New York, Bergman grew increasingly nervous as the Broadway opening date approached. Used to film acting, she had problems projecting her voice. When she asked Margo for specific directions, Margo urged her to "just feel it," or suggested that she try something and told Bergman that she would let her know if she liked it, or said simply that she was doing fine. Used to strong, male directors who were very sure of what they wanted, Bergman began to lose confidence in Margo and to depend on Sam Wanamaker for guidance. Wanamaker had fallen in love with his co-star and although Bergman wasn't in love with him, they had developed a close rapport. "Bergman wanted a director who made hard and fast decisions," Wanamaker says now. "Margo was the kind of director who allowed actors to blossom as they felt in rehearsal under her guidance."

According to stage manager Alan Anderson, during the Washington tryout Margo began to have problems working with the two stars in their scenes. "She didn't push actors around," Anderson recalls. "Margo was careful, quiet and subtle." In a sense, her work as director had become superfluous—the world of the play had taken over and Bergman leaned more and more on Wanamaker, who, of course, played the tough, decisive director in the play within the play.

Blooded on Broadway

Maxwell Anderson watched developments from the sidelines, and he too began to believe that what the production needed was a strong, masculine director —someone like Masters, the director he had created. Pressures on Anderson were enormous; a great deal of money was at stake as well as his reputation. Reviewers had been less than complimentary about his play—one critic had called it "boring." He could not bear another flop like *Truckline Café*. He had to do something, to take some kind of action, or perhaps he needed a scapegoat. Whatever the reason, on Saturday, November 9, with one week of tryouts left, he fired Margo.

Later, both Bergman and Wanamaker expressed shock and surprise at her dismissal. Bergman recalled incorrectly that it happened on opening night in Washington, not two weeks later. In her version, Maxwell Anderson told her that he had fired Margo. Bergman did not understand why, she felt that Margo had been doing a good job. "How cruel can you be," Bergman thought. "Yes, everything is lovely they say, you were great, and then out of the blue they are plotting behind your back, and you're fired." However, even though Bergman's contract did not give her control over the choice of a director, it is highly unlikely that Anderson failed to consult with her before firing Margo. Possibly to protect Bergman from bad publicity, Anderson and the Playwrights' Company took full responsibility for the decision.

Anderson named his stage-manager son and, ironically, Sam Wanamaker, the man Margo had pleaded with him to cast, as co-directors. Neither man had any professional directing experience, but if Wanamaker could play a tough, Broadway director convincingly onstage, Anderson perhaps felt he could become one in reality. Wanamaker called Margo and said, "Look, I don't want to do this if you feel it would be disloyal to you."

"What's the difference?" Margo replied. "They've fired me. I think it's wonderful that you should do it."

"For me it was an incredible opportunity," Wanamaker recalls.

On the surface, Margo was composed and professional, accepting Anderson's decision with equanimity. Within, she was devastated. For months she had nurtured the play. It had become her life and now it had been taken away. She found little consolation in the fact that she received all her contractual benefits—full fee, full credit in the Broadway playbill and publicity, and her percentage of the gross for the run of the play. She was fortunate in these respects; at the time, directors were unprotected by a union, and producers often fired them without compunction, refusing to pay fees and percentages. In Margo's case, to all appearances she was still the play's director. Audrey Wood, her powerful agent, probably had a hand in settling the contract with the Playwrights' Company, but the primary reason for the Company's seeming generosity was simply this: Margo had done her work. The production was set. According to Alan Anderson, Lee Simonson, and Joanna Albus, nothing about the production changed after Margo left and the play moved to New York. Only her personality was absent. Her work had been perceived as too gentle, too womanly, not tough enough to shepherd Anderson's play to Broadway, and she had failed to inspire belief and confidence in her two leading actors. And Margo knew—perhaps better than anyone involved, since one of her acting maxims was "just believe, baby"—that in the ephemeral world of the theatre, belief was at the heart of a successful production.

The day after her dismissal Margo labored over a letter to Maxwell Anderson. The strongly worded first draft of the letter, written in bold, slashing script, told Anderson that his move was "very wrong" and "unwise." In the next draft, Margo kept the strong wording, but added that she hoped it would work out. Her finished, typed letter omitted any criticism of Anderson's actions and simply summarized their agreement. Diplomatically, Margo wrote, "[W]hat you consider is for the good of the play I will do and will follow your suggestions of procedure." Even at this low point, she did not want to appear less than gracious and buried her anger in polite phrases.

Although her firing was not announced publicly, Margo knew that the theatre grapevine would quickly carry the news. Rumors would spread like wildfire, adding to her humiliation and embarrassment. Without saying good-bye, she left the *Joan of Lorraine* company. What had begun as a joyous adventure had ended in bitter failure. It was a new experience for her—one that would take some getting used to.

Toward a National Theatre

*J*oan of Lorraine opened on Broadway on November 18, 1946, and although audience members complained about inaudibility, calling out to Bergman, "Speak louder, we can't hear you," the play would run 201 performances, closing May 18, 1947. Critics praised Ingrid Bergman's acting but were less than enthusiastic about Maxwell Anderson's play, finding it decidedly inferior to George Bernard Shaw's masterpiece, *Saint Joan*. Although she didn't paste these clippings, painful reminders of her firing, into a scrapbook, Margo's work earned good notices. Brooks Atkinson in the *New York Times* said, "Under Margo Jones' direction, the performance makes fascinating use of the form of the play." Robert Garland in the *Journal-American* wrote that her direction was "admirable and assured"; however, Howard Barnes of the *New York Herald-Tribune* reported that "the staging of the two acts has been adroit, whether accomplished by Margo Jones, or Wanamaker who took over for her." Ticket sales soared as Bergman's fans, many of them screaming bobby-soxers, jammed the theatre and waited on the sidewalk outside to see their movie-star idol. By the end of 1946, Margo had earned over seven thousand dollars from the play, which may have assuaged her disappointment.

Any disappointment or depression she felt about the firing, however, she kept to herself. Even Joanna Albus did not recall her discussing the dismissal. Although Albus blamed Ingrid Bergman, who she felt had "stabbed Margo in the back," if Margo shared that opinion she kept it to herself. Conciliation rather than recrimination was her style, a prudent course of action in the small world of the theatre, where this year's adversary may become next year's co-worker. That Christmas, Margo and Bergman exchanged letters and gifts. *Variety*, the show business paper that reports rumors as well as hard news, asked, "Will Margo Jones share co-billing with Sam Wanamaker—he thinks he's entitled?" Margo did not share credit, but did send Wanamaker a Christmas gift, and he wrote her saying that he had enjoyed working with her and hoped to have her as a friend. She did not dwell on past problems or nurse grudges, and she masked any pain she felt. One of her Houston friends recalls that "Margo wanted everyone to think she was in complete control." Significantly, following her firing from *Joan of Lorraine*, she would work only for herself. In the future she would be in control, as much as possible, and not at the mercy of a capricious producer or a volatile star.

Courage, Margo felt, was the most important personal trait. In fact, she prided herself on her strength—she took care of others—and there was a core of self no one could penetrate. One friend characterized her as "the cat who walked alone." Tennessee Williams, perhaps her closest friend at the time, said, "She always popped up at times of depression and lifted me out of it. If she was ever depressed or discouraged herself, she never showed a sign of it." Like Williams, who felt that his writing was his true self and the rest shadowy and incidental, Margo's work was her life. Once when a friend asked how she was and he didn't mean theatre, she told him, "That's a hard one to answer . . . because I'm so mixed up with theatre that I can assure you there's no place where I begin and it stops or the other way around."

IN LATE NOVEMBER she attended the annual meeting of the National Theatre Conference at the Hotel Piccadilly in New York. The NTC supported Margo's effort to decentralize the theatre and encouraged her plan to begin with a fully professional repertory theatre producing new plays and classics. She met with colleagues Gilmor Brown and Frederick McConnell and had dinner with Hallie Flanagan. She also spent time with Manning Gurian. They walked in Greenwich Village, enjoyed Japanese and pushcart food, and explored side streets and the subway. When it came time to leave, Margo continued talking to "keep the tears back."

To alert Dallas to her return, Margo spoke with Clay Bailey of the *Dallas Times Herald*, who wrote on December 1 that she was "determined to fight the battle solely on the Texas front . . . turning down all future lures in the form of directorial offers."

Once again Margo and Joanna headed for Dallas, with an overnight sidetrip to visit Tennessee in New Orleans. Williams and his handsome, fiery-tempered lover, Pancho Rodriguez y Gonzalez, lived in a second-floor apartment on St. Peter Street, near the main street of the French Quarter where Williams would watch the two streetcars—one named Desire, the other called Cemeteries— go by. He read them a draft of a new play he was writing called *A Chart of Anatomy*. Although some of Tennessee's friends didn't like the play and had told him to set it aside and concentrate on his half-finished script *The Poker Night*, Margo became obsessed with *A Chart of Anatomy* and with the character of Alma Winemiller and thought that Tennessee's writing was "more exciting than ever." In fact, seeing Tennessee and hearing his script lifted her spirits and focused her energies on creating a theatre where she could produce his new work.

Toward a National Theatre

Back in Dallas, Margo met with the Operating Committee of the board of trustees to discuss plans for submitting a new slate of officers and to consult on building plans. The cost of remodeling the Museum of Natural Resources was found to be too high, and various other possibilities she investigated like high school auditoriums, town halls, and former movie theatres were either impractical or too expensive. Board vice-president E. L. DeGolyer began calling her "Crisis" Jones, telling her, "Anytime you get into a crisis, just yell for me." He couldn't help her with a building, however, since most theatre space in Dallas was controlled by movie chains. The Circle Theatre, with a proscenium stage, was available, but the lease cost fifty thousand dollars, and monthly rent must still be paid. Margo learned that to build a suitable concrete block building would cost approximately fifty thousand dollars also, including the land but excluding air conditioning, heating, carpeting, electrical equipment, and seats. She applied for a building permit from the Civilian Production Administration and waited for approval from Washington. With a population of 350,000 people, many nightclubs, five country clubs, four hundred churches, eighty-four public schools, and fifty-two movie theatres, Dallas couldn't seem to find space for even one professional theatre.

Although reading plays, entertaining visitors, attending meetings, looking at buildings, and writing letters continued to occupy her in December 1946, Margo was really waiting, an activity she hated, for her dream to come true, but with "some real outsmarting," she said, "we're going to pull this off." Convincing others to share her dream was a process she found "tough as hell. . . . The entire system is geared to one conception as far as theatre is concerned—money and stars and long runs and what 'goes' and 'nothing if not done in New York first' and 'what do you want to be so idealistic about?' and 'why don't you go to Hollywood?' "

All these were questions she probably asked herself as well, since three years had passed since that night in December of 1943 when she had first articulated her ideas for a national theatre to friends Ed Torrance and Maudee Carron in her room in Austin. Although her last experience in New York had been unpleasant, Margo still felt that old pull between the commercial theatre and her regional art theatre. Broadway was an established fact, her art theatre just a dream. Was she pursuing a child's fantasy? Now she was thirty-five years old, 1946 was ending, and the reality still eluded her.

SHE WENT HOME to Livingston to celebrate Christmas with her family, but her spirits were less than joyful. She wouldn't be seeing her dependable admirer Sonny Koch that Christmas because he planned to marry. Although she was happy for Sonny, she must have felt a pang of regret when he wrote, "Well, bebe, my love for you has altered, tho not my affection. . . . I've found a fine girl, Ferne Goodman, who has consented to be my wife . . . and who I'll be proud for you to know." At home with her straightlaced, conservative parents, Margo could not indulge in smoking or drinking, both of which helped her to relax. Preoccupied with their own lives and concerns, they saw Margo just as their daughter, and while they encouraged her work in the theatre, they did not understand the life she led. Her mother, now in her late sixties, had returned to Livingston after an extended stay with her sister. Although Margo and her mother chafed each other's nerves and often failed to connect, they attempted to smooth out their differences in letters. After Margo's brief visit, Martha Pearl wrote to her "precious Margie," whom she still treated as a little girl, "Oh how I longed to hold you tight against my lonely old heart and kiss you again & again to try to make up for the hundreds of times I had longed for you"—words sure to inspire guilt in her absent daughter.

For relaxation and an opportunity to be herself and talk theatre, Margo visited Tennessee, who had invited her for a long weekend visit after New Year's. New Orleans was cold and wet, but her reception was warm. Tennessee had been depressed, plagued with thoughts of death and disease, and he needed Margo's encouragement as much as she needed his. Pancho brought her breakfast in bed, toast and coffee with a whiskey chaser. She walked with him and Tennessee in the rain, went to the ballet and a party with their friends, and "let her hair down and relaxed." Sunday afternoon was set aside for a reading of Tennessee's new play, formerly *The Poker Night*, now titled *Paper Lantern*. Margo thought the whole play magnificent and the character of Blanche Dubois perfectly drawn. "There is nobody living who can write like you do," she declared. She couldn't contain her excitement and told Tennessee that his two new plays, *A Chart of Anatomy* and *Paper Lantern*, "have got to be done just as you want them to be done." If only she had a theatre, she thought, she would option them immediately or maybe they could produce them together. Perhaps she had the wealthy DeGolyer or Mrs. Braniff in mind when she told him, "As far as being able to get the money for such a venture, it could be done with one telephone call."

Discouraging talk began to circulate about the future of her theatre, however, as several board members whose terms of office were going to expire wanted to resign. Margo believed that Eugene McDermott, the board president, who was often out of town and perhaps not as attentive as she might have wished, wanted to end the project. "Now's the Time for All Good Men To Help Theatre," an unattributed article in the *Dallas Morning News* probably written by John Rosenfield to support Margo and put some pressure on the board, featured a picture of Margo and Eric Capon, the director of England's Old Vic Company, who was visiting Dallas. Theatre '47, the article said, was "more closely watched by professional and academic circles of New York and London than by Dallas."

Margo called a meeting of the board for February 11, 1947—exactly two years after the 1945 founders' meeting at the McDermotts' home. Her aim was to present a new slate of officers, an action Gene McDermott opposed, and to prod the board into accepting responsibility for building a new theatre. On the night of the meeting, only sixteen members of the forty-five-person board attended. Both Margo and McDermott rose to chair the meeting. Margo, who was afraid that McDermott wanted to end the project, spoke first and dominated the meeting for two hours, talking about her activities in the past months and the plans for building a theatre. She told them that she wanted this meeting "to have finality," but voting on a decision to continue and for new officers could not proceed without a quorum. She felt that she had raised the level of enthusiasm about the theatre, but the finality she sought had not been achieved. There would have to be more meetings, more indecision, more talk.

The next day she heard from the Civilian Production Administration in Washington that her application to build a new theatre had been denied so that "the construction of homes for veterans of World War II may proceed as rapidly as possible." After days of soul-searching, Margo wrote to her agent, Audrey Wood, asking her to find her a directing job somewhere—in New York, Hollywood, television, or radio. "As far as my dream," she wrote Audrey, "it's still the same—I still want to work in a permanent, professional repertory theatre—I still want to see good professional, resident theatre in all the large towns of America but I know now beyond a shadow of a doubt why such theatres do not exist. . . . I'm willing to forget these dreams for the moment and put my whole self into commerce and make me a new set of dreams about that." She wrote an almost identical letter to Jo Mielziner, telling him that she "was a Pollyanna by nature and [could] hang on with faith for a mighty long time but there comes a time when it is sheer nonsense not to face facts." Margo knew that in the nonprofit setup she had envisioned, a board of directors to raise money, provide leadership, and use power in the community to obtain land and support was essential. Yet her board was stymied. There wasn't a suitable building in town for a theatre, and they were not permitted to build one. She didn't want to spend her life talking about directing, she wanted to work on her art. "For me this is a very strange letter," she wrote

Toward a National Theatre

Mielziner, "for I've always known exactly what I wanted and went out after it. I still know what I want but have found out that it cannot be gotten in this way."

Audrey Wood told Margo that she was saddened by her letter, and said that she would talk to people about a directing job for her. So it was over. Margo decided not to tell the board right away—perhaps she could take another long leave of absence, and when they had built a theatre or found one, she could come back.

In late February, however, with most of the members present, the board of trustees voted to continue the project. Eugene McDermott, who was in New York and did not attend the meeting, said that he had not wanted the project to end and was pleased that it would continue. With the board's vote of confidence in her ability to do the job, Margo felt a renewed "physical and spiritual determination," willing herself to make a "last violent effort to pull this thing through." She wrote Audrey Wood and told her to forget her earlier letter, saying, "I will not let this thing whip me." Margo's plan—her dream for a resident professional theatre and many others like it—wasn't ready to die.

"When there is no theatre available," Margo asked herself, "and yet you must start a theatre, what do you do?" Had she been talking about a building, she wondered, or about an idea? Conventional solutions had been considered, but "when one runs out of solutions," Margo thought, "the unusual solution will save the day." What about theatre-in-the-round? It had worked before in Houston, why not here in Dallas? With the approval of her board, Margo began to look at a different type of building. Until a more permanent situation could be found, the air-conditioned Palm Garden Room at the elegant Hotel Adolphus would do just fine. With over twenty thousand dollars in the bank from fund-raising, Margo began to plan a short ten-week summer season, advisable she felt because she wanted to have enough money in the bank to ensure the completion of the season.

EARLY IN MARCH, Manning had sent her his new script, a comedy called *God Bless Them All*. He hoped to be a playwright and wanted Margo's opinion of his first play. If he had counted on love blinding her critical eye, he was wrong. In a three-page letter, Margo said that she liked the title, encouraged his writing, damned him for making "this so difficult for me," but after reading and rereading his play, admitted she found little to praise. She said that his story was not interesting enough to hold an audience and his characters were "so unpleasantly superficial that I simply cannot like them." She suggested cutting one character because he wasn't funny (the cut thus saving an actor's salary), and said she found the character of a "goon southern girl" somewhat amusing, but useless in the play unless Manning "just let her do a strip tease and be done with it." She told him that a play was like "a person: some people look at it and love it; some look at it and loathe it." She also shared the knowledge she had gained after years of reading and evaluating plays. "For a play to be a good one," she told Manning, "it must have either one or a combination of the following: (1) A story that in itself is so interesting that nothing else matters; (2) Characterizations that are so fascinating, different, individual, fun, sad or tragic that the characterizations alone hold interest; (3) Create a mood that can be so projected into an audience that the mood itself can hold a sort of fascination; (4) Dialogue that is either so witty, intellectual, gaggy, poetic that the very stringing together of the words holds an audience with the style. Now any one of these things can carry a play; but of course if you combine two or all, then I think you have something."

Her description of a good play was encompassed in the work of Tennessee Williams, a playwright who she felt "hung the moon." In March she flew to New Orleans to talk to him about producing one of his new scripts in Dallas. They spent three days drinking in quaint little bars, driving through the park enjoying the spring flowers, feeding the monkeys at the zoo, and discussing *A Chart of Anatomy*, which Tennessee had retitled more evocatively *Summer and Smoke*, a phrase taken from Hart Crane's poem "Emblems of Conduct." With Audrey Wood's approval, modified by stipulations that Margo give the play a first-class production and consult with her about casting, Tennessee agreed that she could give his script its world premiere in Dallas that summer. His other play, *The Poker Night*, which he had renamed *A Streetcar Named Desire*, he sent to Wood, who would try to sell it to New York producers.

Meanwhile Manning had received her letter and responded by sending her a lavish spring bouquet of white gladiolas, pink carnations, and pale blue iris. Margo was touched and charmed by the gesture because she loved flowers, but more importantly because she felt now that she could tell the truth to Manning, be herself with him and, she recalled later, because "we completely understood each other." Earlier, Manning had written that although he was manager on Norman Krasna's new comedy, *John Loves Mary*, a "simple play with a thin excuse for a story," he wished he could help her with her theatre, adding, "but commercial me. Maybe if I get restless."

Although the Hotel Adolphus had been announced as the site of Theatre '47, Margo was not satisfied with the makeshift arrangement and continued to look for a suitable theatre space. She found it on the grounds of Fair Park, fifteen minutes from downtown, in a sleekly modern stucco-and-glass-block building designed in the International style by Swiss-born architect William

Toward a National Theatre

Lescaze. Built in 1936 for the Texas Centennial, the structure was one of the first International style buildings in the country. Although it had been originally designed as a "comfort station," a euphemism for restrooms for State Fair visitors, the building, leased by Gulf Oil Corporation, had evolved into an exhibits area with a small auditorium and stage, ideal for adapting to theatre-in-the-round. A large foyer suitable as a theatre lobby opened onto a lovely landscaped terrace. Fair Park with its grand ceremonial plaza, massive desert-colored exhibition buildings decorated with flags and colorful banners, heroic sculptures, large murals, sparkling fountains, and thousand-foot-long reflecting pool all bathed in a gleaming array of colored lights provided spectacular surroundings. Designed by Dallas architect George Dahl, the architectural motif of the 277-acre Fair Park was a combination of Art Deco, International style, and Moderne with a southwestern flavor—a dramatic, vivid setting for the small new gem of Theatre '47.

WITH THE ASSISTANCE of board member Arthur Kramer, Jr., Margo received permission from Gulf Oil to use their air-conditioned building at no charge except payment of utilities. Although both John Rosenfield and Eugene McDermott warned against opening during the hot Dallas summer when many people, including her major contributors, left town, Margo had had enough of waiting and planned to open the ten-week summer season on June 3. She had two months to remodel the building's auditorium for theatre-in-the-round, install lighting equipment, platforms, and seats, make final decisions on five plays (four new scripts and one classic), hire an acting company and staff, and mount a publicity and subscription campaign.

The news of the long-awaited opening of Margo's theatre circulated rapidly in the theatre world, and letters of application from actors, playwrights, technicians, and designers poured into her office. Her ideas influenced and inspired a whole generation of young theatre people, mostly trained in colleges and universities, who wanted to work but found little opportunity in the limited confines of the commercial theatre. One young man, a student at Bard College, wrote, "My main interest in the theatre is in the type of work you are doing in Texas. I never have had, nor do I now have any desire to work on Broadway. . . . The idea of taking Theatre outside of the narrow limits of New York, where, I feel, Drama has lost its integrity and purpose and has become merely another business, is a definite challenge to me as well as the challenge of starting a permanent theatre in a fundamentally non-theatrical section of the country." Margo didn't have a job for him, but although the young man went on to work successfully in the commercial theatre as a production manager, he held on to his youthful dreams, and in 1963 co-founded the Guthrie Theatre in Minneapolis. Peter Zeisler later became the director of Theatre Communications Group (TCG), a national service organization of the nonprofit resident professional theatre.

At Jo Mielziner's suggestion, Margo hired Joseph Londin as her technical director. Londin had worked as a stage manager in New York and was currently technical director at Hunter College. With the assistance of Mielziner and Ed Kook of Century Lighting, Londin began working out the seating arrangements and lighting plan for the theatre.

When it became clear to Joanna Albus that Margo would not ask her to be a member of the acting company, she requested the job of production and stage manager. She supervised the technical details, renovations, and promotional activities in Dallas while Margo flew to New York to select the acting company and option the scripts. Margo's primary task, however, was to hire a "first class business manager." She felt that to have the respect of the community, her theatre "must be run in as businesslike a fashion as a department store" by an experienced manager with "hard-boiled business sense." Theatre '47 had already hired a business manager, a local man recommended by a board member, but after complaints from Joanna that he was late for meetings, unprepared, and never had anything with him "but that eternal briefcase, I wonder what in the hell he has in it," Margo fired him.

When she arrived in New York, she called Manning Gurian, and they saw each other every night. Although Manning was still employed as company manager of *John Loves Mary*, Margo began to work on persuading him to join her in Dallas as her company manager. She respected his expertise and wanted him to set up her theatre financially. She couldn't match the money he earned in the commercial theatre, but Manning took the job anyway, drawn both to Margo and her ideas for a new kind of theatre. Also, he had another, more capitalistic motive: he wanted to make money by finding "good plays and bring[ing] them into New York." Margo's ambition was just the opposite—to find good plays and present them in Dallas, to do something about the unhealthy centralization of the theatre in New York— but she shrewdly lured Manning with the possibility that money could be made in developing new plays. And she was in love with him, "full-fledged one hundred per cent in love," she said. "All the physical feelings, all the jealousy and everything else." Certain associates of Margo's, well-aware of her ability to find people who could do multiple jobs—the assistant stage manager who could play walk-ons, the secretary who was also a playwright —chuckled at her romantic efficiency. How convenient and how typical that her lover was not only a budding playwright but also a highly skilled business manager!

With Audrey Wood's assistance and with the cooperation of Actors' Equity and the Dramatists Guild, Margo hired a company of eight actors and signed contracts on four new plays in just three whirlwind weeks in New York. She used the standard stock tryout contract for plays, paying a $150 advance against a royalty of 5 percent of the gross. William Inge's first play, *Farther Off from Heaven*, would open the season, followed by *How Now, Hecate* by Martyn Coleman, Ibsen's *Hedda Gabler*, Tennessee's *Summer and Smoke*, and *Third Cousin* by Vera Mathews.

She auditioned hundreds of actors, looking for the right combination of talent, character, and experience. And, since her budget limited her to only eight actors, she needed to find people who could play a wide age range. Casting *Summer and Smoke's* Alma Winemiller proved especially difficult. Margo and Tennessee had seen Lillian Hellman's play *Another Part of the Forest*, featuring Margaret Phillips as Birdie. This performance had earned Phillips critical accolades and awards, and Tennessee wanted her to play Alma. It is likely, though, that Phillips was not available for a summer repertory season, because after seeing a number of women, Margo chose Katharine Balfour, a tall, brunette actress with a febrile, nervous manner, to play the neurotic Alma. She auditioned for Margo and Tennessee in Margo's hotel room. "I'll never forget the way Tennessee listened to me. He helped me on with my coat when I left, like a real southern gentleman," Balfour recalls. "I hope I get it," Balfour told him. Tennessee gallantly replied, "I hope so too. I think you will."

The eight-member acting company, selected for their ability to play a variety of characters, would have their acting expertise and their stamina severely tested at salaries of sixty to seventy-five dollars a week. The character men were Geoffrey Lumb, who had worked in New York and London, acting with Helen Hayes, Peggy Wood, and Clare Luce; Raymond Van Sickle, who had worked on Broadway with Eva Le Gallienne; and Wilson Brooks, an experienced actor in New York and Chicago stock. Young, handsome Tod Andrews, who had appeared in stock and on Broadway in *Storm Operation*, would play the male lead in *Summer and Smoke* and Eilert Lövborg in *Hedda Gabler*. The character women were Carole Goodner, a veteran of New York and London theatre who was in her early forties but could look younger; Marga Ann Deighton, who was recommended by Will Geer and who had acted with the Theatre Guild and with Noel Coward and Sir Herbert Beerbohm Tree in London; and Betty Greene Little, who had been in *On Whitman Avenue*.

Smaller parts would be taken by Rebecca Hargis, Marilyn Putnam (a student of Londin's who was attending Hunter College on a Rockefeller Fellowship), and four production assistants, Jonathan Seymour, Frank Amy, Clinton Anderson, and Jack Warden. The production assistants would receive a salary of forty dollars a week supplemented by the valuable acting experience they would gain. Margo, Manning, and technical director Joe Londin collected the top weekly salary of one hundred dollars each. Stage manager Joanna Albus earned seventy-five dollars a week.

During her New York stay Margo attended Broadway productions of Elmer Rice's *Street Scene*, Wilde's *The Importance of Being Earnest*, and the musicals *Brigadoon* and *Finian's Rainbow*. All fine theatre, she thought, but unavailable to most Americans. In 1946 Margo had become a member of the board of directors of the American National Theatre and Academy, an organization chartered by Congress in 1935 to stimulate a national theatre that would further the production of theatre of the past and the present throughout the United States. The Federal Theatre Project eliminated the need for ANTA in the 1930s and then World War II interrupted, and it was not until 1946 that ANTA became a working institution. Supported by an impressive list of theatre notables, including Brooks Atkinson, producer Cheryl Crawford, playwright Moss Hart, actress Helen Hayes, and designer Robert Edmond Jones, and with Robert Breen as executive secretary, ANTA served as a clearinghouse for theatre, provided a placement service and a speakers and conference bureau, published a newsletter, and supported close ties between the professional and nonprofessional theatre. At an ANTA dinner meeting where she preached to the already converted, Margo pounded out her favorite theme, which had become a steady drumbeat, a call to battle. Like the herald of a new age she told her audience that "a nation's drama will shrivel and die from too intensive centralization. Good theatre entertainment must be made available to people outside the narrow confines of Broadway."

While Manning stayed in New York arranging for the actors' transportation to Dallas and finalizing contracts with Actors' Equity and the Dramatists Guild, Margo flew back to Texas. Work had progressed on transforming the auditorium of the Gulf Oil building into a 198-seat theatre-in-the-round. Seats mounted on carpeted, stepped platforms surrounded the twenty-four-foot-by-twenty-foot playing area on four sides, with three rows of seats on two sides and four and five rows of seats on the other two sides. An unexpected windfall was the donation of upholstered theatre seats by Dallas residents Phil and Dolly Isley, the parents of actress Jennifer Jones. Although Margo would have liked the flexibility of six, three aisleways provided for entrances and exits. Since she believed that the chief virtue of theatre-in-the-round was intimacy, the first row of seats was on the same level as the stage, giving the audience the feeling that they were in the same room with the actors.

In theatre-in-the-round, lights serve as a curtain to open and close scenes, suggest the physical setting, and create atmosphere and mood. With the help of production assistant Jack Warden, Joe Londin installed the Mielziner-designed lighting system, which was controlled from a booth behind the last row of seats. A three-turntable sound system and amplifiers would supply pre- and post-show music, sound cues, and musical bridges between scenes. In a theatre without realistic settings, Margo knew that imaginative and artistic lighting and sound design were essential.

The acting company arrived on Monday, May 12, after a two-day train trip, and were greeted at the station by Margo, Manning Gurian (who had flown in the day before), board president Gene McDermott, Ross Lawther, and Clinton Anderson. Jean Baptiste Tad Adoue III, just Tad to his friends, the dark-haired, sardonic scion of a prominent Dallas family (his father founded the National Bank of Commerce), was also on hand to welcome the actors. He had become a close friend of Margo's and volunteered his time as an assistant to Manning Gurian, and he often served as Margo's chauffeur. Several board of trustees members were also present to help transport the company to their rustic lodgings, air-conditioned cabins at a local tourist hotel called The Last Frontier—a name that immediately inspired bad jokes and black humor among the transplanted New Yorkers. After a quick lunch, the company reassembled at Margo's house for a three o'clock rehearsal.

Margo liked to say that a day without a rehearsal was a day wasted. After years of planning and working and riding an emotional roller coaster, the first rehearsal of Theatre '47 had arrived. It was a warm May day, and Margo wore one of her favorite sundresses and her comfortable old ballet slippers. She pushed her short dark hair behind her ears, brandished her pencil, smoked cigarette after cigarette, and beamed enthusiasm and energy at the actors. This was her world, the world she had worked so hard to create—encircled by a company of actors, reading a brand-new script.

The first play they read was William Inge's *Farther Off from Heaven*, a realistic drama set in a small midwestern town during the 1920s. Written out of Inge's experience growing up in Independence, Kansas, the play involves the problems and frustrations of the Campbell family—a mother and father who bicker over money, a son who is afraid of the dark at the top of the stairs and is hounded by bullies who call him a sissy, a daughter convinced she is homely, and Mrs. Campbell's chattering sister and her long-suffering husband. With compassion and a delicate comic touch, Inge transforms the story of an ordinary family into compelling theatre. Although Margo was advised to open with *Summer and Smoke*, she felt that that would have been cheating somehow. By beginning her season with William Inge's play, she would immediately communicate that her theatre's purpose was to help unknown playwrights.

After a break for cocktails and a picnic dinner, the company read *How Now, Hecate* by Martyn Coleman. Although Inge would not arrive in Dallas until Thursday, playwright Coleman was present at the first reading of his play, a farcical spoof of supernaturalism involving a writer, an unscrupulous actress, and a sorceress who appears every seven years.

The next morning the company rehearsed in the studios of WFFA, a local radio station, since the theatre was still being renovated. They read *Hedda Gabler*, the third play and the only classic of the season. *Hedda* was a touchstone for Margo: in her college thesis she had examined the play as a cautionary tale of thwarted hopes; she had directed it in Ojai, California, her first community-theatre production; and she had chosen it for the inaugural season of the Houston Community Players. Margo empathized with Hedda, saying that Hedda had a potential for stature and a "passionate desire to find great beauty in life," but was destroyed by "her fear of scandal, her concern with other people's opinion and above all, by her lack of interest in anything her environment can provide."

In the afternoon the company moved on to *Summer and Smoke*. As his contribution to the theatre, Tennessee had waived all royalties on the play during its Dallas run. Set in two moods, a summer and a winter in Glorious Hill, Mississippi, the play focuses on the character of Alma Winemiller, a minister's high-strung daughter who embodies the "smoke" of the title. Alma (Spanish for "soul") lives in an idealized world of the spirit and rejects the physicality, the earthiness of the wild young Dr. Buchanan, the "summer" of the title. In the course of the play the characters change, but Alma's realization that a life spent denying sensuality is inhuman comes too late for her to find happiness with Dr. Buchanan, who plans to marry someone else. Margo considered this play the jewel of her season, calling it a "sensitive drama about the quest of the spirit and the flesh and their battle as they meet and part and meet again."

That evening the company read *Third Cousin* by Vera Mathews, a light farce with a slight story. The plot involves a widow who is suddenly given mystical powers by her dead third cousin. This play, typical summer-stock fare, was not Margo's first choice but was selected after negotiations for another play fell through.

Toward a National Theatre

"I honestly wish I were five people," Margo told a friend. A daily rehearsal schedule of nine to twelve hours rehearsing three plays at once, supervising construction on the theatre, overseeing the publicity and ticket campaign, making phone calls, writing letters, and playing peacemaker to an overworked staff whose tempers and patience were stretched thin filled her days and nights, giving her little time to sleep or eat. A happy result, she felt, was that she lost ten pounds.

Playwrights William Inge and Martyn Coleman lived in the Burford estate guest cottages (Margo had moved to an apartment above the garage) and were constantly available for rehearsals as well as late-night script conferences. Two years younger than Margo, Bill Inge was overwhelmed at actually seeing his first play produced. He sat in rehearsals chewing his fingernails, and couldn't think of anything to say when she asked his opinion on script changes or production decisions, usually deferring to her suggestions. To support himself, Inge had accepted a teaching job at Washington University in St. Louis, but like Margo he loathed the academic life. With this production of his first play, he began to believe that he could be a writer. English-born Coleman, who had recently become an American citizen, revised his play during rehearsals, cutting out repetitive scenes, but Margo was not pleased with the cluttered plot and all the stage business, complaining that there were "too many things to drink—coffee, sherry, brandy, brew, castor oil." Tennessee, who was in the middle of casting A Streetcar Named Desire for a December opening in New York, wrote that it broke his heart to miss the rehearsal period in Dallas because he felt very hopeful about Summer and Smoke, even though he thought its romantic qualities expressed Margo more than they did him. He told her that she would have first option on bringing the play to New York, but he wanted her to wait until the following year so that his two plays would not be unfairly compared and he would have time to make revisions.

As usual Margo enjoyed her work with playwrights, but perhaps because of last-minute planning and inadequate preparation, she had managed to hire a group of temperamental actors who complained continually about their accommodations, the grueling schedule, the Texas heat, their roles, and their billing, their complaints taxing her formidable patience. Many of them were not used to working in a company, and a three-week rehearsal period was certainly not enough time to foster a unified feeling. In small, "sweet-spirited" ways, though, Margo tried to bring the company together. Birthdays were celebrated, and she urged her board members to entertain the actors and make them feel welcome. These considerate touches were little compensation, however, for actors who felt they were sentenced to thirteen weeks in the blazingly hot and boring boondocks.

On the other hand, the young production assistants, who scoured Dallas for properties, furniture, and secondhand clothes, prepared and rehearsed their small parts faithfully, cleaned bathrooms, and ran errands, managed despite all this to bristle with high spirits, energy, and enthusiasm. Margo thought that red-headed, blue-eyed Jack Warden, the waggish prankster of the group, was a "talent in the rough" who had "that rare wonderful quality known as charm plus comedy sense and timing . . . a real potential personality." The athletic Warden, a New Jersey native who later became a successful movie actor, says now, "Let's face it—I was a lifeguard in a pool—Margo gave me the first break I ever had."

Although Margo tried to maintain a cool, noninterfering profile in the technical and production management areas, which were Joanna Albus's responsibility, she often had to play diplomat when Joanna's short temper alienated and irritated her staff. Joanna wanted recognition in her own right but again found herself in Margo's shadow. At one point in 1946 she had been considered an associate director, but despite her role in founding the theatre, she did not have a top position and made less money than Margo, Manning Gurian, and Joe Londin. While Joanna certainly had the organizational skills for her job, successful stage managers need to be unflappable paragons of tact and good humor. With no formal theatre training and only one assistant stage-managing job to her credit, Joanna lacked experience. When faced with tension and disorder, she tended to become hysterical. The two women presented a united front in public, but privately they often didn't speak for days. Finally, when the situation became intolerable, Margo moved from the Burford estate into an air-conditioned apartment at the Stoneleigh Hotel, where Manning Gurian had a room one floor down.

Settled at the Stoneleigh, Margo hired Floyd McDaniel, short, stout, and warm-hearted, to take care of her personal needs. Floyd worked Monday through Friday buying groceries, cooking meals for Margo and her guests, washing clothes, and cleaning. Often she stayed late to serve drinks and pass hors d'oeuvres when Margo entertained. Blacks were not allowed in the hotel's main elevator, so if parties lasted past 10:00 P.M. when the service elevator had stopped running, Margo would accompany McDaniel downstairs and past the disapproving looks of the hotel manager. In 1947 Dallas was a segregated city, and while Margo never overtly challenged the ingrained racism, she invited members of the black community to preview performances at her theatre, hired the first black actors ever to appear professionally in a civic theatre in

Dallas, and helped found a black community theatre. Through Floyd McDaniel, who provided a sane, nurturing center for Margo's erratic lifestyle, made her favorite black-eyed peas and cornbread, and teased her about Manning, Margo met other black people who became her friends. McDaniel said later that it was "the easiest work I ever did," and Margo paid her the top wage for domestic labor. Their relationship was more than a business arrangement, however; it was a loving friendship that would last for years.

AT THE END OF MAY, the company began rehearsing in the theatre, setting entrances and exits, timing sound and light cues, making final adjustments on costumes. Most of the costumes for the season were rented from Brooks Costume in New York, others were purchased, and board member Jed Mace, a Dallas designer, volunteered his time and staff to fit and freshen the clothes. He also consulted on set design and helped to locate antique furniture and properties.

Business manager Gurian reported to Margo that every opening night was sold out, and six hundred season subscriptions had been purchased. Reservations for the June 3 opening had been made by playgoers from as far away as Los Angeles, New York, and Mexico City, as well as from Oklahoma City, Houston, and Fort Worth. Messages flooded in from around the country. Vinton Freedley, president of ANTA, wired, "We are confident that your theatre will be recognized as one of the first important moves toward a truly national theatre."

In her modest 198-seat theatre, Margo had united two major forces in twentieth-century theatre—the aspirations of the art-theatre movement launched in the beginning of the century by the Provincetown Players and continued in the 1930s by the Group Theatre, and the move toward decentralization of the theatre that had reached its height in the 1920s with the community-theatre movement and then in the 1930s with Hallie Flanagan's Federal Theatre Project. To this synthesis she added her own unique contributions, and a new pattern began to emerge. Margo's theatre, the prototype for a national theatre, was incorporated as a nonprofit institution—the first modern nonprofit, professional resident theatre. The temptation to reduce artistic standards in order to earn larger profits was thus avoided. The staff and company, hired for an entire season, had stability and permanence. Supported by subscriptions, the theatre was ongoing, escaping the "hit or flop" syndrome of the commercial theatre. Artistic success, not just success at the box office, determined a play's worth. Her theatre grew out of its Dallas community, supported by donations and subscriptions. Margo had learned from the Federal Theatre Project that there was a vast national audience hungry for quality theatre in their own communities. The noncommercial status of her theatre allowed her to take risks and in particular to present new plays, producing the first tentative work of new playwrights and thereby giving them a chance to learn and grow and go on to write their mature work. She knew that without developing new playwrights and without productions of the classics of world drama, theatre would wither and die. Although her choice of theatre-in-the-round, which eliminated the proscenium stage that was a standard of the commercial Broadway theatre, was purely a practical, economic decision, the arena stage of Theatre '47—the first professional arena theatre in the United States—led to increased intimacy between actors and audience, innovations in lighting and set design, and offered an inexpensive way to create a theatre.

Even while Margo was consumed with the task of opening her theatre, she continued to focus on the horizon, on larger issues facing the American theatre. Under the boundless, piercingly blue Texas sky, a sky which invited grand dreams, she produced press releases, publicity articles, and speeches promoting Theatre '47 and pounding out the theme that had become part of her pulse, a steady rhythm, a cadence repeating over and over—"national theatre . . . every large city . . . decentralization . . . nonprofit, resident company . . . new plays and classics—we have to have it . . . we must have it."

To honor Margo on the opening of Theatre '47, Gilmor Brown of the Pasadena Playhouse wrote to say that she had been awarded the Playhouse's Gilmor Brown Medal for "outstanding creative and artistic achievement," especially in her work with new playwrights. The McDermotts delivered a note to Margo and the company saying, "From the shades and shadows of a dream, you have made possible the sunlight and substance of a reality." Tennessee sent a letter and a wire wishing her a brilliant opening and telling her that she was a girl who could do anything. Her parents and brothers did not plan to attend the opening. In fact, not one member of her family ever attended a production at her Dallas theatre. Of course, in 1947 a trip from Livingston to Dallas seemed out of the question for her parents, who rarely traveled far from their own little town. But the distance between them was more than just geographical. Margo lived in another world, a world they did not share. This fact did not change their feelings for her or their pride in her accomplishments, however, and they sent her an opening-night gift they knew she would cherish—a box of fresh flowers from Martha Pearl's garden.

On June 3, opening day, Margo distributed personal notes to each member of her staff and company. While they made last-minute preparations, Margo, dressed in a new low-cut, sand-colored tulle evening gown, her hair freshly styled, went to the foyer to greet her audience. Arms outstretched, she welcomed George Freedley, the critic of the *New York Morning Telegraph*, who had flown out to review this first performance of Theatre '47. Other old friends arrived, including playwright Ted Apstein and actor Sidney Holmes and his wife Malvina from Houston. Board members who had enjoyed cocktail parties and dinner parties prior to the 8:15 opening arrived in expansive, buoyant spirits. Margo welcomed the McDermotts, the DeGolyers, Elizabeth Ann McMurray, Sam Acheson, the Braniffs, the Kramers, and was introduced to all their guests. Board member Betty Winn recalls that Margo "wanted the theatre to move into people's lives as it had into hers. She drew out of people a kind of dedication to the theatre. . . . And she did this by standing at that front door and personally greeting everybody who came to every play. She was remarkable at remembering names and faces." When she couldn't remember a specific name, she disguised that fact by using endearments like "baby" or "darlin'" or "honey." To all the newspaper people Margo gave special smiling attention, seeing that John Rosenfield quickly found his aisle seat on the second row next to the lobby entrance.

At a time when gasoline sold for seventeen cents a gallon and cigarettes for seventeen cents a pack, Theatre '47 ticket prices of $2.50 for evening performances and $1.80 for matinees were a bargain compared to Dallas road show prices of $3.25–$3.60 a seat. Season tickets for all five plays were available as well, but were not discounted. John Rosenfield told his readers that Theatre '47 offered Broadway-quality productions at substantially less than the Broadway price of $3.60–$4.80 a ticket. Production assistant Clint Anderson took tickets and ushered audience members to their seats, reminding people on the front-row aisles to keep their feet tucked under the seats "because the actors might trip over [them] on their entrances," and guiding others across the stage and around the furniture to their seats.

With all of the 198 seats filled, Margo took a place on the steps, and the houselights dimmed. They came up on the dusty, faded living room of the Campbell house in Kansas. A hand-crank phonograph (actually played onstage), a worn rug, a sewing basket, and well-used furniture provided the setting, achieved at a cost of $134.19—the eight-dollar phonograph the most expensive prop. The beginning of a staircase was suggested by three steps at the end of one of the aisles. Betty Winn said that when she saw *Farther Off from Heaven*, with the action two feet away from the audience, with "a husband and wife bickering right in front of our eyes; it was almost too poignant, too intimate." The play, George Freedley observed, "completely won the hearts of the audience in this new theatre in the round experiment."

At the end of the performance, the audience burst into prolonged applause, calling for the author and Margo to take a bow. A greatly embarrassed William Inge rose to his feet for a quick bow, and Margo ducked out of the theatre with a wave. Carole Goodner and Wilson Brooks, who played husband and wife Sarah and Andrew Campbell, received mixed reviews, some critics feeling that the glamorous Goodner was miscast as a Kansas housewife, but Rebecca Hargis was singled out for her performance as daughter Irene. Mr. Inge, said John Rosenfield, "has a sure instinct for punch scenes and also a good ear for colloquial speech." George Freedley wrote that while the play "would probably seem too slight for Broadway were it removed from the arena and hidden behind footlights," Inge could "write excellent comic dialogue and invoke a mood of nostalgia through his well-articulated characters." Freedley also praised Margo's staging and handling of the actors. "More companies of this sort should be founded," he said. "If Margo Jones has the success she deserves, it will undoubtedly be an encouragement to other communities."

After the opening, the exhausted but exhilarated company and staff celebrated at a party given by a board member at Brook Hollow Country Club. It seemed they were a success, but could they continue to draw an audience? The well-established Starlight Operettas with summer productions of *Showboat*, *Blossomtime*, *No, No, Nanette*, *The Student Prince*, *The Desert Song*, and even Margaret Truman in concert brought huge audiences to Fair Park, but would people come to see straight drama?

In its week's run of eight performances, *Farther Off from Heaven* played to two-thirds capacity, the amount budgeted by Manning Gurian to meet operating expenses. Martyn Coleman's farce *How Now, Hecate* opened June 10. Coleman had lived in Yugoslavia for two years and had studied black magic there. His play required stage trickery and occult effects, mostly created with colored light, dry ice, and an offstage thunder sheet. In the play a sorceress turns an actress into a cat. As Margo said later, "It is possible to use animals in theatre-in-the-round, but they will drive you insane." A cat they named Hecate rehearsed like a trouper but on opening night, when she heard applause for the first time, clawed the actress who was holding her and sent them both into the lap of a gentleman who kindly escorted them to an exit. The theatre was so intimate, one writer noted, that during a backgammon game in *Hecate*, when a character announced "six and four" after a roll of the dice, a man on the first row who could see the game clearly muttered, "Craps." While John Rosenfield called the play little more than a diversion, Margo felt that it needed great farce acting, something it was not getting in her production, and believed that she had failed to find an appropriate style for the play. Again, audiences were at two-thirds capacity, and the theatre was barely hanging on financially.

The difficulty, summed up by one observer, was selling "Dallas theatre-goers schooled for years in nothing more than the traditional Broadway hit roadshowing the sticks" on "first-run plays, appearing out of nowhere without the benefit of a couple of years of build-up from a Broadway run." If she couldn't lick this problem, Margo knew that her entire project was doomed. The board agreed to spend more money on promotion, and during the third week, with *Hecate* and *Farther Off from Heaven* in rotating repertory, they boosted sales by buying blocks of tickets and inviting guests. One writer felt that the public must be "fast asleep not to be flocking to Theatre '47."

In the fourth week, however, Ibsen's classic *Hedda Gabler* attracted audiences to the theatre, responding to a title that they recognized. Carole Goodner and Wilson Brooks played husband and wife again, this time Hedda and George Tesman. The 1890s period was depicted through costumes, hairstyles, and borrowed antique furniture and props. In his first unqualifiedly enthusiastic review for Theatre '47, John Rosenfield said that the arena stage "may be just the milieu *Hedda Gabler* has needed for half a century." "Never before," he wrote, "had we found *Hedda* so natural and so human, a story of persons instead of a saga of personages. To the surface came the Ibsen humor; not hearty fun, to be sure, but humor, nevertheless, or rather mordant wit. The audience discovered it could laugh with Ibsen at Professor Tesman's naivete, at Hedda's outrageous perverseness . . . at Judge Brack's cynical gallantries." At the end of the play, Margo found it most effective to eliminate Carole Goodner's curtain call after Hedda's suicide. The production proved to be so popular that twenty-five to fifty people were turned away at seven out of the eight performances.

While final rehearsals continued on *Summer and Smoke*, the fifth week offered a rotating repertory of the first three plays. Attendance took a downward slump that week during the Fourth of July holiday but hit its peak during the sixth week with the world premiere of *Summer and Smoke*.

Williams's play strained Margo's ingenuity and the technical capacities of the theatre and the staff to the limit. The play has four settings: the stone angel fountain, the Winemiller rectory, Doctor Buchanan's office, and the arbor at Moon Lake Casino. Williams also asked for a great expanse of sky in the background which, in the night scenes, would be splashed with familiar constellations and the Milky Way, and he wanted a Fourth of July fireworks scene. On a small twenty-four-by-twenty-foot arena stage, four distinct sets and a sky cyclorama would be impossible. Instead Margo staged the scenes with a minimum of set pieces and properties, like the small stone birdbath with its carved angel. Guided by Williams's suggestion that "everything possible should be done to give an unbroken fluid quality to the sequence of scenes," Margo melded the prologue and thirteen scenes of the play into a seamless whole, primarily with flexible, imaginative use of light and music to bridge scenes and the use of actors in character to shift props and furniture. For the most part, she did not impose detailed blocking but instead worked improvisationally with the actors to find staging patterns that pleased her. She moved around the house, looking down on the action, visualizing the play from above as the audience would see it, allowing the movement to flow from the four points of the compass. She coined terms to describe her direction on the arena stage. "Making the rounds" meant that an actor should find a motivation to face in more than one direction during a scene, while making the movement appear natural. Or she might tell actors to "pull down the girdle," which meant that if they were getting laughs with a funny facial expression, they should add comic body movements so that audience members sitting behind them could be amused as well. Envious of the continuous, unbroken quality of motion pictures, she sought to achieve a similar effect with her staging, eliminating waits and shortening pauses between scenes.

Audiences and critics raved about Katharine Balfour's lyrical portrayal of the neurotic Alma Winemiller. One audience member who found the character remarkably believable exclaimed, "Why, she's just like my aunt!" Rosenfield felt that *Summer and Smoke* was Williams's best play, his pure essence. Soon, Margo would find out how Tennessee and Audrey Wood felt about her production. Although she had asked Tennessee to come for rehearsals and the opening, he felt overworked and tired, and said that he would come with Audrey Wood for the final repertory week in early August.

The last play of the season, *Third Cousin*, a lighthearted romp for actors and audiences, became the season's comedy hit, finishing second to *Summer and Smoke* in ticket sales. The last two weeks of the season, July 29–August 10, were devoted to a festival presenting all five plays. Production assistant Jack Warden, who played several small roles in addition to his technical duties, recalls that during repertory "you'd wonder sometimes—which play are we doing now?"

On Wednesday, July 30, a contingent of influential theatre people flew into Dallas's Love Field. Brooks Atkinson of the *New York Times*; Vinton Freedley, producer and president of ANTA; Robert Breen, executive secretary of ANTA; Sherman and Marjorie Ewing, Broadway producers; and Milton Lewis, a talent scout for Paramount Studios, were met by a reception committee of

Margo, Gene McDermott, John Rosenfield, and Arthur Kramer. They were whisked out of the Texas heat to their cool hotels and a luncheon hosted by McDermott.

"Something of consequence is rising here in addition to the thermometer," announced Brooks Atkinson to his New York readers. He told them he found theatre-in-the-round refreshing, establishing a "wonderful feeling of intimacy with the audience" and having the practical advantage of making silly plays more bearable in the theatre. Although he sat through *How Now, Hecate* and *Third Cousin* without groaning, they were merely tolerable, he said, to a "heat-stricken visitor." He imagined, though, that to the rest of the audience these two plays must have offered more excitement than staying home with the radio. To William Inge he offered encouragement for a sincere effort at presenting homely truths. Theatre '47 merited distinction, he wrote, for its production of *Hedda Gabler*. "The characters of Hedda and George Tesman have never seemed more vivid, immediate and vital to this day than in the acting of Carol Goodner and Wilson Brooks." It was to Williams's script, however, that he gave the highest praise, saying, "This is a lovely play. He has drawn the characters with tenderness. The dramatic ideas are mature and honest. The writing is perfect in lucidity and tone." Atkinson, aware of Margo's desire to bring the play to New York, warned of a danger, a calculated risk, in bringing the play to Broadway. "Its buoyant loveliness," he said, "might disappear into the fly loft. For the magic of the informal staging in Theatre '47 has completely unpacked the heart of Williams's poignant narrative. The Broadway style is seldom that sensitive."

TENNESSEE, PANCHO, AND Audrey Wood arrived for the Saturday performance of *Summer and Smoke*. Although Tennessee had told Audrey Wood earlier that he would not take Pancho to conservative Dallas where their relationship would not be understood, Pancho did accompany him, probably after assurances from Margo that there wouldn't be any problems. An astonished and impressed Wood noted the "smart crowd" gathered at the theatre — producers, show business people, even Brooks Atkinson. "The night was truly remarkable," she said. "Margo was a pioneer." She enjoyed the performance, which was well received by the audience, including Williams, who shouted "bravo," applauded the actors, and later assured Margo that she had given his play a brilliant production. Afterward, the McDermotts gave a gala garden dinner party for the company and staff, visiting critics, New York and California theatre people, Wood, Tennessee, and Pancho. Audrey Wood marveled at the elegant surroundings, the orchestra, and the servants passing food and champagne. Seeing the New Yorker's amazement at the gathering, an amused Dallasite with tongue firmly in cheek told her, "Why, it's just a small Texas party."

Another party for just Margo, Tennessee, Pancho, and company members followed in Williams's Hotel Adolphus suite. Tennessee had ordered lots of food and pitchers of martinis. Rebecca Hargis, barely out of her teens, who had been given her first drink of Scotch by Margo, was now given her first martini by Tennessee. "Lethal," she remembers. The party raged all night, turning into a bacchanalia, releasing the pent-up stresses and strains of the season. One actor lost his false teeth down the toilet, others gave up more than teeth, and everyone reported to work the next day with a throbbing hangover. They deserved a celebration—Theatre '47 had ten thousand dollars in working capital to launch the fall season, a scrapbook filled with favorable press clippings, and a growing audience.

Weeks of constant production had left Margo with an office piled with neglected correspondence. First, she wrote to ask audience members if they preferred classics or new scripts and also which production of the season they had liked best. Then she wrote letters thanking everyone who had supported her theatre—to Gilmor Brown, for his inspiring example; to Jo Mielziner, for his practical design assistance and high standards; to Audrey Wood, for casting and script consultations. She urged the play editors at Warner Brothers and Columbia Pictures to consider William Inge for a Hollywood writing job. Reporters, critics, friends, actors, playwrights, contributors, technicians all heard from her. Ignored for weeks, a request for advice on how graduates could "break into theatre" from her college newspaper at Texas Woman's University was given special attention. She wrote that she detested those words, that there was no reason to "break into" anything. "What you should do," she said, "is sow some seeds . . . and let them grow."

She had done just that. She needed and deserved a vacation, but her seedling, still small and tender, demanded constant care and attention. And why take a vacation when you were already doing what you loved? She and Manning planned to return to New York to organize the fall season, and then she would visit Tennessee in Provincetown to discuss *Summer and Smoke* and read plays. Yes, work was recreation enough. She didn't have time to rest or reflect. When a reporter asked her to review all the obstacles that had hindered the opening of Theatre '47 since its birth in 1945, Margo wouldn't oblige. "Forget it," she told him, her cat's eyes burning with intensity. "What we are going to do is more important."

Man of the Year

ARGO WAS falling in love, and she brought to romance the same passion and sense of drama she brought to theatre. She told Manning, "I breathe, think, dream, and live through you." She saw him as one who not only shared her love of the theatre but also seemed to share her vision of its future. Here was a man she could pour out her soul to, she thought, a writer—an artist —who would listen to her dreams and share her deepest longings. As with Jerry Coray, she cast herself as a romantic heroine, even at times a breathless ingenue, and she played the role to the full, sometimes sounding in her letters to Manning like a character Tennessee might have created. "You'd think I'd grow up . . . ," she wrote, "but there's something about articulation in any form—be it your voice on the phone—your words when we're together —your letters and wires when we're apart—there's something definite and wonderful about it—it's like some kind of extra special ceremony—with fanfare and banners flying—sky rockets and bands playing—yet it has the feeling of a pipe organ echoing in a high cathedral—or a natural ceremony like a little silver slipper of a moon coming up or a high wind blowing through the pines or rain falling on shining city pavement or sunshine glistening on telephone wires or the odor of wild violets nestled deep in the shadows of trees—I have come to value articulation very highly—natural beautiful words that come because of feeling and thought—I want to be with you as much as I can—I want to work with you—live with you—love you—be all things to you—." Love like this was a miracle, she thought, a miracle of "real happiness and faith and trust and hope and inspiration and wonderment and truth and beauty." But love implied responsibility too, real responsibility, and she vowed they would give back this miracle to the world in full measure. They would work together, create beautiful plays together. They talked about marriage but were so busy, it seemed the "love and obey" life would have to wait.

IN MARGO'S SINGLE-MINDED pursuit of her vision, her affairs with Jerry Coray, with Paul Moor, with Sonny Koch had been secondary to her work. In Manning Gurian she had found both a professional partner and, she thought, the love of her life. At thirty-six, she realized that she was no "spring chicken." Her firing from *Joan of Lorraine* and Sonny Koch's marriage had left her contemplating her future and feeling more vulnerable. She had succeeded in creating her theatre and now she was ready to fall in love, and it couldn't be an ordinary love affair, it had to be a great romantic dream of love, like Alma's love for Doctor Buchanan in *Summer and Smoke*. Although she knew that Manning's background in the New York commercial theatre was vastly different from her own experience, and while she realized that their "deep down philosophies were different," she believed "one thousand percent" in the possibility of their happiness. It was a welcome release for her to have someone to share intimate moments and her theatre plans and burdens, and Manning played his part with consummate skill, the handsome, soft-spoken hero who awakens his beloved to passion.

Outwardly Margo gave little indication that she had fallen in love. She did not confide in her women friends, especially not Joanna Albus since she had been involved with Manning first. Joanna said later that she never knew Margo on a personal level, that Margo did not confide in her except about the theatre. Mabel Duke, the theatre's publicist, recalled, "I don't think Margo really knew the kind of friendship most of us know. She wasn't capable of meeting a girlfriend and going to lunch—that would have been killing time and out of the question." Friends like Elizabeth Ann McMurray, the energetic bookstore owner and Dallas tastemaker, were either on her theatre board or were workers at her theatre, and with members of both groups she maintained affectionate but not intimate relationships. She thought of the actors in her company as her family, her children. Actress Louise Latham recalls that "Margo was everyone's mother and good mothers tend to take it all on themselves and don't lay their own pain on other people." Houston friends Malvina Holmes and Dr. Jean Barraco knew the dynamic theatre leader who was sensitive to their personal problems, but Margo rarely shared her own doubts with them. To be successful in Dallas, an effective leader, she had to remain aloof from the petty squabbles, the gossip, and the factional disputes. She remained in control, above the social "ladies-who-lunch" crowd while still currying their favor. In truth, the "daddy's girl" from Livingston preferred the company of men, surrounding herself with attractive men who adored her, like Tad Adoue and production manager Jonathan Seymour and, of course, Manning and her old pal Tennessee.

It was to Tennessee that she confided her unhappiness with Joanna's work at Theatre '47. In turn Tennessee, who liked Joanna, advised her to make a life for herself in New York, and secured for her a position as assistant stage manager of A *Streetcar Named Desire*. Although publicly Margo acknowledged Joanna's contributions in starting Theatre '47, she did not like sharing the spotlight with another woman. Understandably, Joanna wanted to make her own way, free of Margo's shadow, and she accepted Tennessee's offer. Before Joanna left for New York, she and Margo had a talk that, Margo said, meant "a chance for some real understanding." Apparently Joanna felt differently: she told Tennessee that a "mysterious wall" had come between her and her old friend.

A N   O B L I G A T O R Y   three-day visit with her mother and her frail Aunt Stella in Amarillo in August did not quell Margo's good spirits. She endured a party given for her by the Amarillo Little Theatre, ate jello and peaches and pink ice cream, sneaked cigarettes, drank coffee instead of Scotch, and went to bed every night at nine o'clock. In the middle of August, she traveled to New York for a two-week stay to confer with Manning about their commercial production of *Summer and Smoke*, to gather new scripts, and to make plans for the twenty-week 1947–48 season.

While she was in New York, Margo joined Tennessee, Pancho, and Joanna on Cape Cod, where Tennessee had rented a beach house near Provincetown. Manning, who was working now behind the scenes as Margo's producing partner as well as the business manager of the theatre, urged her to get the contracts on *Summer and Smoke* finalized while she was there. Tennessee had assured Margo that she would produce and direct the play, and he wanted the two of them to work together without outside interference. He asked her to keep quiet about their arrangement so that he could enhance his bargaining position with Irene Selznick, the producer of A *Streetcar Named Desire*.

The group relaxed in Tennessee's ramshackle beach house, settling in to some serious drinking. The highlight of Margo's four-day stay was the arrival of Marlon Brando, who had been sent to Provincetown by *Streetcar* director Elia Kazan to read the part of Stanley Kowalski. Brando hitchhiked to the Cape, arriving just at dusk. He found the fuses in the house blown out and the plumbing stopped up. In less than an hour, he had everything working again. Tennessee said, "You'd think he had spent his entire antecedent life repairing drains." Around midnight, Brando sat down with the script of *Streetcar* and read the part of Stanley. According to Tennessee, after less than ten minutes Margo jumped up and shouted, "Get Kazan on the phone right away! This is the greatest reading I've ever heard. . . ." Tennessee shared her feeling, and cast the young actor immediately.

Man of the Year

ON HER TRIP HOME, Margo stopped in New Orleans to pack Tennessee's papers and the personal effects that he had left behind in his subletted apartment. She arranged for storage of his and Pancho's trunks and sent the receipts and keys to Audrey Wood. Back in sweltering Dallas, thankful to be in her air-conditioned apartment, she began reading scripts and applications from over two hundred actors. The opening of the theatre was scheduled for early November, when the building would be available following the State Fair. Rehearsals would begin October 7, allowing Margo only a month to option new scripts and hire a company of actors. She had already decided on three Tennessee Williams one-acts and Manning's new comedy, *Lemple's Old Man*. William Inge had sent her *Front Porch* (an early draft of *Picnic*), and although Margo told Inge that she was "quite moved by parts" of the play, she felt that it needed more work before it would be ready for production. Tennessee wrote from Provincetown that he was working on a new play called *Quebrada*, set in a hotel on a cliff overhanging the Pacific. The play would illuminate the moral dilemmas of the times, he said. Margo didn't get excited about this new script, though, since she knew that soon the pressures of rehearsals for *Streetcar* would consume all Tennessee's energy, leaving him little time to write.

Before she returned to New York to option scripts and hire her company, she wrote her Houston friend Dr. Barraco a chatty letter, inviting her to the November opening of the theatre. Margo said that while she was sleeping just fine now and was not under any pressure, she wanted to keep her weight down. Could she have some more of those "get thin—keep awake" pills that Doc had prescribed for her in Houston? She promised to take only half a pill, twice a day.

IN HER ROOM at the Royalton Hotel in New York, Margo interviewed actors, many of them sent by agent Audrey Wood. Tod Andrews, Wilson Brooks, and Betty Greene Little stayed on from the summer season, along with production assistants Clinton Anderson, Jack Warden, Marilyn Putnam, and Rebecca Hargis, all of whom would also play small acting roles. Jonathan Seymour moved up to become production and stage manager, replacing Joanna Albus. Five new actors were hired to fill out the company.

Margo lauded the group that she had assembled as "healthy and sane and sweet with no temperaments except talent." The new members included Mary Finney, who had acted at the Pasadena Playhouse and on Broadway; Frances Waller, a blonde ingenue who had begun her career at New York's Neighborhood Playhouse and appeared on Broadway in *Deep Are the Roots*; experienced character actor Vaughan Glaser, who had acted in motion pictures and with Minnie Maddern Fiske in *Hedda Gabler*; actor and singer George Mitchell, who had played on Broadway and at Carnegie Hall; and Mitchell's wife, Katharine Squire, a gifted actress who had performed with the Theatre Guild, played Mrs. Elvsted to Eva Le Gallienne's *Hedda Gabler*, and received critical acclaim for the best performance on Broadway as Miss Sally in *Chicken Every Sunday*. The National Theatre Conference awarded Theatre '47 five hundred dollars for an acting fellowship, and Margo split the award between Charles Taliaferro and her former University of Texas student Louise Latham, who had been working as a model at Neiman-Marcus and waiting for an opportunity to act.

Margo and Manning met with designer and board member Jed Mace at New York's Plaza Hotel to discuss the costumes and sets for the new season. The choice of Mace as designer was a shrewd business and artistic decision. With his partner Bob Rodgers, Mace owned a successful interior design firm and had decorated many showplace estates in the Dallas area. He had invaluable contacts with antique dealers and store owners, and a full-time staff to sew costumes and refurbish furniture. Previously he had designed costumes for the Dallas Little Theatre, but later, after achieving national recognition at Theatre '47 and '48, he also designed for Broadway and touring companies.

With the imaginative and talented Mace as designer, the productions would have a finished, polished look, essential in intimate theatre-in-the-round where the closeness of the audience demands subtlety, precision, and authenticity of materials and construction in costumes and set pieces. Margo told Mace that she had decided to open with Ibsen's *The Master Builder*, hoping to repeat the success of their summer production of *Hedda Gabler*. *The Master Builder* would be followed by the three Williams one-acts. Originally she had also planned to produce Irish writer Vivian Connell's violent, controversial play *The Nineteenth Hole of Europe*, possibly presenting it behind a cocoon of scrim. Nervous about the audience reaction to the gore in this pessimistic play about the future of Europe, she gave the script to critic John Rosenfield and board members Eugene McDermott and Lon Tinkle, who all said that the play was unsuitable for intimate theatre. Consulting with her board about play selection was unusual for Margo, who claimed, not entirely in jest, that she dealt with them best by having two meetings a year, one at the beginning of the season to tell them what she planned to do, and another at the end of the season to tell them why she didn't do it. *Throng O' Scarlet*, another new script by Connell, replaced the controversial play.

Shakespeare's *The Taming of the Shrew* was set for the holiday season, then

Man of the Year

Manning's new play, followed by Wilde's *The Importance of Being Earnest*, Joseph Hayes's *Leaf and Bough*, and Barton MacLane's *Black John*. The season would close with a four-week repertory of the four most popular plays. The season included three classics, four world premieres, and the previously produced Williams plays. Audrey Wood told her that the program she had scheduled was a mighty one, saying that she believed that Margo was one of the few people with enough energy even to conceive of such a season.

In presenting the lineup to designer Jed Mace, Margo rarely gave specific instructions or particular concepts that she wanted him to achieve. Instead she trusted Mace's ability and rarely disputed his design decisions. At the beginning of each season of their working relationship, which spanned several years, Margo would discuss the plays with him, and Mace would come up with a design concept and detailed watercolor renderings. They would go over his work, usually for about an hour, then Margo would say more often than not, "Fine, baby." Mace remembers that he sometimes wanted to talk aesthetics with her, but Margo had little time for theory, relying instead on her instincts and his expertise.

REHEARSALS OF *The Master Builder* began with a reading and dinner afterward for the company and board members at Margo's Stoneleigh apartment. The actors settled in to their various rooms in a local boardinghouse, the cool October weather helping to ease their adjustment to Dallas. Board members welcomed the acting company, inviting them to their homes for dinner, often forming lasting friendships.

Charming Raiberto Comini, a talented portrait photographer and composer who also tutored in French, Italian, and Spanish, and his Irish wife Megan, who had worked for a time as Ernest Hemingway's secretary, had befriended Margo and opened their spacious, elegant home to her actors, indulging the homesick easterners with home-cooked Italian cuisine. When Margo needed new portraits made for publicity purposes, Comini not only took her picture, but reshaped her image into a more glamorous one, teaching her how to apply makeup skillfully and suggesting changes in her hairstyle. To keep her figure, Margo attended modern dance classes every week with Megan Comini. The Cominis' young daughter, Alessandra, enjoyed staying up late for her parents' parties, and especially liked watching her father and Margo dance. Fascinated by the woman with the bright eyes who loved to move to the music of a sensuous tango, Alessandra thought Margo looked just like a large slinky cat.

While she continued to dress casually for rehearsals, usually in basic black slacks and blouse or stretch top and her favorite ballet slippers, for public occasions Margo now wore beautiful, expensive clothes usually purchased from Neiman-Marcus. She insisted that her staff too present a tasteful, suitable appearance in public. Undoubtedly, her relationship with Manning had contributed to her new interest in her looks. For the first time she experienced jealousy when she saw other women admiring or flirting with the handsome Gurian. He liked women, and she suspected that he strayed from time to time, but right now she felt fulfilled and happy anyway.

On opening night of the new season the enthusiastic audience, led by board president Eugene McDermott, who loyally stood and applauded every opening whether he liked the play or not, leapt to their feet shouting, "Margo!" But Margo felt that the stage was the place for actors, and she slipped out of the theatre to the foyer to receive congratulations there. Despite the applause, Ibsen's *The Master Builder* received a lukewarm critical reception. The play tells the story of the successful architect Solness, an artist who, Margo said, "at the pinnacle of his career, begins to disintegrate because he is afraid that he will never again be able to build churches and climb the steeples to place upon them the wreaths of achievement." The play's combination of mysticism and realism appealed to her. John Rosenfield compared Francis Waller, who played the hitchhiking young Viking seeking communion with the architect, to Ingrid Bergman, except for Waller's disconcerting habit of slipping occasionally into an Alabama accent. The audience didn't care, Margo said, they were completely in love with Francis.

Her theatre was a hit. Programs billed her as a Broadway director who chose to work in Dallas. Brooks Atkinson, the critic of the *New York Times*, the newspaper that arbitrated the taste of the country, had decided that Margo Jones was important, and this was good enough for Dallas. Everyone called the theatre simply Margo's, even though the official name was Theatre '47. The theatre *was* her and she was the theatre and everyone knew it.

Board president Gene McDermott hosted a lavish opening-night party, and Margo wore her new red dress, an off-the-shoulder gown with a huge net skirt. A week later she wore the same dress to Dallas's debutante ball at the Baker Hotel, where she said the people looked like *New Yorker* cartoons. Since the event had nothing to do with the theatre, she wondered how "anybody could stand much of this so-called social life in Dallas."

She preferred dinner with Manning at Mario's, their favorite Italian restaurant near the fairgrounds. There they grew friendly with the owners, Mario and Christine Vaccaro, and their young daughter Brenda. Except for company theatre parties, Margo and Manning rarely socialized with the actors or staff.

While she was warm and supportive in her position as managing director, Margo felt that it was necessary to maintain a certain distance. Tad Adoue often joined them, or Elizabeth Ann McMurray, whose bookstore had become the downtown box office for Theatre '47, or sometimes a wealthy patron treated them to dinner. Manning recalls that Margo loved to dance, especially after she had had a few drinks. She didn't care who was around, he says, and would "twirl and twist and be Salome and Isadora." She also liked to read plays or her favorite Tagore poems to him while sitting on the floor of her apartment.

Rehearsals of the three Williams one-acts, preparations for the six other plays she had to direct, and theatre business occupied most of her time. Deciding on the season so late had left her without adequate time to prepare the plays, even though she had directed *The Master Builder, The Taming of the Shrew*, and *The Importance of Being Earnest* before in Houston. Rehearsals, often interrupted by phone calls and meetings, never seemed to be long enough. All she needed, she thought, was more time.

It didn't help that Joanna wrote her ecstatic letters, filled with exclamation marks, raving about her work on *Streetcar*, the brilliance of Elia Kazan, the cast, the play, her new closeness to Tennessee, her terrific crush on Karl Malden, who played Mitch, her meeting with writer Albert Camus, and her total happiness with everything in New York. Joanna also mentioned that she thought sometimes about what was happening below the Mason-Dixon line and wondered how Margo's theatre was doing. The friendship of the two women had always had a strong element of competition. Joanna's job with *Streetcar* was her first theatre position working for someone other than Margo. The friendship that had been on an employer-employee level, with Margo dominating the relationship, had undergone a shift. Having lost Manning to Margo and feeling wronged by Margo's failure to give her equal billing in Dallas, Joanna now relished the opportunity to tell Margo of her experiences working with really important people in New York. It's a sad fact of theatre life that self-esteem often depends upon who's talking to whom, who's in favor and who's out of favor, and personal contact with the people in power is pocketed like currency to be brought out for display and self-aggrandizement and used to purchase new alliances.

For this reason true friendships are extraordinarily precious to theatre people, because they are so difficult to sustain in that ephemeral world. Professional jealousy, distance, insecurity, and lack of time to nurture a relationship play havoc with friendships. During the intense rehearsal period and run of a production, intimate friendships are often formed only to die of neglect when the production closes and everyone moves on to another life and other relationships. Or many theatre artists, like Margo, devote themselves to work, leaving little time for a personal life. Tennessee once told an interviewer that his few close friends—Audrey Wood, Margo Jones, and Jay Laughlin—were all connected with his career. In a statement that was misinterpreted by those who didn't understand the difficulty of sustaining lasting friendships in the theatre, he added, "I am gregarious and like to be around people, but almost anybody will do."

Jo Mielziner, *Streetcar*'s designer, wrote more restrained letters about their problems out of town with finding endings for Tennessee's scenes and about Jessica Tandy's efforts to overcome vocal monotony as Blanche. Along with Manning's eagerness to return to New York whenever possible, these letters only heightened Margo's ambivalence about staying in Dallas with her theatre. It was her dream, what she had wanted, but the problem was she was the only one doing it. Everyone else who mattered in the theatre seemed to be working successfully in New York. One consoling fact was that next year she would be there herself with the production of *Summer and Smoke*.

PERHAPS UNCONSCIOUSLY, Margo had chosen to produce three Williams one-acts while *A Streetcar Named Desire* was in tryouts before its Broadway run. In that way she could feel a part of Tennessee's world. Manning felt, jealously and accurately, that Margo placed Tennessee on a pedestal, and he faulted her for feeling that the playwright could do no wrong. She gave in to Tennessee's every request, Manning complained.

Critic Rosenfield reported that the Williams plays were a welcome change from the plot-heavy, overpopulated traditional one-acts of Ruth Draper and Cornelia Otis Skinner. *The Last of My Solid Gold Watches*, which takes place in a shabby hotel room in Mississippi, centers on the character of Charlie Colton, a seventy-eight-year-old shoe salesman who is talking to a black porter about the good old days. The room was created quite simply with an old-fashioned iron bed, a worn-out rug, a cuspidor, a rocker, and a washbasin. Vaughan Glaser played the old man, and Will Bryant acted the porter, marking the first time a black actor had appeared onstage in a professional Dallas theatre. Publicly the event passed unremarked. John Rosenfield, who attended the Sunday preview performance of each play as well as the opening, never mentioned that blacks were in regular attendance at the preview performances. Board member Betty Winn recalls that blocks of seats were occasionally given to people in the black community, especially when a play was not selling very well. Although Dallas was a segregated city, playgoers somehow accepted that Margo's theatre was governed by her rules; they knew that theatre people were a bit eccentric. When actress Katharine Squire took a bus one day and sat in the section marked "Colored," the bus driver asked her to move into the white section. "I wouldn't move," Squire recalls. Rather than argue with one of Margo's actors, the bus driver just moved the sign instead.

Rebecca Hargis played Willie in the second Williams one-act, *This Property Is Condemned*, a touching play, really an extended soliloquy, about a thirteen-year-old girl who glamorizes the cheap and tawdry life of her dead sister and dreams of following in her path. The previous play's hotel-room furniture and properties were cleared, leaving the stage completely bare. The shadow of a water tank and that of a house with a sign declaring "This property is condemned" were projected on the walls of the exits, providing the only set. Atmosphere was created primarily through lighting, Rebecca Hargis's inventive performance, and the music of a steel guitar.

Katharine Squire played Lucretia, an old maid, in the last play of the evening, *Portrait of a Madonna*. Again the setting was a hotel room, but this time the stage was cluttered with the debris of the aging spinster, who leaves for a mental institution at the end of the play under the delusion that she is expecting a child.

While critics felt that the plays were artistically a success, praising the acting and direction, the public had difficulty accepting an evening of one-acts. In fact, rarely has the professional theatre ever made a success of an evening of one-acts, and Theatre '47's attempt was no exception. Margo believed that while the plays were not united by story, the writing quality would organize them, and that in any case the effort was a worthy one.

The next play, *Throng O' Scarlet*, Vivian Connell's lusty Irish drama set in the fox-hunting country of South Cork, Ireland, challenged the company with its four distinct settings—an upper-class drawing room, a pub, a saddle room, and a slaughter-shed. Margo spent hours rehearsing the complex organization and shifting necessary for the scenes to flow smoothly and thus maintain the necessary illusion. To speed changes, she used a camouflage method for certain scenes, simply covering furniture with burlap. The effect apparently worked, since one audience member recalls the scene in the saddle room as "so realistic . . . you could almost smell the stables." During the slaughter-shed scene when an actor stamped his feet and shouted, "Can't we do something about these rats!", every woman on the first row, Margo reported, "drew up her feet at least fourteen inches from the floor."

Actor Jack Warden, previously unnoticed by the audience except as "a rather plain nondescript creature who had been moving furniture on and off stage," gave an outstanding performance as Mikey in *Throng O' Scarlet*, his first important role. Warden drew the attention of both critics and audience members, who realized that here was an actor to reckon with.

George Mitchell also received good notices for his performance. He was at last getting used to the new experience of theatre-in-the-round. Since Margo's theatre was the only professional theatre-in-the-round in the country, Mitchell's initial introduction to the arena space was frightening. "There is no scenery to turn to in embarrassing moments, no wings to escape into . . . no curtain . . . no nothing but a circular sea of leering, peering faces often closer to you than the nearest actor's," he wrote in an article for the *New York Times*. During his first entrance onto the stage at Theatre '47, he said that his "hands felt enormous, swollen, awkward beyond belief. . . . When another actor leaned over me, I stared intently at him, trying to blot out the mass of eager, bulbous faces right behind him." Soon, however, he began to appreciate the "great freedom of movement, the break from the classic face-front technique . . . and far better try lying to your own mother than attempt to give a false performance before the searching eyes of such a proximate audience."

DURING REHEARSALS OF *Throng*, Margo had been in close touch with Tennessee. He had written about the progress of *Streetcar* and about his difficulties with what he called his "Mexican problem." Pancho, the "problem," had become violent and destructive and given to jealous rages (usually for good reason), and on one occasion had even thrown Tennessee's typewriter out the window. Williams confided that his feeling for Pancho had flown out the window with the typewriter. Margo, who couldn't bear seeing her idol ill-treated, wrote a letter filled with advice, telling Tennessee that he didn't owe anything to Pancho, that he owed himself "every moment of the day to be given to your work and to the people you respect . . . and to someone that you can love and respect too. . . . I've told you before that I think the child is dangerous. . . . He's a leach [sic] and will only bring trouble. . . . Anyone who brings ugliness into life so often shouldn't be allowed to. . . ." Finally Tennessee paid Pancho off with money for a new start and a train ticket to New Orleans. Weeks later, Pancho wrote plaintively to Margo, reminding her of their good times in Provincetown, when Tennessee had painted a bust of a woman with long flowing hair, all done in yellows, greens, and blues and captioned "by that time *Summer and Smoke* were past." Loyal to Tennessee, Margo did not reply.

While Tennessee confided the problems and joys of his love affairs to Margo, she, tellingly, did not do the same. Williams seems not to have known about the extent of Margo's involvement with Manning. The playwright's relationship with his old friend was complex. Margo adored Tennessee as a writer and as a man. In turn, he admired her energy and ability to accomplish things and called her "dearest" and "honey." When they were together, Tennessee was the courtly southern gentleman, flirting and affectionate. Because he had not publicly acknowledged his homosexuality and had a masculine, virile presence, this behavior, of course, led to speculation among Margo's acquaintances that they were having a love affair and to fear among Tennessee's acquaintances that Margo wanted to marry him. In truth, they did love each other, although it was not romantic love but rather a deep friendship based upon similar backgrounds, a satisfying artistic relationship, a respect for each other's talents, and a mutual appreciation of a good time. They had fun together. In a sense, though, Margo was Tennessee's "girl," often serving as his public "date," and she knew instinctively that he would not have welcomed a competitor for her affections.

Almost immediately after *Throng* opened on December 1, Margo flew to New York for the December 3 opening of *Streetcar*. A huge crowd attended the premiere at the Barrymore Theatre, including luminaries like Dorothy Parker, Lillian Hellman, Gypsy Rose Lee, Ruth Gordon, Garson Kanin, Cole Porter, David O. Selznick, Olivia de Havilland, George Cukor, and John Garfield. Margo sat next to Tennessee, across the aisle from Elia and Molly Kazan. The presence of the optimistic Margo did little to soothe Williams's anxiety about the reception of his play, and fraught with worry made worse by a tension headache, he, along with Margo, treated himself to double Scotches at intermissions. He needn't have feared. At the end of the performance, the audience applauded for a full half hour, and later at Williams's apartment, his friends read aloud the glowing reviews, which universally trumpeted the greatness of his play. While Margo celebrated and enjoyed Williams's success with *Streetcar*, she felt that *Summer and Smoke* was the better play. Soon she would have a chance to prove this to a New York audience.

F O L L O W I N G *Streetcar's* triumphant opening, Margo rushed back to Dallas to continue rehearsals for *The Taming of the Shrew* and for Manning's play *Lemple's Old Man*. Directing Shakespeare was a joy for her; she believed that he was the greatest playwright of all time, but she did not "approach his work with awe." She eliminated the play's prologue—a decision that disturbed certain audience members who came to the theatre with tiny pen flashlights and insisted on following the text in their personal copies of the play. The setting depended entirely on fluid lighting and lush Renaissance costuming. Jack Warden, wearing a ridiculous parody of Petruchio's costume, played

Grumio. The women wore outlandish headgear concocted by designer Jed Mace. Four white benches and a table were the only set pieces used.

As Margo gained experience directing in the round, her technique became more assured. In an article for *Theatre Arts*, she wrote that Shakespeare's plays were ideal for the round, for just "doing what comes naturally." Unlike the proscenium stage, which presents a flat picture to the audience, theatre-in-the-round resembles a sculpture. Whenever possible, Margo incorporated dance or stylized choreographic patterns of movement into her direction. She found the use of comic dance movement in some scenes of the *The Taming of the Shrew* very effective.

Because of the intimacy of Theatre '47's stage, she did not have a problem with finding a focus for the action. The size of the playing area, however, limited the choices for placement of furniture and set pieces. Although she used the aisleways and corner spaces, action moved quickly through these weaker areas. A play set on a proscenium stage creates a single effect—that is, everyone in the audience sees the same action. A comic movement elicits a simultaneous reaction. In theatre-in-the-round, however, the same comic movement may have a ripple effect—members of the audience see the movement and laugh at different moments. In theatre-in-the-round, half of the audience may see an actor talking and the other half may see another actor reacting to the conversation. Focus is divided. On the other hand, the proximity of audience and actor permits a subtlety of gesture and emotion difficult to achieve when viewers and players are separated by a proscenium arch.

Margo rarely discussed the negatives of theatre-in-the-round, but in making plans for a new theatre she wanted a larger, more flexible space with at least six entrances and exits.

Lemple's Old Man, Manning's play, opened on December 29. The slight plot involves a spry old man who demonstrates that the old can enjoy life just as much as the young. He makes his first entrance circling the playing area on a bicycle, a novelty for the audience but not enough of a diversion to sustain what is basically a weak play. Set in Brooklyn, the play depends on local color and atmosphere. Although Margo and her actors made a valiant effort to recreate the accents and maintain the illusion of a Brooklyn street scene, the play, critics agreed, needed a few more drafts and some ruthless editing. Manning watched it every night, his stomach in knots, groaning at the audience's cool response to his script.

Although it was little consolation to Manning, Margo realized that the failure of one play wouldn't hurt the theatre. In fact, in this theatre, failure was planned for, expected from time to time, even honorable. To celebrate the theatre's stability and to mark the beginning of the new year, Margo planned a ceremony that became a yearly tradition. Typically, it was an event that involved the audience. On New Year's Eve, the performance began at 9:30 and ended about 11:30 P.M. When the play had ended, the actors passed out paper hats, noisemakers, colorful streamers, and champagne, and invited the audience to join them at the entrance to the theatre. At midnight, Margo, wearing the new full-length mink coat that indicated her arrival as a success in Dallas, where all the important women wore full-length mink coats, and board president Gene McDermott stood on ladders and changed the sign from Theatre '47 to Theatre '48. The audience and the acting company cheered, lifting their glasses in a toast.

John Rosenfield had his tradition too. At the close of each year, in imitation of *Time* magazine, he announced in his *Dallas Morning News* arts column his choice for the city's Man of the Year. On December 31, 1947, he proclaimed that the Man of the Year this year was a woman—Miss Margo Jones of Theatre '47. He wrote, "On the last day of 1947 we can say that we have got Margo's idea at last. She has pursued it with a persistence that could conquer worlds or a steel plant. She has implemented the idea with a practicality that could institute an airplane factory in Grand Prairie. She has done this at small reward to herself financially and at the sacrifice of many opportunities to grow richer if hardly more famous as a director of Broadway plays, several of which she has directed anyway." In case his Dallas readers did not know the significance of her accomplishment, he told them. "The fact remains," he wrote, "that Dallas in its postwar adjustments has come up with a resident theatre that is both radically new and providentially solvent. There is nothing else quite like it in America. In its conception reside the hopes of public-spirited Dallasites for a living stage, the dreams of everybody who writes plays in English and of actors who want to act. This statement is not rhapsody."

It is a credit to John Rosenfield that he never sought to publicize his own role in creating the Dallas theatre, but it is highly doubtful that without his powerful support the theatre could have survived. He was Margo's severest critic in terms of play selection and direction and was sometimes so scathing in his dismissal of an unworthy effort that he outraged her board members. But Rosenfield simply respected Margo enough to tell her the truth, and he carefully separated his criticism of individual productions from his feelings about the theatre as an institution. He was undemonstrative in his manner, unlike Margo, who hugged the roly-poly critic and called him "Rosey" when she was feeling particularly affectionate or when she wanted something. Still,

Martha Pearl Jones and Richard Harper Jones. *Jones Family Archives (JFA)*.

Margo playing in her mother's flowers. *JFA*.

Playing dress-up in her uncle's clothes. *JFA.*

Margo, *l.*, and her sister Stella Nell. *JFA.*

Margo at Texas Woman's University. *JFA.*

Jones family home in Livingston after an ice storm. *JFA.*

Celebrating the Texas Centennial, 1936. *JFA.*

Brooks Atkinson. *From the collection of the Texas/Dallas History and Archives Division, Dallas Public Library (T/DHAD, DPL).*

Arthur "Sonny" Koch. *Courtesy Arthur Koch.*

Margo in 1941. *JFA.*

Gertrude Levy and Bill Goyen, *standing*, at a Houston Community Players audition. *Courtesy Malvina Holmes.*

Del Peppin, *l.*, and Ray Walston in Houston Community Players production of Maxwell Anderson's *Winterset. Courtesy Ray Walston.*

Director of the Houston Community Players. *JFA.*

Richard, Martha Pearl, Richard Harper, Margo, and Charles Jones, 1942. JFA.

Richard, Margo, Bea, and Charles Jones, 1942. JFA.

Eddie Dowling and Margo. *JFA.*

Margo and Laurette Taylor. *JFA.*

Tennessee Williams relaxing in Dallas. *T/DHAD, DPL.*

Margo rehearsing with Canada Lee and *On Whitman Avenue* company. *JFA.*

Ingrid Bergman and Margo. *JFA.*

John Rosenfield. *T/DHAD, DPL.*

Margo surrounded by new scripts—wonderment! *T/DHAD, DPL.*

Rebecca Hargis, Marilyn Putnam, and Joanna Albus, *l. to rt.*, backstage during Theatre '47's opening summer. *Courtesy Rebecca Hargis Turner (RHT)*.

Carole Goodner in Theatre '47 production of *Hedda Gabler*. RHT.

World premiere of William Inge's *Farther Off from Heaven*, with Carole Goodner, *l.*, Wilson Brooks, and Rebecca Hargis. *RHT*.

Young Alma and John—Rebecca Hargis and Martin David—at the angel fountain
in the Theatre '47 world premiere of *Summer and Smoke. Courtesy
Mabel Duke (MD).*

Changing the sign on New Year's Eve. Margo, in her new mink coat, on the ladder; Eugene McDermott, Theater '47 board president, assisting. Tod Andrews (with raised glass), *l.*; Jack Warden and Manning Gurian (in dark suit), *center*; *Louise Latham, far rt.* (behind boy in cap). *MD.*

Manning Gurian. RHT.

Margo with Tennessee Williams during 1948 Broadway production of *Summer and Smoke. NYT Pictures.*

Jack Warden surrounded by Moliere's "learned ladies." *RHT*.

Margo with her staff: *l. to r.*, Tad Adoue, Manning Gurian, Jonathan Seymour.
T/DHAD, DPL.

Theatre '49's world premiere production of Dorothy Parker and Ross Evans's
The Coast of Illyria. RHT.

Dorothy Parker, *center*, at a cocktail party in her Dallas hotel room. *RHT*.

Theatre '52. *JFA*.

Raiberto Comini portrait of Margo in her red evening dress. *JFA*.

A surprise birthday party for Margo, December 1953. Jim Field, *far left*; Ramsey Burch, *fifth from left*, Fred Hoskins (in bow tie), *center. Courtesy Fred Hoskins.*

Reading scripts in her Stoneleigh apartment. Note turtle ashtray. *T/DHAD, DPL.*

Margo with Eugene McDermott. *Courtesy Margaret McDermott.*

Margo rehearsing Charles Braswell and Louise Noble in Harry Granick's *The Guilty.*
Courtesy Harry Granick.

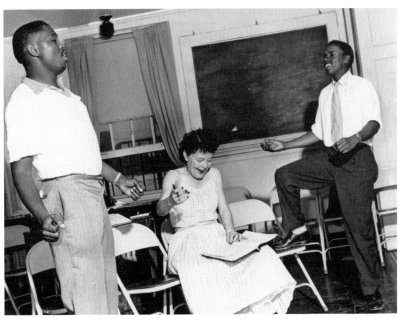

Margo directing members of Dallas's Round-up Theatre. *T/DHAD, DPL.*

Jerome Lawrence and Robert E. Lee confer with Margo about *Inherit the Wind.*
T/DHAD, DPL.

The prayer meeting—world premiere of *Inherit the Wind* at Theater '55.
T/DHAD, DPL.

Margo Jones. *JFA*.

Rosenfield had a fatherly fondness for her. From time to time, he and Margo lunched, or he stopped by her apartment for a visit and a drink, but he never attended theatre parties. He liked to say, "The only people I owe anything to are the people who pay five cents a copy for the *Dallas Morning News*."

THERE WAS little time for resting on laurels or for medal polishing at Theatre '48. Oscar Wilde's perfect gem, *The Importance of Being Earnest*, the third classic of the season, opened on January 12. It was a hit. Margo's direction was highly stylized, with choreographed, comic movements and colorful, elegant, beautifully detailed costumes. The antique English Regency and French Empire furniture was custom-upholstered in corresponding plaids and stripes, giving a flippant air to the production. Louise Latham, who played Gwendolyn, all blonde loveliness in ruffled pastels, received critical raves for her performance, as did the entire production. Rosenfield called it "easily one of the most brilliant and successful plays in Margo Jones' repertory." While the promoter in Margo was often given to hyperbole, the artist in her, like all searching artists, was a perfectionist, and a play never lived up to the ideal production she had created in her mind. Despite the brilliant success of *Earnest*, she felt it merely came close to having the finish that she wanted her productions to have.

With barely two weeks' rehearsal for each play, it is remarkable that the theatre's productions had any polish at all. While one play was running for fourteen days, another was in rehearsal, but matinees during the two-week period eliminated four days of rehearsal time and the actors had one day off every two weeks, which cut another day, thus leaving just nine days for rehearsal. "Not enough time to do a play anywhere near right," Margo complained and began planning how she could have more rehearsal time in the next season.

PLAYWRIGHT JOSEPH HAYES and his wife Marrijane, who lived in Brookfield, Connecticut, had arrived in Dallas in the middle of January to participate in the rehearsals for *Leaf and Bough*. A native of Indiana and a 1941 graduate of Indiana University, Hayes had moved to New York and worked for publisher Samuel French as a reader. Although he had written a number of plays for high school production, *Leaf and Bough* marked the thirty-year-old playwright's first professional production and his first experience working with a director. When he saw the stucco-and-glass-block theatre in Fair Park, his memory was jolted. He remembered that in 1936, while bumming across the country riding the rails, he had stopped in Dallas to earn some money. There he had found a job pushing wheelchairs around Fair Park during the Texas Centennial celebration. At every opportunity, hot and sweating, he had taken refuge in the only air-conditioned building on the grounds —the small stucco-and-glass-block building that was now Theatre '48.

At his first meeting with Margo, Hayes learned what every writer who ever worked with her discovered, that the playwright was the most important person in the production. And he was struck by her energy. "With all her vitality," he recalls, "she never overwhelmed anyone—it was all gentle." His experience with Margo, Hayes says, "spoiled me completely for the rest of my career. The work was collaborative, quiet and friendly, with no tensions in the company. As we got closer to opening, however, her direction tightened down and her instructions became more and more specific."

Leaf and Bough is a story about two families, the Warrens and the Campbells, who live in an Indiana farming community. The plot concerns the love between the two children of the families and their effort to break away from the narrow dullness of their surroundings. Four simultaneous sets suggested by a few pieces of furniture and a platform combined elements of realism and symbolism. Lighting and music were used to weave the scenes together. The play was the favorite new script of Margo and her company that season, although she felt it was the most difficult in terms of production. Because it had some talky scenes, revisions and cutting continued after the play opened. Hayes says now, "If I could have worked with more directors like Margo, I would have written more plays instead of the fourteen novels I did write."

A monster snowstorm hit Dallas during the week of the opening, forcing many businesses to close, but Theatre '48 remained open, though playing to small houses. At the opening, Hayes recalls that "tough-looking, barrel-chested oil men" came up to him moved to tears by the poignancy and gritty reality of his farm folks. They told him that when they could see plays like his they didn't mind going to the theatre. Jack Warden, who played the part of the brother to one of the young lovers, "made his role so understandable," Hayes says, that he gained immediate audience sympathy.

Critical reception was mixed as usual for an untried new play, the reviewers' vocabularies seemingly limited to that tiresome phrase "needs work." Critic John Mason Brown, who had never seen a production in arena theatre, covered the performance for the *Saturday Review* and called Margo's direction "unfailingly sure and inventive." He discovered that at Theatre '48, "performers were merged to a degree not even guessed at in our customary auditoriums. More than being spectators, playgoers had for once come close to being participants." He felt that theatre-in-the-round would "open windows wide on what can be stuffy and is seldom ventilated in theatre practice."

Man of the Year

Despite the mixed reception, producers Rouben Mamoulian and Charles P. Heidt optioned *Leaf and Bough* for Broadway. Directed by Mamoulian, it opened there in January 1949—and closed after only nine performances. Frustrated and disappointed, Hayes watched as his play became something else entirely on the New York theatre's large proscenium stage cluttered with scenery and furniture. "Mamoulian had a heavy touch," Hayes remembers, "and he didn't get any of the emotion out of it that Margo got. On Broadway the play was overburdened by sets and furniture. In Dallas we got more reality by just the suggestion of sets on that bare stage." Plays are more than scripts; they are living, volatile events that often change radically when the physical space is altered. Director Mamoulian encountered the problem with *Leaf and Bough*, and soon Margo too would learn this important lesson.

Undaunted by his Broadway failure, Joseph Hayes went on to become the only playwright ever to write the play, the novel, and the screenplay of a single work. He accomplished this feat with *The Desperate Hours*, which won the 1955 Tony Award for best play, and this time he produced the play himself. Hayes and his wife maintained their friendship with Margo for several years. She spent weekends with them at their Connecticut home; they corresponded, then gradually lost touch.

MARGO HAD CHOSEN to end the season with *Black John* by Hollywood screenwriter Barton MacLane, a light comic farce set in a saloon in the Yukon that is populated by improbable "type" characters. She had searched futilely for that elusive chimera of all producing directors, a good comedy with one set and a small cast, but *Black John* would have to do. Margo thought the play corny and melodramatic, but at this point in the season, after three classics and four new plays, she and her exhausted company were ready for something superficial. Her directing challenges were physical this time: she had to hang a man onstage and drop several others through a trapdoor. Rosenfield thought the play pure nonsense; the critic from *Variety* wrote that it was slow and unoriginal; but the tired businessmen of Dallas chomped on the corn, roaring with laughter. The same audience of subscribers that sat respectfully through Ibsen's tragic drama *The Master Builder* especially relished the scene in *Black John* where several characters place bets on whether a fly will light on a lump of sugar.

At season's end the four most popular plays of the season—*The Taming of the Shrew*, *The Importance of Being Earnest*, *Throng O' Scarlet*, and *Leaf and Bough*—played for four weeks in rotating repertory, attracting New York producers and Hollywood talent scouts. When the season officially ended on

March 20, Manning reported that they had made expenses and a profit of twelve thousand dollars. In addition, fifteen hundred people, responding to a subscription campaign during the audience-pleasing production of *Black John*, had already bought their tickets for the upcoming season.

Dallas patrons were disappointed when they learned that the theatre would be dark that summer because Margo would produce and direct *Summer and Smoke* on Broadway. In less than a year, she had presented thirteen plays, nine of them world premieres, and she had taught her audience to enjoy the excitement of watching a new script come to life as well as to appreciate a theatre classic. Theatregoing had become a habit. Rosenfield grumbled in his column that Dallas needed a theatre in July too, conveniently forgetting that he had advised Margo the year before that no one would attend theatre during a hot Dallas summer. Aware that Margo and Manning had been contacting local people, including board members, to raise money for *Summer and Smoke*, he also voiced the concern that they, the people of Dallas, were being used as Broadway "angels" or suckers. Part of Rosenfield's disgruntlement stemmed from the fact that he didn't like Manning Gurian or his influence on Margo. He and his wife Claire believed that Gurian was a Broadway character, an opportunist out to make a buck.

Margo thought differently. She brought out another side of Manning. True, he wanted security and hoped to make money on *Summer and Smoke* and other plays that they would produce together, but she worked a kind of magic on him; she encouraged his dream of becoming a writer and caught him up in her vision of creating a national theatre. With his background in commercial management, Manning could have worked in New York for far more than the one hundred dollars a week he earned in Dallas. "I was still an idealist then," he recalls now. He loved Margo, and if he wanted to be a part of her life, he had to share her kind of theatre. At times he felt that he was losing his identity in her powerful presence; after all, his lover was also his employer. But he brushed these feelings away even as he teasingly called Margo "Boss."

DURING THE 1947–48 Dallas season, Margo devoted her free moments, which usually occurred in the middle of the night or in the early hours of the morning, to answering her mail. The recent purchase of a dictaphone made this task immeasurably easier since now she could simply talk her letters into the machine and Ross Lawther would type them up from the tapes. Much of her correspondence dealt with plans for the New York production of *Summer and Smoke*. The first step was securing her old friend Jo Mielziner, the busiest designer on Broadway, to do the lights and sets. Manning delivered the script to him while Mielziner was on the road with Josh Logan's production of *Mister*

Roberts. Mielziner wrote Margo that he thought the writing was Tennessee at his best, and while the directing and design problems would be difficult, as they usually were in a Williams play, he would take the job. He also mentioned that he thought Manning was a wonderful fellow for her personally and professionally.

The designer met with Williams about the play in late December 1947, just before Tennessee was scheduled to sail to Europe. Mielziner told Margo that he went to Tennessee's apartment and found fourteen people who seemed to be playing a sort of perverse game in which half of them competed to get Tennessee packed, in the process destroying stacks of unopened letters, while the other half concentrated on drinking quarts of champagne out of a communal brown bowl since all the glasses had been smashed. Mielziner lamented that it had taken two hours to achieve what might have been accomplished in twelve minutes of serious conversation with the unshaven but strangely calm and sober Tennessee. In brief, Williams told the designer that he wanted an unrealistic set, with lots of romantic sky.

T E N N E S S E E, who had been without a typewriter since Pancho had tossed his out the window, wrote Margo from Paris on the new portable Swiss-made typewriter she had given him for Christmas. She had sent the gift to New York with actor Montgomery Clift, who had passed through Dallas in December and taken in a performance of *The Taming of the Shrew*. Margo loved Tennessee's return gift to her, a blue blouse emblazoned with a golden cock, which she wore with a full black ballet skirt.

In his long, newsy letter, Williams admitted that he felt lonely now, so far from his few dear friends. Joanna seemed to blossom in New York, he told her. Pancho, he said, was living in Miami Beach. He continued to insist that no outside producers be included in the production of *Summer and Smoke*, that he wanted just the two of them involved. Of course, this meant that Manning could not be credited publicly as co-producer. Not wanting to jeopardize her relationship with Tennessee, Margo continued to keep silent about her professional and personal partnership with Gurian.

After the January 12 opening of *The Importance of Being Earnest* and the cast party, Margo stayed up all night answering personal correspondence, typing the letters herself. At 4:00 A.M. she wrote a long letter to Tennessee. She thanked him and Elia Kazan for recommending her for a job as head of the drama department of Bennington College, but told him that she had already heard from the school and promptly turned them down. Hadn't Tennessee been listening to her for the last four years? Margo must have wondered. When would everyone finally get what she was about?

As she had to do so many times, she repeated her theme, her driving ambition. "This theatre here is the beginning of my dream and I believe in the idea here heart, mind, soul, and body," she wrote Williams. "More and more I feel that good really good permanent, professional repertory theatres in all our large cities are the real answer to the life of theatre in this country . . . provid[ing] dignity and security for that enormous number of good actors who have no jobs in New York and provid[ing] a place where new scripts can be done by fine companies with good direction without the enormous outlay that New York productions require."

Lecture delivered, she continued their discussions about where *Summer and Smoke* should try out. Remembering his unfortunate experience with *Battle of Angels*, Tennessee wanted to avoid the Boston–New Haven circuit and instead open in Chicago, where *The Glass Menagerie* had premiered. Margo felt that while Chicago was a possibility, production costs were high there, and her schedule would not permit a long run in Chicago before moving into New York.

Margo's letters to Tennessee during this period communicate her unwavering belief in his writing and in the upcoming production. After reading Hart Crane's poetry late one night, she also made a confession to Tennessee. "I would give my soul," she wrote, "if I in some permanent way—some actual record of articulateness—if I could express beauty I feel—I think I do in my direction—and that is good—perhaps its fleeting quality lends it enchantment—but surely its only permanence is in the mind of the audience." She assured him that their experience of working together on *Summer and Smoke* was going to be beautiful.

In his next letter, Tennessee burst her bubble of optimism, telling her that while he had been working on the play, adding the character Rosa Gonzales, revising and tightening, he felt that it was a bitter failure, dead and lifeless and decidedly inferior to the passionate *Streetcar*. He believed that if the play opened in the East it would suffer from a comparison to *Streetcar*. Although Williams told Donald Windham that he had tried to talk Margo out of producing the play at all, he did not go so far in his letters to her. Rather he told her not to tell anyone about his misgivings and not to be discouraged by his news—maybe he could rework the play, and if the production values were right, especially the set and the music, they could create some beauty. Audrey Wood had advised Tennessee that Margo was not capable of both producing and directing *Summer and Smoke* on Broadway. As Margo's agent, Wood knew of her difficulties with *Joan of Lorraine* and felt that Margo lacked the necessary toughness to achieve success on Broadway. Wood felt that while the play worked in Dallas, the New York audience was "an entirely different breed." Later, Wood recalled, "I expressed my doubts to Tennessee, but he merely shrugged them off. Margo was his friend and he would remain loyal to her."

BY EARLY FEBRUARY 1948, Margo and Manning had accumulated the full hundred thousand dollars needed to capitalize *Summer and Smoke*. Because of the success of *The Glass Menagerie* and *A Streetcar Named Desire*, they could literally choose their investors from dozens who wanted to be a part of another Williams triumph. To keep operating costs low, they would not use stars and Margo would not take a producer's salary. Manning, of course, was paid for his position as general manager. The production plan was limited partnerships, offered at two thousand dollars each. Margo asked publisher Jay Laughlin to invest because she and Tennessee wanted people who believed in theatre, she said, not the "usual bunch." Laughlin did not buy in, but some of the usual bunch did, including producers Sherman and Marjorie Ewing and Charles Heidt. Tad Adoue, board member Arthur Kramer, Jr., actor Clinton Anderson, and her old friend Frank Harting all bought shares. Manning sold partnerships to two of his brothers, but when Jo Mielziner wanted to be included, the Gurian brothers gave up a share to him.

In March, Audrey Wood wired that she and her husband wanted to invest up to five thousand dollars, but Margo wrote back that they were too late, financing was set. There had been tension between the two women. Failing in her attempt to persuade Tennessee to take the play away from Margo entirely, Wood had pushed for an experienced Broadway producer to work with her on the production. Herman Shumlin, who had produced and directed on Broadway since 1927, had offered his services. But Margo firmly insisted that she would be sole producer-director. After all, Tennessee wanted the two of them to have complete working autonomy. To protect Tennessee's rights and his play, Wood expected to be deeply involved with the casting and with all the production details, but Margo was determined to run the show herself. Perhaps for this reason, she and Manning did not offer Audrey Wood the same courtesy they had given Jo Mielziner. Wood kept her five thousand dollars. It was an unfortunate decision that resulted in increased coolness between the two strong women.

IN APRIL 1948, Tennessee wrote from Rome asking Margo to come to Italy to talk about the play. He wanted her to give herself plenty of time and take a real vacation. Margo had been in New York beginning preliminary casting work for the play and for her fall Theatre '48 season. Tennessee was pleased at her report that Margaret Phillips would be available, but urged her to tell the other actors that they were not finally cast until after at least five days of rehearsal, so that he would have time to see if they were right for their parts.

With her entire vacation wardrobe of three dresses in one suitcase, Margo flew to Rome. There Tennessee met her at the airport accompanied by his young Italian lover, Salvatore Maresca. They had long conferences about the play and made frantic efforts to contact writer-composer Paul Bowles, who seemed to have disappeared in Morocco, to discuss the music for the play. At Jo Mielziner's request, Margo consulted art dealers, looking for detailed photographs of the sculptured angels from the Cathedral of Lucca that Mielziner wanted to use as models for the stone angel of the fountain symbolizing eternity in *Summer and Smoke*.

After two weeks in Rome, Margo, Tennessee, and Salvatore drove wildly to Naples in Tennessee's backfiring Jeep. Margo said later that the trip was fun, but certainly not comfortable. They spent a few days in Capri and Sorrento, swimming and relaxing. They got lost in the mountains and spent a night in a small village sleeping in one room because, Tennessee reported, Margo was afraid to be by herself in such strange surroundings. Tennessee wrote Donald Windham that Salvatore giggled in wonder at this arrangement and at Margo, who loved talking and drinking and eating but didn't seem to care about lovemaking. Margo found Italy beautiful, but Tennessee observed that she was distracted and inattentive. He sensed her restlessness, but didn't know that Margo wanted to accomplish the script work on *Summer and Smoke* as quickly as possible because she longed to be in New York with Manning. He had written her in Rome: "Boss . . . one thing that makes me happy is that you love me enough to make everything twice as good. The things you see, the things you do . . . everything. I see Rome through you. . . . I see heaven. If this gives you any notion that I might be in love with you . . . you're right. I do, Baby. . . . I sure do."

To expedite matters, Margo had taken over their travel arrangements, even packing Tennessee's luggage and making their train reservations to London. Although Tennessee had not written in weeks, her energy stimulated him and in England he began writing every day. She saw five plays in London, including Sartre's *Passion Processional*, which she thought was the most interesting. She met with producer Hugh Beaumont and gave him a copy of Edwin Justus Mayer's script for *The Death of Don Juan*. Finally, in June, her business completed and Tennessee settled in London, Margo flew back to New York. The playwright planned to return to the States in August for the rehearsals of his play.

Man of the Year

MANNING MET HER at the airport and, happy to be in New York and together, they began pre-production work on *Summer and Smoke*. Margo had again sublet Rosamond Gilder's Gramercy Park apartment for the summer months. It had a lovely view of the park, high ceilings, spacious rooms, and Gilder's huge theatre library. Complete comfort was assured with the arrival of Margo's housekeeper, Floyd McDaniel, from Dallas. To handle her correspondence and appointments, she hired a full-time secretary.

Margo worked on casting for *Summer* and for her Dallas season, read new scripts, and during that summer and fall saw most of the shows that were running in New York. She visited with Robert Morley and Peggy Ashcroft backstage at Morley's play *Edward, My Son*. She thought Judith Anderson's performance in *Medea* "very fine." She went back to see *Brigadoon* several times because she loved it, but left "bored to death" after the first act of another popular musical, *Love Life* by Alan Jay Lerner and Kurt Weill. She thought Tallulah Bankhead overplayed in Noel Coward's *Private Lives*, "turning it into a vaudeville act." She also visited summer theatres around New York to see actors but, she wrote, she found the "summer theatre set-up . . . really terrible. The star system is ridiculous, the choice of plays almost always very cheap, the [week's] rehearsal schedule completely inadequate."

By early August, casting was set for *Summer and Smoke*. Margaret Phillips, a slim young actress from the tongue-twisting town of Cwmgwrach in Wales, would play Alma Winemiller, and Tod Andrews would repeat his Dallas performance as Dr. Buchanan. Raymond Van Sickle and Marga Ann Deighton would reprise their Dallas roles too as the Reverend Winemiller and his demented wife. Betty Greene Little would again play the gossipy Mrs. Bassett. Margo chose the fresh-faced, buoyant young actress Anne Jackson as Nellie Ewell, the girl from the wrong side of the tracks who ends up marrying Dr. Buchanan. And she called Ray Walston, who was currently acting in East Hampton, and said, "I have a part for you." She cast him in the small but crucial role of Archie Kramer, the traveling salesman who, at the end of the play, takes Alma with him to the notorious Moon Lake Casino. Walston was thrilled with his part, achieved without an audition but simply on Margo's faith in him. He had previously played only walk-ons and a small part in *The Front Page* in New York, and he felt that this was his chance at last to prove himself on Broadway.

Margo met Tennessee's boat from London at New York harbor and took him to the apartment she had found for him, the first floor of a brownstone on East 58th Street. She had paid his first month's rent and arranged for Audrey Wood to sign the lease. Margo didn't mind taking care of these personal details for

Tennessee; she wanted him happy and ready to work. Unfortunately, like his creation Alma Winemiller, the hypochondriacal playwright began to complain that he had problems with his heart—symptoms, he fretted, of a life-threatening disease.

Rehearsals began at the Music Box Theatre on Sunday, August 15. The next day George Freedley interviewed Margo over breakfast at her apartment. She told him that *Summer and Smoke* was a delightful reunion of the *Menagerie* team of herself, Tennessee, Jo Mielziner, and composer Paul Bowles. Of course, she did not divulge Tennessee's doubts about the play. She had pledged to keep quiet about his despair over the script, an easy task since she believed it was a masterpiece and told him so. Freedley, a board member of ANTA as well as a critic for New York's *Morning Telegraph*, turned the topic to her Dallas theatre, asking, "Do you believe in trying out your plays in Dallas before Broadway?"

Margo indignantly replied, "Absolutely not. I don't try out plays. What is good enough for Dallas is good enough for St. Louis, San Francisco or New York. I just find the best play I can and do them the best way I can. If New York is interested in them later so much the better."

AN UNPLEASANT SURPRISE came early in the rehearsal period: Tennessee informed Margo that *he* wanted to direct *Summer and Smoke*. Clearly, Williams, tutored in the commercial theatre by Audrey Wood, had begun to doubt Margo's ability to direct his play in New York. His experience with Elia Kazan on *Streetcar* had been extraordinarily positive. Although Kazan has often been given credit for saving *Streetcar* by reshaping it, the director wrote later, "We cut five pages out of the last scene and that was it." By his own account, Kazan was rude, often arrogant, in pursuit of what he believed was right for the production. But Williams felt that Kazan had "the dynamism my work needs." While Margo certainly was dynamic, she did not have Kazan's leathery, ruthless style. Margo wrote Jo Mielziner that with *Summer and Smoke*, she wanted to "prove that it is possible to get on a big New York show with understanding, decency, fineness, honesty, integrity, creativeness, and pure joy—to say nothing of hoped for success." Statements like these must have terrified sensible Audrey Wood, who believed that the last thing *Summer and Smoke* needed was a cloudy dreamer given to phrases filled with sweetness and light. Tennessee persisted in his demands that Margo turn the directing over to him while she concentrated on producing, but Margo continued to brush him off.

Still, there were clashes. At one point, during a rehearsal of the traveling-salesman scene, Tennessee leapt onto the Music Box stage and began acting out the way he thought Ray Walston should play the part. He asked Walston to imitate him. Walston thought that Tennessee looked ludicrous, but was at a loss as to how to proceed without insulting the playwright. He fumbled for words but was interrupted by Margo's voice, screaming from the house. "Now, Tennessee," she shouted, "I am the director of this play. You get yourself off that stage right this minute. I am the director and you better know that. You get off the stage, Tennessee."

Williams left the stage and stormed out of the theatre. Shaken, Margo returned to work, upset that she had quarreled with her most cherished friend. But Tennessee had challenged her, attempting a power play in front of the actors. Undoubtedly, Margo was aware of his insecurity with her direction, and felt that she had to make a strong stand. In fact, some of Williams's friends believed he had changed after his breakup with Pancho and the success of *Streetcar*, growing colder and more self-centered. The tension between Margo and Tennessee tainted the atmosphere and damaged the trust that is so important for a successful production. They would smooth over their differences, but this argument, their first major disagreement, would have lasting effects.

Elia Kazan had received billing over the title of *Streetcar* and thus paved the way for other directors who would insist on the same treatment. As producer-director of *Summer and Smoke* Margo was to enjoy the same above-the-title credit. Tennessee, on the other hand, perhaps still smarting from his confrontation with Margo, snappishly announced to the newspapers that he did not want his name above the title of the play, but under the title the same size as the actors' names. He said everyone knew he had written it, and he wanted the producer's name to be the only name above the title.

THE PLAY OPENED its pre-Broadway tryout in Buffalo, New York, on September 9, 1948. The fifteen scenes of the Dallas production had been cut to twelve. The character of Rosa Gonzales, the sensual consort of Dr. Buchanan, had replaced the earlier, sketchy character of Jessie Serio; a scene had been added between John Buchanan and his father; a long scene between Alma and her suitor, Roger Doremus, had been cut completely; and other scenes had been trimmed and tightened. The heart of the play, its basic feeling and language, had not changed from the Theatre '47 production.

Jo Mielziner was in Buffalo to supervise installation of his set. Mielziner had not seen the Dallas production, and in his design of *Summer and Smoke* he had not deviated from Tennessee's description of the set. To eliminate delaying set changes, the entire set was onstage from the beginning of the play.

Man of the Year

In the center of the stage loomed a large stone figure of a kneeling angel on a fountain pedestal, which would be spotlighted during the scene changes. The interior of the rectory with several chairs, a love seat, a table, piano, and piano bench was on stage right, and the doctor's office with a couch, large desk and chair, folding screens, and a table, all dominated by a huge chart of anatomy, was on stage left. The Moon Lake Casino scenes were played center-stage in front of the stone angel. A sky cyclorama with delicate outlines of distant buildings provided the background.

On opening night in Buffalo both Tod Andrews and Margaret Phillips had problems with audibility in the enormous Erlanger Theatre, and there were a few minor lighting mishaps as well. However, critic Mary Nash of the *Buffalo Evening News* enthused that "Tennessee Williams has written another beautiful and exciting drama, which can proudly take its place beside its two celebrated predecessors. . . ."

The company moved to Detroit and the Cass Theatre. On opening night Tennessee and Margo jokingly battled over who had the right to sit in the aisle seat, in order to beat a hasty retreat if necessary. They need not have worried. The critics and audience, one writer reported, "not only liked it, but loved it." Both Margo and Tennessee were interviewed by the local paper. Margo talked about the play and her turtle collection, now numbering over six thousand—from a tiny turtle the size of her little fingernail to a large china one whose shell flipped up to reveal a spittoon. Although he had warned Margo not to express doubts about the play, Tennessee himself told a reporter that his play was "just beginning to take shape" and admitted that he didn't know if what he wanted "to say would come across." *Variety* picked up the quotes from the Detroit papers—sincere comments, no doubt, but certainly not designed to build interest in a New York premiere.

DURING THEIR STAY in Detroit, the company was invited to a Sunday supper party in a wealthy suburb. Margo and Tennessee relaxed by the bar, enjoying the free drinks and a moment of harmony. Then they were approached by several of the guests, eager to ask questions about the play. Tennessee reported later that he and Margo were backed up against the bar like a "pair of antlered beasts." Taking a plate of food with him, he retreated to an alcove but was soon surrounded, he said, "by three women in basic black who had been to the Saturday matinee and had apparently thought of nothing since except the problems of Alma Winemiller." They bombarded him with questions: "What is the theme of your play? What happens to the characters after the play is over? Why do you write? Why do you always write about frustrated women?" Tennessee said later that he stood with his mouth full of food, confronted by these questioners, and pondered: "Was Blanche of *A Streetcar Named Desire* frustrated? What is frustrated about loving with such white hot intensity that it alters the whole direction of your life, and removes you from the parlor of an Episcopalian rectory to a secret room above Moon Lake Casino?" But before he could put these thoughts into words, Margo arrived at the alcove and shouted, "Tennessee does not write about frustrated women!"

"Oh," said one of the ladies, turning to Margo. "Then what does he write about?"

"People!" said Margo. "Life!" While she was talking, Tennessee slipped quietly away, leaving Margo with the women, once again to fight his battles for him.

THEIR LAST STOP before taking the play to New York was the Hanna Theatre in Cleveland. Ray Walston remembers that Audrey Wood and her husband William Liebling joined the company there, and sat like "stone figures in the back of the theatre." Margo had known Wood and her husband since 1942; Wood had served as her agent and advisor, and they had established a warm friendship. But their once warm friendship had chilled. Now the older woman resented Margo's influence over her playwright, and most assuredly she thought that Margo did not understand what she, Audrey, knew so well, the commercial New York theatre. By the time Wood and her husband arrived in Cleveland, the two women were "at dagger points" arguing over details of the production. Later, Dakin Williams, Tennessee's brother, asked William Liebling about his and Audrey Wood's relationship with Margo during *Summer and Smoke*. "That woman!" Liebling said angrily. "They call her the Texas Tornado, but I tell you if she was standing right here beside us, I would pick her right up off the ground like a real twister and I would throw her down this elevator shaft."

W. Ward Marsh reviewed the play for the *Cleveland Plain Dealer*. "*Summer and Smoke*," he wrote, "is no ordinary play and cannot be judged by ordinary standards. It seems tenuous and frail, at times full of words but, say anything against it you like, it still remains a powerful, magnetic and beautiful piece of playwrighting." And he said, "Margo Jones's direction is brilliant. I do not think that she always has the best with which to work, but in the main her players have responded accurately."

With the opening only a week away, Margo took time off during their few days in Cleveland to look for a dress for the New York premiere. The lines of the play echoing in her mind, she walked into a shop where she was met by a saleslady who looked, Margo said, "as if she had no poetry in her soul."

"I want a *Summer and Smoke* dress," Margo told her, "summer-yellow and smoke-gray. I want it to look like a sky rocket that has burst into a million stars, and I want it to look like a water lily."

"We haven't got any yellow and gray dresses," the saleslady said rudely, turning away.

"Please, won't you look?" pleaded Margo.

The woman stomped off and returned moments later, her face filled with amazement. "Here it is," she said, holding out a filmy yellow and gray dress.

It looked, Margo thought, like a beautiful water lily on a Chinese lagoon, and the top part of it was just like a million stars.

THREE DAYS BEFORE the October 6 opening of *Summer and Smoke*, the *New York Times* published an article entitled "Questions Without Answers" by Tennessee Williams. The tone of the article varied from pretension, to archness, to defensiveness, to condescension, to honest entertainment in his depiction of bullying theatre ladies attempting to wring answers out of him. He criticized newspaper reviewers for stating the themes of his plays, remarking with irony that he was "thankful for these highly condensed and stimulating analyses." He suggested that the all-inclusive theme "life" would sum up his plays nicely. The man who had just had an overwhelming success with his last two plays wrote, "Inflated reputations and eclectic styles have cast an aura of gravity over much that is essentially vacuous in painting, obscurity has disguised sterility in a good deal of verse. But the theatre, which is called the charlatan of the arts, is paradoxically the one in which the charlatan is most easily detected." To the New York critics who would surely read this article he was suggesting the possibility—a possibility that probably would not have occurred to them—that he might be a charlatan and his play a trick. And a rich one at that: on the day of the opening *Variety* announced that with the premiere of *Summer and Smoke*, *Streetcar* on Broadway and on tour, and *The Glass Menagerie* with Helen Hayes playing in London and in amateur productions around the country, Tennessee Williams was now taking home a whopping amount of money for the times—approximately seventy-five hundred dollars a week.

MARGO'S FRIEND Frank Harting, who had invested five thousand dollars in the play, entertained her, Manning, investors, and assorted friends at a black tie, pre-theatre party in his apartment on opening night. Tennessee, who had dedicated *Summer and Smoke* to Carson McCullers, would attend the opening with the writer. They had met during the summer of 1947, and McCullers had shared his beach house in Provincetown, writing her play *The Member of the Wedding* while he worked on *Summer and Smoke*. Tennessee had grown increasingly close to the tall, gifted southern writer, who was both mentally unstable and physically debilitated by strokes.

Crowds lined 45th Street to watch the notables of theatre and society enter the Music Box for the 8:00 P.M. opening. Irene Selznick, the producer of *Streetcar*; Vinton Freedley, president of ANTA; actresses Celeste Holm and June Allyson; George Freedley; and Brooks Atkinson were all part of the first-night audience, which filled the 1,010-seat theatre to capacity.

After distributing her personal notes and gifts of silver angel key rings to the company, Margo, wearing her special dress, took her seat. At the last four openings of Tennessee's plays, her place had been beside the playwright, giving him courage through each wrenching experience. Now she sat apart, with Manning and Frank Harting. During the performance, the audience occasionally burst into applause and women were moved to tears, but during intermission some wisecrackers in the lobby were heard to retitle the play "A Kiddy-Kar Called Conversation."

Faced with writing that could not be easily categorized except for comparisons with Williams's own *A Streetcar Named Desire*, most reviewers heaped abuse on the play. "A pretentious and amateurish bore," said Howard Barnes of the *New York Herald-Tribune*. "Mawkish, murky, maudlin, and monotonous," alliterated John Chapman of the *Daily News*. Robert Garland of the *Journal-American* told his readers that if they enjoyed *Streetcar* they wouldn't like *Summer and Smoke*: "The stock Tennessee Williams figures are up on the stage. Especially the females of the deep Deep Southern species. The Alma Winemiller played by Margaret Phillips is . . . the Blanche DuBois played by Jessica Tandy . . . who is the Laura Wingfield played by Julie Haydon." And he told them, "I beg you, do not let Mr. Williams' apologetic pieces in the Sunday papers persuade you otherwise."

While most of the reviews were in this vituperative vein, several critics disagreed with the pack. Robert Coleman of the *Daily Mirror* wrote that *Summer and Smoke* "has been given a superlative production by Margo Jones. . . . Williams has no peer among modern dramatists at creating a mood. In *Summer and Smoke* he not only has achieved mood beautifully, but beyond any previous attempt, has probed human values. Though this is a verbose play, its verbosity is eloquent, searching and moving. *Summer and Smoke* thrilled us. It proves for us that our so-called tributary theatre is the real home of the American theatre." The *New York Times* review by Brooks Atkinson called the play a tone poem, and Williams a poet of the theatre. "*Summer and Smoke*," Atkinson wrote, "is a theatre piece charged with passion and anguish. Margo Jones, who directed the original performance in Dallas, has brought it to the stage with infinite respect for its delicate qualities. On a large stage it loses some of the moving intimacy that it had in the cramped quarters of the Dallas theatre. . . . Mr. Williams and his two principal actors have performed the miracle of translating a drab corner of life into something that is tremulous with beauty."

The morning after the opening and after reading all the reviews, Margo called Frank Harting. He picked her up, and they put the top down on his convertible and drove up and down the Hudson River, wondering, Harting says, "how [the play] could have been such a smash hit in Dallas and fallen flat on Broadway." Harting felt that "the set was so dazzling—with cloud effects and star effects and sky effects and fountains splashing—that you found yourself concentrating on [it] more than on what the actors were doing." Those who had seen the play in Dallas agreed with him, preferring the intimacy of that production and its understated setting, comparing, for example, the Theatre '47 angel on the small stone bird bath to the grand Broadway angel that towered over the actors. Although Jo Mielziner got excellent reviews for his setting and lights, which were beautiful, he had failed to achieve his own first precept of design, "to aid and abet the actors." This time, instead of questioning Tennessee's design concept as he had done during *The Glass Menagerie*, Mielziner and Margo had followed the playwright's directions exactly. The result was that the characters were dwarfed by an overproduced set that had a kind of grandeur and formality unsympathetic to the delicate moods of the play.

Of course, the most important difference between the successful Dallas production and the Broadway version was the difference in the theatres, in both type and scale. Drama historian and critic John Gassner believed the reason for the failure of *Summer and Smoke* on Broadway was that the proscenium stage at the Music Box Theatre "forced the action toward the wings and failed to center the heroine on the stage. . . ." Seated at a distance from the actors, seeing them in only two dimensions, the audience had a difficult time identifying with or caring about the characters. Perhaps a director like Elia Kazan might have surmounted the production problems—Tennessee believed that he could have. The playwright thought that while Margo brought out the romantic, pure qualities of the play, her direction was mediocre, lacking in vitality. Used to the sculptural style of theatre-in-the-round and more adept at directing in that medium, Margo did not find a production style for *Summer and Smoke* that suited the standard proscenium arch of Broadway.

And perhaps the failure of the play had to do too with the intangible qualities of belief and faith, values that cannot be forced or faked but must be honestly felt. From the beginning, the commercial production had been under a cloud of doubt—unlike the relatively risk-free Dallas premiere where the production had had a patina of confidence and assured success. When the stakes were raised to Broadway with all the accompanying tension and uncertainty endemic to that world, the production and all those involved in it never seemed able to rise above their own fears. And audiences and reviewers sometimes seem able to smell that fear when they walk into a theatre. Perhaps unconsciously, critics picked up the scent of Williams's terror over *Summer and Smoke*, and went baying after him.

MARGO TOLD JUNE and Jim Moll that she was prepared for the conflicting critical opinions. "To the very best of my ability I did not compromise," she said. In a follow-up article in the Sunday *Times*, Brooks Atkinson wrote a mini-lecture explaining Williams's art to the public. It would take other critics and scholars several years to concur with him, but eventually they would share Atkinson's opinion that *Summer and Smoke* was a masterpiece. He called the play "as intangible as a piece of music" and said, "these qualities are a rare treasure in our workaday theatre. . . . As far as spiritual tumult is concerned, *Summer and Smoke* is the most eventful drama on the stage today . . . a work of art."

Margo clipped his article and carried it with her on the plane back to Dallas, then home to Livingston, where she sat on the broad front porch in the shade of the chinaberry tree and read his words aloud to her family. She savored the phrase "work of art." Those words said everything she wanted to hear, she told Atkinson.

In her own mind, Margo had succeeded with *Summer and Smoke*, maintaining her faith in the play when Tennessee had lost his. It hurt her that many thought the play and her production of it a failure, but her faith was not shaken. In one way, she was like the tough Elia Kazan—she had an arrogant belief in her own judgment. In a few years when her belief in *Summer and Smoke* was vindicated, she didn't even say, "I told you so."

Mixer of Truth and Magic

URING THE early weeks of its run, *Summer and Smoke* played to capacity houses (primarily pre-booked theatre parties), giving the backers a 10 percent return on their original investments. When the group sales ran out, however, single-ticket buyers, influenced by the play's damaging reviews, chose to spend their money elsewhere. Many lined up for tickets to *A Streetcar Named Desire*, which had been playing for over a year to full houses. After all, why attend a less than successful play when you can see a hit by the same playwright? Tennessee's instinct to hold *Summer and Smoke* out of New York to avoid comparisons with *Streetcar* had been proven correct. While Margo's decision to bring the play there may have been the appropriate decision artistically, it was a financial disaster. To save an extra seventy-five dollars a week, she replaced actress Ellen James (who played the small part of Rosemary) with Margaret Phillips's understudy Leslie Paul—a decision that annoyed Tennessee, who accused her of acting as highhanded as the Shuberts and insisted that James be rehired. Margo maintained that she had discussed the problem with him and that as a producer responsible for a large investment she had an obligation to cut costs whenever possible. Hurt at what she felt to be Tennessee's lack of understanding, she wrote him using his own words from *The Purification*: "Since honor is more than a word between us there must surely be a way to understand each other." Again, they patched up their differences, but after the turmoil of *Summer and Smoke* their friendship would never be the same. Her relationship with Audrey Wood had changed too. Soon after *Summer and Smoke* opened, Wood had written Margo a straightforward letter, briskly touching on their different approaches to the New York commercial theatre and, in closing, terminating their professional relationship, saying that it would be foolhardy for them to work together again. The letter came as no surprise to Margo, who certainly shared Wood's sentiments.

The 1948–49 Broadway season was a dismal one for many producers, except for those of long-running hits like *Mister Roberts, Born Yesterday*, and *A Streetcar Named Desire*. Although musicals *South Pacific, Kiss Me, Kate*, and *Where's Charley?* and dramas *Death of a Salesman, Anne of the Thousand Days*, and *Edward, My Son* drew capacity crowds, Broadway was in a serious slump. The road companies were also having a difficult time. Margo and Manning had hoped that business might pick up over the Christmas holiday, but a major snowstorm hit the city, discouraging ticket sales even more, and on January 1, 1949, after only 102 performances, *Summer and Smoke* closed. About seventy thousand dollars of the initial one-hundred-thousand-dollar investment was lost.

Ray Walston probably benefited most from his involvement with *Summer and Smoke,* winning the 1948 Clarence Derwent Award for the best performance by a newcomer to Broadway as well as *Variety's* Drama Critics Poll Award. The awards brought him attention from directors and producers and led to more work and the beginning of a long and fruitful career. The talented redhead, who had begun as a skinny, scared kid with only one word to say in Margo's Houston Community Players, found the words to tell her what she had meant to him in a letter much like hundreds Margo received over the years from people she had helped:

> I did want to say how grateful I am to you for all this, because without you it would not have been possible. And I don't just mean about your giving me the part. I mean about all the years you have encouraged me, championed me, loved me, and held me close to your heart. . . . As for your handing me the sides even without a reading and being directly responsible for this Award, well you know how I feel about that. . . . For the part of the Traveling Salesman I had to learn a few Spanish words. Not listed among them was the word "Gracias." I am learning that word now.

O B V I O U S L Y, the backers of *Summer and Smoke,* who would not recoup their losses until almost thirty years later, were not as thankful for the experience. Margo's Dallas investors, however, like theatre board member Arthur Kramer, Jr., took the failure philosophically. The loss of several thousand dollars would not seriously affect these wealthy Texans, who had invested in the first place, according to Kramer, "because we loved Margo."

When asked by a reporter how she felt about her experience with *Summer and Smoke* on Broadway, Margo replied, "Broadway? It's the most courageous place I know. It takes immense courage to put on a play in New York, with costs so high and risks so great. But if you love a play and it fails, that's not a tragedy. You've had all those weeks—perhaps months—immersed in something you cared for." On the other hand, although Manning Gurian took the failure of *Summer and Smoke* "like a gentleman," Margo said, she knew that he was bitter about the experience. Since Manning had not been acknowledged publicly as a co-producer or even as Margo's professional partner, he had achieved nothing from the production except his salary. His contributions to *Summer and Smoke* and Theatre '48 had received no mention at all in an article on Margo that appeared in the October 1948 *New York Times Magazine* under the title "A Texas Tornado Hits Broadway." While Manning had a strong ego, and as a business manager was accustomed to staying in the background in a supporting role, he must have felt overshadowed by this woman who expected him to share convictions about the theatre that were not truly compatible with his own. Trained in show business, not art, Manning measured success in the theatre by how much money a play made. Margo felt quite the opposite. She wrote June and Jim Moll that "perhaps the strongest thing that came out of the production for me was to reaffirm beliefs that I have always had regarding the essentials of our theatre here. I am convinced . . . that for real . . . fineness in the theatre, the apprehensive shadows cast by commercialism do not make for growth."

W I T H   T H E   W O R K on *Summer and Smoke* behind her, Margo concentrated on the November opening of a new season at Theatre '48. The schedule had been extended to thirty weeks, with each of the eight plays running for three weeks (and six weeks of repertory at the end of the season), allowing for three weeks of rehearsal for each play—the standard amount of time for most Broadway productions. The transfer of *Summer and Smoke* to New York had enhanced the prestige of the theatre, and almost two thousand season subscriptions had been sold, representing 37 percent of the theatre's house. Again, Manning planned a budget based on two-thirds capacity. To break even in the 198-seat theatre with a play running for three weeks, fifteen hundred single tickets in addition to the two thousand subscriptions must be sold. Of course, to ensure stability and start-up money for the next season, a surplus was mandatory. The stakes were higher for Margo than a balanced budget, however. She had set out to prove that Theatre '48, her nonprofit theatre, without warmed-over Broadway hits, without stars, with a low ticket price, and presenting new plays and classics only, could survive and even flourish, artistically and financially, serving as a blueprint for others to follow.

As managing director of Theatre '48, Margo headed a primarily male staff: company manager Tad Adoue, with his comically broad drawl, who had left the banking milieu of his wealthy family for the theatre; the young production manager Jonathan Seymour, who considered himself fortunate to work with Margo and hoped to move up to a directing position; and general manager Manning Gurian, her lover, whose ambition was to write and produce plays.

Mixer of Truth and Magic

Smiling serenely, wearing a ribbon in her dark, wavy hair, Margo posed for publicity photographs for Theatre '48 encircled by these three men. The picture ran in *Theatre Arts*, where the caption identified only Margo. Although she was devoted to playwrights and concerned for the welfare of her actors, considering both writers and actors to be "artists," Margo often seemed curiously blind to the ego needs of her staff. Perhaps she viewed them as extensions of herself. Certainly she expected them to work long hours with the same total dedication that she gave to the theatre, at the same time failing to recognize that they were not receiving the attention or personal gratification that she received. In a sense, Theatre '48 *was* Margo Jones—she embodied the institution. Although at first June Moll and Joanna Albus worked well with her, the two women soon discovered that to work with Margo, they had to submerge their own identities. Unhappy with this choice, both women left Margo's theatre to work elsewhere.

Now, with a support staff of men united in their affection for her, Margo opened rehearsals for the Theatre '48 season. Production manager Seymour and actors Frances Waller, Mary Finney, Jack Warden, and Clinton Anderson returned from the previous season. Despite Margo's admonition that she was throwing away a promising career, Louise Latham had left the company, gotten married, and moved to Brazil. Good-looking John Hudson replaced leading man Tod Andrews, who was in *Summer and Smoke*. Harold Webster and Edwin Whitner, veteran Broadway actors, and ingenue Romola Robb, who had just finished a year acting in *Harvey* with Frank Fay, completed the company. Area actors, some of them college students, would fill in throughout the season.

"Learning to know members of your cast and understanding them is a fascinating job," Margo wrote her parents. "I guess I treat them like children; and just as the temperaments of one's children are often different, so the temperaments of each member of the company are a new and challenging experience." Although many established New York actors were unwilling to devote almost a year of their lives, leaving apartments and loved ones, to join a resident company far from the theatrical center, the wide attention Theatre '48 received and Margo's national reputation, coupled with the scarcity of jobs in New York, lured some talented actors to commit to a season of repertory. Their salaries were not high, but living expenses in Dallas were low, and they could play a variety of good parts in both classic and new plays. They were treated handsomely by the locals, who were fascinated with them. Also, Margo made sure that each of the resident actors had several important roles during the season and was pictured on the cover of the playbill at least once.

Mixer of Truth and Magic

To open the season she again chose a classic, but this time a comedy she had directed in Houston—Molière's brilliant satire *The Learned Ladies*. She and designer Jed Mace moved the period of the play from the reign of Louis XIV to the 1780s to take advantage of the passion for pastoral life that swept France at that time. Using glazed chintz, organdy, and net in a pastel color scheme, Mace costumed the actors in the shepherd and shepherdess fashions that the upper classes of the period affected. To create the setting, he borrowed a few pieces of French provincial furniture, upholstered them in white quilted chintz, and hung a papier-mâché balloon and a basket of flowers from the center of the acting area. Margo directed the action like a dance, "for these people," she wrote, "were like graceful marionettes in a ballroom environment."

The elegantly dressed opening-night audience loved the play, as did the critics. John Rosenfield announced drily, "Theatre '48 Starts With a Hit for a Change." Molière had been largely relegated to the classroom and was rarely seen onstage, and Rosenfield felt that Margo's decision to present the playwright's work was "showmanship at its best. All too few in the trade realize that the public never knows what it wants until it sees it." He singled out Jack Warden for particular praise in his character role as Trissotin, a foppish poet dressed in lace and ribbons and infatuated with his own verses. "Although a wrestler or left tackle by nature," Rosenfield wrote, "Warden's gifts of timing and his insight enabled him to create a convincing portrait and only occasionally did he labor with a polysyllable as if he had never met it before."

SINCE SHE WOULD be in final rehearsals of the next play during the Thanksgiving holiday, Margo wrote her family, who wanted her to join them for the special day, that she would be arranging a dinner for her company at the theatre. Her housekeeper Floyd McDaniel prepared two turkeys with all the trimmings, and they all sat down together "like a great big family," Margo wrote. She worked at creating an atmosphere of trust and closeness in the company. "She talked about love and togetherness—we'd all sing happy birthday for each other—she was turned on by loving her neighbor," recalls actor Clinton Anderson. Martha Bumpas, an actress who worked at the theatre during the early 1950s, felt that Margo "was unique in that she could create a magic moment." However, when she tried to create similar rituals for her Broadway companies, for example having a wishing well constructed backstage for the *Summer and Smoke* cast in New York and then sending them daily good wishes for a successful performance, her efforts, out of place in the hard-boiled, more cynical world of the New York theatre, were sometimes met with derision and laughter from actors and crew members. In a business that batters self-esteem, Margo's style was an attempt to create a safe, harmonious working environment. With deliberate calculation, masked by her considerable charm, Margo sought to discover what motivated other people, and used that knowledge to gain what she wanted. While this behavior could be called hypocritical, it is behavior familiar to every good director, who must manipulate actors to achieve a desired effect. At times Margo would drive her actors to their limit, and the mask would slip a bit. One actress who glimpsed the force underneath the mask was reminded of a great volcano that might explode at any moment.

Here's to Us, a contemporary comedy by Shirland Quin (pen name of British writer Enid Guest), followed *The Learned Ladies*. The setting, a Gramercy Park apartment in New York, was home ground for Margo, but the characters, drawn from the worlds of radio and literature, and the plot, mundane drawing-room-comedy material centering on the actions of literary agent Kit Tremaine, who sublets her apartment from 5:30 P.M. to 10:00 A.M. to a former test pilot while she occupies it the rest of the time, held little interest for the Dallas audience. The critics thought it frothy and mildly amusing. The play wasn't particularly popular, but many women in the audience did admire the Neiman-Marcus costumes, not to mention Jack Warden's athletic physique when he appeared wearing nothing more than boxer shorts comically decorated with a pattern of glaring, three-inch-long red ants.

Since a comedy by Shakespeare had been popular the previous season, Margo chose *Twelfth Night* as the holiday show. She and Mace arrived at a production style in the spirit of Mardi Gras, relying on costuming and lighting to create the atmosphere. Three black benches, a table, and a stool, easily set or removed by actors in character, were the only set pieces. Music, both recorded and live, was incorporated throughout the play, which opened and closed with Feste, the fool, singing and accompanying himself on a mandolin. Jack Warden appeared in yet another guise as Sir Toby Belch, padded to gargantuan proportions.

On New Year's Eve, in keeping with the tradition established the year before, *Twelfth Night* ended shortly before midnight, and the actors threw colored streamers to the audience and led them outside in a serpentine dance to change the theatre's sign from Theatre '48 to Threatre '49, then back inside for an eggnog party. All three weeks of *Twelfth Night* were sold out, proving again Shakespeare's popularity with the public. The critics liked the production too. Rosenfield felt that it was superior to *The Taming of the Shrew* of the previous year, writing that the "company reached a singleness of style" that "did not wash out into something blandly literary. Instead it was lusty and boisterous as intended."

After three comedies, Margo felt that her audience was ready for the poetic drama *Skaal*, by Wisconsin native Vivian Johannes, a theatre director turned playwright. Set in a Norwegian settlement in the big-woods country of the Mississippi Valley, the play, despite the cheer of its title, was a "nightmare of dullness," according to one playgoer. Critics concurred, calling it wordy and dreary. Rosenfield poked fun at the clichés that told the audience, "pine trees are tall, smoke is black, fire is red, the sea is wide, skies are blue and so are you." The actors weren't too happy about the play either. Clinton Anderson, who played Young Thor, the hero of the piece, announced to Margo one day during rehearsal, "I think this is one of the worst plays I've ever tried to do."

"Well," Margo replied, "I think it's one of the best plays I've ever read in my life." Actually, she realized that the play had weaknesses, writing Tennessee that "it doesn't have enough body for a real play, but it has moments of rare beauty." Expressing doubts to her company was not her method. Keeping her enthusiasm and belief intact or seeming to do so exacted a toll in energy and spent emotion, but she considered it an essential part of her work as a director. Poetry, mood, atmosphere all appealed to her in play selection, and she did not apologize for choosing a script that others considered lifeless. She wrote George Freedley that "[*Skaal*] is a beautiful example of why a theatre like this must exist . . . to do a script that we want to do, even though the appeal is limited." Of course, she was also shrewd enough to sugarcoat the bitter pill of *Skaal* by placing it after three lively comedies and following it with a comic farce.

The third new script of the season was *Sting in the Tail*, a farce–murder mystery by British writer Tom Purefoy. Although Margo kept her misgivings to herself, at the final dress rehearsal she thought that the production needed a week's more work, and at the preview performance she felt physically ill. "You would think that I would get hardened and not take the opening of a play so seriously," she wrote a friend, "but I am afraid I get worse instead of better." However, Jack Warden, wearing a stiffly starched collar and a false moustache for his role as a Victorian scoundrel, and Mary Finney, playing the old lady who finds him out, both gave outstanding performances and made the play one of the most popular of the season.

As his gift to Theatre '49, Stark Young waived the royalties on his translation of Chekhov's *The Sea Gull*, originally made for Alfred Lunt and Lynn Fontanne. To accommodate the small playing area, only two settings were used: the garden and a room in Sorin's house. Rare antique chairs made in 1870 for

Mixer of Truth and Magic

the Emperor Franz Joseph of Austria and valued at three thousand dollars each, an empire sofa once owned by one of Napoleon's marshals, and Directoire candlesticks (an identical pair was owned by the Duke and Duchess of Windsor) decorated the set and received almost as much publicity as the actors. Margo felt that Chekhov's play, "in which every character's movement and the rhythm of every word count, [was] ideally suited for an intimate theatre." Although the production was not popular with audiences, critics thought it one of the best of the season.

When efforts failed to find another new play (that elusive comedy with one set and a small cast), Margo chose instead to present a classic, *She Stoops to Conquer* by Oliver Goldsmith, which opened March 14, 1949. She treated the play as a broad, comic romp, staging it with a few benches and stools moved by the actors. Although written for the eighteenth-century picture-frame stage, the action adapted easily to theatre-in-the-round. Jack Warden, playing the absurd Tony Lumpkin, delighted audiences with his antics and earned the title "Comic King of Theatre '49." Single-ticket buyers besieged the box office, making up for the poor attendance during *Skaal* and *The Sea Gull*.

IN FEBRUARY, Margo had rushed home for a quick trip to see her parents and Charles in Livingston. Her brother Richard, his wife, Bea, and their baby, Judy, now two years old, also visited from Houston. Margo doted on her niece, indulging her with presents, often turtle toys, and attention. When she visited her family, Margo seemed to close a door on her life in Dallas. Her brothers and Bea knew of her involvement with Manning, but she did not discuss this relationship with her parents—to do so might lead to uncomfortable questions. While Manning introduced Margo to his family, he never accompanied her to Livingston and never met any member of her family. He recalls, "I didn't know anything about her family or remember her ever talking about them except that she was proud to be from the piney woods of East Texas." He told Margo about his family history and relationships, but she did not share her background with him. "It wasn't part of her life," he believed.

Although she only saw her family a few times a year for brief visits, they were in her life and her thoughts. Her mother, now white-haired and past seventy, wrote frequently, often enclosing pressed flowers and religious sayings, her handwriting shaky and almost illegible and her news primarily of deaths and her own fears. In one letter, she expressed her hope that her "little girl [would] never be left alone and lonely anytime anywhere." Margo's father, still vigorous and active, accepted that his daughter was a woman in her late thirties, and wrote with practical advice and encouragement. "Learning to say 'No' is best many times," he counseled. "You are your own boss now. So watch your step and don't let any one side track your plans." Margo's relationship with her family mirrored the experience of countless others like her who leave rural backgrounds to form new lives in cities far from home, only to find in time that they have little in common with the parents who raised them. In regular, detailed, always cheerful letters, Margo attempted to bridge the communication gap with her family, describing her daily activities and justifying and defending them as well.

FOR WEEKS the Theatre '49 company had immersed themselves in the literary atmosphere of the Romantic period in nineteenth-century London in preparation for the final play of the season, *The Coast of Illyria* by Dorothy Parker and Ross Evans. Margo had asked Parker and Evans to come to Dallas a week before their play opened to work on the script. The company was eager to meet the wisecracking, witty Miss Parker, famous for her best-selling poetry and short stories and for her image as queen of New York's fabled Algonquin Round Table.

That cynical flapper with a repertoire of smart sayings, the darling of the 1920s, never arrived in Dallas. Dorothy Parker did, a short, overweight, fifty-five-year-old "shrinking violet" of a woman, her mouth drawn into a thin, tight line. A fringe of brunette bangs framed her round face, which was puffy from lack of sleep and too much alcohol. Accompanying her was her thirty-one-year-old lover and co-writer, tall, dark, and handsome Ross Evans, an alcoholic, who had been so eager to work with her, he said, "I'd have been glad just to sharpen her pencils."

During the 1930s and 1940s, Dorothy Parker and her husband Alan Campbell had collaborated on a series of successful screenplays. After their divorce in 1947, she had written a screen adaptation of *Lady Windermere's Fan* with Ross Evans, and they had co-authored *The Coast of Illyria*. Probably through their mutual friend playwright Edwin Justus Mayer, Parker had heard about Theatre '49 in Dallas and had submitted the script to Margo. Although celebrated for her prose and poetry, collected in *The Portable Dorothy Parker* in 1944, Parker yearned to be a playwright. Her first play, *Close Harmony*, written with Elmer Rice, had failed on Broadway in 1924. Margo's optimism and her reputation with new plays fueled Parker's hope that *The Coast of Illyria* might make it to New York.

Parker and Evans had wanted to come for the full three-week rehearsal

Mixer of Truth and Magic

period but Margo put them off, saying that she needed the first two weeks to pound in characterization and stage business. Instead she asked them to stay for a week before and after the opening. Greeted by the dynamic Margo, Parker told a Dallas reporter, "I've never met anyone like her," then added, probably with more tact than sincerity, "She's wonderful."

Although the two women both preferred to live in hotels and enjoyed a taste for liquor, there the resemblance ended. Parker was an avowed pessimist who, according to her biographer Marion Meade, wondered, "What fresh hell is this?" when she was confronted with a ringing telephone or a doorbell. Margo was an optimist, a self-confessed Pollyanna always looking on the bright side. Parker needed to be driven to work and had had to be prodded by her former husband and partner Alan Campbell into turning out screenplays; Margo, on the other hand, lived to work and had boundless energy and tenacity. While the two women were certainly cordial, even quite friendly, both in correspondence and in their working arrangement, their relationship was one of necessity.

Margo, usually eager to have playwrights present for rehearsals, complained to her parents that she had the double responsibility of taking care of the authors of *The Coast of Illyria* and having them at rehearsals. "They are not accustomed to the pace I have to keep, so I find myself having to keep them organized all the time to get the work done," she said. The main problem was the script—it was much too long, running about three hours. Since Parker did not write quickly or easily, the revising process was, Margo said, "extremely tedious."

The title of the play was inspired by Shakespeare's *Twelfth Night*, and his story of a brother and sister who are shipwrecked off the coast of Illyria. In the Parker and Ross play, however, the brother and sister are Charles and Mary Lamb, nineteenth-century English writing collaborators best known for their *Tales from Shakespeare*, who are battered by storms of poverty, insanity, and alcoholism. Drawing on a well of pain from her relationship with Alan Campbell, Parker tells the story of Mary Lamb, who in a moment of madness years earlier had killed her mother with a kitchen knife. To save her from Bedlam, Charles had promised to take care of her for the rest of her life—a decision that leads to his sacrificing his romance with actress Fanny Kelly. That sacrifice sends Charles to the brandy bottle and Mary Lamb back into madness. The Lambs' home is the gathering place for the literary lights of London, who are afflicted with various neuroses and addictions. They include Samuel Coleridge with his tinctured laudanum, Thomas De Quincey with his opium habit, and the bitter critic William Hazlitt. The characterizations, part his-

Mixer of Truth and Magic

torical, part imagined, are rich and complex and the language sparkles from time to time with Parker quips such as "hisses come more deeply from the heart," the description of Wordsworth as "up to his rump in sunsets," and this introduction of Coleridge: "[H]ere comes Coleridge, who has dropped the world from his shoulders and is dragging it behind him." When the poet recites "Kubla Khan," Hazlitt, ever the critic, sharply observes that it's no "Ancient Mariner."

Designer Jed Mace and Margo wanted the audience to feel that the Lambs' London flat was an actual room where they lived, worked, and entertained. They devised a naturalistic setting, furnished with antiques of the Empire Period, including a complete library loaned by a local bookstore that filled low bookcases set against the imaginary four walls. Every volume was carefully chosen to represent books that the Lambs and their contemporaries might have been reading. Two precious Royal Crown Darby mantel figures were placed onstage only after the audience had been seated. The theatre carried additional insurance for the use of these valuable antiques.

A great deal of advance publicity stimulated interest in the play, and ticket sales boomed. On opening night April 4 every seat was filled. The audience was eager to catch a glimpse of the famous writer. Unfortunately for them, the shy, frightened Parker scurried backstage during intermissions, murmuring Margo's standard phrase "Bless you" when complimented. Theatre '49's publicist, Mabel Duke, had envisioned capitalizing on Parker's clever repartee and acerbic wit but was disappointed that she "never heard a sharp crack from her all the time she was here." The opening-night audience gave the play an ovation which, John Rosenfield reported, brought "a shaky Miss Parker and a pale Mr. Evans" to their feet. The local critics considered the play to be the find of the season, sure to go on to Broadway. The reviewer for *Variety* told his readers that *The Coast of Illyria* was a hit, "written with intelligence and taste, sharp-edged and convincing."

Despite the good critical response, Margo felt that the script needed more work before it would be ready for further production. Brooks Atkinson and his wife Oriana traveled to Dallas to see the play and left disappointed, having found it, Atkinson wrote, "an ordinary drama about some extraordinary people . . . not very vigorous or searching. . . . "

W H I L E   H E   D I D N ' T respond positively to the play, Atkinson, like John Rosenfield, continued to report favorably on Margo's unique theatre. "In its third season," he wrote, "Theatre '49 is a genuine artistic, economic and cultural success. The arena style of acting is enjoyable and artistically legitimate. The productions and acting are professional. And the fare Miss Jones serves in Dallas is no insipid imitation of Broadway but original, nourishing and uncommonly well-balanced." He also continued to support the decentralization of theatre, urging others to follow Theatre '49's example. "All a theatre needs is a playwright, a director and some actors," he wrote. "The impulse for theatre comes from within."

In addition to her work at Theatre '49, Margo continued to be active in the American National Theatre Academy, serving as vice-president and as ANTA's primary spokesperson for the decentralization of theatre and seeking out and talking with theatre leaders around the country. She visited Houston, advising Nina Whittington Vance's Alley Theatre, primarily urging Vance to follow Theatre '49's example and present new plays and classics. Inspired by Margo's success in Houston with the Community Players, Nina Vance had begun the Alley with a $2.14 investment in penny postcards sent to 214 people, including many like Dr. Barraco, Sidney and Malvina Holmes, and Sonny Koch who had supported the Community Players. Although the theatre was currently strictly amateur and many of the supporters liked it that way, Vance had other ambitions, and in the 1950s the Alley would become fully professional.

In December 1948, Robert Breen, executive secretary of ANTA, and Richard Coe, the theatre critic of the *Washington Post*, approached Margo about starting a theatre-in-the-round in Washington, D.C. Coe said that Washington had plenty of money for a theatre. She replied that since she didn't have an assistant director at her theatre, she couldn't leave. She told them that they needed to find one committed person, a leader, and said she would be glad to help by phone, letter, or wire.

IN MARCH 1949, Margo attended a three-day conference on the state of the theatre sponsored by ANTA and Actors' Equity at the Hotel Astor in Manhattan, overlooking Broadway and Times Square. The hotel teemed with middle-aged theatre people. The women sported hats of every type—soft berets, wool cloches, veiled hats, jeweled hats, even bonnets with chin ties. They tossed thick furs carelessly over their padded shoulders and accented their attire with necklaces, earrings, and gloves. The men were more subdued in their dark business suits with wide ties or an occasional ascot. Everyone seemed to be puffing on a cigarette. These were the men and women of the commercial theatre, embodying the image of sleek prosperity.

Margo, who was not wearing a hat or any makeup except lipstick and who wore a dark simple dress and at thirty-seven was several years younger than most of the participants, must have looked as though she had entered the wrong club. In fact, although a sometime commercial director and producer, Margo belonged to another kind of theatre world, undeveloped but growing, that was based on art not profits, and that key difference set her apart from the Hotel Astor crowd. However, among the well-known theatre figures like Helen Hayes, Richard Aldrich, Agnes De Mille, Kermit Bloomgarden, and Robert Morley, she saw old friends Rosamond Gilder and Vinton Freedley, and she soon sat down next to Brooks Atkinson, a familiar sight in his trademark bow tie and with his ever-present pipe.

While many of the people attending the conference were actually there to find new jobs or to make contacts, most pretended that the conference's business was their first priority, showing up at committee meetings and listening to speeches. Aline MacMahon of Actors' Equity reminded the group of a shocking fact. As of March 2, 1949, she told them, of Equity's six thousand members only 572 were employed in the thirty-one theatres on Broadway. After hearing this depressing statistic and other dire warnings from agents, playwrights, producers, scene designers, stage managers, composers, directors, and critics, the conference participants agreed on one thing: the state of the theatre was not good.

Margo had been invited to speak. A pioneer to the core, a believer in the axiom that if you want something done, you have to do it yourself, Margo had little faith in committees and conferences. She knew that others felt that theatres could be founded and theatre people employed by state governments or the national government or by a consortium of producers, but she believed along with Brooks Atkinson that "the theatre impulse comes from within." One person, one leader, could make a difference.

Standing at the front of a huge meeting room decorated in traditional eighteenth-century style, Margo spoke of the future and of leadership. Speaking without notes, since hers was essentially the same message she had delivered since 1944, she urged her audience of avowed New Yorkers to leave that city, establish theatres across the country, and make their own jobs. She said, "To me the pertinent factor in the establishment of a successful theatre is . . . getting one person who is a combination of business and artistic leadership, or of getting two leaders, one first-class business manager and one first-class theatre person, who can work together in every large town in America. If we are to have first-class professional theatres all over the country, we must have the people who can do it wanting to do it." She talked about practical matters —budgets, salaries, unions, ticket prices, and start-up costs—and about a total commitment to a life in the theatre, telling them that "the glamour and

Mixer of Truth and Magic

excitement of the theatre comes from working in it all the time, every day. The sorrows of the theatre come as a result of not working in the theatre."

At the close of the conference, it was resolved that a standing committee be formed to study all the resolutions presented. In a few months another conference would be called to discuss the committee's findings. John Rosenfield grumped that it would take dozens of conferences on the state of the theatre to make New York theatre professionals understand what the rest of the country wanted and needed. "The trouble with the legit business," he wrote in his column in May 1949, "is the narrow vision of the Broadway promoters and producers. . . . The stage audience can not be limited to resident New Yorkers or transients on expense accounts."

THEATRE '49 closed out the season with a six-week festival of six plays. Instead of scheduling the unpopular *Here's to Us* and *Skaal*, Margo revived *The Importance of Being Earnest* from the previous year. Although the classics had been popular, *Twelfth Night* and *The Learned Ladies* especially, the new plays had been less successful at the box office. Still, Manning Gurian calculated that on average Theatre '49 had played to 85 percent capacity and had grossed twenty-six hundred dollars a week, leaving a profit of fifteen thousand dollars to begin the fall season.

To take advantage of the promotional opportunity afforded by the two-year anniversary of the theatre's opening of its first play, Margo and Manning met with the mayor of Dallas and the president of the Chamber of Commerce on June 3, 1949, greeting them with a large placard saying, "Thank you, Dallas." In response, the mayor held up a sign that said, "Thank you, Margo." While the signs were probably lettered in the theatre scene shop and the event directed by Margo, the sentiment expressed was sincere. Margo brought honor to Dallas, and she was someone they understood, a good old girl who liked to drink and work hard and was their own star in the vast blue skies of Texas.

She couldn't wait to get back to New York.

TWENTY-FOUR GRAMERCY PARK had been Margo's home away from home since 1941, a refuge from Texas and a cool, quiet oasis amidst the clamor of the city. She spent long summer evenings reading scripts there, or sometimes she went to the small private park across the street, unlocked the ornate iron gates, and walked about, enjoying the flowers and the solitude.

In July, she and Manning toured the straw-hat circuit scouting acting talent for Theatre '49. At Tufts Summer Theatre in Medford, Massachusetts, they visited with Jonathan Seymour, who had directed several in-the-round productions there. At Lambertville, New Jersey, they saw a production of *The Vagabond King* at St. John Terrell's Music Circus, a tent theatre-in-the-round inspired by Theatre '49. It was a lazy time, a time for doing nothing at all, Margo wrote June Moll.

The idyll was brief, however, for she and Manning had negotiated an agreement with the Shuberts to take a new production of *Summer and Smoke* on the road. Since the Shuberts owned theatre buildings across the country, many of them empty, they had decided that it would be in their interest to back a road tour, thereby receiving rent on their out-of-town theatres. When the Shuberts had recouped their investment in the play, all profits would then be split with Margo, who planned to share the proceeds with the original investors.

In the first two weeks of August 1949, Margo cast the company, primarily choosing actors from the original Dallas production and from the New York production. Katharine Balfour would again play Alma, the role she had created in Dallas, to Tod Andrews's Dr. Buchanan. Since Ray Walston was working in another play, Jack Warden would act the role of the traveling salesman Archie Kramer. After rehearsals in New York, the first week in September the company moved to the Harris Theatre in Chicago, where the play would open as the first attraction of the Theatre Guild's Theatre Society subscription series.

Tennessee, taken aback by Margo's whirlwind decision to restage the play, suggested changing its title to *August Madness*. He continued to work on the script: for the touring production, he cut the prologue with the two children completely, reinstated a scene between John's father and Alma, and revised the first act. On opening night in Chicago, Margo insisted on dining at Riccardo's, the restaurant where the company had gathered after the opening of *The Glass Menagerie*. Again, the city was receptive to a Williams play. The reviews were excellent, especially the notices for Katharine Balfour. Critic Claudia Cassidy wrote that Balfour's portrayal of Alma was vastly superior to Margaret Phillips's version. Business was good too, despite the competition of touring productions of *Death of a Salesman*, *Brigadoon*, and *Kiss Me, Kate*, and the Chicago run was extended.

Tennessee continued to talk to the newspapers, this time in a more affable if still defensive mood. He wrote Ashton Stevens of the *Chicago Herald-Tribune*, "I believe that you and several other critics insist on regarding *Summer* as an earlier work because it is the most romantic of the three and because romanticism is thought of as a juvenile quality. Actually, I feel that cynicism is the more juvenile quality though I admit that it can be expressed in a more adult sounding way and is more acceptable to most adults. Also I think it is very optimistic of critics to suppose that the latest works are always the best. Often a poet's early lyrics are his most intense."

Summer and Smoke moved on to Cleveland, Milwaukee, Pittsburgh, St. Paul, Minneapolis, and St. Louis. Margo flew from Dallas to St. Louis for a Saturday reunion with the company and for a party given by Tennessee's mother, Edwina, and his brother, Dakin. The tour continued, playing Louisville, Springfield, Indianapolis, and Columbus, and eventually closing in Boston on January 7, 1950. Margo then sold the amateur rights, making the play available to nonprofessional theatres and colleges. The original investors did receive a return from the tour and dividends from amateur performances, but it would take yet another production several years later to ensure the place of *Summer and Smoke* in theatre history.

IN APRIL 1952, a group calling themselves the Loft Players at Circle-in-the-Square, a tiny amateur theatre housed in a former nightclub at 5 Sheridan Square in Greenwich Village, presented *Summer and Smoke*. Founded in 1951 by José Quintero, a young native Panamanian and graduate of the University of Southern California, and Ted Mann, a Brooklyn lawyer who had worked out the financial set-up for the theatre, the Loft Players' plan was to present unusual plays for runs of at least two months. Like Margo in Dallas, they had faced the problem of lack of theatre space and for practical reasons had decided on a three-quarter-round stage in the center of the nightclub's ballroom. The group worked cooperatively, taking turns tending bar, selling tickets, and checking coats, with actors in the company alternating in leads, supporting roles, and bit parts—all for a salary of ten dollars a week plus a place to live in the theatre. Unlike countless other off-Broadway groups that sprouted in New York only to die of neglect or lack of funds or inexperience, the Circle-in-the-Square would flourish. Although many of the original members left the theatre life for various reasons, José Quintero boasted later that "those of us who stubbornly stuck it out have enriched contemporary theatre by being willing to pledge heart, soul, mind, strength and loneliness to the sometime wickedness of that whore. It can kiss you and applaud you and at the same time break your heart, but there is nothing you can do about it. Nothing you want to do about it. You are in love. What else is there?"

Margo saw the Circle-in-the-Square production of *Summer and Smoke* in June 1952 with her old friend, writer Bill Goyen, and artist Joseph Glasco. They sat in the front row of the two-hundred-seat theatre; the stage was surrounded on three sides by tables and chairs. As Margo watched the play unfold in a theatre very much like hers in Dallas, with minimal settings and properties, the action flowing fluidly from scene to scene, the audience not detached observers but involved participants, a wave of memories rushed back to her. At the end of the play, with tears streaming down her face, she congratulated Quintero and the talented young actress Geraldine Page, who had played Alma. Joseph Glasco remembers, "Margo adored the play and she told them and they were thrilled. She was not a bitter woman—there wasn't a mean bone in her body."

Perhaps Margo wondered how things might have been different if her original production had been seen in New York. Or if she had heeded Brooks Atkinson's warning against a standard proscenium-stage presentation. Atkinson, who had trekked downtown to attend the opening night of the revival of *Summer and Smoke*, gave the production and particularly Geraldine Page excellent notices. The fact that he wrote about the little-known theatre at all was even more significant; of course, he had been drawn more by a desire to see Williams's play than to see Quintero's or the actors' work showcased. Margo believed that the off-Broadway groups would have "more continuity in the theatre if they realized that their main aim is still to produce a good play in the best possible manner and not be a showcase for actors and directors. If their productions are good, they will automatically function as showcases. . . ." As he had for Margo's Dallas theatre, Atkinson used his powerful position on the *New York Times* to bring public attention to a noncommercial theatre outside the mainstream. Atkinson argued, as he had earlier, that the play was superior to *Streetcar*, illuminating a wider range of human experience. He wrote that "Circle-in-the-Square is an arena-style playhouse for a small audience and a simple production, and *Summer and Smoke* comes alive in that environment." Quintero's production gave the play a new life, launched his professional directing career and Geraldine Page's acting career, and brought real distinction to an off-Broadway theatre. In a sense, the off-Broadway movement, the revolt of artists against the commercial theatre, sporadic at best during the 1940s, really began with the major triumph of Circle-in-the-Square, with the unorthodox (to New York eyes) production of *Summer and Smoke*. And the group continued to succeed with revivals of *Our Town*, *Children of Darkness*, and most importantly with Eugene O'Neill's *The Iceman Cometh*, another play that had failed on the proscenium stage but found a new, more intimate life in the round.

In fact, a theatre environment modeled on the work and writings of pioneers like Margo in Dallas, Gilmor Brown at the Pasadena Playhouse, and

Mixer of Truth and Magic

Glenn Hughes at the University of Washington was finally taking root in New York. In the summer of 1950, a theatre group based at the Hotel Edison brought arena theatre to New York, but failed after six months. Director Albert McCleery, who had worked extensively in theatre-in-the-round in universities, wrote about this event for *Theatre Arts*. Gilmor Brown, Glenn Hughes, and Margo Jones, he reported, have finally been heard. "During this past summer of 1950," he said, "we watched bemused as the inestimable New York critics discovered a 'revolution' in the Hotel Edison. The pioneers watched with a sense of irony, for it was an old, old story to them." While Margo must have taken some comfort in this interest in theatre-in-the-round and in the success of *Summer and Smoke*, which had come full circle for her, she also learned the lesson that recognition, acceptance, and success in the theatre meant Manhattan. In the solipsistic world of New York theatre, the rest of the country simply did not matter.

IN OCTOBER 1949 Margo returned to Texas for the upcoming season while Manning remained in New York supervising the tour of *Summer and Smoke* and functioning as the theatre's general representative there. He had trained Tad Adoue to take over his position as business manager at the theatre. Jonathan Seymour would again be stage manager and would also serve in the new position of assistant director. Jed Mace's increasing freelance-design obligations as well as his decorating business made it impossible for him to continue as resident designer although he did stay on as a board member. Other designers replaced him, but the look of future productions while serviceable was not noteworthy, lacking Mace's visual wizardry.

With the exception of Mary Finney and Edwin Whitner, who were returning from the previous season, the company members were all new, mostly from the New York stage. Jack Warden had left the company permanently, acquired a New York agent, and would go on to a successful television and film career. He said later that the diverse experience gained at Margo's theatre, playing the classics and new plays, "was great training, the best training anyone can have." New members included Peggy McCay, Joe Sullivan, Virginia Robinson, John Denney, Gregg Juarez, Ben Yafee, and Louis Veda Quince, who had been Margo's teacher years earlier at the Southwestern School of the Theatre. Eighteen-year-old Larry Hagman, the son of actress Mary Martin and Ben Hagman of Weatherford, Texas, joined the company. He was on leave from his drama studies at Bard College and would serve as a production assistant and play small acting roles. J. R. in the popular television series "Dallas," Hagman recalls, "My career has really come full circle, because all the training, all the discipline, started right there at Margo's theatre in Dallas. She was a woman of great force."

Five new plays and three classics would be presented during the thirty-week season. This represented, Margo claimed, "the greatest variety and finest dramatic values of any of the four seasons to date."

The season opened on November 7, 1949, with George Bernard Shaw's comedy *Heartbreak House*, written in 1916. Margo felt that the play was "incredibly timely for a drama written before World War I, and it is as prophetic today (if not more so) as when it was first conceived." For this reason, she directed the play using a contemporary set and modern costumes.

During the final dress rehearsal of *Heartbreak House*, Margo was notified that her old friend, actor Sidney Holmes, had died of a heart attack. Sidney had been the mainstay of the Houston Community Players and had performed at Nina Vance's Alley Theatre, while all the time holding down a full-time job as a salesman. He had dreamed of working for Margo in Dallas or New York, of devoting himself to acting full-time. Fearful of the lack of security this would provide for Sidney's family, Margo had always discouraged his ambition. She took the midnight plane to Houston to spend the night comforting his wife, Malvina, and their three small children.

The next day she returned to Dallas for the opening of *Heartbreak House* and to greet Manning, who had arrived accompanied by their New York lawyer, gray-haired, distinguished Jonas Silverstone. Margo missed Manning's presence in Dallas, but they talked on the phone often—she kept the light on beside the telephone, waiting for his 1:00 A.M. call from New York. Manning continued to be thoughtful, sending flowers and wires, telling her, "You have nothing to worry about. I am the best hand holder in the world."

SARI SCOTT, a native of Pittsburgh, a graduate of Carnegie Tech, and a former assistant to Max Reinhardt, had arrived in Dallas six weeks prior to the opening of her new play, *An Old Beat-Up Woman*. To fund playwrights' residencies at the theatre, the Rockefeller Foundation had awarded Theatre '49 a two-thousand-dollar grant for the season. For the next four years, Margo applied for grants from the Rockefeller Foundation, eventually receiving a total of eighty-five hundred dollars to support her work with new playwrights.

Margo had worked with Sari Scott for months developing her original one-act play into a full-length script. Set in the Texas Panhandle in a one-room shack, the play has three characters: Joe Neal, a drunken truck driver; Utah, his lusty, loyal wife: and, to complete the triangle, Pete, their truck driver friend who falls in love with Utah. The plot is the stuff of country and

Mixer of Truth and Magic

western songs—a good woman wasting her life on a good-looking, no-good man. After years of beatings by her husband, Utah leaves him, and Joe commits suicide. John Rosenfield criticized the expansion of the one-act into a full-length play, feeling that much of the added character development and plotting were unnecessary; however, George Freedley argued that the acting was weak but the play powerful. Despite the homegrown characters, the Dallas audience didn't care for the play.

In the face of the poor response to the production from critics and audiences, Margo chose to produce the play in New York anyway, probably for several reasons. Manning was in New York, eager to produce, and *An Old Beat-Up Woman* with its three characters and one set would be a relatively inexpensive undertaking. Also, she wanted to maintain her position as a Broadway producer, not just as a regional-theatre leader. Finally, she believed in the play and its author and rationalized that with casting changes the play would succeed.

In early December she placed Jonathan Seymour in charge of directing Theatre '49's third production, *Romeo and Juliet*, and traveled to New York to cast *An Old Beat-Up Woman*. She hired Jack Warden to play Pete, taking him out of the *Summer and Smoke* tour. Donald Curtis, who had been in over eighty films and recently appeared on Broadway in *Good-Bye, My Fancy*, would play the drunken, abusive Joe. Carol Stone, who had acted with Paul Muni in *They Knew What They Wanted* and had toured the summer-theatre circuit with Thornton Wilder, playing Sabina to his Mr. Antrobus in *The Skin of Our Teeth*, would play Utah, the tough but downtrodden wife. Frederick Fox, a Broadway designer currently working in television, signed on to do the set and costumes. Capitalized at forty thousand dollars, backed by Dallas residents as well as New Yorkers like George Freedley, the production marked Manning's first credited producing effort. A publicity release (perhaps written by Manning, certainly approved by him) announced, "from usher to general manager, Manning Gurian knows every phase of show business. In the latter capacity he has served Margo Jones long and faithfully. With her, he will be billed formally for the first time as co-sponsor of *An Old Beat-Up Woman*."

Margo and the cast returned to Dallas for rehearsals, in the process surely lowering the morale of the Theatre '49 company members who had been judged unacceptable for the Broadway production. At the same time, she rehearsed the theatre's upcoming play, *My Granny Van*, by Texas author George Sessions Perry.

An Old Beat-Up Woman began tryouts at the Shubert Theatre in New Haven, Connecticut, playing there for three days. While Margo was in New

Haven, she met playwright Thornton Wilder, a resident of nearby Hamden. Wilder attended rehearsals and grew fond of Margo, whom he recognized as a fellow enthusiast. He wrote her later thanking her for the rehearsal sessions and saying, "especially I want to thank you for the wonderful work you are doing in discovering new playwrights—in being a Divining Rod for American drama. I must give a lecture tonight—about Melville, and Emily Dickinson, and Thoreau—people whom a Margo Jones would have espied before their death and posthumous consecration!"

Sari Scott continued to work on the play in New Haven, where it was not well received. While praising the forceful acting, the local reviewer found the play slow and too wordy. Although the production moved to the Wilbur Theatre in Boston, it closed there on January 28, 1950. Margo told George Freedley that the play *was* too talky, with "literally no action from the beginning to the end dissipating into a Western melodrama with no heart or soul." She blamed herself for not seeing the problems earlier. To playwright Scott she confessed that "the play that you wrote and the play that I fell in love with is not the play that we saw on the stage. The fault may be completely mine."

Tennessee wrote her teasingly that she must be feeling like an old beat-up woman herself after the grueling schedule she had been following. He felt wonderful, he told her, had lost thirteen pounds and was at peace for the first time in years. Although *My Granny Van*, which had opened January 9 at Theatre '50 and which was the first truly regional play the theatre had produced, was breaking attendance records, Margo was depressed and discouraged —and for good reason. *An Old Beat-Up Woman* had failed, losing thousands of dollars of her investors' money, almost certainly because of her poor judgment. And John Rosenfield had warned her about taking the play to New York, insinuating that Manning's influence over her was misguided.

After the play closed, she wanted Manning to join her in Dallas, but he told her that he had lost his perspective and needed some time away. "I don't want anything from you," he wrote. "It's not the show that failed, it may be partly financial, but it's something, and I must do something about it. I must." Ironically, while Rosenfield blamed Gurian for the failure, Manning held Margo partly responsible. He felt that she was the kind of director who never went beyond the play, and he believed that "a director has to go beyond the play. She didn't try to improve the play or change it." To find his perspective, he vacationed in Florida for several weeks, writing Margo about his lazy days basking in the sun, and putting her off about when he would join her in Dallas.

During this time of despondency, on a gray February day in 1950, on "the day I needed it most," Margo said, she received a postcard from her new friend Thornton Wilder. It was just a note, but a note filled with Wilder's largeness of spirit and with a prescient understanding of Margo's feelings. "What amulet do you use in moments of discouragement?" he asked. "Even Texans must have such moments." Then he gave her a charm fashioned of his words. "Just murmur to yourself: in fifth-century Greece, the people arrived at the theatre soon after dawn, saw 3 tragedies in the A.M. and a steel-broom of a comedy in the P.M.; that Goldoni wrote 33 plays in a single season, all good and two of them masterpieces; that Lope de Vega was so idolized by the people that the word 'lope' came to mean 'excellent' . . . your beads. Your tonics . . . To you = fighter, builder, explorer, and mixer of truth and magic. Greetings. Selah, Mizpah, etc. Thornton Wilder."

Mixing truth and magic, creating plays, escaping her own life to live in the theatre, in the art she said "had given [her] a chance not only to live [her] own life but a million others" as well restored Margo, giving her renewed vigor. Hardy and healthy, blessed with physical well-being despite her sometimes poor eating habits, Margo was rarely ill. With Manning absent, however, she increased her consumption of liquor and possibly her "get thin–keep awake" pills as well. The pills kept her up, sometimes for twenty-four to thirty-six hours at a stretch, and the liquor relaxed her, countering the effects of the amphetamines. When she had a day off or had caught up with correspondence or play-reading, she would sleep for twelve to twenty-four hours, getting up at Floyd McDaniel's urging to eat a home-cooked meal and drink great quantities of milk and orange juice.

WITH JONATHAN SEYMOUR'S assistance, Margo directed the world premiere of Sean O'Casey's *Cock-a-Doodle Dandy* as the first play presented by Theatre '50. The play opened on January 30. The Irish dramatist's first play, *The Shadow of a Gunman*, had been presented in 1923 by the famed Abbey Theatre, the national theatre of Ireland founded by Lady Gregory and William Butler Yeats in 1904. When the rough-looking O'Casey, a construction worker wearing hobnailed boots, appeared at the Abbey with his script, Lady Gregory said that the theatre would "put on the play for three nights only, in order to let the poor fellow see how bad it was." O'Casey went on to write his masterpieces, *Juno and the Paycock* and *The Plough and the Stars*, but when Lady Gregory and Yeats rejected his more experimental work, *The Silver Tassie*, O'Casey severed his ties with the Abbey and lived as an expatriate in London. Now in his seventieth year, O'Casey had given Margo the rights to his latest play, saying, "I hope your gallant theatre will live long and bless many good work in production during the years to come."

The play is a comic, poetic fable that celebrates the joy of life primarily through the central figure of the Cock, a gorgeous, enchanted bird who can transform into a top hat or a beautiful woman, collapse chairs and tables, make liquor change color, even create thunder, lightning, and wind. Margo believed that with the active imagination of the audience, coupled with clever lighting, this magic could be created on a small arena stage. However, the production of *Cock-a-Doodle Dandy* on the intimate stage of Theatre '50 failed to create the fantastical visual feast the play required. While the acting and the script were praised, the critics agreed that the style of presentation was inadequate. The production of the play was a significant theatrical event, but it barely broke even at Theatre '50's box office.

Margo felt that Ibsen's *Ghosts*, the final classic of the season, which opened February 20, was better suited for their stage although somewhat dated. The critics liked this production and exhorted the public to go and "relax and enjoy it," but the public didn't listen and the production lost money at the box office. *The Golden Porcupine*, a new play by Muriel Roy Bolton about the rise of the "bastard king" Louis XII to the throne of France, opened next. The reviewer for *Variety* wrote that it was a "lavish and fast-moving play, though . . . overloaded for the small theatre-in-the-round."

The final play of the season, however, a comedy-satire titled *Southern Exposure* by Hollywood screenwriter and producer Owen Crump, broke all box-office records at the theatre. Demand for single tickets was so high that Margo decided to run the play for a fourth week, moving into the time scheduled for the end-of-season repertory festival. She explained her change in policy to John Rosenfield. "We couldn't turn people down at the box office, could we? It might make them mad and we don't want anybody, not anybody, mad at Theatre '50. So we are going to sell them tickets to keep them happy."

The plot of *Southern Exposure* is melodramatic with a satirical edge. A sweet old southern lady, Miss Penelope Mayweather, can't pay the mortgage on her antebellum mansion and is forced to open her home to the hordes of Yankee tourists who descend on Natchez, Mississippi, during an annual pilgrimage to view old southern homes. Miss Penelope tolerates the intruders in her home but doesn't know that a charming young writer, John Salguod, who has rented a room in her house, is really John Douglas (Salguod spelled backward), the author of a scathing book about racial relations that has been banned in Natchez but is a best-seller everywhere else. Of course, Miss Penelope has a lovely, liberated young cousin who fights with John but secretly

Mixer of Truth and Magic

yearns for him. In the end Miss Penelope sells her steamy memoirs (conveniently discovered by John) and pays the mortgage. John marries Carol and all ends happily. The Dallas audience howled at the sight of gawking northern tourists making vulgar idiots of themselves and at the ladylike Miss Penelope tippling wine and swooning at the mere mention of the nasty word "Vermont."

Although Margo called the play a "light, charming little piece of fluff," she felt that its enormous popularity in Dallas practically guaranteed a success in New York. With Manning and Tad Adoue as co-producers, she decided to open the play on Broadway in the fall without a tryout. Enthusiasm was high, and they had no trouble raising the sixty thousand dollars necessary to finance the production.

While the fourth season ended triumphantly for Margo's nonprofit resident theatre—attendance had grown dramatically and five of her eight plays had been financial successes, thereby validating her policy of presenting only new work and classics—the 1949–50 season had not been good economically for the commercial theatre. Postwar inflation combined with the competition of radio, television, and the movies continued to contribute to the decline. When the Theatre Guild cancelled its 1949–50 Dallas road tour, John Rosenfield noted the passing of an era; no longer could Dallas depend on art from the East. "We must make the shows we expect to see," Rosenfield wrote. On Broadway, only fifty-six shows were produced, and according to the chronicle *Theatre World*, that was the "smallest number of productions to reach New York . . . during the past fifty years."

After four continuous seasons, Theatre '50 had stability and continued to grow artistically and financially. In speeches and articles, Margo had talked about the growth of her theatre and the vision she had for a national network of theatres. As a result, John Selby of Rinehart & Company Publishers had asked her to write a book about theatre-in-the-round, her philosophy, and her plans for the future. June and July were free of theatre obligations (*Southern Exposure* rehearsals would not begin till August), and that would be an opportune time, Margo felt, to write the book she had been threatening to write for years. Realizing that even she couldn't write an entire book in two months without assistance, she contacted her old friend and former student, playwright Ted Apstein, who lived in New York. She split her advance with him, and he agreed to help her.

A L T H O U G H   M A R G O had directed his plays at the University of Texas and the Pasadena Playhouse and her respect for his work was, he said "flattering and gratifying," Apstein was disheartened that she rejected play after play he submitted to her Dallas theatre. "She would say how much she enjoyed reading a play of mine, but she could never really tell me why she didn't want to do it," he recalls. To support his wife and children, Apstein took a teaching job at Columbia University but continued to write plays. Although his early years in New York were a struggle, he became a successful playwright. (Eight of his one-acts were published in the *Best Short Plays of the Year* series.) In addition to screenwriting, he penned adaptations for television's "Hallmark Hall of Fame" and original scripts for a number of other television series, including "Studio One," "Alcoa Playhouse," "Dr. Kildare," and "The Waltons."

They worked in the Gramercy Park apartment on the book they had titled *Theatre-in-the-Round.* Ted arrived in the mornings and, he recalls, "There was a restlessness about her—she always had something to tell me, part of my job was pulling her back to the book." Margo talked the book, pacing around the room with cigarette dangling or sitting on the floor while Ted took notes. "We had a fairly easy time of outlining it," he remembers. The title of the book is something of a misnomer since ideally Margo advocated a physical theatre space that will accommodate flexible staging. Theatre-in-the-round, however, was a practical, inexpensive alternative to the picture-frame stage. They divided the book into six major sections, first touching on the history of theatre in general and theatre-in-the-round in particular; then focusing on Margo's background and the story of Theatre '50; developing a guide to creating a resident, nonprofit professional theatre from philosophy to organization and finance; discussing the techniques of producing theatre-in-the-round; chronicling the plays produced by Theatre '50; and concluding with "The Future: A Dream and a Plan."

During the summer she worked on the book, Margo met the future in the person of a young woman named Zelda Fichandler from Washington, D.C., in a meeting arranged through ANTA. Several years earlier Margo had advised ANTA secretary Robert Breen and critic Richard Coe that to start a theatre in Washington, D.C., they needed a leader. She had offered to help, but she believed that the drive and determination to create a theatre came not from outside forces but from within. Zelda Fichandler, fresh out of George Washington University, wanted to create a theatre in the nation's capital and had sought out Margo for advice. Fichandler's former professor, Edward Mangum, had attended *Romeo and Juliet* at Theatre '49 and had come away impressed with the fluid staging, which used just four benches. He became convinced that an arena stage was the answer to their problem of creating a theatre in Washington.

"I remember feeling that I was going to meet the Queen," Fichandler recalls now. To prepare for her introduction to the famous Margo Jones, Zelda felt that she must wear a hat. The problem was she didn't own one. So "I went out and bought a hat," she remembers, "a dark navy ribbon hat with a large brim which dipped engagingly over one side of my face." Wearing a long navy knit dress, stockings, high heels, and her new hat—costumed appropriately, she thought, for the meeting, but certainly unsuitably dressed for a hot New York summer day—Zelda arrived at ANTA headquarters. There she waited in a small, empty office, feeling uncomfortable and slightly foolish in her unaccustomed finery.

Margo breezed into the room wearing a cotton skirt with a faded yellow cotton blouse and open sandals. She perched on the edge of a desk dangling her bare legs and smiled at the young woman sitting nervously in front of her, a girl really, with huge dark eyes. They talked, and Zelda remembers that "she was open and giving and generous and sure of what she believed in. Her advice was totally inspirational, but she had a really solid view of reality. She told me that she emptied the mailbox herself every day to see what new plays had come in . . . and she would read them during the performance at night."

At the end of the conversation, Margo said, "Well, honey, there just isn't any reason in the world why you can't do it. . . . You have to have faith in yourself and go right ahead."

Zelda Fichandler went back to Washington, D.C., and with Edward Mangum founded Arena Stage. Years later, she speculated that without Margo's pioneering example and her willingness to talk to a frightened young girl, "Maybe we would never have had the courage to go ahead."

IN WRITING HER BOOK, Margo sought to reach countless others that she could not touch personally. Her book, however, is an intensely personal document. Like Margo herself, it is a combination of the practical and the romantic, the doer and the dreamer. Chapters crammed with concrete information about budgets, boards, sets and costumes, personnel, plays, and fund-raising written in down-to-earth prose are counterpointed by chapters dreamlike in their prophetic vision and written with evangelistic fervor. In every section of the book, Margo's voice rings clear and true. It was easy for her to talk the book—she was simply telling her own story.

"We must create the theatre of tomorrow today," she proclaimed. "What our country needs . . . is a resident professional theatre in every city with a population of over one hundred thousand. . . ." Margo recognized that her dream was not new; in fact, Lady Gregory on a speaking tour of America in 1915 had declared that what America needed was a national theatre, "a tree with a root in every State." The difference, Margo wrote, was that "today it does not have to be merely a dream because there is a way to do it."

Margo found the process of writing the book enormously satisfying and inspirational, giving shape and substance to long-held thoughts. "I am not interested in dreams without action," she wrote. "I will be impatient no longer. I have a definite plan for the future."

She imagined a cross-country trip she might take in 1960. "I could stop in every city . . . and see a good play well done. I would like to see *Othello* in Philadelphia, and a new play by a promising young American author in Pittsburgh, and *Tartuffe* in Detroit, and a new play by an established American playwright in Dayton, and *The Wild Duck* in Kansas City, and a new play by an interesting European author in Oakland. . . . My dream for the future is a theatre which is a part of everybody's life. . . . We can, if we will, create a golden age of the American theatre."

After almost two months of nonstop work, she and Ted Apstein had finished the manuscript. John Selby at Rinehart & Company was pleased with it and planned to bring the book out in the spring of 1951. In July 1950, using material from the manuscript, Margo wrote a long article for the *New York Times* titled "Central Staging," which helped to stimulate interest in arena theatre. In it she said, "There is no difficulty in choosing plays for theatre-in-the-round if you have the courage of your convictions. Theatre is theatre, whether it has three walls or four or none, and a good play well done looks wonderful from all directions."

She felt wonderful too. The gray days of January and February were behind her, and she and Manning were together in New York working on a play that promised to be the success they both hoped for. Ted Apstein recalls that when he met Margo's lover that summer, he thought Gurian was "very good-looking, one of those men who really know how to be attentive to women. And he had a way of looking at [Margo] as if she were the only person in the world."

O N O N E W E E K E N D that summer, Margo took a break from writing, or perhaps Manning had other plans for the weekend, and she visited her old friend Frank Harting, who now had a country house in northern New Jersey complete with trout stream. On this particular weekend, Harting served Margo's favorite meal of fried chicken, black-eyed peas, and cornbread to her and his other house guests. They stayed up for hours, talking and drinking and, Harting recalls, "It got to be bedtime and Margo wouldn't go to bed."

"I'll lie down in the hammock," she said.

The next morning Harting went outside and saw that the hammock had been burned completely, with a turned-over glass resting beside the ashes. Surmising that Margo had fallen asleep with a lighted cigarette, Harting decided to play a practical joke. He happened to have an exact duplicate of the destroyed hammock. After carefully clearing away the ashes, he put up the new hammock. About midmorning Margo staggered out of the house, coffee cup in hand, and stared at the hammock hanging between the trees.

"I had the goddamnedest dream last night," she said.

"What did you dream?" Harting asked innocently.

"I thought I was in that damned hammock and it burned up!"

Harting laughed, enjoying her confusion, not telling Margo about the trick he had played until a year and a half later. Then he told her the story as a warning, late one night when he thought his old friend had been drinking too much.

IN LATE AUGUST, rehearsals of *Southern Exposure* began. Margo had assembled an excellent cast, including Cameron Mitchell as John Salguod. He had played Willy Loman's youngest son in Broadway's *Death of a Salesman*. Betty Greene Little and Mary Finney would act Penelope Mayweather and Mary Belle Tucker respectively, recreating the roles they had played in Dallas. Pretty, blonde, twenty-year-old Pat Crowley would play the feisty ingenue Carol Randall.

The Broadway season of 1950–51 offered nearly twice the shows produced the previous season, but many of them quickly closed. Only one drama, *The Country Girl*, became a hit. Perhaps audiences had had their fill of real-life drama. On June 25, 1950, the North Korean Army had crossed the 38th Parallel and overwhelmed the South Koreans. American forces, led by General Douglas MacArthur, with the support of United Nations troops, had rushed to their aid, plunging the country into an unpopular war. The public, reading about war in the newspapers and hearing daily about the Communist threat, wanted escapist entertainment like *The Moon Is Blue* and *Bell, Book, and Candle* and the popular musicals *Guys and Dolls* and *The King and I*.

Before the premiere of *Southern Exposure*, Margo talked to the press about the play and about Theatre '50. Brooks Atkinson said that whenever she visited New York she was "constantly exploding. . . . She zips into the office, talks theatre a blue streak for an hour and then she's gone."

"Ah can't stop thinkin' of Broadway as The Road," she quipped to two reporters. "Dallas is mah town!" Probably because of the southern setting of the play, when talking to New York reporters who didn't know her Margo changed her normally fast-paced, well-articulated diction to a thick southern drawl. She shared a pint of bourbon with one reporter, and drenched him in good-old-girl charm. "Honey," she told him, "theatre is business to me in Texas just as it is up here at the Biltmore. Since 1947 . . . ah've never had a losing week. . . . No mattah what happens to the play, ah've done the best ah can . . . and ah've had the time of my life doin' it." Aware of the importance of image and the value of generating positive press, in New York Margo played the part of a down-home southerner, while in Texas she acted the role of the sophisticated Broadway director who chose to work in Dallas.

Southern Exposure premiered at the Biltmore Theatre on September 26, 1950. Margo issued her usual opening-night notes along with a nervous truism to the cast that "the theatre is one place you can't ever predict what's going to happen, so you just do your best and pray." Dozens of Dallasites who had formed theatre parties to attend the opening loyally supported the play, laughing and applauding in all the right places. Later, Brooks Atkinson observed that the Texans present "were the people who enjoyed Mr. Crump's lampoon of Natchez most thoroughly. . . . They know the Natchez private jokes more intimately than we do away off in little old up here." Richard Watts of the *New York Post* allowed as how the play should have stayed in Dallas instead of traipsing off to New York. Most of the reviewers found the play mildly agreeable, somewhat charming, with pleasant acting, directing, and sets, but concurred with Atkinson's opinion that *Southern Exposure* was "a regional joke that loses savor the further it travels from home." The production managed to limp along for twenty-three performances, closing October 14, 1950, at a loss of fifty-two thousand dollars.

MANNING STAYED in New York to close the play, taking care of the paper work, the costumes, properties, and sets. Disillusioned by yet another producing failure, in November he planned to follow the smart money, the big money, and enter television school on the G.I. Bill while keeping his long-distance position as general manager of Theatre '50. Millions and millions of dollars were being poured into the new television industry, attracting young playwrights like Ted Apstein and Horton Foote and established playwrights like Maxwell Anderson and other members of the Playwrights' Company. In 1949 *Theatre Arts* had followed the money too, becoming a glossy entertainment monthly with features on theatre, film, television, fashion, and personalities that attracted the advertising dollars of the broadcasting networks and even the insurance industry. Editor Rosamond Gilder, her scholarly, serious approach inappropriate for the new format of the magazine, had moved to a full-time position at ANTA. With continuous publication since 1916, the journal that had introduced

Mixer of Truth and Magic

Margo to the world of the theatre with its slightly breathless devotion to high art had vanished, remaining in name only.

Before she faced a new season at Theatre '50, Margo visited her family in Livingston for two days, telling a friend later that she had enjoyed getting reacquainted with her "wonderful gawky adorable six feet two brother" Charles. En route back to Dallas, she spent a few hours in Houston with Dr. Barraco and other friends, only to be told later by Doc that she felt Margo had been rude and selfish during her visit. Margo apologized, insisting that it had meant a lot for her to be with her friends. Increasingly, though, some of her Houston friends had grown irritated with her, feeling that she was brushing them off, rejecting them. Among the vast number of letters Margo received, only a few of them were bitter or venomous and those were often written by friends who, perhaps unaware that she had constant demands on her time, continued to tug at her, requesting letters or visits or recommendations or introductions or theatre tickets or some other small favor that only Margo could provide. Joanna Albus, however, who had moved to Houston from New York, did not ask for advice or favors or inform her of her plans. Margo had to read the newspapers to learn that Joanna, with her lawyer partner Bill Rozan, planned to build a professional theatre-in-the-round in Houston. The theatre opened in 1951, presenting for the most part name stars in recent Broadway hits—a departure in philosophy from Margo's theatre. Clearly, the competition between the two women had reached a new level. Years later, Joanna recalled that Margo was upset, "in all kinds of ways without saying it," that she had started her own theatre, even though, as Joanna remarked with bitterness, "her theatre succeeded, mine didn't."

Margo didn't have the time, the inclination, or the temperament to ponder the vagaries of the new decade, the failure of *Southern Exposure*, or the fickleness of friendship. In fact, she joked that she didn't even have time to go to the "johnny." Intuitive, nonintellectual, driven by her inner vision, she lived moment to moment, the way actors live in plays, concentrating on the present and the tasks at hand. Vernon Rice of the *New York Post* called her "Speed" Jones. Obviously taken with Margo, he raved about her trim figure and her exuberance. "Texas Tornado just won't stop," he announced in his column, then went on to relate a story that Margo had told him about herself. A rehearsal had run long at Theatre '50, she said, and she was late for a date. A taxi took her back to the Stoneleigh, where she asked the driver to wait while she ran upstairs to shower and change clothes. "When she returned in less time than it takes most women to powder their noses," Rice wrote, "the man at the wheel, who had settled down to wait the usual time it takes a girl to dress and fix a new face, and who hadn't bothered to look at the young woman dashing toward his car, said, 'Sorry, lady. I've already got a fare.'

"'Honey,' replied Margo, 'I'm your fare.'"

STARTING A NEW SEASON in the cool Dallas fall with her company of actors stimulated her—even the prospect of directing eight plays in just thirty weeks. In October she wrote Frank Harting thanking him for the summer visit and saying, "I have never felt better in my life."

To replace Jonathan Seymour, who was working in California, Margo hired Spencer James, the *Southern Exposure* stage manager, as production manager and assistant director. Betty Greene Little, Edwin Whitner, Charles Proctor, and John Denney returned to the resident acting company, and new members included Richard Venture, a popular radio actor who had recently toured with Katharine Cornell; Mady Correll, a stage, film, and television actress who was married to Spencer James; and Karolyn Martin, a young actress hired at the recommendation of Mary Martin. Richard Venture's wife, Grayce Grant, and Charles Braswell would serve as production assistants and play small acting roles. Margo wrote Ted Apstein, "I am crazy about the company—Spencer James is saving my life." Apstein and his wife had recently had a baby and several of her company members or their wives were expecting as well. "Personally I feel like I am having all of your babies," Margo said.

With Spencer James assisting her, directing two of the plays, and her New York secretary now working for her full-time, Margo felt that she could concentrate on other important priorities. While she was in New York, she had lunched with Charles Fahs, Director of the Humanities at the Rockefeller Foundation, and discussed the possibility that the Foundation might fund a drive to create a national theatre. She also began negotiations with the Columbia Lecture Bureau to schedule a program of lectures across the country based on material taken from her book, especially the last chapter, promoting her idea for a network of theatres throughout the U.S. To raise money for Theatre '50, she organized an Audience Guild series that would bring well-known speakers to Dallas. She started a subscriber newsletter, which she edited and filled with material about playwrights and actors who had worked at Theatre '50. Tad Adoue, who had moved to New York, helped compile information for the newsletter and functioned as a play reader. At Manning's urging, she began to investigate the possibility of a television program originating from Dallas. She started working with the board to plan a new 400-500–seat theatre building with a flexible stage. She supervised the day-to-day operations of the theatre herself as well as reading plays, conducting rehearsals, and attending most performances. To work even more efficiently, she turned her apartment into an extension of the theatre, creating an office in the dinette area, where her secretary reported to work every day. That October she entertained visitors from around the world who wanted to study her theatre, including Allan Davis of England's Old Vic; Emilio Carballido, a Mexican playwright; Mashe Shamir, an Israeli playwright; and Els Vermeer, a Dutch director. And there were her usual social obligations, several cocktail parties or dinners or events to attend each week, plus company parties and get-togethers.

THE FALL SEASON of Theatre '50 opened on November 6 with Oscar Wilde's comedy *Lady Windermere's Fan*, which criticizes hypocritical morality and presents a fallen woman sympathetically. Spencer James directed the following production, a new script titled *A Play for Mary*, a comedy by William McCleery dealing with New York theatre people. McCleery had two Broadway productions to his credit and hoped to move his new play to New York. However, critics and audiences gave the play a poor reception. Margo blamed the bad business on the Korean War, but more likely the audiences just didn't care for the script or its New York subject matter. The third production, however, Shakespeare's *The Merchant of Venice*, directed by Margo, was a success critically and at the box office. Charles Laughton, who was in Dallas with his one-man show, attended the production and visited rehearsals, treating the company to his readings of Shakespeare.

During rehearsals of *Merchant*, Tallulah Bankhead arrived in Dallas to kick off Theatre '50's Audience Guild lecture series. On tour with *Private Lives*, the star had visited Theatre '50 earlier that year, attending a performance of *My Granny Van*, her husky, booming laughter filling the small theatre. Margo had given her Edwin Justus Mayer's play *I Am Laughing*, which she and Manning hoped Tallulah would agree to do in New York. To supplement her erratic income from the theatre, Bankhead had begun hosting NBC Radio's "The Big Show," interviewing guest stars, cracking jokes, and singing, one wag said, "in a voice that almost had more timbre than Yellowstone National Park." The Alabama-born Bankhead, the bitch-goddess of Broadway, had never lectured before, was frightened of the thought, but her friends screamed at her that she had been "lecturing every night of her life . . . in hotel lobbies, in restaurants, on railroad platforms, in smoke-filled cellars, in Congressional committee rooms."

The lecture, titled "Tallulah Tells All," held at McFarlin Auditorium on the campus of Southern Methodist University, drew twenty-eight hundred people, almost three hundred more than the auditorium could seat. They had paid a dollar a ticket and braved snow, sleet, and icy roads to come and hear the famous Tallulah. She didn't disappoint them. Wearing a clinging black velvet gown, Tallulah slinked onto the stage, blowing kisses to the wildly applauding audience, and drawled into the microphone, "Thank you, dahlings." Then she ad-libbed for ninety minutes, danced the Charleston, sang "Give My Regards to Broadway," chain-smoked, confided that she wasn't the beauty she used to be, that she wore lots of makeup and a phony bracelet, chided Margo for not finding her a Confederate flag, and imitated Katharine Hepburn but refused to do Bette Davis, saying, "Why should I? She's been imitating me long enough." After paying Bankhead fifteen hundred dollars, Theatre '50 had over a thousand dollars profit. Tallulah's two-day stay in Dallas, Margo told Tad Adoue, "wore me to a nub, but it was worth it."

WITH TALLULAH safely out of town, Margo took a flying trip to Phoenix, Arizona, to meet another larger than life figure with a colossal ego—the architect Frank Lloyd Wright. Margo and her board planned to replace the present theatre with a larger, more flexible space, and they had heard that the eighty-one-year-old Wright wanted to design a theatre. Margo was to talk with Wright about the possibility of his designing that theatre in Dallas. Board president Eugene McDermott paid her travel expenses out of his own pocket.

In 1949 Wright had hoped to build a theatre in Hartford, Connecticut, but funding had fallen through. He wanted to design a theatre that would be successful at "freeing the so-called legitimate stage from its present peepshow character," he said, "and establishing a simple workable basis for presenting plays as a circumstance in the round, performers and audience in one room, more like sculpture than, as it is now, a painting."

Margo spent the day at Taliesin West with the architect, finding her desert surroundings "beautiful and awe-inspiring." They talked for hours in Wright's stone office and walking around the grounds. Wright loved to go to the theatre, and he had definite opinions about theatre architecture that he wasn't afraid to express. A friend recalled that during performances, he would often shake his cane at the proscenium arch and whisper loudly, "Botch—anachronistic botch!" While Margo and Wright agreed on the value of arena stages, they argued about practical matters like offstage working space, dressing rooms, and scene shops. Margo returned to Dallas convinced that Wright was a genius, but doubting that he really understood "the needs of our specific form of work."

Mixer of Truth and Magic

ON DECEMBER 12 the company surprised her with a birthday party, cake, and presents. Margo, who had just turned thirty-nine, was feeling lonely and nostalgic, remembering her birthday six years earlier when she had been in Chicago with *The Glass Menagerie*. She wrote Tennessee a long, wistfully affectionate letter, telling him her news and saying that she would love to see him. Williams, who was living in New York and preparing for a production of *The Rose Tattoo*, wrote back almost immediately, with warmth and fondness, encouraging her to pursue her dream of a network of theatres across the country. He told her that the Broadway theatre that ANTA had opened was just the same old story—a showcase for stars. He also made the generous offer to travel with her and make speeches in support of her ideas.

She heard from another old friend, writer Bill Goyen, who had recently finished his first novel, *The House of Breath*. For several years Margo had helped support Goyen's work by giving him cash gifts and stipends for play-reading as well as by providing emotional support. During his visits with her in Dallas, she had introduced him to John Rosenfield, to Lon Tinkle, who reviewed books for the *Dallas Morning News*, and to the influential Elizabeth Ann McMurray. In fact, *The House of Breath* had been awarded the McMurray Prize for best novel from Texas. But Goyen was in low spirits, disturbed by criticism of his novel. Literature was his life, art his ecstasy, and he railed against the Philistines, who did not understand artists.

Margo soothed his anger with a long letter filled with gentle advice. "Baby," she said, "don't let anyone rile you so. Obviously we are fighters, both of us, and always will be, and we will use the weapons of 'love, faith, belief, tough-ness, and a stubborn-headed stand for the true and the beautiful,' but don't use your energies, dear, getting into a turmoil over anything anybody says. You know it happens everywhere. It's awful, and it is stupid, but you haven't got the time to pay any attention. This may sound unprofound, but I believe I am right. I swear you should stop, relax, and smile maybe—even laugh out loud—drink a cup of coffee or a glass of milk, and get back to your typewriter. I wish you a really happy holiday. I won't drink an egg nog for you, but I promise I'll swig a straight jigger of bourbon."

While company members celebrated in her apartment on Christmas Eve, Margo hurried home to be with her family, then returned for Christmas Day rehearsals of the second new script of the season, *The Willow Tree* by A. B. Shiffrin. The play is the story of a psychologically disturbed twenty-year-old man who has been overprotected by his widowed mother and who kills five women before he is discovered. John Rosenfield called it "much ado about an inferiority complex," but the other critics and the public found the terror thrilling. The production marked the professional debut of nine-year-old Brenda Vaccaro, the only child of Margo's restaurant-owner friends Mario and Christina. She had one line, "Papa, Papa, Mama's dead, you better come home now," but that moment, Vaccaro recalls, "gave me my start in the theatre." With a new title, *Twilight Park*, and starring Walter Matthau and Nancy Kelly, the play opened in New York later that year, there disproving the Shubert Alley adage that "any murder melodrama, any mystery play, is good for six weeks' minimum run on Broadway. And after that, the movies'll buy it." On Broadway this murder melodrama lasted just eight days.

Spencer James directed the third new play, *An Innocent in Time* by Edward Caulfield, a dramatization of the life of Lord and Lady Byron that was also well received by the audience. During the bleak days of January, Margo rehearsed the fourth new script, *One Bright Day* by Sigmund Miller, scheduled to open February 17. And she made a flying trip to Chicago to visit Tennessee and see a tryout performance of *The Rose Tattoo*.

STELLA NELL had died on January 1, and the beginning of the new year usually brought on depression and despondency for Margo, and a physical and emotional letdown. By January 1951 her unrelenting workload had begun to take its toll. Since the fall of 1947, in a little over three years, she had directed twenty-nine plays in Dallas, plus three Broadway shows that had been judged failures and a national tour. She had lost over $150,000 in investors' money, had been fired by her agent Audrey Wood, and had clashed with Tennessee, till then her dearest friend. She had traveled to Europe, made dozens of cross-country trips, written a book, a number of articles, and hundreds of letters, given speeches and interviews, served on committees, managed a theatre, attended parties, smoked thousands of cigarettes and consumed vast quantities of liquor, played mother to a company of actors, counseled writers, and read hundreds of plays. And she had fallen passionately in love.

After four years, however, her relationship with Manning had begun to change. Separated by distance, the gulf between their basic values became wider. As their partnership continued to lose money, Manning began to reconsider his idealism. Although he had planned to visit Dallas during Christmas, he had changed his mind and stayed in New York. Margo wanted him in Dallas, missed him desperately, and the telephone became her lifeline to him. They talked, often late at night. Manning pushed for her to get involved in television—a medium Margo knew nothing about. He wanted money and security, and having found neither in his professional partnership with Margo, had entered television school feeling that perhaps in that medium he could make his fortune. He wanted her in his life, yet resisted her dependence on him, felt smothered by her need, jealous of her success, and overshadowed by her personality. He did not want to be "Mr. Margo Jones" or to live in Texas.

Unable to leave her theatre in Dallas to go to him and try to bridge the chasm that had opened between them, Margo, who had always been positive and sure, began to experience the wracking pain of conflicting feelings and the need to reach out for intimacy, but she was without the acquired habit or skill of seeking closeness. For most of her thirty-nine years, she had defined herself through her work and her single-minded obsession to create a national theatre. She had turned her apartment into an extension of the theatre, a home where tables overflowed with scripts and letters and dictaphone tapes and other evidence of work. She had played so many roles—nurturing mother and little girl, country bumpkin and Broadway sophisticate, driven workaholic and hard-drinking good old girl, searching artist and flamboyant huckster, Gene Autry and Joan of Arc. But who was she?

When she fell in love with Manning, finding a passion that competed with her obsession for the theatre, Margo began to question her choices—understandably, since many of her friends were marrying and having babies, sharing their lives. As a person driven by absolutes, with one center to her life, she found herself now off-center and drifting, not knowing what she believed or what she wanted. The lack of certainty terrified her.

She talked to no one about her problems. Who could she talk to? She lived in a city and a section of the country, the great Southwest, that prided itself on, had been built on, pioneer spirit, self-reliance, individualism, and strength. With her position of power and respect in Dallas as the much-loved, celebrated theatre leader, how could she reveal her weaknesses, the doubts like tiny cracks in the mask of her public personality? The truth was Margo didn't have anyone to talk with, no women she looked up to or intimate female friends who could guide her through the crisis that many people face when they approach their fortieth year. Beginning with her lawyer father, her heroes had all been men: John Rosenfield, Gilmor Brown, Jerry Coray, Brooks Atkinson, Eugene McDermott, even her favorite playwrights and writers Robert Edmond Jones, Tagore, Tennessee Williams—all male. If she had reached out to Tennessee, who had tremendous compassion and empathy, most assuredly he would have welcomed the opportunity to help his old friend. Adept at asking for help for her theatre or for writers or actors, she did not know how to reach out for help for herself. So she turned inward—like a cat that has been hurt and seeks out the darkest corner to lick its wounds. She tried to take

Mixer of Truth and Magic

care of herself, to stay in control, to fix things, to alleviate her pain and make everything work out. Outwardly she continued her frenetic pace, with pills to keep her awake and liquor to comfort her.

On Thursday, February 8, Margo went to the theatre and rehearsed Sigmund Miller's play *One Bright Day*. Its main character, the president of a large drug company, must decide whether or not to inform the public that one of the company's pain-killers contains a toxic poison. Sometime that night, on a chilly, gray Thursday in her Stoneleigh apartment, exhausted and overcome with stress, Margo stopped her efforts to shape and control her world, and turned to a proven pain-killer of her own—a bottle of liquor and a handful of pills.

Was she still trying to take care of herself when she ran some bath water, stripped herself naked, and lay down in the tub? The mask was dropped now, exposing a distraught woman approaching mid-life, her body limp, lacking in animation, her square face careworn and marked with deep lines, her eyes swollen with fatigue.

Or perhaps she had gone past caring, sunk so low in unaccustomed melancholy and pain that she had reached for another drink and another pill, again and again until the pain was gone and she fell into darkness.

Is It Worth It?

"**I**LLNESS FORCES Margo Jones to Take Time Out" reported the *Dallas Morning News*. Mabel Duke, Theatre '51's publicist, told the press that Margo had fainted at the theatre on Friday morning February 9, succumbing to overwork, influenza, and, she added, "a mysterious virus attack." She did not disclose that on Friday morning Margo's secretary had found her passed out in the bathtub and had called Mabel in a panic. Dr. Howard Aronson, the Stoneleigh house doctor who was also Margo's personal physician, examined her and prescribed bed rest with a nurse in attendance. While Mabel tried to keep the incident as quiet as possible, rumors abounded. Some said that Margo had gone on a drinking binge, others speculated that the "mysterious virus attack" was a euphemism for a suicide attempt.

In her most personal writing, Margo never mentioned the possibility of suicide, and it is highly unlikely that she ever consciously considered suicide as a way out of her pain. Although Mabel Duke believed that Margo did attempt suicide, she could not really be sure, since they never discussed the incident. "She wanted Manning with her all the time," Duke recalled. "It was a serious depression. After that we were always afraid." The collapse frightened Margo as well. Following her breakdown, she hated to be alone, often urging friends to stay with her until the early hours of the morning. "I am optimistic by nature," she liked to say about herself, but she had another side too —darker and despairing. "I feel like a failure," she told Mabel. Margo's self-imposed remedy was to go back to work; she took less than a week off.

To actor Edwin Whitner, who expressed the acting company's concern for her, she said, "I have been an extremely lucky girl all my life in the fact that I have had remarkable health which has given me lots of vitality. I simply did not know what it was like to be really sick." Physically run-down—her body abused by alcohol and amphetamines—she suffered from lack of appetite and fatigue, but she also recognized that her problems were deeper than her physical health and so began seeing Dr. Joseph Knapp, a local psychiatrist, for weekly sessions.

Her assistant, Spencer James, had assumed directing responsibilities for *One Bright Day*, but soon Margo was back on schedule rehearsing George Bernard Shaw's *Candida*, the third and final classic of the season, which would open March 12. As she worked on Shaw's intelligent comedy, which advocates self-knowledge and exposes hypocrisy, and made plans for the final new play of the season, Margo began to heal. She was thin, somewhat shaky and vulnerable, but she noticed the arrival of spring in the brightness of the redbuds, in a bed of blooming pansies in front of the theatre, and in a pot of blue iris and tiny wild roses given to her by a neighbor across the hall.

TO CLOSE THE SEASON, Margo had chosen *Walls Rise Up*, a new musical based on Texas writer George Sessions Perry's comic novel of the same name. Frank Duane of San Antonio adapted the novel, writing with the arena stage of Theatre '51 in mind, and Richard Shannon of Houston composed the music, heavily influenced by what John Rosenfield called "race records . . . the music by some crossroads guitarist, taped, waxed and pressed into millions. Record reviewers never receive them or hear them. Big city shops stock them incompletely. But they sell like nails, pins and needles in village drugstores and places where merchandise still prices for five and ten." Set in the Brazos country of Texas, the action of the play centers on three wandering tramps who fall in and out of love, worry over their supply of whiskey, and wonder if they should attempt to find respectable jobs. "The walls rise up from the earth to protect the pure in heart," Jimmie the hobo says. Rosenfield called the musical "lowdown, primitive, natural as sunbathing and a bit poetic," and said that it was the most valuable play presented by the theatre since its opening in 1947. The *Variety* reviewer concurred, calling it the best comedy to premiere at Theatre '51. The musical, the first ever produced at the theatre, equalled the success of the previous year's hit, *Southern Exposure*.

The season concluded with six weeks of repertory of the four most popular plays, *Walls Rise Up*, *The Willow Tree*, *Innocent In Time*, and *The Merchant of Venice*. Two of the five new plays, *The Willow Tree* and *One Bright Day*, had been optioned for Broadway. Attendance by out-of-towners had expanded considerably, and once again the theatre closed with a surplus in the budget to fund its next season.

After several months of concentrating on her health and neglecting her correspondence, Margo wrote to the many friends who had expressed concern about her during her "illness." She told Bill Goyen that she had "been good and sick for a couple of months and I just felt so stinkin' that I didn't do any of the things I really cared about. I am fit as a fiddle—feel simply marvelous now."

She felt well enough to attend public functions, even judging a samba contest at the Baker Hotel, and she entertained Rosamond Gilder, who visited

Is It Worth It?

Dallas in April as the third speaker in Theatre '51's Audience Guild lecture series. George Freedley had been the second speaker in late February. Gilder spoke at Scott Hall about the problems of the American theatre. "If Dallas has a successful theatre, why not every city?" she asked. "Is it possible that there are other Margos who will pioneer and overcome the economic problems of the legitimate stage?"

In early May, Margo visited New York for two days to confer with Manning and Jonas Silverstone about a prospective all-star in-the-round television production of Tennessee's play *The Purification*. As usual, New York energized her. With Tad Adoue and Mary Martin she attended a performance of *The Taming of the Shrew* at the City Center, and enjoyed seeing Larry Hagman, her former production assistant and Martin's son, in a small role. She spotted Tennessee lunching at the Algonquin, and they visited at Bill Goyen's apartment late one night. On her way back to Dallas, she stopped in Livingston for a brief reunion with her family, saw Richard, Bea, and their daughter Judy in Houston, and attended a production at Joanna Albus's Houston Theatre.

Theatre-in-the-Round had been published—it would even be translated into Japanese—and Margo basked in its excellent reception from friends and critics. When a Houston reviewer wrote a few critical words about the book, Martha Pearl was upset, but Margo told her mother, "I have been in this business now for a long time, and honestly darling, so much more is said that is good than otherwise, and it's so much better to pay no attention. I really think the smartest thing I have ever done is to never, never answer anybody back. . . ." The *New York Times* reviewer observed that *Theatre-in-the-Round* appeared to have been "hastily assembled . . . [but] Miss Jones has written a fine success story . . . [and] honestly reports that bringing theatre to a wider public is the chief mission of [theatrical] circles." Later that year a reviewer for the *New York Herald-Tribune* wrote that "if the book lacks discriminating advice on the choice of plays, it more than compensates in enthusiasm. It ought to be read by all the young theatre aspirants across the land. . . ."

In fact, many young theatre leaders were inspired by the book. "[M]ore than a handbook," resident-theatre historian Joseph Zeigler has written, "it is also an apocalypse." Zelda Fichandler at Arena Stage in Washington read the book and wrote later that "I knew that she, the mother of us all, could not be dreaming in vain." Alley Theatre leader Nina Vance told Margo that she had read and reread *Theatre-in-the-Round* and had been inspired by her example. When Vance asked for advice on obtaining new plays from agents, Margo promptly wrote all the agents she knew and introduced Nina to them. She sent her a list of new plays that Theatre '51 had read but not presented, and also suggested that Nina consider repeating some of their successes, although she understood that it would probably be better for Vance to present plays that had not been presented elsewhere. "I think you are doing such a grand job," Margo told her. In addition to helping the Alley Theatre, she also flew to Oklahoma City in late May to assist a theatre group called the Mayde Mack Mummers. She appeared on local radio and television shows, attended a luncheon, autographed her book at a bookstore, went to a dinner, saw a play, and made a ticket sales speech—all in one day.

H E R   S E A S O N had been a success, her book well received, and Manning had joined her in Dallas to help close the theatre. According to Manning, Margo did not discuss her breakdown with him, and she exuded her usual high spirits.

"The season is ending in a festive manner," she wrote a friend. The company celebrated with a picnic in the country, spending the day riding horses, wading in the creek, and eating too much. The highpoint of the outing was Manning's dash to Dallas with Richard Venture and his wife, Grayce Grant, who had gone into labor with their first child.

After closing the theatre, Margo and Manning borrowed a friend's car and drove cross-country to New York. It was the first leisurely automobile trip she had ever taken, and her first vacation since her visit to Mexico City twelve years earlier. They drove to Tennessee and then through the beautiful Cumberland Mountains and into the Blue Ridge Mountains of Virginia. She wrote her parents, "I found myself becoming so interested in different kinds of trees and flowers [that] you would have died laughing at me trying to remember the names. . . ." In her letters to them, she discreetly did not identify Manning as her traveling companion, signing her letters "love, from your little girl." As she and Manning drove through historic areas, Margo began to wish that she knew more about history. Was Stonewall Jackson the same person as Andrew Jackson? she wondered. Her historical knowledge had mostly been gleaned from plays like Eddie Mayer's *Sunrise in My Pocket*. She knew from that play that Andrew Jackson had been president in 1835, but to find out about Stonewall she had to ask questions of helpful southerners.

P R O V I N G   T H A T   T H E Y could be successful business partners was the way to ensure their personal happiness, Margo believed, and so she and Manning together had optioned Mayer's latest play, *I Am Laughing*, about the life of a glamorous actress and her many lovers. One of their objectives during the summer in New York was to convince Tallulah Bankhead to star in a Broadway production. Manning later recalled that the summer of 1951 was the best time, the happiest time they ever had together. Margo agreed, writing Liz Ann McMurray that she and Manning had been having "a simply perfect time."

Freed from the pressures of constant rehearsals and openings, Margo relaxed and enjoyed everyday, normal activities like dinners with friends and going to the movies. In long weekly letters to her parents, keeping carbon copies for herself, she wrote detailed descriptions of her days, almost as if she wanted to document each moment in order to savor the experience and somehow hold on to it. Brooks and Oriana Atkinson invited Margo and Manning for dinner in their elegant old apartment, which had a magnificent view of the Hudson River and was filled with roses from their country garden. They had several visits with Burl Ives and his wife and talked about a production of *Sunrise in My Pocket* using ballads of the period. In New York on a book-buying visit, Elizabeth Ann McMurray was Margo's house guest for a week. The two women shopped for clothes, lunched together, and had their hair done. McMurray remembers looking out of the living room window of the Gramercy Park apartment with its view of the park and a lighted tower and feeling "that it was the embodiment of the whole city to look out that window." Theatre '51 board member Arthur Kramer and his wife visited New York for a few days, and Margo and Manning joined them for dinner at a Japanese restaurant. Afterward they walked in Central Park, and Margo expounded on the beauties of the park—the lovely lakes, the zoo, the trees and flowers, and the people. "It is wonderful," she wrote her parents, "to look at the faces of all of the different kinds of people sitting and resting in a cool and beautiful place." On Wednesday evenings, Margo and Manning, sometimes accompanied by Tad Adoue or George Freedley, drove to Westport, Connecticut, to see performances at the Westport Country Playhouse and scout acting talent for Theatre '51. They also saw a number of Broadway shows. Margo liked *A Tree Grows in Brooklyn*, found *Darkness at Noon* "moving and stimulating" and *Guys and Dolls* entertaining, but wrote Bill Goyen that "many of the things we have seen seem utterly insignificant."

In her elation at being with Manning, Margo found happiness in everything, including the Connecticut highway system—"no advertising and one-way traffic"—and a Long Island dinner party in honor of her southern roots where she "shocked everyone by putting pot liquor on her cornbread and eating three pieces."

On July 2, Margo and Manning drove to Poundridge, New York, for a visit with Tallulah Bankhead to persuade her to star in *I Am Laughing*. The visit was a memorable one. When they arrived, Tallulah invited them to go for a cooling swim in her pool. Margo and Manning demurred, pointing out that they hadn't brought swimsuits. Tallulah laughed huskily at their modesty, and insisted that they strip and swim. She would watch from the side since she only swam at night. Eager to please, they gave in, and after their swim had drinks and dinner and endured a recorded speech by Bankhead's father, who had been Speaker of the House of Representatives for some years. Tallulah also played a recording of Ethel Barrymore reading a poem, then phoned Barrymore in Hollywood so that Margo could tell her how much she enjoyed it. They talked about *I Am Laughing*, but while Bankhead liked the play, her weekly radio program made it impossible for her to commit to a Broadway production. At the end of the evening, Tallulah announced that now she would go for her swim. "She was past her prime," Manning recalls, "but she lit up that pool like a circus, took off all her clothes and went swimming."

To gain backing for *I Am Laughing*, they would have to find another star for the all-important lead. Margo told a friend, "[W]e will not do this play until we can do it right," but with a fall production now unlikely, Manning began to feel financial pressures and decided to look for a job in commercial theatre management. Clearly, while there was a possibility of co-producing with Margo, Manning, a self-confessed opportunist, was her charming, attentive lover, but when he knew she would again return to Dallas and focus on Theatre '51, he began to pull away from her and to seek to establish his own identity. Since Margo was well connected in the theatre world and had strong ties to wealth, especially Texas oil money, he was careful not to break with her completely, maintaining their sporadic love affair. Supported by her helpful sessions with Dr. Knapp, Margo accepted this arrangement. She had an enormous amount of pride and did not want to become what she called "one of those awful women" who clings to a man, but she loved Manning, romanticized their relationship, and so refused to give up hope.

J U S T   A S Margo had made a new start with her personal life, regaining her health and good spirits and spending a bittersweet summer with Manning, her theatre too would undergo a transformation. Margo replaced her old publicity photographs with a glamorous new Comini portrait picturing her in her favorite red evening dress. "I just cannot stand for a brochure to go out with a picture of me looking like such an old, haggard Peter Pan," she told Mabel Duke. Theatre '51 had grown shabby, with peeling paint, falling plaster, and a leaking roof. During the summer, Margo convinced her board and the State Fair Association, which owned the building, to commit to the necessary improvements. With no thought given to preserving the historic International style design of the building, two large square rooms, a storage room, and a dressing room that would accommodate thirty actors were added to the back of the structure. During the summer and early fall, workers, many of them volunteers, painted the building inside and out, installed new carpeting in the theatre and new tile floors in the lobby and green room, re-covered the seats, improved the air-conditioning system, updated the electrical wiring, and landscaped the theatre grounds. As usual, Eugene McDermott stood firmly behind Margo, supporting whatever she proposed not only with financial contributions but also with his time, which had become limited since the incorporation of Texas Instruments that year. Exhilarated by the renovation of the theatre, which had provided an opportunity for her to exercise her talent for getting things done quickly, Margo wrote her thanks to her board president: "Gene, I have never told you how much it has meant to us having you as our president. Again, I say I hope I can show my appreciation by creating the finest theatre in the world." She had regained her health and renewed her sense of mission—had rediscovered the purpose that had driven her in years past. In her book's final chapter, "The Future: A Dream and a Plan," she had written, "It is easier to have ideals when you are nineteen, but if you have them fifteen years later or thirty years later, they are most valuable because with them is the wisdom of experience. . . . In certain fields age seem to defeat people. It should not be that way in the theatre, for we must combine the wisdom of age with the enthusiasm of youth."

DURING SEPTEMBER in New York, working out of producer Roger Stevens's Fifth Avenue offices, Margo hired a new company and a new staff. After her breakdown in January, it had become clear to her, perhaps at the gentle prodding of Eugene McDermott or John Rosenfield, that she needed someone to share the burden of work and responsibility for the theatre, which she hoped to expand now into a year-round operation. She also wanted to spend more time away from Dallas. She had signed on with the Columbia Lecture Bureau to give lectures all over the country promoting *Theatre-in-the-Round* and her plan outlined in the book to create twenty resident theatres modeled after Theatre '51. In addition, and primarily at Manning's urging, she planned to begin producing original work for television, a medium she rarely watched and knew little about. She didn't seem to pause to question whether she might be trying to do too much, but at least she knew that she needed a reliable, devoted staff and an associate director.

At Jonas Silverstone's office she met his efficient legal secretary, Violet Burch, who had extensive theatre experience not only with Silverstone's theatrical law firm but also as private secretary to director Rouben Mamoulian. She had worked on the Broadway production of *Leaf and Bough*, which had originated at Theatre '48. Violet Burch remembers that "upon meeting Margo there was an instant sympatico between us—I felt as if I had known her all my life. She was the friendliest and most vivacious woman I had ever met, and thus began an association that made her a part of our family." Violet's husband, Ramsey, serious and soft-spoken with a dapper moustache, was an actor and director who had been "doing the old summer stock deals, tangling with stars," he said, and finding the work artistically unrewarding. After seeing Ramsey's work at a summer theatre, Margo hired him as associate director and actor, and Violet as her personal assistant. The Burches had one small daughter, and another child on the way, and saw the opportunity to work in Dallas as an exciting challenge and a place to have a real home.

In July 1951 Michael and Mary Dolan, a young couple who had been active with the Little Theatre in Tacoma, Washington, had left their paid jobs there, sold their house, and packed all their worldly possessions into their beat-up 1939 Oldsmobile in order to go take jobs as apprentices with a theatre in Florida. The day before they were to leave, they received a wire that the theatre had closed. "We had to leave," Mary remembers. "They had already given us a farewell party." The pair drove to Florida and tried to revive the theatre. When their efforts failed, on a whim they decided to call Margo Jones in Dallas, whom they had only read about in *Theatre Arts*. Dallas Information supplied her phone number, and Margo happened to be in town for a short stay. Charmed by their story, she asked, "Honey, could you be in New York this weekend?" The Dolans drove from Florida to New York and met with her at her apartment. Mary Dolan recalls that Margo was fascinated with "these two nuts" who had called her out of the blue, and told them, "I'll see you two in Dallas." Transplanted to Texas, Mary became the box-office treasurer and Michael was assigned a job as production assistant.

Other new staff members included Jim Pringle, a rangy young man who had heard Margo speak at Fordham University about arena theatre and had been struck by her enthusiasm. Margo hired him to assist the new resident designer, Tony Deeds. Fred Hoskins, a recent graduate of Texas Christian University with an impish sense of humor and an unwavering devotion to theatre in general and Margo Jones in particular, signed on as a production assistant. Since Manning had taken a job managing the commercial New York production of *I Am a Camera*, starring Julie Harris, Margo needed a full-time general manager and hired Roy Somlyo, who had worked in New York and at the Cape Playhouse in Massachusetts. For the company she also hired Roy's wife, Mary Dell Roberts, who had acted in radio and television.

The only company members returning for the new season were Evelyn Bettis and Edwin Whitner, who had played in twenty-two productions in his previous three years at the theatre. New actors included the talented character actress Norma Winters; Peter Donat, a native of Novia Scotia who had acted with the Provincetown Players and was the nephew of screen star Robert Donat; Marion Morris, who had acted primarily in France; John Munson, who had worked in film and touring productions; and Mary Dell Roberts. Minor roles would be taken by the younger members of the company, including Charles Braswell, who had grown up professionally in Margo's theatre; Bernadette Whitehead, a recent graduate of Southern Methodist University; and Salvatore Amato, a former airline steward whom Margo had discovered on an Eastern Airlines flight to Dallas in 1950. Drawn to his dark good looks and desire to follow in his actor father's footsteps, Margo had encouraged him, giving him lists of plays to read, arranging for acting lessons, and finally hiring him for her company. Margo told Tad Adoue that she loved her talented, *sane* company. "[W]hen a neurotic son-of-a-bitch shows up, I will let you know," she said. Although Adoue lived in New York, he remained close to Margo as her script reader and devoted friend and confidante. With her actors and young staff, she played the role of theatre guru or nurturing mother, but she let Tad see the forceful, strongminded woman.

In addition to hiring her new company and staff in September, she optioned several new scripts and, to bolster her depleted bank account, appeared on two television programs, "Elaine Salutes the Stars" and General Electric's "Guest House." (One of the great compensations of being a prominent Dallasite, she felt, was that the local bank allowed her to overdraw her account. Her New York bank, the Irving Trust Company, was not as accommodating, and she relied on Tad to deposit the necessary cash to cover her overdrafts.)

In early October, after completing her work in New York, she traveled to Livingston for a visit with her family. Her father was not well. He had written Margo early in the summer that Martha Pearl was visiting her sister in Amarillo and he was leading a narrow existence, with "only thoughts of you children and my work [to] keep me going." At the insistence of his sons, he had agreed to go to a hospital in Houston for tests. A cancerous tumor as well as an enlarged artery had been discovered. The news served to bring Richard, Charles, and Margo closer together. Richard's wife, Bea, who had married into a family of stubborn, strong-willed people, pointed out that they should all practice what they preach, take care of themselves, and get their own ailments fixed. Margo had grown fond of her gentle sister-in-law, who seemed to understand her better than her brother Richard, who frowned on her drinking and cigarette smoking. She vowed to Bea that she would take care of herself, and arranged to have her sinuses repaired and bought reading glasses. Margo felt guilty that Richard and Charles bore the responsibility of caring for her parents. "I do not do my share and I want to very badly," she said. "Please, please, no matter how busy I may seem, let me know anything I can do at any time."

On November 10, five days after the opening of the new season, Margo's father died. She had hoped for a miracle, writing her father frequently with news of her activities and prayers for his recovery. His death devastated her —she found it difficult to talk about the loss, writing to her mother and Charles, "I know you understand why there is so little I can say today. The sun is shining brightly and I do have real faith." After he died, her letters home became less frequent, more cryptic, as if she had always been writing primarily to her father, for she had identified closely with him and constantly sought his approval.

THE NEW acting company at Theatre '51, many of them visiting Dallas for the first time, were welcomed by board members and made to feel at home, but for the moment the city cared only about football—was in a euphoric uproar celebrating Southern Methodist University's victory over Notre Dame and the University of Texas's defeat of their traditional rival the University of Oklahoma.

This season Margo planned to present six untried new plays and just two classics—a risky decision given the continued box-office appeal of classic plays. However, subscription-ticket sales were up almost 20 percent over last season, her theatre was now an established Dallas institution, and she believed in the new plays and trusted her audience to give new work a hearing. She would alternate the direction of the plays with Ramsey Burch to accommodate her lecture tour, although initially she did not publicize this fact to her Dallas audience. They thought of the theatre as "Margo's" and might not take kindly to another director.

As usual, Margo consulted with John Rosenfield about her play selection. After reading all the scripts, he spoke vehemently against her first three choices, "sternly advised against them," he said, but she ignored his advice. She chose plays intuitively, and often couldn't explain her choices intellectually except to say that a play had moved her. If she believed in a play nothing could shake her faith. The playwrights she had nurtured, Tennessee Williams, William Inge, and Joseph Hayes, had no problem finding commercial producers for their work, and while Margo knew that most of the plays received by Theatre '51 had already been rejected by Broadway producers, she read them anyway, always searching for what she called "wonderment." She advised Nina Vance that "it takes reading hundreds to find one, which we do not feel is discouraging, but an exciting challenge."

To introduce her new acting company, Margo opened the season with a large-cast play, *The Sainted Sisters* by screenwriter Alden Nash. An original version of the play had been made into a 1948 movie but, according to the author, the Dallas script had been substantially rewritten. Set in the tiny fishing village of Sandy Creek, Maine, the comedy revolves around two female confidence artists with good hearts who are hiding from the law in Sandy Creek, and who use their stolen money to benefit the town. Critics and audiences agreed that the play wasn't much, but praised the new acting company.

Ramsey directed the second play, *One Foot in Heaven* by Irving Phillips, a nostalgic comedy about the family problems of a Methodist minister in a small town in Iowa. Rosenfield reported that the script was the "sort of American village anecdotage that makes Margo's best box-office material," but felt that the play owed its success primarily to the stellar acting of Edwin Whitner as the minister and Norma Winters as Sister Lydia, his antagonist.

For the holiday play, Margo had chosen Shakespeare's *A Midsummer Night's Dream*, a decision that horrified John Rosenfield, who questioned her sanity in presenting a spectacle play on the small stage of Theatre '51. "How did Shakespeare manage it?" Margo said. "Only an outer and inner stage were needed for the 'Dream' originally," she reminded him. "It is very simple as to setting and stage properties. The Elizabethan audience and the Dallas audience of 1951 need little in the way of scenery. Costumes must tell more, but the lines of the play tell the most." Unfortunately, Rosenfield was right, and the play was not popular. The reviewers found the lavish costumes, some with appliqués of velvet flowers and tree branches, quite gaudy, and the set of plain gray platforms bland and boring. Margo saved the play financially by offering a series of matinees for schools.

DURING LATE NOVEMBER, with Ramsey holding rehearsals and Violet overseeing the management of the theatre, Margo traveled to New York for the Broadway opening of John Van Druten's *I Am a Camera*, starring Julie Harris. Manning was serving as company manager of the production and had grown enthralled with the talent of Julie Harris and indignant at the way her husband treated her. "He was awful," Gurian recalls, "came around just to pick up her check." Harris's portrayal of Sally Bowles had earned her rave reviews and secured her place as a Broadway star. Many had recognized her great promise from the start. Several years earlier, when Helen Hayes had seen Harris act the part of the twelve-year-old Frankie Addams in *The Member of the Wedding*, according to *Theatre Arts* Hayes had "rushed home to get a small, white, lace-bordered handkerchief." Originally the handkerchief had belonged to Sarah Bernhardt, who gave it to Julia Marlowe with instructions to "pass it on only to someone who seemed most likely to perpetuate the great tradition of acting." Marlowe had given the handkerchief to Hayes, and Hayes in turn bestowed the theatrical legacy on young Julie Harris. Manning, who had returned to his first home, the commercial theatre, was in his element as manager of this important new play, was smitten with Julie Harris, and felt liberated in a job that he had achieved on his own without Margo's influence.

In late December 1951 Margo received a letter from her lawyer, Jonas Silverstone, containing for her signature a Certificate of Discontinuance of the partnership of Jones and Gurian. The official notice was not a surprise to her, since Manning had prepared her for their professional break-up via late-night long-distance telephone calls, but it was still a shock, since their professional relationship was intertwined with their personal one. It was painful, she wrote, to touch his name in print "as though it were your beautiful face." In their conversations, Manning had told her that he felt she had a destiny and he had none. Without the sense of destiny he saw in Margo, Manning wanted money and security and had found neither in their partnership, but he kept his options open and told her that if she could accomplish something in television, that would give him a feeling of confidence that she could operate successfully in his commercial world too.

Despite her idyllic summer with Manning, the year had been a brutal one for Margo, beginning with her breakdown in February, followed by the death of her father, and culminating with her separation from Manning. A weaker person might have sought the deadening solace of alcohol or drugs, but while she continued her habit of heavy drinking, Margo turned to her own inner resources and found strength and hope, as she always had before, in the power of the written word. To sort out her feelings and organize her thoughts, as she had done so many times for friends who had needed her, she wrote letters, scrawled out her thoughts on pages torn from a yellow pad, but this time she wrote to herself, to Manning, and to God.

Her career in the theatre or Manning? New York or Dallas? Art or money? Love or loneliness? Personal life or her cause?

Is It Worth It?

In the early 1950s most women did not struggle with Margo's dilemma, for they had accepted the traditional female role of wife and mother. But just as Margo had served as a pioneering theatre leader, clearing the way for others to follow, in her personal life too she found herself alone, ahead of her time in undiscovered country. The pages she wrote for herself, outlining her conflicts, make a remarkable document, revealing a tormented, proud, extremely earnest woman with a touching, childlike faith.

Dear God, she wrote, *I know that you will show me how to live a great love story.*

What do I really want—that I think is clear—I want to be needed and loved by M—If he could get success & security with me in such a way to give him real identity I believe it would solve his problem.

Real trouble—Joy gone out of work because no chance of personal satisfaction which comes two ways—through job well done and through sharing it with someone you love.

Important Points.

1. Spent my entire life on making this job come true.

2. Have a kind of standing & represent something in this period of American theatre.

3. Do still believe all the things I ever did about possibility of theatre.

4. Know if I give up Theatre will be set back—

5. All my contacts & people's belief in me is tied up with this.

6. Really want to be great theatre director.

Point 1. Must learn how not to be possessive—

Point 2. Must learn how not to need to lean on him.

Point 3. Must be able to prove that partnership is possible . . . The reason he has wanted to break it is because he has lost confidence in himself because it seems everything we did I was given credit.

Point 4. He must have chance to do something that will give him real credit—

Point 5. I must really be successful & happy on my own—he must be sure of this—so I must be . . .

Ways of Solving

1. Going on—alone

2. Trying to figure way to combine our work

3. Could I attack television to help theatre?

4. Could I leave the theatre for a year?

5. Could I remain in any way a person working on decentralization & hope to have any life of my own or real security for future?

6. Should I try taking on Rockefeller television plan—

Is It Worth It?

7. If I make a clean break what is our future—
My Personal Attitude
1. With you—I think I can do anything—if it's for us.
2. We have to both be 100% sure that it's right.
3. New way—can still direct in New York—can be something to new writer.
4. The heart of the matter—the person must want to do it more than anything in the world—I do but not alone & not like I used to—
5. I have always loathed people losing their ideals as they grew older.
MARGO MUST
1. Keep humor.
2. Weigh all problems.
1. Sacrifice personal life to cause.
2. Take chance on all beliefs & personal life.
3. Try to make the two work out together.
IF I STICK TO MY GUNS
1. Loneliness and doing it alone—necessary—
2. Seeing you in summer—your way of life would have to gradually be without me.
3. If I feel like I do now I'll become a nervous & bitter person—try as hard as I can.
4. I want to share my life.
5. If I do get 20 theatres—if I do create a golden era in the theatre—would it be worth it—
If it seems impossible to run 1 what would happen to 20—
I've got one chance of greatness in the world & it's to prove that each large town can have professional theatre. I don't want a sense of failure—I must get a clear calm peaceful mind about all this—

On the day before New Year's Eve and the traditional party at the theatre with the changing of the sign from Theatre '51 to Theatre '52, Margo stayed up all night and drafted a letter to Manning that she probably did not mail. "I'd like to make this 'writing' a kind of Pirandello's *Miracle*," she wrote. "I believe that I can make what I believe in come true." She told him about going to the Dallas Symphony with actress Greer Garson. "Being a celebrity of her calibre is tough—even in my stupid little way—tis tough—that is wrong to say that—I say it because—thinking of Greer now—I saw how impossible it was for anyone to come up to her without her having to put on an act (a very good one—a wonderful one—even a true one in a way) everyone acting so humble—everyone wanting something from her." She spoke of her inability to think clearly about their involvement. "My mind jumps," she said. "I know I have meant what I have said, I love you enough not to love you . . . but I have my doubts now. Somehow I still believe that men and women are not so different—we all have our hopes and our dreams and our needs. . . . It's 20 minutes after 4 in the morning—I'm sure you are asleep—tis 5 there—and I'm the night owl—There is a wind blowing up—tomorrow night is New Years '52. . . . THIS WILL BE OUR YEAR."

S H E T O O K immediate action to make the new year theirs. On January 5, she flew to New York to finalize contracts on several new scripts, to confer with Burl Ives about a possible production of his children's musical in Dallas, and to see Manning. She had not given up on their relationship. After all, Manning had always claimed that Margo was the only woman close to him, even when she knew he was seeing others. She understood him surprisingly well. Soon after she arrived in the city a little item, with no basis in fact, mysteriously appeared in *Variety* announcing that Margo Jones was there for meetings about a proposed Broadway production. While Madison Avenue suggested that a woman use an enticing perfume to lure a man, Margo knew that money and business deals were aphrodisiacs to Manning, and she didn't hesitate to use both in her campaign to regain his love.

During her ten-day stay, she visited with Tad Adoue, who presented her with a gift of white Alfred Orlik cigarette holders that she delighted in using. She attended the theatre and especially liked *Antony and Cleopatra*, starring Laurence Olivier and Vivien Leigh, and the new musical *Pal Joey*. Before returning to Dallas she traveled to Fayetteville, Arkansas, for a lecture. Her three-week absence was the longest time she had ever spent away from her theatre, and "it was a real joy to get back," she said.

Under Ramsey Burch's direction, the new play, *A Gift for Cathy* by Ronald Alexander, was ready to open. In 1950 the Alley Theatre in Houston had presented Alexander's second play, *Season with Ginger*, then had followed that popular production with his next play, *Angelica*, written for their arena stage. Margo had tried to convince the Rockefeller Foundation to fund a playwright-in-residence position for Alexander at Theatre '52, but they had rejected her proposal because of a negative reader's report on *A Gift for Cathy*. Set in the present in a tenement in a large American city, the play tells the story of a young Irish-American girl, Cathy O'Donnell, who decides to become a prostitute but is saved by marrying a millionaire. Rosenfield liked the play, finding the scenes "bright and sharp, often [taking] literary flight." The production drew the largest audiences of the season. The following year on Broadway, Alexander's *Time Out for Ginger* (a revamped *Season with Ginger*) became a hit, and later enjoyed a long life as a perennial favorite of community theatres across the country.

Is It Worth It?

In February, Brooks Atkinson arrived in Dallas for a three-day visit to see a new play, talk with Margo, and subject himself to constant Dallas hospitality. Eugene McDermott hosted a dinner party in his honor and a luncheon at the Brook Hollow Country Club. Rosenfield gave a lunch at the *Dallas Morning News*; Margo, McDermott, and E. L. DeGolyer took him to dinner before the performance; and Clifford Sage, entertainment editor at the *Dallas Times Herald*, snagged him for an interview. Atkinson told Sage that "he had reviewed more than 2,700 Broadway plays during the past 27 years. . . . We used to have as many as 200 openings a season during the '20's," he said. "Sometimes we had three reviewers working every night. And once, I remember covering three shows in the same issue. That was the famous night in December of 1929 when we had 11 legitimate openings just after Christmas."

Atkinson saw the fourth new play of the season, *The Blind Spot* by Edward Caulfield, who had written last year's *Innocent in Time*. Margo directed the play, and probably chose it because of the central character of an idealistic, if masochistic, playwright who refuses to accept a fortune he has earned for a popular play, saying that his success was undeserved good luck. He even demonstrates his disdain by burning a fifty-dollar bill. In the end, though, the playwright compromises his principles, illustrating the author's theme that life sometimes demands small dishonesties and petty compromises. Roundly condemned by reviewers as inept and hackneyed, the play pleased audiences well enough to fill the house most performances, an example of regrettable "public lawlessness," quipped Brooks Atkinson. Word of mouth was the most powerful advertisement the theatre had, and even when the reports on the plays were not good, people bought tickets anyway, because going to "Margo's" was the thing to do and hers was the only professional theatre in town. In 1951 and 1952 Dallas audiences saw two of their favorite actors in road shows—Tod Andrews in *Mister Roberts* and Mary Finney in *Gentlemen Prefer Blondes* —but visits from touring companies were infrequent now, despite Dallas's population of 434,000.

THE REMAINDER of the season proceeded routinely. Ramsey and Violet Burch had proven to be invaluable to Margo. While Ramsey's directing technique lacked the fire and spontaneous creativity of Margo's style, the acting company appreciated his workmanlike approach to a script and the consistency of his direction, very unlike the constant changes Margo demanded. His low-key manner, quite different from her own, did not represent a threat to her position at the theatre or in the community, and Margo often trusted him to fill in for her at speaking engagements or to manage the day-to-day business of the theatre when she had to travel on her lecture tour.

While she had final say on script selection, she allowed Ramsey complete freedom to conduct rehearsals in his own way. He continued Margo's practice of greeting the audience at the theatre when they arrived and chatting with them after performances. Margo spoke of Ramsey and Violet as her dearest friends, but she was not truly intimate with them. Their relationship, though warm and affectionate, largely remained professional.

Violet's office was in the dinette area of Margo's apartment at the Stoneleigh, and her job included driving Margo to her weekly session with psychiatrist Dr. Knapp. Observing positive changes in her employer, Violet felt that these sessions "helped her tremendously." Despite their close working arrangement, Margo did not confide in either Violet or Ramsey. They knew of her involvement and break-up with Manning only through Jonas Silverstone. "One thing Margo never did was speak disparagingly about anyone, even those who may have treated her shabbily," Violet recalls. Writing about Margo years later, Violet and Ramsey remember her as "dear, loving, vivacious, considerate, and the most caring theatre devotee we have ever known. A true Texan. The best times we had together were our family gatherings of which she was always a part. . . . She loved [our daughters] Pamela and Gigi and they in turn adored her."

ON MARCH 10, Theatre '52 presented Strindberg's *The Father*, directed by Ramsey. It was the first play by Strindberg ever to be produced in Dallas. Critically well-received—Rosenfield called it "an educational event of some significance"—the difficult drama succeeded financially as well. Dallas audiences were always eager to prove their cultural sophistication. Margo then staged Eddie Mayer's *I Am Laughing*, which opened March 31 and divided the critics. Clifford Sage of the *Dallas Times Herald* called it extremely boring and trite, while John Rosenfield hailed it as one of the most important plays Margo had ever premiered. To close the season, Ramsey directed *So in Love*, a small musical by Vera Marshall (formerly Vera Mathews, who had written the first season's *Third Cousin*). Set in New Orleans in 1825, the play was dubbed "A Perambulator Named Desire" by John Rosenfield because of its gentle approach to sex. Few of the players had adequate singing voices, but they were good actors, and had fun with lyrics like "Our cheeks are pink, our lips are red / We'd like a little bedroom sport before we're dead," and "I'm Sally, the maid, but I've never been made."

Following the final weeks of repertory, Theatre '52 again closed with a budget surplus and theatre capacity over 80 percent, but the season sparked a public argument between the entertainment editors on the rival local newspapers. Sage of the *Dallas Times Herald* announced that he could care less about box-office receipts. He denounced the poor selection of plays presented, finding only A *Gift for Cathy* worthy of production. Who chooses these plays? he wondered, knowing very well that Margo read and selected each play personally. He called for a qualified committee of play readers to improve the quality. If something wasn't done, he hinted darkly, the theatre's days were numbered. A few days later John Rosenfield presented his rebuttal to Sage's article and reminded the critic and his readers of Margo's mission. He agreed with Sage that A *Gift for Cathy* was first-rate but praised also *I Am Laughing, The Father,* and *One Foot in Heaven.* "The astute Broadway producer," he wrote, "lands one hit in ten tries. Margo's record any season is sensationally better. . . . And what she is doing is a fantastic challenge. She is not conducting her business among proved and tried stage hits. . . . She is dedicated to new and hitherto unproduced plays, largely by unknown authors." At the same time Rosenfield criticized Margo for not insisting on rewriting new plays in rehearsal and for sometimes valuing "specious theatricality, sex situations and melodramatic corn above challenging ideas."

While the critics argued about the merits of past seasons, a restless Margo thought about the future. Diversification, growth, new projects beckoned. She wanted to operate year-round, but the State Fair Musicals had use of the theatre during the summer. It was suggested that she use a tent, and move to different places around town. "I'll think about it," she said, "but not very hard." She did think about building a larger, more flexible theatre.

Two other projects occupied her. Inspired by Albert McCleery's television series "Cameo Theatre" and motivated by Manning's interest in working with her in producing for television, she wanted to create an hour-long series, in the round, originating from Dallas, to introduce new writers and actors. The title of the series would be "Discovery '52." With the assistance of Jonas Silverstone and her agent at William Morris Agency, she had already begun initial discussions with the networks and had proposed dozens of script possibilities. She had also launched preliminary discussions with arts leaders in San Francisco about opening a resident professional theatre in their city. Her former assistant, Jonathan Seymour, a native of San Francisco, planned to work with her on the founding of the theatre and to be its resident director. Clearly, Margo knew the pace she would have to keep to accomplish these objectives. But she was a workaholic, addicted to work, needing it as much as she craved liquor or the soothing effects of nicotine. When her own buoyant optimism wavered, she read the work of Norman Vincent Peale avidly, attended his lecture appearances in Dallas, and often sent his pamphlets to her mother. She believed in the power of positive thinking and in her force of will. Perhaps all her professions of optimism and faith and Pollyanna gladness were efforts to silence a voice inside her that had begun to raise a crucial question—Is it worth it?

M A R G O S P E N T the summer of 1952 again in Gramercy Park. She liked her familiar neighborhood. The tradespeople all knew her, especially the liquor store owner and the local hairdresser, whom she saw often. They exchanged Christmas cards, and Margo sent them theatre brochures. In June, July, and early August, she observed rehearsals and broadcasts of all types of television shows, even the news and sports, from the control booths at the various networks. She continued with correspondence about the founding of the San Francisco theatre and explored other opportunities as well—Kansas City had expressed an interest in her starting a resident theatre there.

One early summer evening, Margo joined Manning for dinner at a vegetarian restaurant, then went to the pier with him, where he sailed on a Cuban freighter for an extended vacation in the West Indies and Haiti. With Manning gone, Margo abhorred the thought of being alone and went out almost every evening. She spent a great deal of time with her favorite writers. One of her oldest friends, Bill Goyen, had an apartment in the city, and they whiled away the hours talking about their childhoods in East Texas, his writing, and the theatre. Goyen grew infatuated with Margo, hooked on her excitement about his work and dependent on her belief that he was a great writer. She visited briefly with Tennessee, and then saw him off as he and his lover, Frank Merlo, sailed to Europe. William Inge, who had established his reputation with the Theatre Guild's 1950 production of his second play, *Come Back, Little Sheba*, gave her his new play, *Picnic*, to read, and she thought it was "simply terrific."

Ramsey and Violet Burch had an apartment in town; Tad Adoue lived close by; Frank Harting again welcomed her for country weekends; the Ray Walstons and the Ted Apsteins invited her for dinners; she lunched with ANTA colleagues; and she attended the summer theatres to spot new acting talent for Theatre '52. She drove out to Westport to the White Barn Theatre, established by Lucille Lortel on the grounds of her estate. "It was an interesting experience," Margo wrote. "A very rich lady who obviously has a heart of gold has just formed a kind of community with many small guest cottages and when she finds talented young writers . . . who need help and encouragement, she provides a place for them to live while they work creatively."

Although the country was gearing up for the presidential election, Margo paid little attention. She did watch the Republican National Convention, primarily to observe the television techniques used to cover the event, and she heard General Douglas MacArthur address the convention. The frustrated Republicans had been out of office for twenty years. The moderates who backed Eisenhower were fearful that MacArthur would repeat the success of his earlier "Old soldiers never die" speech, which when delivered to a joint session of Congress caused even Democrats to shed tears. However, MacArthur's long speech bored the delegates, failed to stampede the convention, and Eisenhower was duly nominated. After listening to MacArthur's speech, Margo wrote her mother that she didn't approve of the general's attitude or think that he was sincere. One evening at her apartment over drinks and dinner, she had listened as Brooks Atkinson and Tad Adoue talked about the Republican vice-presidential nominee, and the accusation that he had created a campaign slush fund for his personal use. "Now, tell me," she had asked, "who is this Richard Nixon?"

FOR THE NEXT two years, Margo confessed later, she "carried on like a maniac," working nonstop, traveling constantly, and consumed "with a hope, with a hope, with a hope" that she and Manning might reconcile and work together again. "I was pretty stupid," she bluntly observed later. She hid her obsession well, except from the perceptive John Rosenfield, who understood exactly why Margo planned to direct only two plays at Theatre '52—she would be free to travel. He knew that Gurian was on the road, touring with *I Am a Camera*.

Despite Margo's involvement with other projects, she kept a close eye on the working of her theatre. When Jim Pringle, who had been promoted to technical director for Theatre '52, suggested that he, Freddie Hoskins, and the Dolans greet the new company and staff with coffee and doughnuts at the train and help them find housing, Margo responded promptly and vehemently. "I am almost violent," she wrote, "in my belief of a certain policy in relationship to our company and staff. One of the things that has happened in so many theatre groups is the kind of Bohemianism brought about by too close association. . . . I think that it is essential that tremendous dignity be maintained in our public relations and that only the press and Mr. McDermott, President of our Board, meet the train and that every effort be made for it to seem as untheatrical as possible. . . . I think your ideas are charming, but not at all suitable."

The popular Edwin Whitner and Norma Winters returned as members of the resident company as well as Mary Dell Roberts, Charles Braswell, and John Munson. New members included Rex Everhart, who had worked on

Broadway and in stock; Dick Ewell and his wife, Patricia Barclay, both of whom had acted on Broadway and on tour with *Season in the Sun*, starring Victor Jory; and Dallas-based actors Louis Veda Quince, Evelyn Bettis, and Martha Bumpas. After meeting the board members at a cocktail party, the actors and staff members gathered at Margo's for a dinner of Floyd McDaniels's southern soul food. Then, according to Martha Bumpas, before they read the first play together, "we would hold hands and it was a very loving moment . . . almost a holy moment. Then we would read the script, exchanging roles."

Five new scripts, Vivian Connell's *Goodbye, Your Majesty*, Robin Maugham's *The Rising Heifer*, Eugene Raskin's *The Last Island*, John Briard Harding's *Uncle Marston*, Rosemary Casey's *Late Love*, Lesley Storm's *The Day's Mischief*, and two classics, Shakespeare's *Hamlet* and Richard Brinsley Sheridan's *The Rivals*, were scheduled for the theatre's seventh season. Four repertory weeks were interspersed throughout the year in addition to two weeks of repertory at the end. Rosenfield noted that "seven seasons in undeviating pursuit of a policy is practically a lifetime in the twentieth century theatre, where nothing else seems to last." As usual, Margo, in her publicist role, enthused that "we have better material, better actors, better facilities and better standing in theatrical centers. So our season should be better."

WITH THE Dallas season safely launched, in November Margo flew to San Francisco for an extended visit to sell her idea of another Theatre '52. Eugene McDermott and two other Dallas board members had provided her with three thousand dollars in seed money. Judge Eustace Cullinan, who had a brother on the Dallas theatre board, drew up the San Francisco theatre's charter, headed its organizational committee, introduced Margo to potential board members and contributors, and helped scout possible theatre locations.

From her sixteenth-floor room at the Clift Hotel, Margo had a marvelous view of San Francisco and the Bay, but she had little time for enjoying the scenery or sight-seeing. She talked to the press at every opportunity. "I first saw San Francisco when I was very young," she said, "and I just fell in love with it. So, when I was ready to open another theatre, I thought, why not in the city I love?" One reporter described her as a "trim, brunette Texas cyclone" who hoped to do what no one else had been able to do—"establish a permanent repertory theatre" in San Francisco. In early December when Manning arrived in town for several weeks' stay with *I Am a Camera*, he found the local newspapers running articles, interviews, and photographs of Margo Jones. It was no coincidence. Margo was quite familiar with his itinerary. After a reunion with Manning, and with the San Francisco project underway, she rushed back to Texas in late December. She made a brief stop in Livingston for Christmas, then hurried to Dallas to direct a new play, supervise the television project, and work on plans for building a new theatre. Like the proverbial cowboy, she had saddled up and was riding off in several different directions at once.

I T H A D B E E N nine months since Margo had directed a play, and she missed the daily rehearsals and contact with actors. Eugene Raskin, who had written *The Last Island*, the fourth play of the season, was in Dallas to work with her on the script. Formerly a practicing architect, Raskin, a native New Yorker, had joined the teaching staff of Columbia University in order to have more time to write plays, compose songs (he later earned a gold record for sales of the popular "Those Were the Days"), and give concerts with his wife, Francesca. Like Ted Apstein, Raskin was a member of New Dramatists, a New York-based organization formed to help playwrights. *The Last Island* was his third play.

As other playwrights had before him, Raskin fell under Margo's spell. "Thirty-six years later," he says, "I think I'm still coasting on that high." He walked into her Stoneleigh apartment, where she was curled up on the sofa surrounded by scripts and her turtle collection. "Hi, honey, come on in," she said, patting the sofa.

"She started to talk to me, in such a warm and friendly manner," Raskin recalls. "She had this little southern trick of ending sentences with a question mark, an upward inflection, [and] this little inflection had the effect of not only sounding warm and friendly, but of drawing you into her thoughts not as a recipient of what she was saying, but as a participant."

"Then the next thing I discovered about her," Raskin remembers, "was that she considered the words written by a playwright to be sacred. That came first, everything else was secondary. Today a play is considered a property, which is a very different point of view—property is something you can chop up, buy and sell—to her a play was a work of art, if it were a painting she would have framed it and hung it on the wall."

Written in blank verse and set in Key West, *The Last Island* is a drama about a retired composer and his ex-dancer wife, who run a small bar and restaurant. While they're awaiting the birth of their first child, the wife's former dancing partner arrives, and when the wife joins him for a last fling on the dance floor, she miscarries. The composer seeks comfort in infidelity. Margo devoted a great deal of rehearsal time to character analysis. When the actor playing the husband had difficulty conveying jealousy, Margo asked, "Haven't you ever been jealous?"

"No," he said.

He happened to be married to an actress who was also in the company. "You mean to tell me," Margo said, "that you haven't ever been jealous of that pretty wife of yours?"

"No, never," he replied.

Both Margo and Raskin turned questioningly to his wife, who shrugged and said with great disappointment, "Yes."

Margo decided to give him a line reading. Then Raskin tried. They both failed and commiserated over drinks. Raskin recalls that Margo drank heavily during his stay in Dallas. "I think when she watched a play she did as many performances as there were actors in the play, which would exhaust her, then she would drink and start to get blurry. Nobody seemed to think much of it."

With several cocktail parties a week and a constant stream of guests, most evenings Margo had a drink in her hand. None of her staff members recall that her drinking affected her work. Jim Pringle once observed her working a cocktail party, "confronting board members and getting them to commit to things by pretending to be tipsy—a lot of times she was acting to get what she wanted—it suddenly occurred to me—she hasn't drunk that much—what is she doing?" At that time Margo's consumption of liquor did not seem particularly unusual. Alcohol flowed freely at most social gatherings, and drinking was considered a relatively harmless habit.

The Last Island opened to good reviews and the critics welcomed Margo's return to directing, but audiences felt differently and ticket sales were down. Margo received a letter from one woman who wrote, "I am returning tickets as such adverse reports have reached me as to the nature of this play. I do wish that others would be as frank in expressing disapproval of the coarse and risqué as found in the modern plays you show. You hear such criticisms in groups at women's clubs, yet they never speak to you. One young woman said today, 'I thought I was quite modern and could take most anything, but I felt unclean for several days after this play.'"

The wife in *The Last Island* takes off her dress to reveal a full-length slip, and there are several profanities. Irate at what he considered a rising tide of prudery and censorship, John Rosenfield published the letter Margo had received, advising his readers that anyone "getting extraordinary sex motivation from *The Last Island* must have a low boiling point and should pitter-patter down to his or her psychiatrist for sedation."

IN OCTOBER 1952, Margo had hired William Dubensky, a young film producer, as the coordinator of "Discovery '52." She contacted dozens of playwrights asking them to submit scripts, and Dubensky worked in Dallas with a local television station on plans for a studio at Fair Park. He had a puppy-like devotion to Margo, drove her 1948 Cadillac around town, and lived at the Stoneleigh—all facts which stimulated gossip among the theatre staff about the real nature of their relationship. By spring of 1953, though, Margo had grown unhappy with Dubensky's work and fired him, gentling the impact by calling it a leave of absence. She decided to manage the project herself.

"Good-looking men were a big attraction for Margo," Jim Pringle recalls, "but her theatre was everything to her—mother, lover, children. She needed people though." Margo even requested that Pringle and his wife Rita move to an apartment directly across from the Stoneleigh. "She used to come over and visit. One night we were sound asleep and all of a sudden we heard, 'Jimmy, we gotta talk.' Margo was on the terrace, and we let her in through the window. We all got up and had coffee. We never knew when she might pop in. But we would never pop in on her—she was our employer."

Margo's relationship with her board of directors, her employers, although it appears she never thought of them as such, was tested that spring. Arthur Kramer, Jr., who served as the business chairman of the board, felt that he was responsible for the financial management of the theatre or his title as business manager was meaningless. He wanted to have authority over how money was spent and accounted for, activities that Margo controlled. Whenever the theatre experienced a shortfall or unexpected expenses, Eugene McDermott simply wrote a check to cover the deficit. The oil business was flourishing, and McDermott's loyalty remained with Margo. Kramer wanted to convert this loose arrangement into a more business-like practice, but Margo interpreted his actions as an attempt to curb her autonomy and even as a move toward firing her. At an emotional board meeting a tearful Margo announced, "I will not be confined!" She demanded 100 percent artistic and financial control. McDermott, trying to keep the peace between two of his closest friends, took Kramer aside and convinced him to stay on the board, although he did give up his title as business manager. "Margo was more important to the theatre than I was. With me, it was a matter of principle," Kramer recalls. "I stayed because of a great personal fondness for Margo, and she did get better at managing the budget."

"THERE IS no healing power quite as strong as really hard work," Margo wrote in April. During the spring of 1953, she kept herself constantly busy with various projects. She asked George Dahl's Dallas architectural firm to draw up rough sketches for a new theatre. And she wrote Tad Adoue that "a piece of property on Blackburn catty corner across from the Jesuit High school right along side [Turtle] creek seems to be available as a gift from its owner. His name is Mr. S. T. Baer. I think it is an exceedingly beautiful piece of property, also very centrally located." However, she soon discovered that Mr. Baer was an eccentric who placed too many restrictions on the use of the property, like demanding unlimited access, and so she refused his gift.

In late March, Tennessee asked that she fly to New York for the opening of his new play, *Camino Real*. The out-of-town tryouts had been a nightmare. Audiences didn't understand the fragmented, poetic play. Margo wrote her parents that "Tennessee is closer to me than a friend . . . almost like family. . . ." When he needed her support, she was there with her unshakable faith in his great talent and to share his anguish over the failure of his play. Margo also helped Tennessee endure a party with his mother and several of her friends, who were in New York for the opening. "Talk about southern," Margo told Tad Adoue. "[T]hey actually talked dialogue right out of *Glass Menagerie*." While she was in town, she also saw William Inge's *Picnic* at the Music Box Theatre and attended a party with Inge where they watched the 1953 Academy Awards on television and saw Shirley Booth receive the Best Actress award for her performance in Inge's *Come Back, Little Sheba*.

She saw Tennessee again in late May when he directed Donald Windham's play *The Starless Air* at Joanna Albus's theatre in Houston. Former members of the Houston Community Players filled the audience, giving Margo a "nostalgic thrill" to see so many old friends.

She gave Ramsey a respite from directing and staged the final new play of the season, *The Day's Mischief* by London playwright Leslie Storm, a drama about a schoolgirl who has a crush on her married teacher that results in a community scandal, unfounded rumors, and the suicide of the teacher's wife. After her season closed, she loaned her theatre and services as a director to a newly formed black community group called the Round-up Theatre, producing a highly popular production of *Walls Rise Up*.

She traveled to the University of Miami in Florida to be the featured speaker at the first arena-theatre conference. Also attending were Joanna Albus, manager of the Houston Playhouse Theatre, Nina Vance of the Alley Theatre, and Zelda Fichandler of Washington's Arena Stage. When Malcolm Ross suggested that the participants at the conference collaborate on a technical handbook for arena theatre, Margo reminded him that she had already written *Theatre-in-the-Round*, and said that "one of the most interesting and exciting things that came out of the conference was the really great differences of opinion not only in technical matters but in an entire philosophical attitude" —a polite way of saying that each woman was an independent leader whose theatre reflected her individual personality.

She spent most of the summer in Dallas reading plays, attending to theatre business and her television plan. In August, she traveled to New York to hire actors for the upcoming season. The San Francisco project was in abeyance since no suitable theatre space had been found. Also, board members had made it clear that they weren't terribly pleased with Margo's extended absences from Dallas and her direction of only two plays during the season. When Jonas Silverstone wrote that CBS was interested in her directing for "Studio One," she replied, "My first responsibility is to the theatre here."

S H E   E X P A N D E D the Theatre '53–54 season to nine productions, eight new scripts and one classic, and planned to direct five of them herself. The eight premieres included the first American production of *The Footpath Way* by British author Burgess Drake; *The Guilty* by Harry Granick; *Happy We'll Be*, a translation of a contemporary Spanish play; *Oracle Junction*, based on the life of Dr. Michael Shadid, a pioneer in community health care; *The Heel*, a farce by Samson Raphaelson; *A Rainbow at Home*, a romantic comedy by television writer Milton Robertson; a new musical, *Horatio*, with book by Ira Wallach, music by David Baker, and lyrics by Sheldon Harnick; and the first professional productions of Tennessee Williams's *The Purification* and Jean Giraudoux's *The Apollo of Bellac*, presented as one evening. Ramsey Burch would direct Shakespeare's *The Merry Wives of Windsor* to close the season. Ticket prices for evening performances were increased to three dollars and matinees to two dollars and fifteen cents. Also, Theatre '53 offered a 17 percent discount to season-ticket subscribers. The season was risky and ambitious, but Margo had decided to refocus her energy on her Dallas theatre. Her enthusiasm and excitement were infectious. For the first time in several seasons, the board planned a gala black-tie party at the Adolphus Hotel to celebrate the opening.

Finding good, versatile actors willing to commit to a season outside New York had been difficult, but Margo was pleased with the quality of actors she had hired. Only Charles Braswell and Martha Bumpas were returning from the previous year. Phyllis Love, who had played the ingenue in *The Rose Tattoo* and understudied Julie Harris in *The Member of the Wedding*, signed on for the Dallas season but broke her contract after appearing in the first production and returned to New York. She was replaced by Jeanne Gal, a dancer who had recently moved to Dallas. Other company members included lovely young Louise Noble, a Boston native who found the adjustment to Dallas difficult; veteran character actor Guy Spaull, who had acted in twenty-six Broadway productions, and his wife, actress Joan Croyden, who had begun her career with David Belasco; leading man James Field, whom Margo had spotted in

Is It Worth It?

The Starless Air at the Houston Playhouse; and Richard Shepard, who had studied with Uta Hagen and had also spent a season at the Houston Playhouse.

She promoted Jim Pringle to technical director and designer and named Michael Dolan as his assistant. With Freddie Hoskins as the production stage manager, and Ramsey and Violet Burch, Mary Dolan, and business manager Vern Armstrong, Margo had assembled an experienced, talented production team. "It's the first time in a long time," she said, "that the entire operation has complete . . . unity."

As usual, Margo's happiness with her professional life had a basis in her personal life. Although Margo was intensely romantic, she also had a practical, down-to-earth side. Separated from Manning by distance and different values, she had finally begun to realize the futility of clinging to a hope that they might reconcile. Tellingly, she did not give up on Manning until another man had entered her life, a man with "a sensitive understanding about my mind, my work, my body, and my soul," she said. She had already begun to create a new romantic drama.

During 1952 and early 1953, she had used every opportunity to see Manning, visiting him in Chicago, St. Louis, or San Francisco, and calling him, often late at night. Their estrangement seems to have been gradual, with few dramatic confrontations, although at one point an angry Margo did toss his pen and handkerchief out the window of her Gramercy Park apartment. During the summer of 1953 in New York, Manning read Margo the first draft of his play *The Way of a Woman*. She had liked it enough to suggest changes and had agreed to produce the play in the 1953–54 season after he had rewritten it. But when she read the final version of the play, which she had scheduled to open on March 29, 1954, Margo returned the script to him and removed it from the season.

The play is fascinating because the central character, Marie, a powerful advertising executive, is obviously based on Manning's view of Margo. Marie works too hard, is driven and ruthless. "There are times I think I'm sane," she says, "when I'm ready to relax . . . but I don't dare. You see, I must build my castle to the sky. If I stop, I'm afraid everything will tumble . . . including me." Marie believes that her lover, George Nelson, will marry her, but he rejects her for someone else. At the end of the play, Marie says that she doesn't need anyone, has always gone it alone, doesn't need George or anyone else.

"Your characters are bitches and bastards—you pull the strings, but I don't believe them," Margo wrote in the first draft of a letter to Manning, her pen cutting through the paper at times. Was this how Manning saw her? she must have wondered. Was this his view of the world—a place where people used one another and were motivated almost entirely by self-interest? In the final typed version of the letter, Margo had composed her feelings and wrote a measured response to the script, choosing her words carefully. She had heard Manning say that he didn't like people, but "I personally believe that you do and that you have real admiration for the good and courageous qualities that can be found in mankind." In summing up her feelings, she wrote, "I think the heart of the matter centers around Marie. This woman should have greatness within her to be able to do what she does. She must have something that makes it possible for her to attract. I feel we must know what her charm is. We need so badly to understand why she can do what she does. To me she is pictured as crude, unkind, ruthless, lacking in charm, and lacking in human decency. How can we pity her and we need so to pity her and have compassion for her. I do not know how valid this analysis is but I do know that it is sincere and from my heart."

Manning wired back that he respected her integrity. Years later he said, "Margo's feeling for me was just too overpowering. I had another life in New York. . . . I knew that she was very unhappy about that, but I had to do what I had to do. Margo wouldn't have been happy in New York—the New York theatre is very cruel. I think she was married to the theatre. . . . She was kind of a Joan of Arc."

Her relationship with Manning, begun in the summer of 1946, had ended for Margo seven years later. She talked about her feelings for him, sometimes addressing him directly (perhaps at the recommendation of her psychiatrist) into her dictaphone, making tapes that she carefully saved. Her recordings capsulize their relationship, make it into a drama with a beginning, a middle, and an end where she says good-bye without bitterness, and thanks him for the happiness he has brought her: "My darling good-bye. . . . Never again shall I call you in the middle of the night. Never again shall I wire you. . . . There is one thing that I suppose I will always do. I suppose here in my apartment in Dallas I shall always leave the light burning above the telephone not now that I ever expect you to call at that one o'clock [but] because it has become such a part of me. . . . You say that you don't like people and I know how much you want security more than anything else and I know the kind of things that you have done. . . . Darling, don't kowtow to names; don't be impressed with people; don't hide yourself up in mountains and say that you are going to write. I'm sorry, darling, when one wants to write, one writes. . . . All that matters right now, dear, is that I'm saying good-bye . . . with all my heart I'm telling you that my entire life is what it is because of you. . . . I now have the capacity to love again. I have no desire for anything from you except your

Is It Worth It?

happiness." Then, on a fresh tape, she says, "[A]nd now . . . and now with such reticence I say hello to you." As the heroine of her own life, she had to have a hero. She found him in writer Bill Goyen.

They had been friends for years, since the late 1930s in Houston, a mutual admiration team writing each other loving, supportive letters, Margo often enclosing money for Bill in her letters. In October 1953, Bill had come to Dallas to spend long evenings and work into the night with Margo on his play—an adaptation of his poetic novel *The House of Breath*. At a time when she was especially vulnerable, Margo could not resist the attractive, articulate Goyen. Unlike Manning, whose background had been antithetical to Margo's, Goyen had grown up in the red dirt country of East Texas along the Trinity River. Although she knew that he had lived with the painter Joseph Glasco for several years, Margo was drawn erotically to the man and to his writing. It is clear from his letters that Goyen was infatuated with her as well. Would Bill Goyen be the love she had been searching for, the person she could share her life with? "I loved your being here. I loved your letters that you have written me. . . . And so my darling . . . I say to you that perhaps, perhaps this, maybe this . . . ," she chanted into the recorder.

The Footpath Way, the first play of the Theatre '53–54 season, was a hit, and the community responded with a round of parties and social events for the company and staff. However, rehearsals of the second play, *The Guilty*, were not going well. The play is a character study of three people who have been involved in a murder and who come before the audience to tell their stories. The presentational style, lack of strong dramatic action, and the necessity of playing characters who age from fifteen to forty in the course of the play—all without properties or major costume changes—frustrated the actors and Margo, who struggled to find a visual style to animate a talky script.

Harry Granick, the playwright, was on hand for all the rehearsals, and he recalls that Margo was full of energy—optimistic and giving—but late at night at her Stoneleigh apartment, where they would adjourn to discuss the script, she would sit on the floor drinking Scotches and growing more and more depressed. Often, she would fall asleep on the floor and an embarrassed Granick would tiptoe out.

The night before *The Guilty* opened, still dissatisfied with the production, Margo kept the company and staff up all night restaging the play. Actress Louise Noble recalls that as the night wore on she felt "bullied" by the director. Wearing black slacks and a black top that exposed her shoulders and arms, with her hair slicked back behind her ears, scrawling notes on her yellow pad, ripping them off and thrusting them at the actors with not a trace of sweetness in her expression, Margo looked like a demonic dancer, intent on perfection.

Her direction received excellent reviews, but her respect for the playwright's words may have contributed to the play's failure at Theatre '53. Following the premiere production, Granick made substantial changes in his play, but during his stay in Dallas, Margo did not ask him to cut or rewrite even one line. She seldom suggested revisions, but when writers wanted to cut and reshape their scripts during rehearsals, Margo cheerfully complied. *Horatio*, a spoof of a Horatio Alger success story that was the first musical for which Sheldon Harnick wrote lyrics—he later won Tony Awards for *Fiorello!* and *Fiddler on the Roof*—opened in Dallas in March 1954. Harnick recalls that he spent most of his time in Dallas writing and rewriting. "There seemed to be no problems [Margo] couldn't solve, no knots she couldn't untangle," he says. "If her staff were having trouble locating some prop or costume, she would disappear for awhile and then return triumphantly in proud possession of whatever it was that was needed." However, he sensed that along with her strength and enthusiasm there seemed to be a great loneliness. "At the end of the day," he remembers, "she didn't want to be alone . . . was constantly inviting us in for drinks and conversation." Margo's turtle collection, which had grown to eight thousand turtles, each one given to her by a friend and each one named, filled her apartment, and made a lasting impression on Harnick. Turtle flowerpots, key rings, ashtrays, pincushions, cigarette boxes, even a spittoon, and turtle jewelry of china, brass, wood, leather, and diamonds—tiny turtle earrings given her by one of her *Summer and Smoke* companies—crowded the floor, tabletops, drawers, and closets. Years later Harnick pondered the meaning, the totemic significance of her collection. Did she see herself as a creature with a tough shell "forever sticking its neck out"? he wondered.

ALTHOUGH SOMETIMES accused of pandering to popular taste in her play choices, Margo attempted to occupy a precarious ground, presenting middlebrow entertainment interspersed with challenging scripts. Dependent completely upon the income from single-ticket sales and season subscriptions ($22.50 for nine plays), Theatre '54 had survived almost ten seasons on a steady diet of new plays. Sometimes Margo used the press to help her raise money. Playwright Harry Granick recalls that during his stay in Dallas, Brooks and Oriana Atkinson arrived at the theatre to see a performance of *The Footpath Way*. At the end of the first act, when Granick went over to say hello to the critic and his wife, he noticed that they were seated in a row of rickety and dilapidated seats. He thoughtfully ushered them to more comfortable seats in another section of the theatre, then found Margo and asked, "How come the Atkinsons were given those terrible seats?"

"Shh," Margo said. "I want him to write that this wonderful theatre needs more money for upkeep."

In May 1954 Atkinson again visited the theatre to see performances of *The Purification* and *The Apollo of Bellac*. "Dallas is lucky to have a theatre where two short plays of literary distinction can be introduced as part of a repertory season," he wrote. Both plays, he said, have been staged by Margo Jones in her best form, *The Purification* "as if it were a religious ritual . . . acted with grace and devoutness." Unfortunately, while the critical response was positive, audiences preferred the lighter entertainment of *Horatio* and the last play of the season, *The Merry Wives of Windsor*.

MARGO ALWAYS DREADED the final production of a season. Each year, during the run of that last play, she had to perform a task she loathed. Throughout the run, every evening during the intermission, she gave a speech to the audience, urging them to use the pencil that had been taped under their armrests to fill out the application for season tickets printed in their playbills. Although the technique was a remarkably effective marketing tool, Margo believed fervently that speechmaking had no place in the theatre. Still, somebody had to do it, and she was certainly the one most qualified. Fred Hoskins, the stage manager, who observed Margo's offstage nervousness explode into a heartfelt sermon, would tell the company before she went onstage, "Now we're going to Come to Jesus!"

At the end of the 1954 season, Margo's friend Megan Comini wrote a three-act parody of the season called *Genital Junction*, which the company performed as a surprise to Margo. Fred Hoskins, warm, funny, and adept at mimicking Margo's rapid speech, acted her "Come to Jesus" speech, which captures the essence of Margo's unique style and even reproduces some of her standard phrases.

Now you all know this is a professional theatre, and we never make speeches. But just once a year—just at this time—I *do* come out and make a speech. We've given you nine plays this year and I hope you've enjoyed them all, but especially tonight's play, Tennessee Shakespeare's "Genital Junction," which I honestly think, so help me God, is one of the finest pieces of theatre ever written. And that's our whole purpose here, folks—to bring you real theatre—not just good theatre, but great theatre.

Is It Worth It?

Our plans for the future are pretty ambitious ones, but I have faith in my people here—my wonderful actors and my wonderful staff. This summer we plan to put on forty-three new plays, one every two nights, and each one different. I haven't chosen the scripts yet, but I plan to start reading next week . . .

Next fall we have an even more ambitious program. I can't tell you anything about it yet, because, quite frankly, I haven't figured it out myself, but it will certainly be ambitious, and will certainly bring you really great theatre. That I can promise you.

Now everybody hates to talk about money, but I'm going to be brave and talk about it. We have a new plan for next year and the years following it. We are going to sell not one-season tickets, but ten-year season tickets and five-year season tickets. The ten-year tickets will cost $750 each and the five-year tickets $450. I can't figure out the difference just now, on the spur of the minute, but Abe Shosid, our wonderful accountant, tells me there is quite a gain. (I forget whether it's for you or for us.)

Anyway, if you'll just reach under the arm of your seat, you'll find a bottle of ink and a pen and blotter for each one of you. Just write your name and address and the location you would like on the place provided for you right here in the program, and how many five- or ten-year season tickets you would like. You don't have to give us the money right away. Tomorrow will be all right, and our wonderful lawyer will get in touch with you if your checks aren't any good.

Go right ahead now, angels. I just love to hear the sound of tearing paper. I had a bet with my staff the other night, and they said I couldn't sell more than two season tickets that performance. I sold three. Now I want to beat that record tonight.

Now, just to make it clear—these are rows 1, 2, 3, and 4 and this is Section A—the uncomfortable one. That's Section B, with the bad acoustics. Over there is Section C—where you snag your stockings, and this is Section D—the drafty one.

Thank you, good people. Bless you.

WHILE THE RAPPORT and family feeling in her company were quite special, Margo felt isolated in Dallas from the theatre mainstream. She didn't regret the choice she had made to stay in Dallas and work on her dream of creating resident theatres around the country, but she was lonely, and missed the stimulation and contact with her peers that New York offered. With her heavier work load in Dallas, her trips to New York became less frequent, and she depended on letters and phone calls to keep in touch with her colleagues. In March 1954, Margo received a letter from Hallie Flanagan. They had worked together on committees in the 1940s and served together on the National Theatre Conference. Margo, along with other women in the theatre, had drawn strength from Flanagan's brave example in heading the vast Federal Theatre Project. In her letter, Hallie shared news about Robert Anderson, a playwright to whom the National Theatre Conference had given a fellowship, wrote about her joy in the marriage of her daughter Joanne to Eric Bentley, and communicated Bentley's wish to direct *Mother Courage* at Theatre '55; but the main import of the letter was Hallie's happiness in Margo's success and her advice that Margo guard her health, and not get too tired as she had. Faced with a degenerative disease and on leave from her theatre at Smith College, Hallie said that while she still believed in miracles, she was under no illusions as to the nature of the adversary.

Margo replied immediately with news about her theatre season, and she wrote, "You are always an inspiration to me, Hallie, and I can't tell you how really thrilled and pleased I was with your letter. . . . I'll try to take your advice, dear, and I, too, believe in miracles. Bless you for being the grand and wonderful person you are."

Rest, however, was not on Margo's agenda. Theatre '54 had become a year-round operation, extending the season for fifteen weeks into the summer, presenting four new scripts and one classic.

An Idea Is a Greater Monument
Than a Cathedral

N THE SPRING of 1954, *Theatre Arts* devoted a special issue to the plight of the American theatre. At the request of the magazine, Dr. O. Glenn Saxon, a professor of economics at Yale University, had prepared an independent report, which contained some revealing statistics. He found that in the 1931–32 Broadway season 195 plays opened, while in the 1953–54 Broadway season only 39 new plays had appeared. Since 1944, total attendance on Broadway had dropped 44 percent. The number of commercial theatres available for production on Broadway had decreased more than 50 percent since 1931, with only 32 theatres open in 1953, and no new theatre construction planned. The low number of touring productions mirrored the decline of the commercial New York theatre. In 1953 the total number of members of Actors' Equity who were working on Broadway or in touring companies was 991, compared to 4,445 working in the 1927–28 season. Dr. Saxon found that the only upward trend in audience attendance was in nonprofit, amateur community theatres scattered around the country. Because these nonprofit theatres did not have to pay the 20 percent federal admissions tax required of all commercial theatres, and because live theatre suffered from the competition of free radio and television, Dr. Saxon concluded that the commercial theatre's tax burden was unfair and had contributed to its decline. His remedy for an ailing theatre was an end to the 20 percent federal admissions tax paid by commercial theatres. If something weren't done, he declared, "the very existence of the living theatre in the United States is now in serious jeopardy."

In 1954 the New York commercial theatre was the central creative force of the living stage in the United States—few states even had one professional theatre. It is not surprising then that Saxon missed the movement toward decentralization, a trend still so tiny that it would have made barely a squiggle on his charts. Margo's Theatre '54 in Dallas, Zelda Fichandler's Arena Stage in Washington, D.C., and Nina Vance's Alley Theatre in Houston—three nonprofit, professional resident theatres not mentioned in Dr. Saxon's study —had found a regional audience for new plays and classics, had given full-time employment to actors and technicians, and were doing something about the existence of the living theatre. Significantly, it was a movement led by women—outsiders who did not belong to the male-dominated commercial theatre—and these women were taking the theatre in a new direction. With Margo they believed that "we will never rejuvenate the theatre by doing the old things in the same old ways."

IN THE SUMMER of 1954, the State Fair Musicals gave up their claim to Theatre '54 and found another space for their rehearsals. Margo's theatre became a year-round operation, playing for a total of forty-five weeks in the 1953–54 season. After closing the regular season in May, the acting company and staff stayed on and immediately began rehearsals of the first play of the summer season. Playwright Ronald Alexander, whose *Time Out for Ginger* had been a hit on Broadway the year before, had brought Margo his latest script, *The Inevitable Circle*, a romantic comedy. She asked him to direct the play, freeing her to read and select the other new scripts of the season. The production received excellent reviews, Rosenfield calling it as relaxing as bourbon and branch water. The play later opened on Broadway as *Grand Prize* in 1955, but closed after only twenty-one performances.

The other new scripts, *The Brothers* by John Rodell, *A Dash of Bitters* by Reginald Denham and Conrad Sutton-Smith, and *Sea-Change* by William Case, were all chosen for their light entertainment value. For the opening of *Sea-Change*, which was set on a cruise ship, the outside of the theatre was decorated with flags, life preservers, and travel posters. Afterward, the audience enjoyed rum punch on the decorated terrace—a treat that at least one reviewer felt was the best part of the evening. The summer season ended with Ben Jonson's classic comedy *Volpone*. Although none of the new scripts were of substance, the productions drew an audience during the scorching Texas summer and made a profit as well.

In July, Margo attended the fourth production of the Round-up Theatre, the black theatre company she had helped to found the year before. The group presented the world premiere of William Saroyan's play *A Lost Child's Fireflies*, and the playwright flew to Dallas for the opening. Margo described the evening to Rosamond Gilder. "It was a very exciting night," she wrote. "There was no such thing as segregation. . . . I had a good visit with William Saroyan, whom I had never met before. I like him enormously."

Also during June and July, Margo received calls for help and advice from Joanna Albus. Her Playhouse Theatre in Houston, which operated as a profit-making venture, was having a serious financial crisis. Joanna had not consulted Margo on the opening of her theatre, wanting to prove her independence from her former mentor, and in recent years the two women had seen each other infrequently. But Margo came to her aid, advising that Joanna change her theatre from a commercial enterprise to nonprofit status, thus avoiding the hefty admissions tax and gaining tax benefits. In addition, Margo packed up the production of *Sea-Change* and took it to Houston, where the company played a benefit performance at the Playhouse. Between the second and third acts of the play, Margo urged the audience to support Joanna's theatre—many wrote out checks and pledges on the spot. Hubert Roussell, a Houston theatre critic who knew Margo from her Community Players days, called her method of stimulating a crowd to unusual enthusiasm something he had given up trying to explain. "The obvious qualities that she brings to the role of promoter are two," he wrote, "an absolute belief in the value and community service of the theatre, and a way of stating her conviction that is so thoroughly genuine, so completely lacking in theatrical chi-chi or pretensions . . . that it often takes the breath out of an audience taught to expect suave and polite nothings when culture is up for discussion." The efforts to save the theatre failed, however, and the Playhouse closed in early 1955 after just three seasons of operation.

SINCE THE OPENING summer of 1947, Theatre '54 had presented sixty-seven plays, including world premieres of scripts by Tennessee Williams, William Inge, Joseph Hayes, Ronald Alexander, Vivian Connell, Sean O'Casey, and Dorothy Parker. Seventy percent of all the plays produced at the theatre had been new scripts, many by unknown authors. Since its opening, the 198-seat theatre had played to a total audience of over 302,000 people, attracting patrons from Texas and surrounding states, from New York and California, and visitors from around the world. The tiny twenty-by-twenty-four-foot stage encircled entirely by the audience had brought national recognition to Dallas. The time was ripe for a celebration.

On November 3, 1954, five days before the opening of the new season, Eugene McDermott hosted a luncheon at the Hotel Adolphus for one hundred civic leaders to honor Margo and the upcoming tenth-anniversary season. John Rosenfield served as toastmaster for the occasion, and for once Margo had nothing to do or say. When she had first arrived in Dallas, she had appeared girlish, if anything too young to head a theatre. Now, just nine years later, she looked every day of her forty-two years and more, although she admitted to being only forty. Her broad grin had grown a little jowly, her narrow cats' eyes were outlined by deep wrinkles, and her once slim figure had given way to plumpness. Still, her youthful enthusiasm remained, and she blew kisses at the mostly male audience and wore an expression, John Rosenfield observed, like "Alice overcome by Wonderland." Following the invocation, Eugene McDermott, who had served as the theatre board's president since its founding in 1945, read a telegram from Brooks Atkinson that said in part, "May Margo always enjoy the mind of an adult and the heart of a girl that has made a dream come true."

Sounding like a roll call of the American theatre, messages were read from Katharine Cornell, Guthrie McClintic, Mary Martin, Jo Mielziner, John Mason Brown, Roger Stevens, Theresa Helburn, Cheryl Crawford, Rosamond Gilder, José Ferrer, Horton Foote, Robert Whitehead, Norris Houghton, Maurice Evans, and many others. William Inge had planned to speak at the luncheon but had to cancel because of illness. There is no record of a message from Tennessee Williams, who had recently returned from Rome to begin filming *The Rose Tattoo* in Key West. Howard Lindsay, of *Life with Father* fame, spoke as a representative of the New York theatre. Lindsay was a strong supporter of decentralization, and told the gathering that "Broadway is only a part of the great American theatre scene." John Wray Young of the Shreveport Little Theatre spoke for the amateur, community theatres. "What [Margo] has done stands unique in the American theatre; a resident company dedicated to the new play. Only she has crusaded for the dual causes of functional theatre and the writing playwright and made it work. . . ." Turning to Margo, Young said, "You have come so far. From this peak you can see the range ahead. You are ready for the accelerated widening of America's cultural horizons. And we of the theatre are determined that it shall be done . . . by civic support." Mayor R. L. Thornton spoke for the community and expressed Dallas's thanks to Margo and her dynamic drive, which had meant so much to the city. He presented her with an engraved placque, which she accepted in wide-eyed amazement. While most people assumed that the city's leaders had decided on their own to pay tribute to Theatre '54, actually the entire event had been staged by Margo herself. The speakers, the invitations, the format, all were carefully planned by her with the assistance of Violet Burch. The one detail she had not scripted was the mayor's presentation. Her amazement at receiving the placque was real.

Later that day, after the luncheon, Margo wrote to Brooks and Oriana Atkinson, thanking them for their telegram. She told them of her surprise at the mayor's placque, and admitted that she had always thought that "this kind of thing was really silly but I did not feel that way today." Eighteen years earlier, in a hotel lobby in Moscow, Margo had boldly approached Atkinson and expressed a promise. Now she made another vow. "I promise you," she wrote, "that I will try with all of my heart to make our theatre an adult theatre and keep the wonderful phrase that you said in your wire — the heart of a girl. Bless you."

WHILE SHE ORGANIZED the tribute to Theatre '54, Margo had reached a difficult but necessary decision. She decided to give up on the San Francisco theatre project. As had been the problem in Dallas, the planning group in San Francisco had been unable to find a satisfactory theatre space. In addition, contributions were low. Without Margo in residence to oversee the fund-raising and direct the search for a building, the project was doomed. According to Jim Pringle, Margo had approached the Theatre '54 board and requested their permission to try to manage two theatre companies, alternating her time between Dallas and San Francisco. The board rejected her proposal, feeling quite correctly that she would be overburdened and the quality of her work in Dallas would suffer, and understandably they did not want to share with San Francisco the publicity and attention she brought to Dallas. "It dashed a lot of hopes for her," Pringle recalls.

Another faint hope was extinguished when John Rosenfield called her in October to tell her that he had just heard on the wire service that Manning Gurian had married Julie Harris. Mabel Duke, who was with Margo when she got the call, said later that "it was just like she had been slugged in the stomach. But then she said she was glad." In fact, although hurt by the news, Margo could not have been surprised. Her friend Tad Adoue was Manning's close friend and sometime business associate, and Margo knew of Julie Harris's divorce and her subsequent relationship with Manning. "I was so happy to hear about Julie and Manning," Margo wrote Tad. "I think they can both be an awful lot to each other." Even in her most private writing and in the personal tapes she made, Margo refused to give way to bitterness or regret. Manning had helped found her theatre and, she said, "The blessed darling brought me more happiness in one hour than I ever had before. I wish for him only, only happiness." In public and in private, she masked any pain she felt with constant work and activity. Since she had problems sleeping, possibly a side effect of her amphetamine use, she often pleaded with friends to stay up with her most of the night, talking and drinking. Ted Apstein recalls that when he saw her in New York in 1953 and 1954, she sometimes lacked her usual energy and high spirits. Once, late at night, she called him at home and said that she had to talk to him. "Right now?" Apstein asked.

"Yes, get in a cab and come over," Margo told him. Apstein went to her

An Idea Is a Greater Monument

Gramercy Park apartment and talked to her for two or three hours. "She had been drinking, but she was not drunk. She was lonely and unhappy. I think she just wanted somebody to be with that she trusted. She was okay when I left."

Although she had stopped seeing Dr. Knapp professionally, he and her physician, Dr. Aronson, were both supporters of the theatre, and kept a kind watch over her. The public perception of her was of a woman who enjoyed her work and her life. Patricia Peck, a local newspaperwoman, recalls that "no one was more fun at a party than Margo." When Liz Ann McMurray sold her bookstore and moved from Dallas, Margo became friends with Bill Gilliland, the store's new owner. "We would have drinks together and talk about music and movies," Gilliland remembers. "She seemed lonesome at times, but she was highly entertaining and very funny." She seemed to know everyone in town. Playwright Harry Granick recalls that she used to pick up the phone and tell the operator, "This is Margo." She had no problem finding escorts. When Bill Goyen was in town they saw each other, and she visited him at his apartment in New York. Actor Jim Field often attended parties with her. Hob Mallon, who was almost fifteen years older than her and was the brother of Dallas businessman Neil Mallon, became a familiar sight around the theatre, doing odd jobs or taking the actors out to dinner. Margo liked his sweet disposition, and because he played the piano beautifully, they often sang favorite hymns together. He adored her, chauffeured her around town, squired her to parties, and served as her drinking buddy. Hob often invited the entire theatre company to the Mallon country home, a former horse farm outside of Dallas, to relax in the swimming pool or play tennis.

MARGO HAD SCHEDULED nine plays in the thirty-week Theatre '54–'55 season. Shakespeare's *As You Like It* and Shaw's *Misalliance* filled the classic slots, and seven new scripts, all world premieres, rounded out the program. Technical director Jim Pringle, stage manager Freddie Hoskins, Michael and Mary Dolan, and Ramsey and Violet Burch all remained on staff. The acting company was a combination of veterans and new faces. Jim Field, Martha Bumpas, Evelyn Bettis, and Edwin Whitner returned from the previous season. After five years in South America and a painful divorce, Louise Latham remembered that Margo had promised her a job whenever she wanted to return to the theatre, so she moved back to Dallas and was welcomed into the acting company. Margo had spotted talented Harry Bergman at the Westport Playhouse and hired him for the season. Bergman, who saw himself as a utility actor, a good team player, recalls that when he stood in the

An Idea Is a Greater Monument

doorway of Theatre '54 and looked at the stage, he couldn't believe how small it was. "But it was enough," he said, "because theatre after all is conjuring up spirits and you can do that almost anywhere." Irish-born Kathleen Phelan, who had extensive experience on the stages of her homeland, England, Canada, and the United States, as well as many television appearances, and Edward Cullen, whose career spanned twenty-five years playing in support of stars like Laurette Taylor, Eva Le Gallienne, and Ethel Barrymore, completed the company.

Ramsey directed the season opener, *Marry Go Round*, a frivolous situation comedy by Albert Dickason, which was followed by Shakespeare's *As You Like It*, staged by Margo. Louise Latham played a radiant blonde Rosalind to Jim Field's slightly jaded Orlando, and John Rosenfield reported that Harry Bergman's Touchstone was "illuminating—one of the best you may ever see." *The Hemlock Cup*, a new comedy-drama about an idealistic high school teacher, written by actor Edward Hunt and directed by Ramsey, opened in late December. Often the season's schedule reflected Margo's attempt to placate her audience with fluff before confronting them with substance—a practical artistic policy that had contributed to her ten successful seasons of operation. Scheduling three comedies to precede the fourth new script, which was planned to open January 10, was a prudent decision.

The new play had been brought to her attention by Tad Adoue, who had "discovered" it in the late summer of 1954 when he was visiting in Malibu, California. One day while walking along the beach he saw two men typing on a patio. Curious, he stopped to ask if they were writers. They happened to be playwrights, and when he told them he was a reader for Margo Jones, they gave him a script. Tad returned the script the next day, told them he hadn't cared for it, and asked if he could see something else they had written.

"No!" one of the writers said. "Now get lost." The other playwright, however, dug out a copy of a play that had been sitting in their files for five years, having been rejected by many Broadway producers, including Elia Kazan, Cheryl Crawford, Herman Shumlin, the Theatre Guild, Josh Logan, Irene Selznick, Leland Hayward, and Alex Cohen. A top motion picture agent had advised the playwrights to burn the script since nobody would ever do it. Tad took the play, read it immediately, then airmailed it to Margo in Dallas with a note saying, "I double-dog dare you to produce this. Will take GUTS to do in the *bible belt*." The writers were Jerome Lawrence and Robert E. Lee, and the play was *Inherit the Wind*.

Margo read the script, then called the playwrights' agent, Harold Freedman of Brandt and Brandt in New York, and told him that she wanted to produce

An Idea Is a Greater Monument

it. He warned her that the subject matter might be too daring for Dallas, but he could not dissuade her. Margo flew to New York for a meeting with the playwrights at the Gramercy Park apartment. She met them at the door, although Jerome Lawrence wrote later that "you can't say that 'you met Miss Jones.' Her flash-flood personality enveloped you." Before Margo said hello, she spoke a few lines of the play that she had memorized. "Is it possible that something is holy to the celebrated agnostic?" she recited. "Yes! The individual human mind. In a child's power to master the multiplication table, there is more sanctity than in all your shouted 'Amens, Holy Holies and Hosannas.' An idea is a greater monument than a cathedral, and the advance of man's knowledge is more of a miracle than any sticks turned to snakes or the parting of water."

Lawrence and Lee looked at each other and thought, "This gal . . . shares our passion."

The prolific writing team, both midwesterners and in their early thirties, had already collaborated on a Broadway musical, *Look, Ma, I'm Dancin'*, won several Peabody awards for their radio scripts, and written for television and film. *Inherit the Wind* was their response to the repression and McCarthyism of the 1950s, and was based on the 1925 Scopes "monkey trial" in Dayton, Tennessee. The trial came about after a young biology teacher, John Scopes, broke a state law against the teaching of evolution. Clarence Darrow, the great trial lawyer, defended the teacher and battled with politician William Jennings Bryan, a three-time presidential nominee, who had been brought in to assist the prosecution. The trial exploded into a clash between the Darwinian theory of evolution and the literal interpretation of the Bible, with Darrow championing the right of free thought and free speech.

Their script brought Margo the "wonderment" she had been searching for. "I will tell you again," she wrote Lawrence and Lee, "that I think *Inherit* is one of the most exciting scripts that I have ever encountered. I live spiritually through you playwrights and bless you both—you have certainly given me life through this script." When Lawrence and Lee arrived in Dallas early one December morning to begin rehearsals of their play, Margo met them at the airport with newsreel cameramen in tow. On New Year's Eve, she invited them to help her and Eugene McDermott change the theatre's sign to Theatre '55. "The playwrights are the stars!" she proclaimed.

For the set of *Inherit the Wind*, Jim Pringle designed and built two plain tables with benches, a judge's podium, and several wooden stools. Since the actors who played the jury sat in the aisles, no other set pieces were needed. Pringle had learned to pare down his design ideas while working for Margo.

Once, he had purchased fake flowers for a play and planted them in boxes placed between the actors and the audience. He soon found Margo tearing them out. Upset that his flowers had been ripped up, Pringle confronted her. "Look, angel," she explained, "I'm interested in the script and the actors. I don't want to see anything else." Years later, whenever stage manager Freddie Hoskins worked on an overproduced show with lavish costumes and sets, he liked to quote one of Margo's favorite sayings: "Honey, we don't do productions, we do *plays*."

To cast the twenty-two-person play, Margo brought in actors from the community, and hired J. Frank Lucas from New York to play the role of the lawyer Henry Drummond. Every member of her permanent company had a juicy role. Edward Cullen acted Matthew Harrison Brady, Harry Bergman played the teacher Bertram Cates, and Louise Latham portrayed Rachel, his fiancée. Jim Field played the cynical reporter E. K. Hornbeck, Edwin Whitner the judge, and Kathleen Phelan acted Sarah Brady. Margo "stumbled into early morning rehearsals a few times a little hung-over," Lawrence recalls. "But she woke herself up and all the rest of us—by waving her arms like a gospel singer, leading the whole cast in singing 'Morning is the Nicest Time of Day,' and convinced herself and everybody else, energized the entire day." As a girl Margo had watched her father try his cases in the courthouse of Livingston and had been moved by the drama of the law. The gospel readings and hymns of her childhood rushed back in a flood of memories as she worked on the play, inspiring her direction. "My God, the rehearsals were exciting," Lawrence recalls. "I'll never forget how Margo whooped up the prayer-meeting. Because she *was* a theatre evangelist. The minister was dead center—and all the participants were in the sloping aisles, so suddenly during a performance, if you were sitting in the audience, an actor right alongside you would leap to his feet and join in their fervor, so that the entire audience got caught up in it."

On opening night, January 10, 1955, the audience watched as a barefoot boy entered the stage and began looking for worms. A pushy little girl skipped on, and the boy couldn't resist chasing her with a worm. He informed her that she was a worm once, in fact, the whole world was once covered with worms and "blobs of jelly." The girl screamed that she was going to tell her pa about his sinful talk. "Ahhh, your old man's a monkey!" said the boy. Begun with children, the debate continued, engulfing the entire town and drawing the audience in as participants in the action. "When the preacher shouted, 'Do you believe?' even the critics shouted back, 'We believe!'" Lawrence recalls. At the end of the play, when Henry Drummond, the brilliant defense lawyer, alone on stage, balanced two books in his hands, the Bible and Darwin's

Origin of Species, then placed them side by side in his briefcase and walked slowly off, the tiny theatre resounded with wild applause and cheers. After the play Margo, as usual, greeted the audience in the lobby. "Bless you," she said, "bless you for coming! Hell of a play, wasn't it!"

The company and the playwrights crowded into Margo's Stoneleigh apartment and waited for the reviews. Virgil Miers of the *Dallas Times Herald* wrote that "Margo Jones directed Theatre '55 through its first premiere of 1955 . . . lighting up a brilliant play. . . . Theatrical sparks flew . . . making the burning issue of the right to think sizzle and explode again. It is simply one of the best plays Miss Jones has staged at her theatre, and one of the best productions she has given to a play." John Rosenfield called *Inherit the Wind* a "new play of power, humanity, and universal truth . . . one of the proudest . . . productions of our unusual theatre devoted sometimes painfully to new plays only." Later, one critic noted that "if nothing else ever has or does, it sturdily justifies Margo Jones' ten seasons of torch bearing." Margo asked that the reviews be read over and over again. Then she "kicked off her shoes and danced and sang in the center of the floor, with tears running down her cheeks." Despite all the warnings about the Bible Belt's expected response to the play, there wasn't a peep of protest.

It didn't take long for New York producers to hear about the success of *Inherit the Wind*. Cheryl Crawford, who had turned down the play several years earlier, wrote asking if she could read the script. However, Margo had requested that Lawrence and Lee ask her friend Howard Lindsay and his partner Russell Crouse if they were interested in co-producing the play on Broadway. Lindsay and Crouse were occupied with their own work, and had to refuse. Apparently Margo did not consider producing or directing the play herself. She wrote her brother Charles, "My trip to New York was based on something I believe in like I did that time I talked with you when you were in the Navy and we were behind the house burning shrubbery and I was telling you about Tennessee Williams. Well, that's the way I feel about this script, *Inherit the Wind*. I knew that I could not be away from Dallas the length of time it takes to produce and direct a show in New York, so I went up there and arranged a production set-up that makes it possible for me to be here and still have a hand in what is going on there." Ramsey Burch took over the directing responsibilities for the rest of the season, staging five plays in a row while Margo managed the theatre and worked on raising money for the New York production.

The last success Margo had had on Broadway was her first New York play, *The Glass Menagerie*. Her subsequent Broadway experiences had not been happy ones: she had been fired from *Joan of Lorraine* and disappointed by *Summer and Smoke*'s New York reception and the failures of *Southern Exposure* and *An Old Beat-Up Woman*. Several factors influenced her decision not to direct *Inherit the Wind* in New York. To begin with, her directing record in the commercial theatre was not one that would inspire confidence in prospective investors. Also, the memory of the overwhelming success of the Dallas production of *Summer and Smoke* followed by the play's Broadway failure probably influenced her decision not to risk staging *Inherit the Wind* in New York. She knew the enormous energy required to direct a large play there, and with the year-round responsibility of her theatre in Dallas, it was energy she simply did not have. It is possible too that she recognized that her directing style had been honed on her own intimate arena stage, that her technique was much less assured on the large proscenium stages of Broadway. Besides, directing plays in the commercial theatre had never been Margo's primary goal. While she and Manning were together, she had shared his objective of staging a money-maker on Broadway, but her own dream had always been different.

Harold Freedman, the playwrights' agent, offered the script to Herman Shumlin, a producer-director best known for his productions of Lillian Hellman's *The Children's Hour, The Little Foxes,* and *Watch on the Rhine* in the 1930s and 1940s. During the late 1940s and early 1950s, Shumlin had not had a successful play and was experiencing a dry spell. After hearing of *Inherit the Wind*'s enthusiastic audience reception and reading the Dallas reviews, he decided to produce and direct the play in New York. Margo served as associate producer and raised 40 percent of the money, primarily from her Dallas supporters. Eugene McDermott invested five thousand dollars—half in Margo's name and the other half in the name of his second wife, Margaret. Tad Adoue, Helen McGibney (the manager of the Stoneleigh Hotel), and Dr. Knapp, Margo's former psychiatrist, were also among the Dallas backers. Although her title was associate producer, Margo gave up her desire to have a hand in the production and agreed (at Shumlin's insistence) to allow him "to function without hindrance" as the producer-director. She would have no say in casting or in any production decisions.

If possible, Shumlin would have eliminated Margo as producer entirely, but he needed the money she could raise, and Lawrence and Lee supported her involvement in the production and kept her informed of its progress. However, Shumlin refused to consider or even to interview any of the actors from the Dallas production. Jim Field, who played E. K. Hornbeck, the writer based on H. L. Mencken, had received outstanding notices for his performance. He and the other actors who had been in the play in Dallas were devastated when

An Idea Is a Greater Monument

they learned that they would not even have an opportunity to audition for roles they had originated.

Therese Hayden, who was Shumlin's assistant on the play, recalls that she met Margo once at a brief meeting at the Algonquin. "Shumlin pushed her out of the New York production. . . . There was no place for her. I'm sure that it was galling to her to have used her energy for a play that Broadway had negated and then to see it snatched away from her. It's bound to have been a wrenching thing for her to be treated that way." Tony Randall, who had been cast as Hornbeck, the role which would launch his career, recalls that he too met Margo only once, as she hurried through the theatre. Shumlin limited her involvement with every aspect of the production, including contact with the actors. He wanted to make it clear that this production would be his alone.

Although she had been shut out of the New York production of *Inherit the Wind*, in the spring of 1955 on her visits to the city Margo saw three other plays that had recently opened — Tennessee Williams's new play, *Cat on a Hot Tin Roof*, William Inge's *Bus Stop*, and Joseph Hayes's *The Desperate Hours*. When *Inherit the Wind* opened, Margo could have taken a stroll through the theatre district and pointed with pride at the marquees of four theatres that boasted hit plays by playwrights who had been nurtured by her faith. While she was in town, she met her old friend Ray Walston for late dinners at Sardi's after his performance as the Devil in the new musical *Damn Yankees*. She also saw Bill Goyen often, and he was her escort to the opening of *Inherit the Wind* on April 21, 1955, at the National Theatre.

Lawrence and Lee had made a few changes in the script for the New York production. Feeling that the opening dialogue between the boy and girl would not be effective on the large proscenium stage, the playwrights cut the scene, but restored it in later productions. The cast had expanded to fifty people, the extras serving as townspeople, jurors, and reporters. "We had so many people in the cast," Lawrence recalls, "that we had long strips of brown paper which we hung on the walls of our hotel room, and for every scene and every character we wrote bits of dialogue and gave each person in the town a character." Paul Muni came out of retirement to play Henry Drummond, and Ed Begley acted William Brady. Their duel, one reviewer said, "was thrilling because it is a duel of ideas, and Muni and Begley fight it magnificently. Muni is slouching, seemingly casual but inwardly aflame with indignation. Begley is benign, pompous and honestly aflame with righteousness." When the curtain closed on the town of Hillsboro, the New York audience shouted, "Author!" startling Lawrence and Lee, who thought at first that they were joking. John Rosenfield was not surprised. In January he had written that "one factor will weigh Broadway sentiment in favor of *Inherit the Wind*. The South is shown up once more as the land of tapeworm, ignorance and bigotry. Not even the fried chicken is good. This is the South as New York loves to have it."

Following the opening-night performance, the company went their separate ways, without a celebration. According to Jerome Lawrence, Herman Shumlin didn't believe in opening-night parties or perhaps just didn't want to pay the liquor and food bill for one of the largest companies on Broadway. Lawrence and Lee, Mrs. Lee, their agent, their lawyer, and Margo gathered at the Lees' hotel suite to wait for the reviews. The *New York Times* review, written by Lewis Funke because Brooks Atkinson was out of the country, was the first to arrive. His assessment of the play was lukewarm—it's about history, he said, has some good performances, a large cast, and is sometimes compelling. The disappointed party soon broke up, but Margo and Jerry Lawrence decided to take a cab downtown and wait for the other newspapers. Sitting in the back of the taxi in the emptiness of Times Square in the early morning, Margo and Lawrence shouted with joy as they read the other notices aloud. "The new play which opened last evening . . . is one of the most exciting dramas of the last decade," said John Chapman of the *Daily News*. "The town has a hit that is distinguished and challenging," wrote William Hawkins of the *New York World-Telegram*. Walter Kerr at the *Herald-Tribune* enthused, "There's a whale of an old-fashioned, free-swinging, suspender-snapping fight going on at the National and Paul Muni wins it."

The joy of that moment was clouded, a little over a month later, when Margo and Herman Shumlin faced each other in a Dallas courtroom to battle over the rights to *Inherit the Wind*. At the end of each season at Margo's theatre it was common practice to present several weeks of repertory of the most popular plays of that season. *Inherit the Wind* was scheduled for eight repertory performances. As part of the standard contract with playwrights, Theatre '55 had the right to repeat productions in repertory at the end of the season. Of course, commercial theatre policy held that while a play was running in New York, no out-of-town productions were permitted. Shumlin asked Margo to cancel her repeat performances. She refused. While he must have known about Theatre '55's contract with the playwrights ensuring the right to produce the play in repertory, Shumlin became enraged, and his lawyers filed an injunction against Theatre '55 to stop the performances of *Inherit the Wind*. It must have been irritating and a blow to Shumlin's ego to read in *Variety* that Margo Jones was staging performances of *Inherit the Wind* in Dallas while his production was playing in New York. Therese Hayden recalls that Shumlin's action was typical. "He would often get involved in legal controversies. But remember, Margo was not just any regional theatre little lady. She was a woman the Broadway theatre was aware of." John Rosenfield called the dispute between the co-producers "the bickeringest piece of Broadway-type litigation [I] ever heard about. And there was once a producer who sued a co-producer over a roll of confetti."

The trial began on Tuesday morning, May 31, in the courtroom of District Judge Dallas Blankenship. Mabel Duke found it quite amusing that New Yorker Shumlin had the audacity to challenge Margo on her home territory and in the courtroom of a judge named Dallas. Shumlin, smoothing his hands over his bald head, identified himself as "a very famous producer" and testified that the "glamour and glitter" of the New York production would be damaged by the Dallas performances. Margo, wearing a suit with a gingham check blouse and employing her best Texas drawl, ridiculed Shumlin's assertion. "We're just a little bitty place," she said, and testified that as a producer she would be "slapping my own face" to stage the play in Dallas if it would damage the New York production. Judge Blankenship refused Shumlin's request for an injunction, and the repertory performances proceeded as scheduled. *Inherit the Wind* ran for several years on Broadway, toured nationally for over a year, became a successful motion picture starring Spencer Tracy and Fredric March, an Emmy Award–winning television movie, enjoyed and continues to have thousands of professional and amateur productions all over the country and the world, and has been translated into thirty-three languages, most recently into Mandarin in the People's Republic of China.

The tenth season had been the most successful in the theatre's history, grossing approximately ninety thousand dollars. *Inherit the Wind* had broken all attendance and box-office records. Ramsey's productions of Shaw's *Misalliance*, staged meticulously with authentic Edwardian furniture and lovely costumes, and *La Belle Lulu*, a new musical based on the life of Offenbach, with music by Offenbach and Charles Previn, were artistic and box-office hits. Margo had every reason to be pleased, but theatre is ephemeral, applause can't be packaged, and her pressing concerns were not the immediate past but the present moment. With barely time to catch their breaths, the staff and acting company charged into the summer season.

I N M A Y, Margo had arranged with Rosamond Gilder once again to sublet her Gramercy Park apartment for June, July, and August, but June found her still in Dallas, reading new plays (she had fallen behind and had not made a final decision on one of the new scripts) and planning her production of *Whisper to Me*. Bill Goyen had given her the script, which playwright Greer

Johnson had adapted from Goyen's short story "The Letter in the Cedar Chest." For years, Margo had encouraged Goyen to write a play or adapt his novel *The House of Breath* for the theatre and was thrilled to be able at last to direct his work.

The ten-week summer season opened with Shaw's *Pygmalion*, directed by Ramsey and featuring Louise Latham as Eliza and Jim Field as Higgins. The schedule had been compressed to two-week instead of three-week runs, which meant a shorter summer season and well-filled audiences; however, the decision also reduced rehearsal time to two weeks. The shortened rehearsal period placed a strain on the actors, the staff, and Margo.

Whisper to Me, set in a small town in East Texas, tells the story of three onely widowed women—Old Mrs. Woman, Sister Sammye, and Little Pigeon—who attempt to create a household where their loneliness and eccentricities will be accepted. The town views them as three insane women living in a haunted house, dancing to an old recording of "Whispering."

Both Greer Johnson and Goyen were in Dallas to work on the script. After the first week of rehearsals, the actress playing the role of the enormously fat Old Mrs. Woman could not learn the lines for the part, and dropped out of the production. Louise Latham, who played Little Pigeon, remembers thinking that the actress could have done it if she had courage, but "she just fell apart. I never heard Margo say a word of criticism." Margo made frantic calls to New York and to Nina Vance in Houston to try to find an actress who could take over the part at the last minute. Her efforts were unsuccessful, and company members agreed that it would be best not to open. Margo said, "I won't change the policy of this theatre; we have to open."

As a last resort, on the Wednesday before the Monday opening, she turned to her business manager Mary Dolan, who had at times acted small character parts. While Dolan struggled to memorize the lines, the costumes were refitted and a suit of padding constructed to change her ninety-eight-pound frame to that of a large, fat woman. Mary remembers "sitting in Margo's bedroom having my costume fitted while Bill Goyen cued me on my lines."

On opening night, Mary had learned Acts I and II, but had to carry the script for Act III. Louise Latham recalls, "We made it through the opening. I remember thinking, 'Well, I have to know everyone's lines tonight.' It was a beautiful play, and devastating to see it crumble because of bad circumstances. Bill Goyen and Greer Johnson were wrecks." The newspaper critics, however, responded kindly to the production. Virgil Miers wrote that Margo's direction was beautiful and heartfelt, while Rosenfield praised Goyen's poetic imagination. Bill Goyen wrote a few days later that he had sat in the darkened theatre with enormous apprehension. "The whole affair before my eyes seemed like a charming and fragile and musical little game, playing itself through with a faraway loveliness and the distant sounds of something long passed away, but as the little boys say at the end, going on and on and on, 'for nobody goes, nobody goes.'"

Overworked, distressed by her failure to bring Goyen's play to full artistic fruition and by their unresolved personal relationship, and disappointed by what she saw as her failures, Margo turned more and more to liquor for comfort. She had always been a heavy drinker, but usually within the bounds of acceptable good-old-girl Texas standards. Now there didn't seem to be any limits. Joe Glasco, who lived in Dallas at this time, recalls that often in the mornings, he and Goyen would drive her to rehearsal. "She would be hung over and lying down all the way to the theatre in the back of the station wagon."

Margo spent many late evenings with Goyen, and he wrote later that they had "desperate" talks. But they also looked at old photographs of Margo's family and she reminisced about her childhood. She told him about the flowers her mother had planted and about the white rosebush next to the door. Goyen wrote later that she had "that Texas girl sweetness and a full-faced smile, that Texas ready belief, that quality of listening, that gentle willingness of Texas youth as I remember it, that courtesy."

Margo had been thinking a lot about earlier years. In the spring, she had written John Stine, whom she hadn't seen since the 1930s and her Pasadena Playhouse days. She told him that she had run into Jerry Coray a few times. "I will never forget the day that the two of us met Jerry," she wrote. She also heard from Doris Porter, one of Stella Nell's childhood friends, who was dying of cancer. Margo answered with a long nostalgic letter, recalling "the first time that I ever saw sheet music straight from a musical show in New York when you visited . . . and brought sheet music. . . . I know that very soon we'll all get together."

In an attempt to relieve tension and take her mind off the theatre, Margo turned to another art, asking artist Joe Glasco to teach her how to paint. He bought her a set of oil paints, and began giving her basic lessons.

On Monday night, July 11, following an opening-night party of Joseph Hayes's new play, *The Girl from Boston*, Margo, Goyen, and Glasco returned to Margo's Stoneleigh apartment, where they continued the party. Margo brought out her oil paints. At some point during the night, Glasco left, and Goyen stayed. According to Louise Latham, "Goyen came on in this fragile, sweet way, but beneath that was ambition and a will. He always clung to powerful women." Almost twenty years earlier, Margo had brought the wonder of theatre into his life, had nurtured him, supported him, and finally had fallen in love with him and his writing. Even with Bill, Margo could not admit that she felt bad or discouraged. Everything was wonderful, she said, but on that Monday night, she let herself go and expressed her need. Years later, Bill Goyen wrote about that night like a scene from hell. For Margo, though, with Stravinsky's *Firebird* playing loud on the phonograph the way she liked it—the Russian music soaring, telling the story of lovers brought together by magic —the night held another meaning. She danced naked, swigging vodka from a bottle, giving way to a frenzied release of feeling, a Maenad paying tribute to the god Dionysus. In her drunken dance, reeling and turning, she took up her oil paints and splashed green, red, yellow, and purple oil paint on the sofa and carpet in a grotesque rainbow. Goyen watched, his writer's eye remembering the details, filing them away, as she drew him down, desperately clinging to him. "Oh baby wait lemme get a cup of coffee please don't leave me alone and mad at me like this, oh baby," she pleaded. He pulled away from her and turned for a last look, then left her alone, drunk and crying on her bed, and returned to New York.

THE NEXT MORNING Margo got up and went to the theatre to work. When Violet Burch arrived at the apartment to begin her day of answering mail, typing, and filing, she called the Stoneleigh's housekeeper to clean up the spilled oil paint. When the housekeeper was unable to remove the stains, the hotel hired a professional cleaning service, who came in and did the job. That evening, Margo invited a few friends in for drinks, including David Blackburn, the assistant manager of the State Fair Musicals. Blackburn recalls a pleasant evening—"she was so fun-loving always"—that ended early. After her guests left, Margo, feeling chilled, turned off the air conditioner, which Violet liked to keep at the highest setting. She settled down on the floor with a drink to read new scripts—she still had not chosen the final new play of the summer season.

Margo woke the next day to find herself on the carpet, surrounded by manuscripts. Although she felt ill, she hurried to get ready for a noon meeting with Eugene McDermott at Texas Instruments to discuss fund-raising plans for a new theatre. After her talk with McDermott, she returned to the Stoneleigh, perspiring heavily, feeling nauseous, with a blotchy rash on her legs and buttocks. She blamed her ill-health on the hundred-degree heat and thought she might be suffering from heat stroke. Phoning Dr. Aronson at home, she told his wife that she felt weak and needed to see the doctor.

Aronson got the message and came to the Stoneleigh, where he "gave her something to quiet her." Floyd McDaniel stayed with her through the night, soothing her fever with crushed ice.

The next morning, unresponsive and semi-conscious, Margo was admitted to St. Paul's Hospital. Because of her drinking problem and the fact that she had been unable to urinate, her illness was diagnosed as a kidney disturbance. A consultant called in from the Southwestern Medical Foundation suspected that her symptoms might have another cause. He went to her apartment, where his suspicions were confirmed. The professional cleaning service had used carbon tetrachloride to clean the carpet and sofa. Margo had spent thirty-six hours in her closed apartment, at times with the air conditioning turned off, with a toxic poison. The action of the poison was exacerbated by alcohol.

During the first days of her hospital stay, Margo, sensing an occasion for publicity, felt well enough to call John Rosenfield and request that he send a photographer out to take a picture of her reading scripts. She wanted the public to know that even though she was ill, she was still working on finding new plays. Rosenfield arranged for the photographer, but Margo called him and cancelled the appointment. "I feel so lousy," she said, "like hell."

Margo did not want her family informed of her illness. However, Vi Burch notified Richard and Bea, and Charles Jones, who told Martha Pearl that Margo had been admitted to the hospital. Vi also wrote to Bill Goyen in New York telling him that Margo was ill, and suggesting that he drop her a note. Soon after she was admitted to the hospital, Margo called Goyen long-distance. "Baby, baby please please listen to me, don't hang up, don't go away, don't leave," she pleaded. Dismayed by her woman's need and frightened by the excess he had seen, Goyen shouted at her and hung up the phone.

Violet stayed with Margo at the hospital, assisting the nurses and monitoring her visitors and telephone calls. At Margo's insistence, Vi did not allow any members of the theatre company or staff to visit her. Margo did not want her children, her babies, as she called the company, to see her less than strong, and she didn't want them to be upset by the hospital paraphernalia —like the jar that collected her urine, turned black by the toxin. During one of Mabel Duke's visits, Margo tied a little ribbon in her hair, and talked of redecorating the room, taking down the crucifix and putting up some of her favorite pictures from her apartment. Richard and Bea drove to Dallas and were cheered by her optimism. They would go home to Houston to pick up their daughter, Judy, then would return to Dallas. Margaret and Gene McDermott visited her and saw her sitting up, with scripts piled on the floor beside her bed. Margo glanced at the plays and told them, "Angels, I'm going to read these in the next few days."

On Sunday morning, July 24, ten days after she had been admitted to St. Paul's, her body bloated with the poison, her lungs began to fill with fluid, and her breathing became raspy and labored. She was transferred to Parkland Hospital, where Dr. Jerry Stirman operated the only kidney-dialysis machine in the city. For a few hours after the dialysis treatment, her prognosis seemed good. Dr. Stirman hoped that the destroyed cells in her kidney and liver might have an opportunity to regenerate. But that evening she lapsed into a coma. Her heart began to fail, and then it stopped beating. For almost an hour Dr. Stirman tried to massage her weakened heart back to life.

At the theatre, the company had completed the final dress rehearsal of a new play, *Cold Christmas.* They were posing for a photographer, who was taking pictures for the lobby display. The telephone rang. Mabel Duke took the call. She gave the message to Ramsey Burch. He sat down on the steps in the aisle and waited for the photographer to finish his work. The photo call completed, the actors and staff gathered together, sitting in the first two rows of the theatre to go over their rehearsal notes.

Ramsey stood up and spoke to the company. He told them, "Margo died at eleven o'clock."

THAT SUNDAY EVENING John Rosenfield could not eat dinner. He had been waiting for a telephone call, and when it came, he asked his wife Claire to fix him a bourbon and soda. He sat down at his typewriter and wrote the obituary for the woman he had known for more than a quarter of a century. He took the copy to the *Dallas Morning News* and space was cleared on the front page of the Monday, July 25, 1955, edition for Margo's photograph and the announcement of her death. In the weeks and months following, distraught at her bizarre, untimely death, he would tell her story again and again. "We guess that Margo Jones thought she ought to be a great woman in the theater," he wrote, "one of historic significance, but never could bring herself to feel that she was. The tragic part is that she was a great woman. For greatness . . . is never the exaltation of one glorious moment. It is the sum of an accomplishment over a dreary span of time."

Richard Jones heard the news on the car radio when he, Bea, and Judy arrived in Dallas shortly after midnight on Sunday. Charles and Lois Jones, who had driven in from Livingston, went to the hospital and were searching for Margo's room. They stopped an intern to ask directions. "Haven't you heard?" the intern said. "Miss Jones just died." Charles and Lois left immediately for Livingston to tell Martha Pearl. Richard and Bea stayed in Dallas to make the funeral arrangements. According to Charles, Martha Pearl, unlike her grief-stricken sons, accepted the news calmly. "She was very religious —she could handle things better than most of us."

The actors and company members were numb with shock. At Margo's request, they had not been informed that her condition was critical. "It was just too terrible for me—I couldn't believe a personality that powerful and strong could be gone," Louise Latham said later. For the first time in Theatre '55's history, a performance was canceled. The opening of the new play was changed from Monday evening to Tuesday, although the company rehearsed on Monday afternoon.

Board president Eugene McDermott announced on Monday that the summer season would be finished as Margo Jones had planned and that "Theatre '55 would continue ad infinitum."

At Parkland Hospital Dr. Earnest Booth, who conducted the autopsy, concluded that the forty-three-year-old woman "with a history of alcohol consumption and poor diet had died of carbon tetrachloride poisoning resulting in acute necrosis of liver, tubule and uremic pneumonitis."

Late Monday night, drunk with grief, Theatre '55 company member Michael Dolan broke into Margo's Stoneleigh apartment, filled his arms full of her clothes, and staggered home.

On Tuesday morning at 11:30 hundreds of people crowded into Sparkman-Brand Funeral Home. Pallbearers were all members of the Theatre '55 company, including stage manager Freddie Hoskins, technical director Jim Pringle, and actors Michael Dolan and Jim Field. Mary Dolan recalls, "I don't know where the family was, they were there, but the company was seated in the separate rows that they usually reserve for the family." Joanna Albus, Dr. Jean Barraco, Malvina Holmes, and other friends from Houston attended. Playwrights, actors, designers, technicians, critics, and friends from around the country—among them William Inge, Jo Mielziner, Nina Vance, Paul Muni and the *Inherit the Wind* company, Lawrence and Lee, Eddie Dowling, Ray Walston, Joseph Hayes, Audrey Wood, and Brooks Atkinson—sent messages of condolence to Theatre '55. Tennessee Williams wired that he was inexpressibly shocked, and hoped that the theatre would be a memorial to Margo. Then he went on a three-week binge. Bill Goyen wrote that his heart was broken.

In the *Dallas Morning News* that day it was announced that a son had been born to Manning Gurian and Julie Harris.

That evening as the Theatre '55 company prepared to open *Cold Christ-*

mas, they received a telegram. "Our thoughts are with you all on this opening night. May it be one of many more successes. The family of Margo Jones."

Her family followed the hearse on the long drive home to Livingston. On Wednesday, hundreds of friends and relatives gathered for a second service in the chapel of the Pace Funeral Home. Kenneth Kennedy, her high school beau, who remembered a dancing, dark-haired girl wearing pink roses, served as a pallbearer. Like almost everyone in Livingston, Kenneth and his wife Mary had followed Margo's career for years, and were proud of her successes. They filed by the open casket, saying their final good-byes. "I'll never forget it," Mary Kennedy recalls. "She wasn't relaxed in the coffin. She looked like she was trying to sit up." Years later, Bill Goyen would write, "They closed your casket as if to hold you in, rising like a loaf, and face like a painting. . . . Indeed, you were your own first and last work. . . ."

With the sun burning in the intensely blue and vast Texas sky, the hearse made its slow way down Main Street, past the courthouse, and turned left on the road up to Cemetery Hill. The flowers wilted in the relentless heat. At the top of the hill, overlooking the piney woods of Polk County, Margo Jones was buried beneath the cooling shade of a live oak tree.

THEATRE '55, renamed the Margo Jones Theatre, continued under the leadership of Ramsey Burch. Floyd McDaniel, since she had worked directly for Margo and not for the theatre, was the only employee out of a job. In his first season as managing director, Burch continued Margo's policy of presenting new plays and classics, but eliminated the weeks of repertory. At the close of the 1956–57 season, board president Eugene McDermott resigned. In December 1957 Burch resigned and Aaron Frankel was hired as managing director. A supervisory committee of board members was formed to help read and choose scripts, undermining the independence of the director. Play selection shifted from original work to previously produced American and European scripts. The theatre also began to use guest stars. At the close of the 1958–59 season, the Margo Jones Theatre moved into the Maple Theatre, a converted movie house with a proscenium stage, which seated 414 persons. The move tripled the operating costs. After four years of steady artistic and financial decline, the theatre closed in December 1959 following a production of *Othello*.

"It seemed to us after Margo's death," wrote Rual Askew in the *Dallas Morning News*, "that the board of directors and its professional artistic-business management got more and more into the deadly rat-race of 'who's boss.' . . . The theater broke out in a rash of almost more bosses and staff salaries than it ever accumulated in its entire span. . . ."

An Idea Is a Greater Monument

John Rosenfield said that the theatre was no longer a playwright's theatre. Eugene McDermott observed that "if you're going to have another Margo Jones Theatre, you've got to have another Margo Jones."

In the years following her death, Margo's work was honored with a number of tributes and awards. In December 1955 a memorial cantata written in her memory by six Texas composers was presented by the Dallas Lyric Theatre. A Margo Jones playwriting competition was established at Texas Woman's University, and Eugene and Margaret McDermott donated two hundred thousand dollars for a Margo Jones Theatre at SMU. In the premiere program at the opening of the new theatre, former board member Lon Tinkle noted that 70 percent of the plays Margo had presented at her theatre were world premieres. "The flame of this faith burned her so intensely that some critics saw in her an evangelical enthusiast rather than a truly searching artist. Margo was well aware of this, but never changed her style. She urged all around her to be affirmative; she was one of the great yea-sayers to life."

Another Margo Jones Theatre was dedicated at Texas Woman's University, and in 1967 the Texas State Historical Commission declared her birthplace in Livingston a state landmark. Feeling that her loss would be felt most by playwrights, in 1961 Jerome Lawrence and Robert E. Lee established the Margo Jones Award, given annually to the producing manager whose policy of presenting new works continues "most faithfully the tradition and vision of Margo Jones." Members of the original judging committee included William Inge, Tennessee Williams, John Rosenfield, and Brooks Atkinson. After more than a quarter-century, Lawrence and Lee are changing the thrust of the award, feeling that it "has accomplished what Margo believed in—the production of new plays." According to Lawrence, the award will now be given to a "theatre statesperson, someone who believes in playwrights and who believes in affirmative theatre. Playwrights will be the judges, but awards may be given to any outstanding theatre person—a playwright, critic, educator, agent, actor, or director."

At the time of her death, however, Margo felt that she had failed in her driving obsession, her "one chance for greatness." The decentralization of theatre, the hope that theatres like hers would flourish around the country, had not become a reality. Her efforts to start the San Francisco theatre had ended in failure, and while she was directly involved in the creation of Zelda Fichandler's Arena Stage, Nina Vance's Alley Theatre, and Mary John's Milwaukee Repertory, they were not the national network she had envisioned in *Theatre-in-the-Round.*

In 1959 when the Margo Jones Theatre closed, the Dallas Theatre Center,

An Idea Is a Greater Monument

built on the same Turtle Creek property originally offered to Margo (a court battle resolved the pre-conditions set by the owner) and designed by Frank Lloyd Wright (the only theatre designed by the architect), was completed. Paul Baker, then head of the graduate theatre program of Baylor University, was chosen as managing director to head the institution. In 1983, the theatre changed direction under the leadership of director Adrian Hall. A second-generation resident-theatre leader, Hall founded the Trinity Repertory Company in Providence in 1964. In 1969 he won the Margo Jones Award for presenting new plays. Hall returned to his native Texas to transform the Dallas Theatre Center, primarily by returning to the policies of Margo Jones. Dynamic, fast-talking, sometimes outrageous in his choice of plays, Hall shook off the theatre's ties to academia, established a fully professional company, and brought the theatre into the mainstream of the resident-theatre movement, producing an eclectic mix of world premieres, classics, contemporary plays, and new translations.

In 1950 Margo wrote, "I . . . like to think that if I decided to take a cross-country trip along in 1960 I could stop in every city with a population of seventy-five thousand and see a good play well done." In the late 1960s her proposed cross-country trip would have taken her to the theatres of her early followers in Washington, D.C., Houston, and Milwaukee, and to the Cleveland Playhouse, which had become fully professional in the mid-1950s, and then on to the Guthrie Theatre in Minneapolis, the Seattle Repertory Theatre, the Mark Taper Forum in Los Angeles, New Haven's Long Wharf Theatre and the Hartford Stage Company in Connecticut, Center Stage in Baltimore, Actors Theatre of Louisville, the Goodman Theatre in Chicago, and the Trinity Repertory Company in Rhode Island. (The full history of the resident-theatre movement is chronicled in *Regional Theatre: The Revolutionary Stage* by Joseph Wesley Zeigler.)

She did not live to see the results of her pioneering work, but slowly and persistently, like her turtles, which had been given after her death to hundreds of her friends around the country, the ideas she had fostered in her book, her lectures, and the example she had set inspired other theatre leaders. Today, over three hundred resident nonprofit theatres in almost every state of the union, America's national theatre, supported by a loyal subscription audience, bring the classics of world literature, the best work by foreign playwrights, and new plays by contemporary dramatists to full performing life. Each of the theatres is unique, but they are united by a common goal to produce theatre that connects with their communities: theatre that is controversial, energetic, beautiful, often political, deeply personal, and powerful. Theatre Communications Group (TCG), the national service organization for the nonprofit professional theatre, functions as a national forum and a communications network for the theatres. TCG publishes *American Theatre*, which, like its forerunner *Theatre Arts*, is America's only national magazine devoted exclusively to theatre.

Since the turn of the century, idealistic theatre people had wanted a decentralized theatre, a theatre that mirrored the diversity of America. During the Depression, Hallie Flanagan's Federal Theatre had come close to that ideal. Margo Jones built on that dream and felt the zeitgeist of a new age, a necessary shift to decentralization, a shift that reflects the varied nature of the United States and the hunger of people outside New York City for live theatre. In the 1940s she had argued that resident theatres would provide large-scale employment, theatre art for millions of people annually, and provide a home for playwrights. She said, "If we succeed in inspiring the operation of thirty theatres like ours, the playwright won't need Broadway." That prophecy has come true. Without the research and development these theatres devote to new work, the American theatre would stagnate and die.

The resident-theatre revolution has been quiet, but the effects have been cataclysmic. During the 1987–88 season, the commercial theatre of Broadway mounted thirty-two productions. In the same time period the resident theatre produced over three thousand plays for an audience of more than fifteen million. The nonprofit resident theatre today employs almost three times as many actors as the commercial theatre and provides steady work to theatre technicians, designers, directors, administrators, and playwrights. For the last twelve years, every Pulitzer Prize–winning play has originated in the nonprofit resident theatre. However, Broadway's huge musical spectaculars, well-known stars, long runs, and mystique keep New York City in the national media spotlight, while the revolutionary work being done at resident theatres around the country is often given short shrift by the press. Despite the emergence of the resident theatre as America's national theatre and its nurturing of playwrights, actors, and directors, that old pull of Broadway and the commercial theatre is still felt by artists who want to make it in New York.

In his 1986 comedy *It's Only a Play*, presented at the Manhattan Theatre Club, a nonprofit resident theatre in New York, Terrence McNally wrote:

PETER: I'll tell you one thing, Mr. Drew. God punishes people who get their plays done on Broadway. He punishes them good.

IRA: That's why he invented regional theatre.

PETER: Don't give me regional theatre. I'll tell you what regional thea-

An Idea Is a Greater Monument

tre is: plays that couldn't get produced in New York with actors who couldn't get a job in New York performed for audiences who wish they still lived in New York.

Peter's view of regional or resident theatre is funny and hugely ironic. The fact is, Broadway as it existed in the 1940s and 1950s as a producing force, the nostalgic Broadway of *Oklahoma* and *Our Town* and *The Glass Menagerie* and *My Fair Lady*, simply has not survived. Today, the commercial New York theatre is actually a showcase for plays from the nonprofit resident theatre or off-Broadway or from Britain. Producers have become increasingly unwilling to risk on an untried work the huge losses associated with a Broadway box-office failure. For example, of the eight new plays presented on Broadway in the 1987–88 season, five originated in the resident theatre, two were British imports, and only one, *M. Butterfly* by David Henry Hwang, was produced directly for Broadway. Producer Stuart Ostrow not only backed the production but also funded the playwright's early research. While the production of new plays on Broadway has steadily decreased, the production of musicals has remained fairly constant—from 1940 to 1988 an average of fourteen musicals premiered annually. Despite this trend, the 1989 Tony Awards nominated only three musicals for the best new musical category, and one of these, *Jerome Robbins' Broadway*, was not new at all, but rather a celebration of musical successes from the past. While New York remains the major cultural center of the United States and the best source of mass-market theatrical entertainment, the most exciting theatre, the best new work, may now be seen in resident theatres like those in Hartford or Chicago or Louisville or Seattle.

The movement toward decentralization has reached maturity and permanence. This is not to say that problems don't exist. Many of the difficulties are the same ones encountered by Margo—artistic isolation; balancing the needs of the artists and the audience in play selection; attracting good actors away from New York and Los Angeles—the centers for commercial and film work important to their livelihood; battling with board members who seek more artistic control; and continuing to build a subscription audience from a populace weaned on television and the movies. Others are problems Margo did not face, including deficit spending brought on by overinstitutionalization, and theatres top-heavy with management. While about 15–20 percent of resident theatres' productions are new scripts—many by unknown playwrights—some resident theatres have tended to make safe choices in play selection, relying on a proven hit or a well-known classic and eschewing the risky new play with its challenging, sometimes non-naturalistic form.

An Idea Is a Greater Monument

Despite the problems, the dangers that lie ahead, the resident theatre today is vigorous and healthy, filled with revolutionaries who will no doubt reshape the theatre of the twenty-first century. Margo Jones's evangelizing work and dedication to a cause helped change the dramatic map of America. Her passion and enthusiasm might seem out of place today, not hip, in the more cynical world of the 1990s, but all those who have been drawn to theatre —artists and audiences—want to enter that world that exists only in the live theatrical moment, immediate and deeply personal. For Margo, like her favorite turtles who carry their home with them, her home was wherever theatre was—a place where life touches life.

Epilogue

For almost five years I worked with Fred Hoskins at the Hartford Stage Company. Fred was a small man with a big, engaging grin, and he loved to drink. A Texan, he had begun his life in the theatre working for Margo Jones in Dallas. He said she used to call him "little Freddie" and tell him that he "belonged to the theatre." After her death, he went to Washington, D.C., to stage-manage for Zelda Fichandler at the Arena Stage, then in the mid–1960s he moved to the Hartford Stage Company as stage manager for Paul Weidner and later for Mark Lamos. His career had followed the rising arc of the resident-theatre movement, and he embodied the passion and idealism of the early days. During his last few years at the Hartford Stage, however, he worked as the theatre's security guard, offering down-home warmth to actors and visitors. He liked to tell "Margo stories," tales of a time when there wasn't as much money, but seemingly fewer problems and more fun.

In the summer of 1985, Freddie Hoskins died. Since he had no family, the Hartford Stage Company made the funeral arrangements. His remains were cremated, and his ashes placed in a special niche in the stage manager's office. How Freddie would have enjoyed the fact that in life and in death, he did indeed belong to the theatre! Later, a memorial service was held at the Hartford Stage, and over a hundred members of his large theatre family gathered to share their favorite "Freddie stories," read poems, and reminisce. His only possessions—his pictures and memorabilia—were distributed among his friends.

I took home a carton stuffed with playbills, photographs, scrapbooks, and letters. I also discovered a small wooden box. Inside rested a polished stone turtle and this note, written with faded green ink in large, sweeping strokes:

> Freddie (I don't want to say "Honey," "Darling," "Baby,"
> "Dear"—or any of those words right now)—I want to say
> something I've no words for—but it's important to me—
> It's all mixed up with God, Faith, Love, and the Theatre—
> Bless you for mixing these things all together and for
> always understanding—   Love, Margo

Acknowledgments

Biography, like theatre, is a collaborative art. I could not have written this book without the assistance of many people. I would like to thank especially the family of Margo Jones—Richard, Bea, and Judy Jones and Charles and Lois Jones—for allowing me unrestricted access to Margo's personal files as well as for their many other kindnesses.

Margo's extended family—her theatre family—was also extraordinarily helpful. Many shared not only their time but also scrapbooks, memorabilia, letters, and photographs. I am indebted to Mabel Duke, Harry Granick, Manning Gurian, Malvina Holmes, Elizabeth McMurray Johnson, Arthur "Sonny" Koch, James Laughlin, Jerome Lawrence, Margaret McDermott, Louise Noble, James Pringle, Rebecca Hargis Turner, Millie Van, Ray Walston, and Peter Zeisler.

I am grateful to the following for interviews: Tad Adoue, Joanna Albus, Alan Anderson, Clint Anderson, Perry Wilson Anthony, Ted Apstein, Mrs. Howard Aronson, Carden Bailey, Katharine Balfour, Harry Bergman, Paul Bigelow, David Blackburn, Dr. Earnest Booth, Ramsey and Violet Burch, Nione Carlson, Jean Carpenter, Alessandra Comini, Jeanne Deis, Mary Dolan, Peter Donat, Randy Echols, Rex Everhart, Zelda Fichandler, Greer Garson Fogelson, Horton Foote, Ruth Ford, Frederick Fox, Michael Garth, Martha Bumpas Gaylord, Bill Gilliland, Olivia Glahos, Joseph Glasco, Willie Gould, David Greggory, Larry Hagman, Sheldon Harnick, Frank Harting, John Harvey, Therese Hayden, Joseph Hayes, Nancy Spencer Heyl, Fred Hoskins, Norris Houghton, Edward Ward Jones, Kenneth and Mary Kennedy, Dr. Joseph Knapp, Arthur Kramer, Louise Latham, Selma Lawther, Lucille Lortel, Jed Mace, Bill Martin, Billy Matthews, Virginia King Mayo, June Moll, Paul Moor, Anne Pitoniak, Ruth Pritchard, Charles Proctor, Marilyn Putnam, Tony Randall, Eugene Raskin, Romola Robb, Claire Rosenfield, Victor Samrock, Katharine Squire, Dr. Jerry Stirman, Haila Stoddard, Patricia Peck Swank, Brenda Vaccaro, Sam Wanamaker, Jack Warden, Dakin Williams, and Mary Hunter Wolf.

I am grateful to Lyle Leverich, whose authorized biography of Tennessee Williams will be published in 1990, for clearing up many points of fact and for sharing both information and his valuable time.

Acknowledgments

I am much obliged to Robert Eason and Cindy Smolovik, who introduced me to the Margo Jones Collection and the Fine Arts Archives at the Dallas Public Library and provided me with professional service as well as encouragement and support. Mary Ellen Degnan, executive director of Friends of Fair Park, guided me through the architectural history of the Margo Jones Theatre and Dallas's Fair Park. My thanks too go to John Broders of *Texas Monthly*; Ron Davis of Southern Methodist University's Oral History Program on the Performing Arts (and Carole Cohen, who conducted the interviews that were so helpful to me); Jeremy Gerard at the *New York Times*; Cathy Henderson at the Harry Ransom Humanities Research Center of the University of Texas at Austin; Ann Holmes at the *Houston Chronicle*; Pam Jordan at the Yale Drama Library; Tom Killen at the *New Haven Register*; Sally Merryman, chief archivist and historian at Texas Instruments; Susan Naulty of the Huntington Library in San Marino, California; Netta Nicewarner of Texas Woman's University; Richard Ploch at the *Washington Post*; Tom Rosenbaum at the Rockefeller Foundation; Del Singleton at the William Inge Collection at Independence Community College; and Jerome Weeks at the *Dallas Morning News*. I am grateful to staff of the Livingston, Texas Public School System, the Livingston Public Library, the Polk County Historical Society, and the *Polk County Enterprise* for their assistance. Barbara Janowitz and Betty Osborne of Theatre Communications Group and Barbara Wolfe of Actors' Equity provided statistical information and support. The book *Regional Theatre: The Revolutionary Stage* was especially useful, and its author, Joseph Wesley Zeigler, gave valuable advice. Reginald Gibbons, William Goyen's literary executor, was very helpful. Don Wilmeth's dissertation, "A History of the Margo Jones Theatre," was an important resource.

I deeply appreciate the suggestions, support, and camaraderie offered by the members of the Amherst Biography Group, who heard the manuscript at our Sunday-night sessions for more than a year: Monie Chase, Sandra Katz, William Kimbrel, Elizabeth Lloyd-Kimbrel, Ann Meeropol, Stephen Oates, and Harriet Sigerman. I owe a special debt of gratitude to Stephen Oates, who first introduced me to the high adventure of biography.

No expression of thanks could ever be enough to repay the encouragement and generosity of my friends. I am particularly grateful to Dave and Linda Keller and Doug and Sue Nelson for their hospitality. My thanks too go to Irwin Beitch, Carol Calkins, Candice Chirgotis, Jane Cohen, Dr. Lawrence Cohen, Dave and Carol Cotton, Wylene Dunbar, Vera Furdas, David Hawkanson, Jerry Jones, Howard Sherman, Leslie Stainton, Jane Tamarkin, Martha Venter, and Dan Zibello. Greg Leaming read the manuscript, offered

Acknowledgments

constructive criticism, and illuminated some of my darker moments with his wit. In countless ways, Pat Sheehy offered help and belief when I needed it most. Connie Congdon and Mark Lamos were a constant source of inspiration in their understanding and faith in my work, and I have been sustained by their theatre artistry. I owe a debt of thanks to Bill Stewart, who read the manuscript and gave me advice and the benefit of his many years of experience in the theatre. My editor, Suzanne Comer, believed in the biography from the beginning, and I appreciate her expertise. This project has been a joy from the start, and would not have been possible without the support of my husband, Tom Sheehy, who listened to "Margo stories" for four years with endless patience and good humor and always gave sensible advice.

Source Notes

ABBREVIATIONS

DMN   *Dallas Morning News*

DPL   Margo Jones Collection
          Dallas Public Library
          Dallas, Texas

DTH   *Dallas Times Herald*

HRC   Harry Ransom Humanities Research Center
          The University of Texas at Austin

JFA   Jones Family Archives
          Richard and Bea Jones and Charles Jones
          Houston, Texas

NYT   *New York Times*

MJ   Margo Jones

MJ Tapes Transcripts of Dictaphone Tapes
          Dallas Public Library
          Dallas, Texas

SMU   Oral History Collection (Carole Cohen interviews)
          Oral History Program on the Performing Arts
          Southern Methodist University
          Dallas, Texas

TITR   *Theatre-in-the-Round* by Margo Jones.
          New York: Rinehart and Co., 1951.

PROLOGUE

1–2 "Babies," "We're doing this," "But darlin's": Author interview with Louise
    Latham. Also, author interviews with Jim Pringle and Harry Granick.
2 "a patron saint of playwrights": Speech by Jerome Lawrence, Texas Woman's
    University, Denton, 16 April 1982.
    "fighter, builder, explorer": Thornton Wilder to MJ, 18 February 1950, HRC.

Source Notes

3 "Texas Tornado": Author interview with David Greggory.
"combination of Joan of Arc": Tennessee Williams to MJ, undated, HRC.

THE HEART OF A GIRL

4 "devilish thing": June Bennett Larsen, *Margo Jones: A Life in the Theatre* (Ph.D. diss., City University of New York, 1982), 7.
5 "we pulled ourselves up": Author interview with Edward Jones.
6 "Try to realize": Martha Pearl Jones to MJ, 8 March 1954, JFA.
7 "I thought that": MJ Tapes, DPL.
8 "sheet music": MJ to Doris Porter, 16 February 1955, DPL.
"was in the presence," "Up went a sheet," "I was lucky": TITR, 40.
"Somehow I got to": MJ Tapes, DPL.
"loved to talk": Author interview with Ruth Pritchard.
"pieces," "a beautiful sunset": MJ to Martha Pearl Jones, 7 August 1930, JFA.
"because they": Author interview with Charles Jones.
9 "socially, terribly inferior," "awful dumb player," "With my family": MJ Tapes, DPL.
"one of the first girls," "already liked": William Goyen, "Margo," *TriQuarterly*, 56 (Winter 1983): 71.
"shame and crime": Emma Haynes, *History of Polk County*, 1937, 91.
"So much was sacrificed": Ibid., 92.
"you were very": Larsen, 10.
10 "All of our family": Ibid., 23.
"You take care": Author interview with Richard Jones.
"I didn't think": MJ to "Rita," 26 October 1950, DPL.
11 "somehow God let me": Ibid.
"perfect goodie-good" . . . "Push, Pull, or Get Out": MJ Memory Book, JFA.
"terribly upset": MJ Tapes, DPL.
"Don't Ever Forget," "great success": MJ Memory Book, JFA.
12 "desire for adventure": MJ to parents, 4 October 1945, JFA.
"a clean town," "woman's sphere," "The spirit": Texas Woman's University History, Denton, undated, 4–5.
"in groups," "provided two": Ibid., 73.
13 "undaunted": Ibid., 77.
"looked like Rudy Vallee": MJ Tapes, DPL.
"made the best": MJ to mother, undated, JFA.
"not like the rest": MJ Tapes, DPL.
"precious Margie": In many letters to Margo from her mother.
"I do love": MJ to parents, undated, JFA.
14 "This was fortunate," "always with the": TITR, 41.

Source Notes

15 "right down to the leaves": "Theatre Time," 14 September 1950, MJ Scrapbook, DPL.
   "New vistas": TITR, 40.
16 "At first it was like": MJ to Frederick McConnell, 31 March 1948, DPL.
   "I know that there": Quoted by MJ in "Theatre '50: A Dream Come True," *Ten Talents in the American Theatre*, ed. David H. Stevens (Norman: University of Oklahoma Press, 1957), 106.
   "lit into the Greeks," "I'm going": TITR, 42.
   "tact, judgment": Shaw pamphlet, DPL.
   "helped me tremendously": TITR, 42.
   "Figure, . . . that I'm 51 percent": Murray Schumach, "A Texas Tornado Hits Broadway," *New York Times Magazine*, 17 October 1948.
17 "The Abnormal Ways," "an emotional conflict," "All our lives": M.S. thesis, Texas Woman's University, 1933.
18 "We were busy" . . . "She got her scholarship": Frank Harting interview, SMU.
   "glorified office": TITR, 43.
   "She was a great": Harting interview, SMU.
   "a source," "to gain": TITR, 43.
19 "the moth-eaten temple": Pasadena Playhouse brochure, undated.
   "has no personal": Harriet L. Green, *Gilmor Brown* (Pasadena: Burns Printing Co., 1933), unpaginated.
   "I think you know": MJ to Gilmor Brown, September 1944, JFA.
   "I don't know," "she was going": Larsen, 37.
   "What am I": MJ Tapes, DPL.
20 "working like mad" . . . "Sex": Ibid.
21 "cute," "was a corn-fed," "It was a strange," "All I know": Ibid.
22 "My first glimpse": Eleanor Clarage, "Main Street Meditations," *Cleveland Plain Dealer*, 2 October 1943.
   "New York made," "It seemed logical": TITR, 44.
23 "Most stage managers": Clipping from unidentified Houston newspaper, MJ Scrapbook, DPL.
   "agreeable to Texans": Sue Dauphin, *Houston By Stages* (Burnet, Texas: Eakin Press, 1981), 72.
   "Texas was a hard": Quoted in TITR, 45.
   "the boys . . . the local": Quoted in *Women in American Theatre*, ed. Helen Krich Chinoy and Linda Walsh Jenkins (New York: Crown Publishers, 1981), 8.
   "Our far-reaching purpose": Dauphin, 69.
24 "dreams without": TITR, 187.
   "She was absolutely": Author interview with Olivia Lockhart Glahos.
   "The moment": Margo Jones, "Houston Girl Finds Russian Theatre Is Vital and Colorful," *Houston Chronicle*, 4 October 1936.
25 "They seem to find": Margo Jones, "Drama Trail Leads . . . ," *Houston Chronicle*,

18 October 1936.
"Though quite an old," "The theatre [in Russia]": Jones, "Houston Girl Finds."
"one great lesson," "the most finished": Margo Jones, "Russian Theatre's Vigor,"
Houston Chronicle, 11 October 1936.
26 "fine and old," "seemed to be," "The Russian theatre," "he would be seeing":
Jones, "Drama Trail."
"It proved," "the great play," "Only the dopes," "the pleasantest job": John
Hutchens, "The Pleasantest Job in the World," *Theatre Arts,* Spring 1948, 36–38.
"the mind of an adult": Atkinson telegram to MJ, November 1954, DPL.
27 "Mr. Atkinson, my name is": Author interview with Claire Rosenfield.

THE SHINING HOUR

28 "Baby, . . . this is Margo": Author interview with Paul Moor.
"I saw no reason": TITR, 45.
29 "founder of the legitimate": William Ransom Hogan, "The Theater in the
Republic of Texas," *Southwest Review,* xix, no. 4 (July 1934): 384.
"Have theatres an immoral": Ibid., 421.
30 "Doc was close": Author interview with Virginia King Mayo.
"God's Chosen": Author interview with Malvina Holmes.
"land man": Author interview with Charles Jones.
"Margo always managed": Author interview with Carden Bailey.
31 "goddess": Larsen, 45.
"I just hint": Clipping from unidentified newspaper, MJ Scrapbook, DPL.
"Turtle Soup": Ms., DPL.
"We'll all make it" . . . "We'll all get": Author interview with Virginia King Mayo.
"sickening pink": MJ to Leola Prestridge, 8 July 1954, DPL.
32 "Only Leola": Author interview with Malvina Holmes.
"because you couldn't do," "off-modern": Author interview with Carden Bailey.
"for each smart": Clipping from unidentified newspaper, MJ Scrapbook, DPL.
33 "ladders, ropes": TITR, 46.
34 "Play after play": Draft of article, undated, JFA.
"talk girl talk": Author interview with Virginia King Mayo.
"I had the devotion": MJ Tapes, DPL.
35 "Twisted Column": Anonymous author, ms., DPL.
"pure energy": Author interview with Olivia Lockhart Glahos.
"always put other people": Larsen, 46.
"Margo worked entirely": Author interview with Olivia Lockhart Glahos.
"If it's that Jones": unattributed publicity article, JFA.
36 "was the most wonderful": Author interview with Malvina Holmes.
"because I thought" . . . "where my Houston theatre begins": Ann Holmes, *Alley*

Source Notes

Theatre (Houston, 1986), 15.
"It's just as important": Larsen, 69.
"Babies, it's two o'clock": Holmes, 14.
"If Margo said": Larsen, 69.
37 "I got the part," "Margo could": Author interview with Ray Walston.
"Of course, . . . that blocking": Author interview with Virginia King Mayo.
"first and foremost," "She could be so": Author interview with Ray Walston.
38 "Culture is getting": Larsen, 38.
"a lot of little," "Everybody just": Author interview with Ray Walston.
"She had complete": Author interview with Virginia King Mayo.
"Oh, Joe": Dauphin, 82.
"You take a ten-gallon": Larsen, 63.
39 "How many of you": Clarage, "Main Street Meditations."
"Margo Jones, the dynamo": *Houston Post*, undated, MJ Scrapbook, DPL.
40 "They hope to": *Special Edition* playbill, MJ Scrapbook, DPL.
41 "This is the first": Clipping from unidentified newspaper, MJ Scrapbook, DPL.
"Why not?": TITR, 49.
"Honey, I don't": Goyen, 71.
42 "No, honey": Virgil Miers, "Good Night Sweet Tornado," DTH, 25 August 1955.
"Why, honey, I just": Author interview with Jim Pringle.
"have been the classics," "Is it perhaps," "young woman": Norris Houghton,
Advance from Broadway (New York: Harcourt Brace Co., 1941), 121.
43 "What's the idea," "It's a halo": Author interview with Paul Moor.
"I know a script": MJ Tapes, DPL.
"a mournful Indian," "condescending," "prudent members": Brooks Atkinson,
NYT, 28 September 1941.
"Think of it," "dear friend": Unattributed publicity article, JFA.
44 "furniture": Atkinson, NYT, 28 September 1941.
"as the worst thing": Author interview with Virginia King Mayo.
"I guess" . . . "what I had with Jerry": MJ Tapes, DPL.
45 "so sophisticated": Author interview with Virginia King Mayo.
"She was not," "On opening": Author interview with Ray Walston.
"good bustling" "the same qualities": Clipping from unidentified Houston
newspaper, MJ Scrapbook, DPL.
"If everybody": MJ to Edwin Mayer, undated, JFA.
"Manuscripts of unproduced" . . . "let me read plays for him": Audrey Wood, "A
Game Called Play Reading," *Theatre Arts*, July 1955, 88.
46 "If you want": Unattributed article, MJ Scrapbook, DPL.
"Please do not leave": Author interview with Paul Moor.
"Who is this": Unattributed article, MJ Scrapbook, DPL.
"I don't believe": MJ to Audrey Wood, undated, JFA.
"I believe in this": MJ to Edwin Mayer, undated, JFA.

Source Notes

"I think we brought": MJ to David Stevens, 20 May 1955, JFA.

47 "place where drama": Ibid.

"everybody knew": Author interview with Nione Carlson.

IMAGES OF MAGNIFICENCE

48 "NEW STAR," "believer in": *Austin Tribune*, 11 October 1942.

"jet planer": MJ Tapes, DPL.

"chucked him": Author interview with Paul Moor.

"Oh no": Louise Latham interview, SMU.

49 "just let things": Author interview with Olivia Lockhart Glahos.

"Kids, you have": Clipping from unidentified New Orleans newspaper, 31 August 1955, JFA.

"of high energy": Author interview with Olivia Lockhart Glahos.

"what I learned," "Someday I'll have": Author interview with Louise Latham.

50 "This isn't staged": Author interview with Ted Apstein.

51 "had a wonderful": Author interview with Paul Bigelow.

"the baby": Unattributed article, MJ Scrapbook, DPL.

"She did restore": Margo Jones Award brochure, undated.

52 "Ah, children": Latham interview, SMU.

"Mother, Dear": MJ to parents, 9 November 1948, DPL.

53 "She was a person": Author interview with Paul Moor.

"tireless striving": *A Tagore Reader*, ed. Amiya Chakravarty (Boston: Beacon Press, 1961), back cover.

"destroyed me": Author interview with Paul Moor.

54 "Darling, I've": Author interview with Ted Apstein.

"pretty excited," "Maybe we could": MJ to Audrey Wood, December 1941, JFA.

"celluloid brassiere": Donald Spoto, *The Kindness of Strangers* (New York: Little, Brown, and Co., 1985), 105.

"completely off": MJ to Tennessee Williams, undated, JFA.

55 "ball of fire," "She was a juggernaut": Author interview with David Greggory.

"I think," "She thought," "poor relation": Author interview with Horton Foote.

56 "wizened Cockney," "Margo was," "practically ironed": Author interview with Nancy Spencer.

57 "grungy old towel," "like honey": Ibid.

59 "The girl is": *Tennessee Williams' Letters to Donald Windham*, ed. Donald Windham (New York: Holt, Rinehart, and Winston, 1977), 101.

"Joan of Arc": Tennessee Williams to MJ, 27 August 1943, HRC.

"too often": *You Touched Me* playbill, Cleveland Playhouse, JFA.

"as good in Podunk": *Cleveland News*, 14 October 1943.

"She spoke," "Although we had": Author interview with Anne Pitoniak.

60 "vague but terrifying": Windham, 109.
"I can't stand": Author interview with Anne Pitoniak.
"turning absolutely": *Cleveland News*, 14 October 1943.
"You remind": Author interview with Anne Pitoniak.
61 "was longing": Author interview with Ruth Ford.
"never had a sober": Author interview with Dakin Williams.
"He had the idea": Windham, 112.
"Margo, . . . I don't," "Oh, I don't": Author interview with Nancy Spencer.
"the old dowagers": Windham, 118.
62 "Margo will not": Windham, 114.
"Life seems unreal": Tennessee Williams to MJ, undated, HRC.
"they do catch": MJ to Tennessee Williams, undated, JFA.
"I don't think," "And I commit," "knock some sense," "Your *Cockcrow*": MJ to Tennessee Williams, undated, JFA.
63 "found out that": TITR, 51.
"restudy every word": MJ to Gilmor Brown, August 1944, JFA.
"we dream beautifully": TITR, 52.
"I sent him": Author interview with Claire Rosenfield.
64 "children would grow": Ibid.
"culture in Dallas": John Rosenfield Collection Register, DPL.
"Why don't you": Author interview with Claire Rosenfield.
"something is wrong," "creative vs. business": *The Daily Texan*, 7 April 1944.
65 "I really felt": Author interview with June Moll.
"keep always": *The Daily Texan*, 7 April 1944.
"I believe passionately," "I believe in decentralized," "This is a job": MJ to David Stevens, 20 May 1944, JFA.
"out of heaven," "steal a plane": MJ to Tennessee Williams, 26 August 1944, JFA.
66 "there is no doubt": Rebecca Hargis Turner to author.
"Do me a favor": MJ to Tennessee Williams, undated, JFA.
"nauseous," "It contains": Tennessee Williams to MJ, March 1944 and August 1944, HRC.
"damn thrilled," "It will be": MJ to James Laughlin, August 1944, JFA.
67 "I'm reading," "I must": Ibid.
"Right after the war": Tennessee Williams to MJ, August 1944, HRC.
"I'm not": MJ to James Laughlin, August 1944, DPL.

LET ME TALK MY DREAMS

68 "It must be great": Rockefeller Foundation grant application, 22 April 1944, JFA.
"I believe": MJ to John Rosenfield, 22 April 1944, DPL.
"I know you have": Charles Jones to MJ, 26 October 1944, JFA.

"talk to every," "learn everything new": MJ to John Rosenfield, 17 May 1944, JFA. "A mere way": Schumach, 60.

69 "freshest cultural": DMN, 1 October 1944.

"the box arrived": MJ to James Laughlin, undated, JFA.

70 "truth in the pleasant": Tennessee Williams, *The Glass Menagerie* (New York: New Directions, 1949), 4.

"exquisitely fragile": Ibid., vii.

70–71 "I left St. Louis": Ibid., 123–124.

71 "She was an encouragement": Author interview with Charles Jones.

72 "be worth its," "I hope": MJ to John Rosenfield, 28 November 1944, JFA.

74 "wraith of God": Author interview with Randy Echols.

75 "I've found it": Marguerite Courtney, *Laurette* (New York: Rinehart & Co., 1955), 393.

"going on the longest": Carole Thompson, *The Acting Technique of Laurette Taylor* (M.F.A. thesis, Yale University, 1955), 32.

"I've just found," "Why not?", "Well, he's": Author interview with Randy Echols.

78 "a strange affair": Untitled clipping, *Variety*, 22 November 1944, Billy Rose Theatre Collection, Lincoln Center Library, New York.

"didn't have a clue": Author interview with Willie Gould.

"to aid and abet": Alva Johnston, "Aider and Abettor," *The New Yorker*, October 1948, 37.

79 "make the tie," "marryin' mood": Sonny Koch to MJ, undated, JFA.

80 "In many cases": MJ to Audrey Wood, undated, DPL.

"I can't light": Clipping from unidentified newspaper, MJ Scrapbook, DPL.

"decided to take": Author interview with Willie Gould.

"this is the most": MJ to John Rosenfield, January 1945, JFA.

"little glass guys," "old-timer": Author interview with Willie Gould.

81 "Tennessee, . . . don't you change," "Mr. Singer, if you": Schumach, 59.

"Could you find," "Yes, Miss": MJ to John Rosenfield, January 1945, JFA.

"It's magic": Author interview with Randy Echols.

82 "They shot," "No, I cannot": Bill Doll, "Ashton Stevens," *Theatre Arts*, July 1951, 94.

"world's best": Richard B. Gehman, "Claudia Cassidy," *Theatre Arts*, July 1951, 86.

"The play leaves": *Chicago Herald-Tribune*, 27 December 1944.

83 "My God," "Julie . . . manages": Clipping from unidentified newspaper, MJ Scrapbook, DPL.

"Eddie [Dowling]": Author interview with Randy Echols.

84 "get going on": MJ to John Rosenfield, January 1945, JFA.

"awful": MJ to "Hazel," undated, JFA.

"wanted to grab this iron": Don Wilmeth, *A History of the Margo Jones Theatre* (Ph.D. diss., University of Illinois, 1964), 27.

85 "Dallas is an example": *Dallas* Magazine Sesquicentennial Edition, Dallas

Source Notes

Chamber of Commerce, 1986, 11.

86 "cultural war horses": George Sessions Perry, "Margo Jones Makes Theatrical History," source unidentified, 10 August 1948, DPL.

87 "didn't think," "oil-derricks," "cotton fields": MJ to Eddie Dowling, undated, JFA. "plain," "looked like": Betty Winn interview, SMU.

88 "Let me talk": MJ Theatre Plan, JFA.
"of the past": John Rosenfield, DMN, 13 February 1945.
"My children have," "bad theatre," "go beyond": MJ Theatre Plan.
"Books!": Theatre '50 playbill advertisement.
"It was riveting": Author interview with Elizabeth McMurray Johnson.

89 "You can feel," "And to prove," "Bless you": Author interview with Claire Rosenfield.
"enthusiasm reigned!": Wilmeth, 36.
"the time will": Author interview with Elizabeth McMurray Johnson.
"Margo had a way": Wilmeth interview with Eugene McDermott, DPL.

90 "had moments," "poetry was": Lon Tinkle, "Gene McDermott Universal Man," DMN, 2 September 1973.
"to run her own," "to keep": Wilmeth interview with Eugene McDermott, DPL.
"marvelous house": Jeremy Gerard, "It Was a World," Dallas Life Magazine, 14 July 1986, 30.

91 "bunch of Texas": MJ to Julie Haydon, 17 February 1945, JFA.
"carry the torch": MJ to Edwin Mayer, 23 June 1945, DPL.
"Margo, I am sure": Mary Morris to MJ, 11 March 1945, DPL.

92 "I can't say": New York World-Telegram, 2 April 1945.
"The craftsmanship": New York Journal-American, 2 April 1945.
"a smooth collaborative": Wilella Waldorf, New York Post, 2 April 1945.
"her one fault": Unattributed article, 5 May 1945, MJ Scrapbook, DPL.

93 "not very lady-like": Tex McCrary and Jinx Falkenburg, New York Herald-Tribune, undated, MJ Scrapbook, DPL.
"Will one of you men": Author interview with Patricia Peck Swank.
"wowed them": Joanna Albus to Maxine Mesinger, undated, DPL.
"the real people," "I told you": MJ to James Laughlin, 23 May 1945, JFA.

94 "a real creative theatre": Conversations with Tennessee Williams, ed. Albert S. Devlin (Jackson: University Press of Mississippi, 1986), 9.

95 "When I pick": John Beaufort, "Theatre in the Round," Christian Science Monitor, May 1954.
"She was always": Wilmeth, 8.

96 "A permanent repertory": "National Press Takes Note of New Theatre '45," DMN, 5 August 1945.
"show Dallas," "if Margo had": "A Playwright's Statement," DMN, undated, MJ Scrapbook, DPL.
"we have won," "attract and nourish": John Lineweave, draft of article, JFA.

97 "rich bitch": MJ to Sonny Koch, undated, JFA.

"What the hell": Author interview with June Moll.
98 "Don't open": MJ to Mary Morris, 8 October 1945, DPL.
"Don't ever do": Author interview with Rebecca Hargis Turner.
"We thought he": Author interview with Jed Mace.
"I can't meet": Gerard, 34.
99 "high-powered business": MJ to Frank Harting, 19 September 1945, DPL.
"Way down deep": MJ to Tennessee Williams, 5 December 1945, JFA.

BLOODED ON BROADWAY

100 "It may seem": MJ to June Moll, undated, JFA.
"real people": MJ to James Laughlin, 23 May 1945, JFA.
"I think": MJ to mother, 25 September 1946, JFA.
101 "kindred spirit": Author interview with Haila Stoddard.
102 "Almost everywhere": MJ to parents, undated, JFA.
"Get him," "very clever," "slick and fast": MJ to June Moll, 13 February 1946, JFA.
103 "managerial headaches," "sweating out": Ibid.
"You can't think": Maxine Wood, On Whitman Avenue (New York: Dramatists Play Service, 1964), 24.
"I feel like": Joanna Albus to June Moll, February 1946, JFA.
"It nearly kills": MJ to parents, February 1946, JFA.
104 "being charming," "a lot of," "We're not resentful": June Moll to MJ, 21 March 1946, JFA.
"kind of person": MJ to June Moll, 26 February 1946, JFA.
"the job": MJ to June Moll, March 1946, JFA.
105 "She had a vision," She was a very": Author interview with Perry Wilson.
106 "a search": Ibid.
"My own theatre": Buffalo, New York News, 9 April 1946, Billy Rose Theatre Collection.
107 "a double victory": Loften Mitchell, Black Drama (New York: Hawthorn Books), 121.
"whites who think": Ibid., 124.
"the dazzling dynamo," "Forgive me": MJ to Mark Marvin, 29 April 1946, JFA.
108 "You ever hear," "I don't know how": Quoted in Mitchell, 127.
"sets out to prove": New York Journal-American, 9 May 1946.
"Negro question," "may be dynamite": New York Post, 9 May 1946.
"the battle": Theatre World, ed. Daniel Blum (New York: Kalkhoff Press, 1946), 4.
109 "swell farewell": MJ to Maxine Wood, 29 May 1946, JFA.
110 "images of magnificence": MJ to Nancy Spencer, 26 June 1946, JFA.
"After World War II," "I finally": Author interview with Sonny Koch.
"sheer exuberance": Undated ms. of article, JFA.

Source Notes

112 "no doubt": MJ Tapes, DPL.

"stimulating and exciting," "wanted nothing": Author interview with Manning Gurian.

"taking pleasure": MJ Tapes, DPL.

113 "good mixer," "put on," "I've never": "Maxwell Anderson," *Current Biography* (New York: H. W. Wilson, 1942), 18.

"devoted entirely," "a play in rehearsal," "I have wanted," "the problem": Souvenir program, *Joan of Lorraine*, November 1946.

114 "as Masters": MJ to Ingrid Bergman, 29 September 1946, JFA.

115 "sun slanting," "ethereal light": MJ to mother, 23 September 1946, JFA.

"Scarcely an hour": MJ to father and Charles Jones, 23 September 1946, JFA.

"extraordinary talent": MJ to William Selwyn, 30 September 1946, JFA.

"No": Souvenir program, *Joan of Lorraine*.

116 "actors should," "But they": Maxwell Anderson, *"Joan of Lorraine,"* Theatre Arts, Spring 1948, 66–67.

"somehow I feel": MJ to Ingrid Bergman, 29 September 1946, JFA.

117 "oil man's technique," "tried to charm": MJ to Ross Lawther, 19 October 1946, JFA.

"very peaceful": Author interview with Alan Anderson.

"I wish": MJ to Ross Lawther, 19 October 1946, JFA.

118 "deplored racial": *Washington Post*, 28 October 1946.

"too much to say": *Hollywood Reporter*, 30 October 1946.

119 "nigger lover": Ingrid Bergman and Alan Burgess, *Ingrid Bergman My Story* (New York: Dell Publishing, 1980), 211.

"All over the United States," "more dynamic": Nelson Bell, "Margo Shoots at Miracles," *Washington Post*, 10 November 1946.

"just feel it," "Bergman wanted," "Margo was": Author interview with Sam Wanamaker.

"She didn't push," "Margo was careful": Author interview with Alan Anderson.

120 "boring": *Hollywood Reporter*, 30 October 1946.

"How cruel": Bergman and Burgess, 212.

"Look, I don't," "What's the difference?", "For me": Author interview with Sam Wanamaker.

121 "just believe, baby": A number of actors who were interviewed quoted this phrase.

"very wrong," "unwise," "[W]hat you consider": MJ to Maxwell Anderson, 11 November 1946, JFA.

TOWARD A NATIONAL THEATRE

122 "Speak louder": *Variety*, 30 March 1947, Billy Rose Theatre Collection.

"Under Margo Jones' direction": NYT, 19 November 1946.

"admirable and assured": *New York Journal-American*, 19 November 1946.
"the staging": *New York Herald-Tribune*, 19 November 1946.
"stabbed Margo": Author interview with Ted Apstein.
"Will Margo Jones": Undated clipping, *Variety*, Billy Rose Theatre Collection.
"Margo wanted": Author interview with Nione Carlson.
123 "the cat": Author interview with Claire Rosenfield.
"She always popped": Margo Jones Award brochure, undated.
"That's a hard one": MJ to Ed Torrance, 20 January 1947, DPL.
"keep the tears": MJ Tapes, DPL.
"determined to fight": DTH, December 1, 1946.
"more exciting": MJ to James Laughlin, 22 January 1947, JFA.
124 "Anytime you get": McCrary and Falkenburg, *New York Herald Tribune*.
"some real outsmarting," "tough as hell": MJ to Ed Torrance, 20 January 1947, DPL.
125 "Well, bebe": Sonny Koch to MJ, December 1946, JFA.
"Oh how I": Martha Pearl Jones to MJ, 30 December 1946, JFA.
"let her hair," "There is nobody," "have got to be," "As far as:" MJ to Tennessee Williams, 7 January 1947, JFA.
"Now's the Time": DMN, 16 February 1947.
126 "more closely": Ibid.
"to have finality": MJ to June and Jim Moll, 12 February 1947, JFA.
"the construction": Wilmeth, 49.
"As far as": MJ to Audrey Wood, 24 February 1947, JFA.
"was a Pollyanna," "For me": MJ to Jo Mielziner, 24 February 1947, JFA.
127 "physical and spiritual," "last violent": MJ to June and Jim Moll, 5 March 1947, JFA.
"I will not let": MJ to Audrey Wood, 7 March 1947, JFA.
"When there is no": TITR, 59.
"when one runs out": TITR, 60.
"this so difficult," "so unpleasantly," "goon southern": MJ to Manning Gurian, 13 March 1947, JFA.
128 "just let," "a person," "For a play": Ibid.
"hung the moon": Schumach, 59.
"we completely understood": MJ Tapes, DPL.
"simple play": Manning Gurian to MJ, 17 February 1947, JFA.
129 "My main interest": Peter Zeisler to MJ, 14 April 1947, JFA.
130 "first class," "must be," "hard-boiled": TITR, 61.
"but that eternal": Joanna Albus to MJ, 20 April 1947, JFA.
"good plays": Author interview with Manning Gurian.
"full-fledged," "All the physical": MJ Tapes, DPL.
131 "I'll never" . . . "I think you will": Author interview with Katharine Balfour.
132 "a nation's drama": DMN, 21 April 1947.

Source Notes

134 "passionate desire," "her fear": TITR, 140.
"sensitive drama": TITR, 146–147.

135 "I honestly wish": MJ to Idabelle Hicks, 20 May 1947, DPL.
"too many things": MJ to Sherman Ewing, 21 May 1947, DPL.
"sweet-spirited": Author interview with Clinton Anderson.

136 "talent in the rough," "that rare": MJ to Warner Brothers, 10 December 1947, JFA.
"Let's face it": Author interview with Jack Warden.

137 "the easiest work": Larsen, 156.
"We are confident": Vinton Freedley to MJ, 3 June 1947, DPL.

138 "outstanding creative": Gilmor Brown to MJ, 12 June 1947, DPL.
"From the shades": Eugene and Ruth McDermott to MJ, June 1947, JFA.

139 "wanted the theatre": Winn interview, SMU.
"because the actors": DTH, 7 June 1947.
"a husband and wife": Winn interview, SMU.
"completely won": New York Morning Telegraph, 6 June 1947.

140 "has a sure instinct": DMN, 4 June 1947.
"would probably seem," "More companies": New York Morning Telegraph, 6 June 1947.
"It is possible": TITR, 139.
"six and four," "Craps": Clipping from unidentified newspaper, DPL.

141 "Dallas theatregoers schooled": Frank Chappell, DTH, undated, DPL.
"fast asleep": Wilmeth, 72.
"may be just," "Never before": TITR, 140.

142 "everything possible": TITR, 144.
"Making the rounds," "pull down": John William Rogers, The Lusty Texans of Dallas (New York: E. P. Dutton and Co., 1951), 219.
"Why, she's just": Frank Chappell, DTH, 14 July 1947.
"you'd wonder": Author interview with Jack Warden.

143 "Something of consequence," "wonderful feeling," "heat-stricken," "The characters of Hedda," "This is a lovely," "Its buoyant": NYT article reprinted in DMN, 10 August 1947.
"smart crowd," "The night was": Audrey Wood, with Max Wilk, Represented by Audrey Wood (Garden City, New York: Doubleday and Co., 1981), 149.
"bravo": Author interviews with Rebecca Hargis Turner and Katharine Balfour.

144 "Why, it's just": Wood, 149.
"Lethal": Author interview with Rebecca Hargis Turner.
"break into theatre," "What you should": MJ to Marguerite Shields, 25 August 1947, DPL.
"Forget it": Clipping from unidentified newspaper, 1 June 1947, MJ Scrapbook, DPL.

Source Notes

MAN OF THE YEAR

145 "I breathe," "You'd think": MJ to Manning Gurian, undated, JFA.
"spring chicken": MJ Tapes, DPL.
146 "deep down," "one thousand": Ibid.
"I don't think": Author interview with Mabel Duke.
"Margo was": Author interview with Louise Latham.
147 "a chance for": MJ to Tennessee Williams, 20 August 1947, JFA.
"mysterious wall": Windham, 203.
"You'd think he": Devlin, 204.
"Get Kazan": Tennessee Williams, Memoirs (Garden City, New York: Doubleday and Co., 1975), 131.
148 "quite moved": MJ to William Inge, 19 August 1947, DPL.
"get thin–keep awake": MJ to Jean Barraco, September 1947, JFA.
"healthy and sane": MJ to Joanna Albus, November 1947, JFA.
150 "Fine, baby": Author interview with Jed Mace.
151 "at the pinnacle": TITR, 147.
"anybody could stand": MJ to Joanna Albus, 10 November 1947, JFA.
152 "twirl and twist": Author interview with Manning Gurian.
153 "I am gregarious": Devlin, 29.
154 "I wouldn't": Author interview with Katharine Squire.
"so realistic": Winn interview, SMU.
"Can't we do": TITR, 153.
"a rather plain": Winn interview, SMU.
155 "There is no scenery," "hands felt," "great freedom": TITR, 128–129.
"every moment": MJ to Tennessee Williams, October 1947, HRC.
"by that time": Pancho Rodriguez y Gonzalez to MJ, undated, DPL.
156 "approach his work": TITR, 154.
157 "doing what comes": "Doing What Comes Naturally," Theatre Arts, June 1949, 55.
158 "On the last," "The fact": DMN, 31 December 1947.
159 "The only people": Author interview with Claire Rosenfield.
"easily one of": DMN, 13 January 1948.
"Not enough time": MJ to Joanna Albus, March 1948, JFA.
160 "With all," "spoiled me," "If I could," "tough-looking," "made his role": Author interview with Joseph Hayes.
"unfailingly sure," "performers were," "open windows": "Seeing Things," Saturday Review of Literature, 3 April 1948, 24–25.
161 "Mamoulian had": Author interview with Joseph Hayes.
162 "I was still": Author interview with Manning Gurian.
164 "This theatre here": MJ to Tennessee Williams, 13 January 1948, HRC.
"I would give": MJ to Tennessee Williams, January 1948, HRC.
165 "an entirely," "I expressed": Wood, 157.

Source Notes

"usual bunch": MJ to James Laughlin, 22 January 1948, JFA.

166 "Boss . . . one thing": Manning Gurian to MJ, 28 May 1948, JFA.

167 "very fine," "bored to death," "turning it into," "summer theatre": MJ to June and Jim Moll, 14 November 1948, JFA.

"I have a part": Author interview with Ray Walston.

168 "Do you believe," "Absolutely not": *New York Morning Telegraph*, 16 August 1948.

"We cut": Elia Kazan, *A Life* (New York: Alfred A. Knopf, 1988), 344.

"the dynamism": Windham, 328.

"prove that it": MJ to Jo Mielziner, 21 February 1948, DPL.

169 "Now, Tennessee": Author interview with Ray Walston.

170 "Tennessee Williams has written": *Buffalo Evening News*, 10 September 1948.

"not only liked it," "just beginning," "to say": Clipping from unidentified newspaper, MJ Scrapbook, DPL.

"pair of antlered," "by three women," "What is the": Tennessee Williams, "Questions Without Answers," NYT, 3 October 1948.

171 "Was Blanche," "Tennessee does," "Oh," "People!": Ibid.

"stone figures": Author interview with Ray Walston.

"at dagger": Harting interview, SMU.

"That woman!": Dakin Williams, *Tennessee Williams, An Intimate Biography* (New York: Arbor House, 1983), 166.

"*Summer and Smoke* . . . is no ordinary": *Cleveland Plain Dealer*, 28 September 1948.

172 "as if she had," "I want," "We haven't got," "Please," "Here it is": MJ to June and Jim Moll, 14 November 1948, JFA.

"thankful for these," "Inflated reputations": Williams, "Questions Without Answers."

173 "A Kiddy-Kar": Robert Garland, *New York Journal-American*, 7 October 1948.

"A pretentious": *New York Herald-Tribune*, 7 October 1948.

"Mawkish, murky": *New York Daily News*, 7 October 1948.

"The stock Tennessee": Garland, 7 October 1948.

"has been given": *New York Daily Mirror*, 7 October 1948.

174 "*Summer and Smoke* . . . is a theatre piece": NYT, 7 October 1948.

"how [the play] could," "the set": Harting interview, SMU.

"forced the action": John Gassner, *Directions in Modern Theatre and Drama* (New York: Holt, Rinehart, and Winston, 1967), 53.

175 "To the very best": MJ to June and Jim Moll, 14 November 1948, JFA.

"as intangible," "work of art": NYT, 10 October 1948.

MIXER OF TRUTH AND MAGIC

176 "Since honor": MJ to Tennessee Williams, 3 November 1948, DPL.

177 "I did want": Ray Walston to MJ, 13 May 1949, JFA.

Source Notes

"because we loved": Author interview with Arthur Kramer.

"Broadway?": Clipping from unidentified newspaper, MJ Scrapbook, DPL.

"like a gentleman": MJ Tapes, DPL.

178 "perhaps the strongest": MJ to June and Jim Moll, 14 November 1948.

179 "Learning to know": MJ to parents, undated, DPL.

180 "for these people": TITR, 165.

"Theatre '48 Starts," "showmanship at its," "Although a wrestler": DMN, 12 November 1948.

"like a great big": MJ to parents, November 1948, DPL.

"She talked about": Author interview with Clinton Anderson.

"was unique": Martha Bumpas Gaylord interview, SMU.

181 "company reached": DMN, 21 December 1948.

182 "did not wash": Ibid.

"nightmare of dullness": Winn interview, SMU.

"pine trees": DMN, 11 January 1949.

"I think this," "Well . . . I think": Author interview with Clinton Anderson.

"it doesn't have": MJ to Tennessee Williams, 16 April 1949, HRC.

"[Skaal] is a": MJ to George Freedley, 10 January 1949, DPL.

"You would think": MJ to June and Jim Moll, 19 February 1949, DPL.

183 "in which every": TITR, 171.

"Comic King": Virgil Miers, DTH, 15 March 1949.

"I didn't know," "It wasn't part": Author interview with Manning Gurian.

"little girl": Martha Pearl Jones to MJ, July 1949, JFA.

184 "Learning to say": Richard Jones to MJ, 23 April 1948, JFA.

"shrinking violet": Author interview with Mabel Duke.

"I'd have been": Marion Meade, *Dorothy Parker: What Fresh Hell Is This?* (New York: Villard Books, 1988), 330.

185 "I've never met," "She's wonderful": DTH, 10 April 1949.

"What fresh": Meade, *Dorothy Parker: What Fresh Hell Is This?*

"They are not," "extremely tedious": MJ to parents, 30 March 1949, DPL.

186 "hisses come," "up to his rump," "here comes": Clay Bailey, DTH, undated, DPL.

"Bless you," "never heard": Author interview with Mabel Duke.

"a shaky Miss": DMN, 5 April 1949.

"written with intelligence": *Variety*, 12 April 1949.

"an ordinary drama," "In its third,": Brooks Atkinson, NYT, 13 April 1949.

187 "All a theatre": NYT, 8 May 1949.

188 "To me the pertinent," "the glamour": Ms. of MJ Speech, JFA.

189 "The trouble with": DMN, 10 May 1949.

"Thank you, Dallas," "Thank you, Margo": DMN, 4 June 1949.

190 "I believe that": *Chicago Herald-Tribune*, 2 October 1949.

191 "those of us": José Quintero, *If You Don't Dance They Beat You* (Boston: Little, Brown, 1974), 95.

Source Notes

192 "Margo adored": Author interview with Joseph Glasco.
"more continuity": TITR, 11.
"Circle-in-the-Square is": NYT, 25 April 1952.
193 "During this past": "An Invitation to Action," *Theatre Arts*, October 1950, 48.
"was great training": Author interview with Jack Warden.
"My career": Author interview with Larry Hagman.
194 "the greatest variety": DMN clipping, undated, DPL.
"incredibly timely": TITR, 175.
"You have nothing": Manning Gurian to MJ, 7 November 1949, DPL.
195 "from usher": Clipping from unidentified newspaper, 7 December 1949, DPL.
196 "especially I want": Thornton Wilder to MJ, 19 January 1950, HRC.
"literally no action": MJ to George Freedley, 1 February 1950, DPL.
"the play that": MJ to Sari Scott, 4 February 1950, DPL.
"I don't want": Manning Gurian to MJ, 11 February 1950, JFA.
"a director has": Author interview with Manning Gurian.
"the day I needed": MJ to Thornton Wilder, 20 April 1950, DPL.
197 "What amulet," "Just murmur": Thornton Wilder to MJ, 18 February 1950, HRC.
"had given": NYT, 26 July 1955.
"put on": Gabriel Fallon, "Pathway of a Dramatist," *Theatre Arts*, January 1950, 37.
198 "I hope your": Sean O'Casey to MJ, 25 April 1950, DPL.
"relax and enjoy": Wilmeth, 111.
"lavish and fast-moving": Wilmeth, 112.
"We couldn't turn": DMN, 25 April 1950.
199 "light, charming": MJ to George Freedley, 6 May 1950, DPL.
"We must make": DMN, 10 May 1949.
"smallest number": *Theatre World*, 1949–50 (New York: Greenberg Publishers, 1951), 6.
"flattering": Author interview with Ted Apstein.
200 "She would," "There was," "We had": Ibid.
"I remember feeling": Author interview with Zelda Fichandler.
201 "I went out," "she was open," "Well, honey," "Maybe we would": Ibid.
"We must create": TITR, 3–5.
"a tree with a root": Kenneth MacGowan, *Footlights Across America* (New York: Harcourt, Brace, and Co., 1929), 3.
202 "today it does not have": TITR, 5.
"I am not interested": TITR, 187.
"I could stop": TITR, 201.
"There is no difficulty": NYT, 16 July 1950.
"very good-looking": Author interview with Ted Apstein.
"It got to be," "I'll lie down": Frank Harting tape transcript, DPL.
203 "I had," "What did you," "I thought": Ibid.

Source Notes

"constantly exploding": Schumach, 59.

"Ah can't stop": McCrary and Falkenburg, *New York Herald-Tribune.*

204 "Honey, . . . theatre is": Robert Wahls, "She's Never Had a Losing Week," unidentified newspaper, 1 October 1950, DPL.

"the theatre is": DMN, 27 September 1950.

"were the people," "a regional": NYT, 27 September 1950.

205 "wonderful gawky adorable": Undated letter to unnamed correspondent, DPL.

"in all kinds of ways," "her theatre": Author interview with Joanna Albus.

"Texas Tornado," "When she returned": *New York Post,* 17 September 1950.

206 "Sorry, lady," "Honey": Ibid.

"I have never": MJ to Frank Harting, 26 October 1950, DPL.

"I am crazy," "Personally I feel": MJ to Ted Apstein, 25 October 1950, DPL.

207 "in a voice": Tallulah Bankhead, *Tallulah* (New York: Harper and Brothers, 1952), 294.

"lecturing every night": Ibid., 296.

208 "Thank you," "Why should I": DTH, 6 December 1950.

"wore me to a nub": MJ to Tad Adoue, 15 December 1950; DPL.

"freeing the so-called": Lloyd Lewis, "The New Theatre," *Theatre Arts,* July 1949, 34.

"beautiful and": MJ to Tennessee Williams, 12 December 1950, JFA.

"Botch": Lewis, "The New Theatre."

"the needs": MJ to Tennessee Williams, 12 December 1950, JFA.

209 "Baby, . . . don't let": MJ to William Goyen, 21 December 1950, DPL.

"much ado": Wilmeth, 139.

210 "Papa, Papa," "gave me my": Author interview with Brenda Vaccaro.

"any murder melodrama": Clipping from unidentified newspaper, MJ Scrapbook, DPL.

212 Information about Margo's breakdown was taken primarily from the author's interview with Mabel Duke, who was on the scene Friday morning, February 9, 1951.

IS IT WORTH IT?

213 "Illness Forces," "a mysterious virus attack": DMN, 10 February 1951.

"She wanted Manning": Author interview with Mabel Duke.

"I am optimistic": *The Zontian,* March–April 1951, DPL.

"I feel like": Author interview with Mabel Duke.

"I have been": MJ to Edwin Whitner, 16 April 1951, DPL.

214 "race records," "The walls rise," "lowdown": DMN, 3 April 1951.

"been good and sick": MJ to William Goyen, 23 April 1951, DPL.

215 "If Dallas has": DTH, 16 April 1951.

Source Notes

"I have been": MJ to Martha Pearl Jones, 25 May 1951, DPL.
"hastily assembled": NYT, 27 May 1951.
"if the book": *New York Herald-Tribune*, 19 August 1951.
"[M]ore than a handbook": Joseph Wesley Zeigler, *Regional Theatre* (New York: Da Capo Press, 1977), 20.
"I knew that she": Zelda Fichandler, "Institution as Artwork," *Theatre Profiles* 7 (New York: Theatre Communications Group, 1986), 2.
216 "I think you": MJ to Nina Vance, undated, DPL.
"The season is": MJ to unidentified friend, 29 May 1951, DPL.
"I found myself," "love, from": MJ to parents, 21 June 1951, DPL.
217 "a simply perfect": MJ to Elizabeth Anne McMurray, 16 July 1951, DPL.
"that it was the embodiment": Author interview with Elizabeth McMurray Johnson.
"It is wonderful": MJ to parents, 29 June 1951, DPL.
"moving and stimulating": MJ to Elizabeth Anne McMurray, 16 July 1951, DPL.
"many of the things": MJ to William Goyen, 16 July 1951, DPL.
"no advertising," "shocked everyone": MJ to Martha Pearl Jones and "Aunt Stella," 13 August 1951, DPL.
218 "She was past": Author interview with Manning Gurian.
"[W]e will not": MJ to unidentified friend, 19 July 1951, DPL.
"one of those awful": Draft of letter, MJ to Manning Gurian, 30 December 1951, Fine Arts Archives, DPL.
"I just cannot": MJ to Mabel Duke, 2 October 1951, DPL.
219 "Gene, I have": MJ to Eugene McDermott, 29 June 1951, DPL.
"It is easier": TITR, 201.
220 "upon meeting Margo": Violet Burch to author.
"doing the old": Undated clipping from *Christian Science Monitor*, MJ Scrapbook, DPL.
"We had to," "Honey, could you," "these two nuts," "I'll see you": Author interview with Mary Dolan.
221 "[W]hen a neurotic": MJ to Tad Adoue, 21 October 1951, JFA.
"only thoughts": Richard Jones to MJ, 14 July 1951, JFA.
222 "I do not do": MJ to Richard Jones, 19 September 1951, DPL.
"I know you": MJ to Martha Pearl Jones, 14 November 1951, DPL.
"sternly advised": DMN, December 1951, DPL.
223 "it takes": MJ to Nina Vance, 29 May 1951, DPL.
"sort of American": DMN, 4 December 1951.
"How did Shakespeare": DMN, December 1951.
224 "He was awful": Author interview with Manning Gurian.
"rushed home," "pass it on only": "Bernhardt, to Marlowe, to Hayes, to Harris," *Theatre Arts*, March 1953, 15.
"as though it were": MJ notes, Fine Arts Archives, DPL.

Source Notes

225–226 "Dear God . . . calm peaceful mind about all this": MJ notes, JFA.
226 "I'd like," "Being a celebrity," "My mind jumps": draft of letter, MJ to Manning Gurian, undated, Fine Arts Archives, DPL.
227 "it was a real": MJ to Martha Pearl Jones, 19 January 1952, DPL.
"bright and sharp": Wilmeth, 147.
228 "he had reviewed," "Sometimes we had": DTH, 26 February 1952.
"public lawlessness": DMN, 27 February 1952.
229 "helped her," "One thing," "dear, loving": Violet Burch to author.
"an educational event": Wilmeth, 148.
"A Perambulator Named," "Our cheeks are pink": DMN, 29 April 1952.
230 "The astute Broadway," "specious theatricality": DMN, 23 May 1952.
"I'll think about": DMN, 27 March 1952.
231 "simply terrific": MJ to William Inge, 29 September 1952, DPL.
"It was an interesting": MJ to Martha Pearl Jones, 14 July 1952, DPL.
232 "Now, tell me": Author interview with Mary Dolan.
"carried on like," "with a hope," "I was pretty": MJ Tapes, DPL.
"I am almost": MJ to Jim Pringle, 26 August 1952, DPL.
233 "we would hold": Gaylord interview, SMU.
"seven seasons," "we have better": DMN, 26 October 1951.
"I first saw," "trim, brunette": Clipping from unidentified San Francisco newspaper, 8 December 1952, DPL.
234 "Thirty-six years," "She started," "Then the next," "Haven't you," "No": Author interview with Eugene Raskin.
235 "You mean," "Yes," "I think": Ibid.
"confronting board members": Author interview with Jim Pringle.
"I am returning," "getting extraordinary": DMN, 23 January 1953.
236 "Good-looking men," "She used": Author interview with Jim Pringle.
"I will not," "Margo was more": Author interview with Arthur Kramer.
"There is no": MJ to William Dubensky, 28 April 1953, DPL.
"a piece of": MJ to Tad Adoue, undated (1953), DPL.
237 "Tennessee is": MJ to parents, 25 March 1953, DPL.
"Talk about southern," "nostalgic thrill": MJ to Tad Adoue, 28 March 1953, DPL.
"one of the most": MJ to Malcolm Ross, 14 May 1953, DPL.
238 "My first": MJ to Jonas Silverstone, 28 April 1953, DPL.
239 "It's the first": MJ to Rosamond Gilder, 30 October 1953, DPL.
"a sensitive": MJ Tapes, DPL.
"There are times": The Way of a Woman, ms., DPL.
"Your characters": Draft of letter, MJ to Manning Gurian, undated, JFA.
240 "I personally," "I think": MJ to Manning Gurian, 16 February 1954, JFA.
"Margo's feeling": Author interview with Manning Gurian.
"My darling": MJ Tapes, DPL.
241 "[A]nd now," "I loved": Ibid.

Source Notes

"bullied": Author interview with Louise Noble.

242 "There seemed to," "At the end," "forever sticking": Sheldon Harnick to author.

243 "How come," "Shh": Author interview with Harry Granick.

"Dallas is lucky": NYT, 6 June 1954.

"as if it were": NYT, 29 May 1954.

"Now we're going": Author interviews with Louise Latham and Jim Pringle.

243–244 "Now you all know . . . Bless you": *Genital Junction*, ms., courtesy of Louise Noble.

245 "You are always": MJ to Hallie Flanagan, 23 March 1954, DPL.

AN IDEA IS A GREATER MONUMENT THAN A CATHEDRAL

246 "the very existence": "The Plight of the Living Theatre in the United States," *Theatre Arts*, April 1954, 64–86.

247 "we will never": TITR, 190.

"It was a very": MJ to Rosamond Gilder, 16 August 1954, DPL.

248 "The obvious qualities": Clipping from unidentified newspaper, MJ Scrapbook, DPL.

249 "Alice overcome": "After Seven Years a Tenth Season," XL, no. 1 *Southwest Review* (Winter 1955), viii.

"May Margo": Telegram, 3 November 1954, DPL.

"Broadway is only": Clipping from unidentified newspaper, MJ Scrapbook, DPL.

"What [Margo] has done": Ms., DPL.

"this kind of thing": MJ to Brooks and Oriana Atkinson, 3 November 1954, DPL.

250 "I promise you": Ibid.

"It dashed": Author interview with Jim Pringle.

"it was just": Author interview with Mabel Duke.

"I was so": MJ to Tad Adoue, 29 October 1954, DPL.

"The blessed": MJ Tapes, DPL.

"Right now?" "Yes": Author interview with Ted Apstein.

251 "She had been": Ibid.

"no one was": Author interview with Patricia Peck Swank.

"We would have": Author interview with Bill Gilliland.

"This is Margo": Author interview with Harry Granick.

252 "But it was": Author interview with Harry Bergman.

"illuminating": DMN, 5 December 1954.

"No," "Now get": Jerome Lawrence, *Actor: The Life and Times of Paul Muni* (New York: G. P. Putnam, 1974), 318.

"I double-dog": Tad Adoue to MJ, undated, DPL.

253 "you can't say," "Is it possible": Jerome Lawrence and Robert E. Lee, "*Inherit the Wind*: The Genesis and Exodus of the Play," *Theatre Arts*, August 1957, 94.

Source Notes

"This gal": Lawrence speech, Texas Woman's University.

"I will tell": MJ to Jerome Lawrence and Robert E. Lee, 10 November 1954, JFA.

"The playwrights": Lawrence speech, Texas Woman's University.

254 "Look, angel": Author interview with Jim Pringle.

"Honey, we don't do": Author interview with Fred Hoskins.

"stumbled into," "But she woke," "My God": Lawrence speech, Texas Woman's University.

"blobs of jelly," "Ahhh, your": Jerome Lawrence and Robert E. Lee, *Inherit the Wind* (New York: Dramatists Play Service, 1986), 8.

"When the preacher": Lawrence Speech, Texas Woman's University.

255 "bless you": Ibid.

"Margo Jones directed": DTH, 11 January 1955.

"new play": DMN, 11 January 1955.

"if nothing else": Wilmeth, 173.

"kicked off her": Lawrence speech, Texas Woman's University.

"My trip to New York": MJ to Charles Jones, 14 February 1955, DPL.

256 "to function without": Jonas Silverstone to MJ, 16 February 1955, DPL.

257 "Shumlin pushed": Author interview with Therese Hayden.

"We had so many": Author interview with Jerome Lawrence.

"was thrilling": *Daily News*, 22 April 1955.

"one factor": DMN, 29 January 1955.

258 "The new play": *Daily News*, 22 April 1955.

"The town has": *New York World-Telegram*, 22 April 1955.

"There's a whale": *New York Herald-Tribune*, 22 April 1955.

"He would often": Author interview with Therese Hayden.

259 "the bickeringest": DMN, 3 May 1955.

"a very famous," "glamour and glitter," "We're just a," "slapping my own": DMN, 1 June 1955.

260 "she just fell," "I won't change": Author interview with Louise Latham.

"sitting in Margo's": Author interview with Mary Dolan.

"We made it": Author interview with Louise Latham.

261 "The whole affair": DMN, 3 July 1955.

"She would be": Author interview with Joseph Glasco.

"that Texas girl": Goyen, 71.

"I will never": MJ to John Stine, 15 February 1955, DPL.

"the first time": MJ to Doris Porter, 16 February 1955, DPL.

"Goyen came on": Author interview with Louise Latham.

262 "Oh baby wait": Goyen, 72.

"she was so": Author interview with David Blackburn.

263 "gave her something," "I feel so": Wilmeth interview with John Rosenfield, DPL.

"Baby, baby please": Goyen, 72.

264 "Angels, I'm": Author interview with Margaret McDermott.

Source Notes

Details of hospital procedure were supplied by Margo's attending physician, Dr. Jerry Stirman, and by Dr. Earnest Booth, who performed the autopsy.
"Margo died": Author interviews with Louise Latham and Jim Pringle.
"We guess that": DMN, 31 July 1955.
"Haven't you heard?": Author interview with Charles Jones.
265 "She was very religious": Author interview with Lois Jones.
"It was just too terrible": Author interview with Louise Latham.
"Theatre '55 would": DMN, 26 July 1955.
"with a history": Margo Jones Autopsy Report, JFA.

Author's Note: When Margo died of carbon tetrachloride poisoning in 1955, little was known about the deadly effects of this toxin. In 1966, the United States of America Standards Institute warned that exposure to a concentrated amount of carbon tetrachloride for even five minutes could result in irreversible injury to the liver and kidneys. The Institute further advised that the odor of carbon tetrachloride, which is not disagreeable, could not be relied upon as a warning. In November 1963, the entertainer Liberace collapsed during a performance after only a few hours' exposure to a cleaning fluid containing carbon tetrachloride. He was immediately placed on kidney dialysis, and did not suffer any lasting effects. Dr. Jerry Stirman believes that if Margo had been placed on kidney dialysis immediately, her kidney and liver cells may have regenerated. However, after her thirty-six-hour exposure to the toxin, it seems clear from all available evidence that damage to her liver and kidneys was irreversible. While the alcohol in her system exacerbated the action of the toxin, even the healthiest person would have succumbed after such a prolonged exposure.
265 "I don't know where": Author interview with Mary Dolan.
266 "Our thoughts are with you": Telegram, 26 July 1955, DPL.
"I'll never forget": Author interview with Mary Kennedy.
"They closed your casket": Goyen, 72.
"It seemed to us": DMN, 6 December 1959.
267 "if you're going": Wilmeth interview with Eugene McDermott, DPL.
"The flame of this faith": Southern Methodist University Margo Jones Theatre Premiere program.
"most faithfully the tradition": Margo Jones Award brochure, undated.
"has accomplished what," "theatre statesperson": Author interview with Jerome Lawrence.
"one chance for greatness": MJ notes, JFA.
268 "I . . . like to think": TITR, 186.
269 "If we succeed": John Rosenfield, "Margo Jones: Theatre Pioneer," NYT, 31 July 1955.
269–270 "PETER: I'll tell . . . still lived in New York": Terrence McNally, It's Only a Play (New York: Dramatists Play Service, 1986), 64.

Source Notes

272 "little Freddie," "belonged to the theatre": Author interview with Fred Hoskins. "Freddie . . . Love, Margo": MJ to Fred Hoskins, undated.

Author's Note: In the years since Margo's death, various rumors have surfaced about her. For example, the circumstances of her death have become clouded, and some have heard she died of alcoholism, others that she was murdered or committed suicide. Rumors have spread about her sexual nature as well. Perhaps because of her association with homosexuals and the fact that she was a powerful, prominent, unmarried woman who lived alone, there has been gossip that she was a lesbian. In my interviews and research, I pursued this rumor, but after talking with those closest to Margo—her lovers, her friends and co-workers, and her family—I could find no evidence of its truth. No mention was made of her rumored lesbianism in my biography because the rumor did not surface until many years after her death. I feel, however, that I must address this issue here briefly, since in his popular 1985 biography of Tennessee Williams, author Donald Spoto describes Margo Jones as "openly lesbian." After spending two years researching Margo's life, I spoke with Mr. Spoto about his statement, asking where he had gotten this information. Had I missed something that he had uncovered? He informed me that he had no evidence, that this was something he had heard somewhere. Then he said, matter-of-factly, "Well, maybe it's not true."

The Margo Jones Award

1961 Lucille Lortel, White Barn Playhouse, Westport, Connecticut

1962 Michael Ellis, Bucks County Playhouse, New Hope, Pennsylvania

1963 Judith Rutherford Marechal/Mrs. Roy McGregor Watt
(University Award: George Savage, UCLA)

1964 Richard Barr, Edward Albee, Clinton Wilder, Theatre '64, New York City
(University Award: Richard A. Duprey, Villanova University)

1965 Wynn Handman, American Place Theatre, New York City
(University Award: Marston Balch, Tufts University)

1966 Jon Jory, Long Wharf Theatre, New Haven, Connecticut
(University Award: Arthur Ballet, Minnesota, OADR)

1967 Paul Baker, Dallas Theatre Center, Dallas, Texas
(Workshop Award: George C. White, O'Neill Theatre Center)

1968 Davey Marlin-Jones, Washington Theatre Club, Washington, D.C.
(Workshop Award: Ellen Stewart, La Mama Experimental Theatre Club)

1969 Adrian Hall, Trinity Square Repertory Company, Providence, Rhode Island
(Workshop Awards: Edward Parone, Gordon Davidson, New Theatre for Now
program)

1970 Joseph Papp, New York Shakespeare Festival, Public Theatre, New York City

1971 Zelda Fichandler, Arena Stage, Washington, D.C.

1972 Jules Irving, The Forum (Lincoln Center), New York City

1973 Douglas Turner Ward, Negro Ensemble Company, New York City

1974 Paul Weidner, Hartford Stage Company, Hartford, Connecticut

1975 Robert Kalfin, Chelsea Theatre Center of Brooklyn, New York
(Citation to AMOCO for its support of the American College Theatre Festival)

1976 Gordon Davidson, Los Angeles Center Theatre Group/Mark Taper Forum

1977 Marshall W. Mason, Circle Repertory Company, New York City

1978 Jon Jory, Actors Theater of Louisville, Kentucky

1979 Ellen Stewart, La Mama Experimental Theatre, Club, New York City

The Margo Jones Award

1980 John Clark Donahue, Children's Theatre Company of Minneapolis, Minnesota

1981 Lynne Meadow, Manhattan Theatre Club, New York City

1982 Andre Bishop, Playwrights Horizons, New York City

1983 Bill Bushnell, Los Angeles Actors' Theatre, Los Angeles, California

1984 Gregory Mosher, Goodman Theatre, Chicago, Illinois

1985 John Lion, Magic Theatre, San Francisco, California

1986 Lloyd Richards, Yale Repertory, New Haven, Connecticut

Note: In 1979, workshop theatres were made eligible for the regular Margo Jones Award.

Index

Index

Index

Index

Index

Index

Index